Now ideas of the pleasure... traumato sail

across the Mediterra... ...

fered a change. Still ... ...

joy every where

Tues 11.   We anchored off Cagliari, this morn
                 at sun rise
ing 'Cagliari, the capital of Sardinia

stood before us rising amphitheatre

like from the waters edge, at the

head of a long bay with distended arm

in either side, to the summit of a hill

governed by its citadel. It said to us after

the last three of storm & tempest here

you will find repose & welcome. Many

ships lay around us, riding calmly at

anchor. Our suffering were soon for

gotten, & when the signal to prepare

for landing. After lessons were over

The Merchant of Naples

James Close (1799–1865) and his Family

IN MEMORY OF JONATHAN

The Merchant of Naples

James Close (1799–1865) and his Family

Edited by Julian Potter

ORFORD BOOKS

First published in Great Britain by Orford Books in 2008

A CIP catalogue record of this title is available from the British Library

ISBN 978-0-9546653-2-6

Designed and typeset by David Roberts, Pershore, Worcestershire

Printed and bound at the University Press, Cambridge

Published by Orford Books, Orford, Suffolk, UK

Contents

Acknowledgements

Thanks are due to:

Joanna and Rosemary Close-Brooks, without whose tireless sorting of trunkloads of family archives this book would not have been possible, and both of whom read the MS at least twice, making many helpful comments and suggestions

Close Brothers plc for making available their archives and office space

Curtis Harnack for permission to make use of his book, *Gentlemen of the Prairie;* and to Barbara Dawes for permission to make use of her book, *British Merchants in Naples, 1820-1880*

Dott. Carlo Knight for his research in Naples

Michelle Froissard of *Services Archives Documentations* in Antibes

Tim Fargher, for the three maps

The Plymouth County Historical Museum in Le Mars, Iowa for supplying clippings from the *Le Mars Sentinel* looking back on the British Colony

The Alaskan Regional Office of the National Park Service for permission to quote from Julie Johnson's *A wild discouraging Mess*

The University of Washington Libraries, Special Collections, for permission to use the images on plates 22 and 23

George Trevelyan, acting on behalf of the estate of Professor G. M. Trevelyan, for permission to quote from *Garibaldi and the Making of Italy*

My wife Valerie, who also read through the original material and the MS, suggesting a number of useful alterations

Most of the illustrations are not attributed as the names of the artists and photographers are in many cases not known. Where they are, the credit is given in the captions.

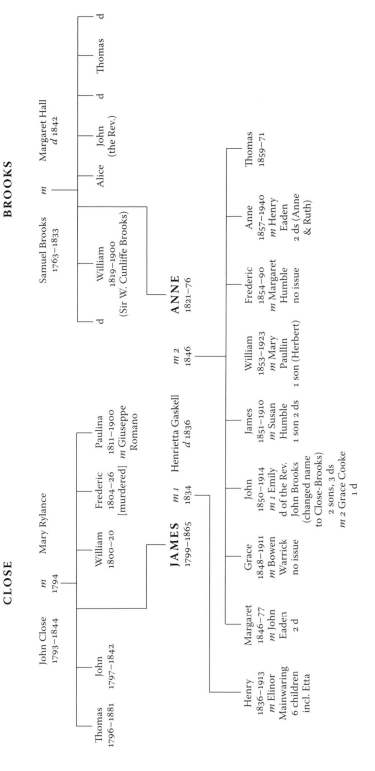

Family Tree

CLOSE

BROOKS

Thomas
1796–1881

John
1797–1842

John Close
1793–1844

m
1794

Mary Rylance

William
1800–20

Frederic
1804–26
[murdered]

Paulina
1811–1900
m Giuseppe
Romano

Samuel Brooks
1763–1833

m

Margaret Hall
d 1842

Alice

John
(the Rev.)

d

Thomas

d

d

William
1819–1900
(Sir W. Cunliffe Brooks)

JAMES
1799–1865

m 1
1834

Henrietta Gaskell
d 1836

m 2
1846

ANNE
1821–76

Henry
1836–1913
m Elinor
Mainwaring
6 children
incl. Etta

Margaret
1846–77
m John
Eaden
2 d

Grace
1848–1911
m Bowen
Warrick
no issue

John
1850–1914
m 1 Emily
d of the Rev.
John Brooks
(changed name
to Close-Brooks)
2 sons, 3 ds
m 2 Grace Cooke
1 d

James
1851–1910
m Susan
Humble
1 son 2 ds

William
1853–1923
m Mary
Paullin
1 son (Herbert)

Frederic
1854–90
m Margaret
Humble
no issue

Anne
1857–1940
m Henry
Eaden
2 ds (Anne
& Ruth)

Thomas
1859–71

Names of offspring given only if they occur in text.

Introduction

*T*HIS book tells the stories of James Close, an expatriate entrepreneur born in Manchester in 1799, and of his wife and children. Possessed by the extraordinary drive and self-belief characteristic of the Victorian age, he was a vivid figure: on the one hand passionate and imaginative and on the other at times sententious.

In his later years James Close wrote a 'History of my Own Life' in which he speaks of his experiences at boarding school with great bitterness. In his view it had taught him very little of practical value and he had suffered deep unhappiness; so much so that he resolved never to send his own children to school but to educate them at home, where they could enjoy each other's company and the care and love of their parents. He would confine their education to subjects that would further their careers in the business and mercantile world and so maintain a suitable station in life. It will be seen that in the case of his sons this decision worked exceptionally well.

JC's father John ran a cotton-exporting firm. Once his son had finished his hated schooling, he started a secondary education accurately geared to his future career: he spent two years at a business school in Frankfurt and two years working with a forwarding agent in Le Havre. He was then summoned home to learn about and work in every department of the family firm. Aged twenty-three, he was sent out to join, and soon to run, the Sicilian branch of the business. His autobiography gives us an intimate picture of a young man's life in all four countries, in the years immediately following the Napoleonic Wars.

Business in Sicily flourished, and soon JC was able to open his own firm in Naples. There he was based for the rest of his working life, during which he became the most successful of the many British merchants in the city. He became a banker to King Ferdinand II, from whom he obtained the royal sailing schooner *Sibilla*, in exchange for two of his own innovatory steamers. His sister married into the Romano family, noted Republicans – yet JC was astute enough to remain on reasonable terms with them while continuing to have dealings with the King. As he neared retirement, he would spend much of his time on board the *Sibilla*, together with his wife, his nine children and a crew and staff of around twenty. The children were given their lessons on board. The hazards of life at sea, the sights they saw and the people they met on shore around the Mediterranean provided the more unusual side of their education. All was recorded in the Journals, a kind of family diary.

At the end of his life JC retired to Antibes. There he bought a large slice of Le Cap, and began to build on it a vast mansion, which he named Antipolis. He did not live to see it completed but he did start off the fashion for going to Antibes: he was the first Englishman to live there.

The final chapter of this book demonstrates the success of JC's experimental method of bringing up his children. Three of his sons went out to America in their early twenties, quickly made a fortune opening up virgin prairies in the Midwest and founded Close Brothers to raise the necessary capital. This was the origin of the firm that still flourishes in the City of London today.

CHAPTER I

James Close's Manuscripts

*J*AMES CLOSE'S origins and early life are well documented – by himself. Aged sixty-three, he wrote two manuscripts for the benefit of his children. The first was the family history, the second an unfinished autobiography. Both were written on board his yacht *Sibilla* while it was moored at Port Ischia and both are dated 18th November 1862.

The two manuscripts have been heavily cut, as otherwise they would be long enough to constitute a book in themselves. The longest excisions have been JC's views on religion, which was an important part of his life. On board the *Sibilla* he preached the sermon every Sunday: he later had a selection of these printed in two volumes, giving a set to each of his children. On shore, the family would listen to the local preacher wherever possible, and if he did not come up to scratch, JC would record his criticisms in the Journal. Above all he detested any kind of sanctimoniousness and cant. He thought religion was a private matter and disapproved of ritual and other forms of display. He disliked the way some of his acquaintances would troop all the family and servants into the drawing room for Sunday prayers. His views on Methodism are made very plain in the following Family History.

Family history

*J*AMES CLOSE'S father and grandfather each had eight children and some of their offspring were equally prolific, so there were plenty of relations to write about. His document covers the lives and characters of some fifty of them, which considering he was aged sixty-three when he wrote it, and had spent very little of his life in England, shows either a phenomenal memory or excellent record-keeping.

His lengthy account of his family background is permeated with the strong views of the writer, so remote from attitudes prevalent today. Hard work, money-making and success are equated with virtue; pursuit of pleasure, shortage of money and failure are seen as degeneracy and vice. He seems to have disapproved of nearly all his uncles, aunts and contemporary cousins. The strength of this antipathy is hard to explain. In part it was due to his aversion to Methodism.

According to JC's mother, her mother-in-law had been a secret Methodist, to which sin JC attributes the many defects and failures of his uncles and aunts. But he had picked this up from his mother, who hated Methodism and disliked her mother-in-law. While she was teaching JC about the evils of the sect, she may have overplayed its debilitating effect on his uncles, aunts and their families. Similarly the responsibility of his grandmother for their decline could likewise be exaggerated.

Another possible cause of JC's resentment might have been that not only had his grandfather and father been over-generous in helping the less successful members of his family when things went wrong, but in spite of this, their shortcomings had led to the near-collapse of the family firm, John Close & Co. JC himself had had a life of labour on the Continent in which to contemplate what his UK inheritance might have been, if these financial disasters had not occurred at home. This would not have mellowed his opinion of those responsible.

These reservations do not cast doubt on the facts in JC's document, but it should be remembered that it was intended in part as a moral tract and warning to his own family; and he wanted to make sure the message was clear. He could not bear the thought that his own nine children might dissipate their talents and opportunities in the same way.

The following is an edited version of JC's family history.
Some passages are in his own words, some summarised.

⚜ Ancestors

At the start of his document JC writes:

> My Great Grandfather, Joseph Close, was a Yorkshire Grazier. He lived I believe in a village named Armley or Idle near Leeds. What I write is from the casual observations of my parents. I have heard them say that the ancestors of my Great Grandfather came originally from Strasburg and that the name was spelt with a K and not with a C. There are still in Strasburg families of the name of Klosen. To judge from the education my Great Grandfather gave to his sons, I conclude that he himself was an educated man and well to do.

JC's grandfather John was the second of Joseph's three sons.

🪶 *Grandparents*

John is described by JC as 'a wealthy and influential citizen of Leeds, a gentleman in education and manners, a man of science and the most extensive buyer and finisher of woollen stuffs of his time'. Unbeknown to her husband, his wife Grace espoused Methodism, instructing her children to conceal visits to their house from Methodist preachers. The 'demoralising consequences' of this 'deceit, false-hood and hypocrisy were unmistakeable, even in the third and fourth generation of the family'. However, in 'deference to the strong prejudices of my mother, her zeal was moderated whilst under my father's roof in Manchester'. She died there, aged eighty, in 1818. Grandfather John died aged sixty in 1793, leaving eight children and a fortune of £50,000. 'He was buried in Leeds parish church under the dais on which the Communion Table rests.'

🪶 *Uncles, cousins and aunts*

The 'demoralising consequences' were soon apparent in the next generation:

Sarah …

… the eldest of my Grandfather's eight children, married William Townsend of Manchester, formerly in the hat manufacturing trade in London, where the elder branch of his family continue that trade to this day [1862]. He was a plodding tradesman in the Home trade, one of those men who work with their hands in their breeches' pocket, and who prefer entering your house by the back door rather than the front. He left £40,000 to his children. My aunt Sarah Townsend introduced into her own family the methodistical impressions my Grandmother had taught her. She like her mother would get one or more of these preachers into her house, whilst uncle was about his business, have prayers and refresh them with warm beer. Such low work is incompatible with good society. The result was that the education of her children was of the worst description. John, Sarah's eldest, was of the best, but he died of consumption. He left an only son Henry, who I believe barely maintained his situation in life. William, Sarah's second son, ruined himself between pictures and parsons, though he inherited the excellent business of his father. His two admirable wives died of anxiety and annoyance at his ignorance and silliness. Thomas, the third son, had the advantage of a few years schooling at Frankfort. He attended to the business his brother neglected and has made a fortune of about £300,000. But his sneaking, pompous, uncertain and methodistical habits were a bar to all good society whilst he remained in Manchester.

Ann, the second daughter, ran away with a 'low fellow, James Appleton of Leeds. She survived her drunken husband but died in low estate'. Her son James is described as a 'scamp, whom I have often relieved and once rescued from arrest for debt'. Thomas, the third child and eldest son, married into a most respectable family, the Cleggs of Oldham, but squandered his fortune in 'country pursuits'. When he died at the age of thirty-four he left no property and no issue.

Betsy was the third daughter. 'In manners and dress she was quite a lady, but in character and habit she was my grandmother over again. Meddling, gossiping, tale-bearing, underhand, critical and untrue'. She married Thomas Coupland, a wine merchant of Rotherham, but 'his affairs went wrong, so he left his family unprovided for'. Their sons, 'unprincipled knaves' had been befriended by JC's father in 1826, but brought ruin to the firm. Thomas committed suicide in the United States after leaving Jamaica with property of his creditors; while John was many times bankrupt in Liverpool. 'Henry, the attorney, the swindler of widows and orphans, died in a Manchester garret of a loathsome disease.' Their only sister, the once beautiful Harriet Coupland, married an attorney of the name of Benson. They emigrated to Canada, where he 'shot himself, perhaps by accident'. Harriet did not long survive her husband. 'Had she told the truth when appealed to by my father, she might have saved my family from ruin and bankruptcy and her own from ruin and misery.'

William, the third son, fared no better:

> He married a Miss Wells, daughter of Dr Wells, rector of Willingham. She was an extravagant and vain woman and he was a dissolute and inconsiderate man, who neglected my grandfather's fine business, became bankrupt and brought ruin on himself and his youngest brother Mathew, who was his partner and whose share of his father's business was vested in the dyeworks. After his misfortunes, Uncle William never rose again in life and he died in Hull, a pensioner of my father's liberality and never-tiring consideration for his blood relatives.

Grace, the fourth daughter, was divorced from her husband, a London solicitor, for adultery with her coachman. She was kept for a time in JC's father's house, then in Liverpool and later in the Isle of Man. Her fortune of £5,000 was kept by 'her husband, a brute and a man in name only. She had no issue.'

Mathew ...

> ... was the youngest of my grandfather's eight children. His fortune was lost in

his brother William's bankruptcy. He went to Rio de Janeiro as agent for several houses, but after prospering at first, 'he went wrong' and as 'a pensioner of my father's for many years he dragged out a precarious existence'.

JC was unhappy about revealing the black history of his uncles and aunts. Two pages of justification boil down to the claim that he did so as a passionate warning to his children:

> … when I contemplate my own eight little innocent children, and when I remember that there was a time when my good old grandfather was as proud of his eight children as I am of mine, I tremble lest from any fault or weakness of their parents a like fate befall my children as befell his! I feel that should my children have no better success in sustaining the honour and dignity of my name than the generality of the children of my Grandfather have had in sustaining his, I could in my vexation and disappointment wish they had never been born.

✿ *Father*

It is something of a relief to get to JC's description of his father John, the second son and fifth child of his grandfather. He relates the little he knows of his father's early life, mentioning that he was sent to the university of Gothenburg in Sweden and that he afterwards spent a year or two in Hamburg. He spoke German and French fluently. Then comes a two-page panegyric, mostly too perfect to be credible. The following short extracts include all the few hints of adverse criticism, because of their possible relevance to his later business failure:

> My father was one of the handsomest men I ever saw … His hair rich in quantity inclined to curl, was fine in fibre and white as silver. … His demeanour in his family was mild and affectionate, persuasive and suggestive; he never commanded. … To his relatives, however poor or unfortunate, he never turned a cold shoulder. … In his politics, he was what is termed a Church, King and State man; an upholder of the constituted authorities, a conservative.
>
> Labour, application and study were hateful to him, nevertheless he had a singular aptitude in acquiring a gentlemanly knowledge of all the leading topics of his day. … Such was his natural indolence in business matters, that he would carry letters and papers in his pocket for months and years without having the energy to dispose of them. Such was my noble and honourable and excellent father! The picture I have drawn is not exaggerated. It is now thirty years nearly since he died, and I am on the wane of life having completed sixty one years.

My children may therefore believe that I can at this distance weigh my Father's comparative merits free from the predilections of a son. He had one defect and one only: he lacked energy, and hated the responsibility of enforcing his own correct and judicious opinions. His affairs were thus abandoned to the management of others, and the misfortunes of himself and family may in a great degree be attributed to this circumstance.

Mother

JC's parents married in 1794. His mother was Mary Rylance, an orphan who had lost her own mother when she was six and her father at seventeen. Through her mother she was connected to the respectable Cleggs of Oldham, one of whom had married JC's uncle. Her inheritance from her father provided a net income of £280–300 p.a. from the rent of houses in Liverpool, Wigan and Oldham. She had few kind words to say about her husband's family on account of her antipathy to Methodism. Sometimes she had sharp words for her husband as well: she is said to have abused him for his want of energy, wishing that she were a man instead of a woman. Impoverished before her marriage, she always kept an exact account of all her expenses and the idea of being in debt was to her intolerable.

Anne Eaden, JC's granddaughter, commented that Mary Close's independence of mind, strength of character and energy, as opposed to her husband's inertia, undeviating conformity and desire to avoid any form of confrontation, made her the stronger partner in the marriage, and it was from her that her son James inherited his immense strength of purpose.

Siblings

Thomas was JC's eldest brother and the only one to survive him. Something of the tempestuous relationship between the two is told in later chapters. In his Family History, JC belatedly puts the blame for the disputes on to Thomas's wife:

> The patience my Brother has exhibited in bearing with his wife's nervousness forms one of the most wonderful features of his forgiving and excellent character. I believe it was she who destroyed the harmony between her husband and his family. During twenty years we never saw nor spoke to each other. Happily these dissensions have been forgiven and forgotten by both of us, as completely as if they had never existed.

Towards the end of his life JC was corresponding with Thomas and, as a dutiful younger brother, asking his advice. It could be that the extract quoted above was composed with an eye to the possibility that Thomas might read what he had written.

JC's other three brothers all died young. **John**, JC's co-partner in business, acted as his assistant. The two were deeply attached and John is described as 'true and honourable'. His health was never robust, and he died of consumption in Naples in 1842, aged forty-five. **William**, 'a noble well-disposed boy', died in Southport, aged twenty. His 'disease was rheumatism in his joints which degenerated into water on the brain.' **Frederic**, the youngest son and his mother's favourite, was murdered. He entered the army as an ensign and was serving at Clonmel in Ireland when in 1826 he was drowned in the river 'together with a beautiful Quaker girl named Grubb. They were thrown into the river by some vindictive Irishman who had been rejected by Miss Grubb. The painful search after him by my brother Thomas, together with the afflicting circumstances which at that period brought my father's house to ruin, form an episode of suffering and interest which will long be remembered by many.'

The Closes' first daughter, **Grace**, had died in infancy. A second daughter, **Paulina**, was born in 1811. JC was to see more of her in later life than any of his other siblings, as she too was to live in Naples. What he writes about her will be found in chapter II.

⁂ *Early life*

*W*RITTEN IN 1862, JC's account of his life up to his early twenties contains his mature comments on religion, love and education, together with appraisals of his own abilities, virtues and failings, all of which he had had a lifetime to consider. Thus it is more than a straight account of his first twenty-three years.

His schooling, as described in this document, is the key to this book and is sufficient explanation as to why he determined never to send his own children to school. The battle of Waterloo was fought during his further education in Frankfurt and his first working years in France and Sicily take us to a Europe in the aftermath of the Napoleonic wars. They were his initiation to a life on the Continent.

The extracts below constitute only about a quarter of the original document.

⚘ *Infancy*

I was born at No. 20 Oldham Street, Manchester, on the 16th February 1799. In those days Oldham Street had a character for respectability. It is now a street of low shops and taverns, a sort of avenue to the Irish purlieus of my native city. I call it city with its 400,000 inhabitants, its corporation and Mayor; but then it was a Town of only 40,000 presided over by a Borough reeve, though really governed by the Lord of the Manor Sir Oswald Mosley. In those days the principal inhabitants resided in the town; now the environs are studded with country palaces. No one lives in the city.

I have no remembrance of Oldham Street as a child. Shortly after I was born, my parents removed to that large and noble mansion at the top of King Street. I have a sort of pride in naming this house for I well remember every room in it. Connected with it I remember my Father in his uniform as Captain of the Militia, receiving his company of grenadiers in this ample Court yard, around which we raced on my cousin Coupland's ponies, when they visited us. [*When Napoleon was threatening invasion, JC's father had volunteered to join the Militia.*]

The following attack on the system of education to which JC was subjected was written with such passion that the early part of it goes on without a paragraph break for four pages and near the start is a single sentence that goes on for twenty-six lines. To make it more digestible it has been broken up and shortened.

⚘ *Boarding school*

I was not quite six years of age, when I was sent with my brothers Tom and John to school at Formby, near Liverpool. From this moment my memory becomes clearer; I can remember well the first impression on arriving; my first fight, on the first day; and my coming off the victor. I can also remember the first book, which Mr. Hodgson placed in my hands, namely the Etonian Latin Grammar. I remember well my sitting on a deal box with my brother John in the corner behind the projecting chimney, studying Latin out of the same book, for he and I belonged to the same class – I remember every battle, every face, friend or foe (for at school we were all friends or foes); every rascality, every trick, every vice which the bigger boys introduced into the school, and which the Master did not, or could not, or would not know.

When I think of my schooldays, days of thoughtless enjoyment in one sense, and of detested application in another; when my young limbs craved for air and exercise, which were denied to them; when feebleness of constitution was unrespected; when education of the heart and affections were neglected by teachers, and perverted by the boys; when the boys were shamed out of every affection for home, and every regard for parental influence; and were taught by example every vice, every folly, every wickedness – I say when I think of my schooldays, and ask myself if I would live them over again in my children or in other terms, if I would send my children to school, my answer is 'no.'

I look upon schools and boarding schools especially as the hotbeds of immorality and dissipation and can trace to those days, irreverence, irreligion, and disregard to all that is holy or sacred or desirable in a parent's eyes. I think that in the great majority of cases the seeds of drunkenness, gambling and lasciviousness are sown in our schooldays. And indeed what right have parents to expect obedience, filial love and respect from children from whom, through their own incapacity or carelessness, or for their own convenience, they separate themselves, weaning them from the attractions of home, severing the ties of nature, and delegating to strangers those duties which can only be truly and well performed by the affection and discrimination of a parent! The whole system is an outrage upon nature. The very beasts of the field set us a different example.

Let us no longer barter the education of our children for such instruction as schools now afford. Instruction! In what? In any thing that may be really useful in the practice of arts? For instance, in agriculture, metallurgy, botany, geology, chemistry, anatomy, medicine, the preparation of food, clothing, or lodging, locomotion and engineering, housekeeping or mercantile accounts? Certainly not. The word 'instruction' or rather scholastic Education conveys to the great majority of people some vague idea of Latin, Greek, Euclid, Mathematics, Algebra, a smattering of sham poetry, a little music, an idea of figuring a dance, or of making a bow, some of the external ceremonies of good breeding, with a painful dilution of French or German. It also comprises a general idea of ancient history, to the exclusion of all others, save the Kings of England down to the accession of the house of Brunswick. But let me ask anyone to point out to me a single eminent discoverer, either in this or in the last century, who could conscientiously say that he traced his special ability to any instruction he received in his schooldays. The men who have conferred real benefit on mankind by their inventions and discoveries were almost universally self-taught.

I, for my part, being as it were on confession in this account of myself, am compelled to admit that when I left Formby, I left there also my Latin and Greek, my Euclid, my Algebra, my Logarithms, my Catechism, which cost me so many years of painful application; and I am moreover obliged to admit that not one of these studies has ever been of any practical use in after life. Yes! I learned at Formby to read, to spell and to write. I also learned arithmetic and plain geography. I am indebted also to Formby for my knowledge of decimals, a system of calculation I have ever preferred to vulgar fractions. I am indebted also to Formby for its fresh sea breezes, and perhaps for the milk diet the boys then chiefly subsisted upon. This is something, I admit; but I fancy all that and more might have been acquired, with far less strain on my young intellect, nay in a pleasurable way, rather than by never-ceasing pain and mental suffering and the sacrifice or at the risk of every natural affection of the heart.

It had been hinted that the school I was at was an inferior, ill-regulated school. I am not of that opinion. I believe Mr. Hodgson was a moral and a kind man, and neither on his part nor on that of his niece Miss Phoebe Barrington was there any lack of attention to the health and comfort of the boys. In those days the school was not of low reputation and other sons of highly connected families were then my schoolfellows. No, I do not abuse the school I was at. I abuse the whole system.

I left Formby in 1814, when I was fourteen years old. My brother John had left the preceding half year. In Manchester my parents provided John and myself with private teachers. I remember well Dr. Holland (he was blind), Dr. Dalton in Mathematics, my tutors in French, Latin and Greek, and old Hughes, who taught me the flute. At this time my mind began to open out: I began to understand what and why I 'laboured to learn'. In this, old Holland rendered me the greatest service. Still I hated lessons of all sorts; I did not give myself up to the opportunities my father at no small expense provided me with. What knowledge I possessed was purely routine knowledge. My convictions had as yet taken no part therein – I had got through most of the Latin classics, but as to what they meant, except perhaps Sallust and Caesar's commentaries, which are written in a more rational and familiar manner, and of which I retain still some slight reminiscence, I was and am still absolutely ignorant. Indeed so great was my dislike of Latin and Greek, though I was by no means the worst scholar in the school, that since I was emancipated from the English system of teaching I have never once opened a Latin or Greek author, nor do I think now I ever shall. Nevertheless such is the fatuity and absurdity of our social system, that unless a young man matriculates at one of our great universities, or colleges, not only is his progress in any of the so termed 'learned professions', Church, Law and Physic, almost completely barred, but his eligibility to serve his country in the higher offices of state is rendered almost impossible by the fact that his social standing in patrician society is disputed on the grounds that he has not the education of a 'gentleman'.

The tirade against Classics and the evils of the system continues, all with the triumphant conclusion that 'I have therefore determined not to send my children to such schools!'. JC's recognition that the lack of classical education was a bar on entry to any of the 'gentlemanly professions of Church, Law and Physic' did not deter him from his belief that instruction for his own children should have more practical value. The following paragraph suggests his idea of worthwhile instruction:

> In my father's solicitude to give us every opportunity of acquiring the means of self instruction, there was one which I much regret I did not value or avail myself of: lessons in shorthand writing. How much time might be saved by its general adoption! How rapidly we could commit our ideas to paper, and render them permanent if we were taught in our schools this most useful art! But indeed how many useful things might be taught at school most profitably for ourselves which are not taught! At Formby I did learn a bit of Carpentering, the use of a plane, a chisel, a gauge and a spoke shave – I could make a boat or a box, I could make snares to catch birds, which we could pluck, gut and roast by twirling them suspended before a turf or peat fire. I also learnt to know the eggs and nests of all birds in that neighbourhood from a wren to a hawk – I also there obtained an idea how to plough, sow, and set potatoes, how to preserve the latter, to reap, thresh and winnow. I am thankful I did learn some of these small important things at that time, for I feel that had I not had that opportunity of seeing them during our play hours (for they were not taught), I should not at this moment have the slightest idea thereof. Shall I be believed when I state, and I do so roundly, that these miserable shreds of useful knowledge have done more for me in practical life as a merchant, than all my Greek and Latin, Algebra and Logarithms to boot!

⚓ *Frankfurt*

At this point JC tells us that he and his brother John left England to continue their education in Germany – in 1814. This was also the year that he left Formby, and the year in which his father arranged private tuition – so the private lessons could not have lasted long.

> In the year 1814 my Father accompanied John (aged 17) and myself (aged 15) to Gravesend where he embarked us on board a sailing packet for Ostend, on our way to Frankfort on the Main – I remember well our stay in London at the York Hotel in Blackfriars. It was illustrated by the hanging of three men in front of

Newgate prison at eight o'clock one Monday morning; John and I saw the hideous spectacle from the corner of the London Coffee House. It was the first and last execution I ever witnessed.

I remember our journey to Gravesend, our having periwinkles for breakfast, and my disgust at their snailish appearance, our embarkation, and my father's tearful embrace and blessing on board the packet. I have no remembrance of our passage, but I perfectly recollect our arrival in Ostend and the kind civilities of the hostess of the Hotel, who treated us as a mother would do, seeing us safely in bed and tucking us in. I do remember also perfectly the peculiar smell of the soap used in scouring the rooms and bleaching the linen – I also remember well how excellent the fruit and especially the pears tasted in comparison with English fruit. I also remember our voyage to Ghent by the canal, our strolling into some great square or market place of Ghent, where we witnessed the punishment of some delinquents who were marked on the back with a hot iron. I also remember my surprise at the chimes of the Town Hall and the curiosity of the crowds to see two English boys, a sight they had not been accustomed to for years, by reason of the war, which had ended a few months previously by the relegation of Napoleon to Elba. At Cologne we parted with our passports, which were not restored to us. In travelling to Mayence [*Mainz*] a friend of my father's took John out of the diligence into his carriage, leaving me alone. On arriving at Mayence and having no passport, I was taken by the police and two soldiers to the commandant, who after questioning me without any other result than that I was a 'Garçon' (such was the extent of my knowledge of French) delivered me to two other soldiers to convey me I knew not where. Fortunately on our road, my father's friend, having heard of my arrest, met us and returned with us to the commandant, at once procured my liberation and took me to his Hotel, where I was overjoyed to find my brother John.

The following day we were transferred to a school [*in Frankfurt*] as Parlour Boarders, under the management of Herr Professor Hadermann, in the Bochenheimer Gasse, where we found some twenty or thirty boys of different nations, as ordinary boarders – John and I had a sleeping room to ourselves, also a studying parlour. We kept ourselves in general at a distance from the boys, for which I feel still thankful, as many of them were coarse and vulgar. Nevertheless we dined at the same table, but breakfasted in our own room, and in general were invited to tea with Mrs. Hadermann, who took a great liking to us and always treated us with marked affection and tenderness. We attended the several lectures by eminent professors, who with a black board and chalk illustrated the subjects treated of by figures and questions addressed to the boys by way of testing their comprehension thereof. I thought and think still that this system was an immense improvement on our English mode of learning so many lines in a book, and then being marched into classes to be heard by the masters. The consequences were natural: little boys at Mr. Hadermann's school were able to give answers to questions which quite bewildered us – and though our ignorance of the German language secured us from open humiliation, I must admit that secretly I felt ashamed and mortified. I retain the most pleasing remembrance of kind good Mr. Hadermann – I see him even now, always more ready to praise than to rebuke, a stranger to coercion and violence, the moderation and simplicity of his habits, his meek submission to his more imperious wife, his delight at a game of chess in the long winter evenings with one of his bigger boys, whom he would seldom beat, with all the lesser boys looking on, the pleasure he showed at the rapid progress I made in German which he undertook to teach himself, the pride he had of showing his two *Engelsmänner*, as he called us to his friends, how can I ever forget the happy nineteen months I spent under his fostering fatherly care!

On my part, I know that I exerted myself to the utmost to deserve his notice and regard. I rose daily at four and oftentimes at 3 o'clock in the morning, to surprise him with my application. Lucifer matches were then unknown – a flint and steel, with some ama [*Amadou: a tinder made from fungi growing on trees*] and a thread of brimstone at my bedside, enabled me to strike a light. I then kindled a fire in the monstrous stove, so heating a cup of cocoa for John, whose health threatened consumption, and when all was ready I awoke him to his studies. Poor Fellow! His strength was unequal to my energy. He used to weep, and say "Jim, I cannot get up, I would but my strength fails me", so I worked on myself, incessantly. In a few months I had mastered this difficult language, and had made great progress in French, and some little in Italian.

My great delight however, was in learning to play the flute under the instruction of Herr Lohwind. During three months I blew at the rate of three hours a day, indeed such was the progress I made that after that period I was invited to accompany a boy named Loupus, who was a sort of prodigy on the piano, and one of my school companions (now a first rate pianist in Frankfort) at some of Mrs. Hadermann's evening parties. I also took lessons in waltzing, in which I afterwards became quite a notability.

John and I took riding lessons also which I found very useful. It is not so much for learning to 'stick on' that lessons are required; a monkey can do that as well or better than a man. Riding lessons properly given teach us something of the nature of the horse, his character, and the best way of managing him – namely by gentleness and tact, not by violence and passion. We are also taught how to hold and handle his bridle, how to mount and dismount, how to use the spur and how the whip, though a good rider seldom requires the assistance of either, for I believe the fact is unquestionable that a horse is always willing to do his utmost if we can only find out the way of making him understand what we want of him. Besides German, French, Italian, Music, Dancing and Riding, we regularly attended the course of Mathematics and Arithmetic in the schoolroom. The professor was an able man. He understood thoroughly the system of European exchanges called on the Continent 'Arbitrages' – which means calculations whereby a merchant can make remittances at a cheaper rate through indirect channels than through direct.

It is clear that Hadermann's lessons were tailored for budding businessmen. JC here went on to show in detail how profit can be made from a normal transaction, adding: 'In these matters we are slow in England. There is not a Jew or German house in London or Manchester that cannot out-calculate every English house.'

At Mr. Hadermann's school several scions of the most respectable houses in Frankfort were brought up. John and I visited chiefly the Herniers, Aubins and Dufays. The Goutards also were kind enough to notice us by inviting us to their Balls. We were also admitted, young as we were, as subscribing members to the Casino, an excellent establishment, where we could read the papers of all countries, and where I tried to learn billiards, a game at which I never succeeded, and which ceased to interest me at all after leaving Frankfort.

The battle of Waterloo took place while we were at Frankfort. I remember well the excitement each successive courier produced as the battle proceeded, commencing with the defeat of Blücher. Politics ran high amongst the boys, amongst whom were two French boys, one an Imperialist named Tosier, the other a Royalist from Bordeaux named Biré. To both however defeat by the English was intolerable. Argument was succeeded by insult to our national pride, and from insult we soon came to blows. John and I licked them soundly, though they were older boys than ourselves. We were, however, all the better friends after.

On several occasions, both in this biography and later in his life, JC resorted to using his fists. Another instance occurs here:

Old Hadermann had an instinctive horror of violence even amongst the boys. I remember one day his favourite chess player, a coarse big hulk of a German from Cologne, a dirty fellow too, with a blue coat and brass buttons which seemed to have been tailored in some country village, and which he wore buttoned under the chin by one button only, to conceal his unwashed shirt; I say I remember this beast laying his ugly hand on Stanius in the schoolroom before all the boys. [*Fräulein Stanius was the housekeeper, about whom JC had romantic thoughts.*] She screamed; in one twinkling both my fists were in his face. [*JC goes on to describe a fierce and bloody fight, from which he emerged victorious.*] Meanwhile old Hadermann presented himself, and in severe terms accused me of brutality, of disregard of the rules of the school, and of want of respect for him. Not a bit daunted I, full of enthusiasm for what I considered a holy cause, stood up, and replied: "Dismiss me if you please, but I here tell Lildai (that was his name) and every other boy in the school, that the same offence repeated shall be visited with the same punishment." I presume Mr. Hadermann was afterwards acquainted with the facts, for not only did I hear nothing more on the subject, but both he and Mrs. Hadermann treated me with more distinction than ever.

I have often tried to bring to my recollection my religious impressions of that period of my life. In vain however. Not that I was without religious habits, for I seldom resigned myself to sleep before kneeling at my bedside in my night shirt, and smothering my face in the eiderdown counterpane, usual in Germany, and repeating the prayers I had been accustomed to from my infancy. I also attended regularly the French reformed service, and I remember one day calling with my brother on the Clergyman who could speak a 'leetle' English, and who praised in unmeasured terms the really splendid, I may almost say inspired, form of our English Litany. I remember also on my return home, perusing the litany, keeping present in my mind the panegyric I had just heard pronounced upon its merits. This was the first time I really comprehended it.

JC goes on to suggest that his religious reactions until now had been unoriginal and humdrum. Even at the time of his confirmation, some years back, he was inspired with 'no born again impressions', which was hardly surprising in view of his account of the event. The boys were led up to the altar in groups of fifty to a hundred and while waiting had been passing the time by changing places with the boys in front and behind by crawling under the pews. He concluded:

First that religious instruction to be effective should be imparted individually and not collectively to children, in the way tender affectionate mothers impress their infant children, and not in the way they are taught at schools and other large establishments by teachers and Clergy.

Secondly, there is nothing so powerfully hostile to these first impressions as to bring a number of boys into contact with each other. The work of a Mother during many years is frequently undone, utterly destroyed on the first evening that a child enters the dormitory of a large public school.

✍ *Le Havre*

It was in the year of 1816 that I received orders from home to proceed to Havre de Grace as volunteer clerk or apprentice in the firm of John George Merian & Co. I cannot say by whose recommendation, but I remember being sent for by Messrs. Rothschild of Frankfort who proposed to furnish a carriage if I would take under my charge two young gentlemen as far as Paris, and to travel post, an arrangement I readily accepted. The young men however were older than myself, wild fellows, whom I had great difficulty in controlling, to the extent of threatening to leave them and the carriage at Nancy, and proceed alone by Diligence – which had the desired effect. I never saw or heard anything of my companions after depositing them and the carriage safely at Messrs. Rothschild's hotel in Paris.

I remained about a week in Paris, seeing the curiosities. I had letters of credit and recommendation, but I don't remember any benefit or kindness they procured me. I indulged in some expense in Paris, I affected the rich young man – visited St. Cloud on horseback with a rascally servant on another horse to attend me. I was much scandalised however by the villain riding alongside me instead of at a respectable distance behind. I quarrelled with him, but to no purpose, whereby my dignity was sorely tried. The ride was long moreover, and I was sore. The next morning I had to pay, and I found out then only, that I had been making a fool of myself even in the eyes of my servant.

I arrived at last in Havre and Mr Merian after introducing me to his partner Mr Pannifix took me to the lodging he had secured for me, in the house of a worthy bourgeois named Feuillet. His family consisted of himself, Madame, and his two daughters, with all of whom I soon became a great favourite. The old man was a gentle, kind, subdued *expéditionaire* [*forwarding clerk*] of near seventy years. Madame treated her good man as an imbecile, and in proportion as he was mild and uncomplaining, so she was imperious and violent. I was lodged and boarded in the family for f1,500 per annum – about £60. The eldest daughter, tall and lank, took after papa, the youngest was as like her mother, as a duplicate. My room was very modest in size and furniture, but I soon set about making it comfortable and cheerful looking. I disposed of my books on shelves, my table in the best light for study. I bought a music stand, and I kept my flute in the most polished order. As I kept uniformly regular hours, I was usually at home in the evenings with a cheerful wood fire to keep me company.

I lodged with the Feuillets the whole time I was in Havre, a period of about two years. I was always considered the senior lodger by the two or three young men who were taken in contemporaneously. I had to make rough days smooth, and generally succeeded in restoring peace to the community. The old Feuillet was never happier than when he could sneak up to my room in an evening, occupy the opposite chair at my little fireside, and with the fire nippers in his hand, heap the live embers into pyramids, or squares, giving me advice from his own experience, and above all recommending me "never to marry".

The bourgeois society of Havre was quite distinct from that of the large Swiss and Paris houses, who since the peace had established themselves there, such as the Hottingers, the Vassals, the Greens, the Merians and others, who considered themselves 'la haute société'; I frequented both classes. Tone and fashion would have preferred the haute société. I suppose, however, that my tastes were not of the very exacting range, for I certainly found myself more at home among the 'dips' of the bourgeois set, than when illuminated by the wax lights of the more pretentious circles. In point of merriment, jollity and real enjoyment the bourgeoisie of Havre had, in my day, no grounds for envy of the more aristocratic classes.

My spare hours were well employed. I still persevered in my habit of early rising. I obtained an alarm, to ensure perfect regularity. I always set it for four o'clock which allowing half an hour for my toilette and half an hour for breakfast, gave me clear three hours every morning for my studies in French, Italian, general literature and other occupations. I sub-divided these three hours, and formed a table for their employment on each day. My only masters were for French, music, and for a short time only dancing.

My music master's name was Walekiers. Quite a young man, I dug him out of the garrison band, where he styled himself 'première flute' of the regiment, but I have since learnt there was no <u>second</u> flute. As a flutist I was quite equal to him, but as a zealous excellent musician he was in every respect a master. I was his first pupil. His charge was f15 for twenty billets. Many a master in London at a guinea a lesson does not understand music half so well as poor Walekiers did even in those days. He took great pains with me, and I rewarded him by procuring so many scholars that I insisted on raising his charge to f50, being the first to set the example. So he flourished in clover, left his regiment, fixed himself permanently in Havre, married, opened a music shop and I have since heard, became a man of substance and consideration in his profession. Some of his compositions are still to be found amongst my collection of music.

My office duties commenced at 8 o'clock every morning and finished at half past four. The post office and letter copying were my charge. I had to 'faire la guerre' at the post office at 8 o'clock amongst clerks and porters, pay postages, register the amount of each letter in a book, and then to transfer the same to a sort of postage account book. I was sometimes sent to receive money which I carried on my back. I had also occasionally to do outdoor work, such as weighing sugar, coffee, sulphur, and to attend with Bills of Exchange at the Timbre (stamp) office. In short I was one step in advance of the porters; and, upon the whole, a willing contented worker.

The corresponding clerk, a fat slow Dutchman, could never finish his letters in time for post hours, four o'clock. He would bring a letter at five to four, I had to copy it, get it signed, fold and seal it, and then off to the Post as fast as my legs would carry me, a sort of neck and neck race. One day I returned breathless with all the letters in my hand – "too late", I said. Furious and breathless, I threw the letters in the Dutchman's face and told him he must play the lamplighter himself another time. He immediately reported me to my chief, Mr Pannifix, who bestowed on me the charming epithet 'polisson'. We have no precise word for it in English, perhaps 'impertinent scamp' comes nearest. I at once dismissed myself from the House, and have never returned to the office. In a few days a friend of mine, an Englishman, a Mr. Noyes, obtained for me a situation as volunteer and corresponding clerk in the House of Vassal & Co., chiefly engaged in the West India trade, and in the importation of Tobacco for the Royal manufactory at Paris. Merian & Co's house soon after went to pieces and Mr. Merian died. I, many years after, found out Mr. Pannifix in Paris. I felt sorry at my impetuosity and I called on him, when I was at the head of three houses in Sicily and Naples, to apologise for my conduct, and to renew my acquaintance with him. He laughed, and appeared pleased. His business then lay in St. Petersburgh. Had it been possible, I would have made myself in someway useful, for he was, doubtless, a most clever merchant.

My expenses in Havre were, I believe, greater than my father approved of. I not only kept a regular account thereof, but I affected, as a matter of experience, to keep them by double entry, as, I had observed, the books were kept in Messrs. Merian's office. Now although I noted down my minutest expenses (as I thought) I always found myself deficient in cash, which deficiency I used to make up, in my accounts to my father, under the head of beggars &c. Thus I would insert, 'washing a pair of leather breeches, f1.50' – and other minute items, then immediately after came 'beggars &c. f4.50' or some such heavy sum; from which my father rightly judged it was time for me to return home – I had been absent nearly four years.

I cannot say that from this distance I view my conduct in Havre with the same satisfaction as I do my general conduct in Frankfort. I had become inoculated with a vast amount of self presumption and self conceit; I had certainly done nothing that was wrong or discreditable – I attended regularly the English chapel there under the ministry of the Rev. Dampierre, but I was irregular in my private devotions. I began to think that they were mechanical, hypocritical and profitless. My expenses too lay heavy on my conscience; they interfered with my peace and happiness. I felt ambitious too; that it was my destiny to become a great man, a member of parliament; and the lord knows how many other vain aspirations at this period occupied my mind! Looking back at the state of my mind after fifteen or twenty months residence in France, I attribute my backsliding in a great measure to the general character of my associates. I cannot detect at this more mature distance of time one single really superior mind amongst all my acquaintances; not one of them had range enough of sterling intellect to make one feel how much I had still to learn, in order to be the superior being I fancied myself or I affected to be. The clerks in a general merchant's office are usually not models of refinement; their inspirations are coarse, worldly, and selfish. Their enjoyments physical and gross; their language vulgarly polite and denoting low tastes. In the midst of such, I hardly see how I could think otherwise of myself than <u>well</u>. I had made progress in French and music. My flute was in general request at Musical parties, where a Mr. Ritter, a Mr. Edwards and myself used to play trios with tolerable effect; I being the third flute, for they were more perfect than myself.

In the midst of all this self complacency I became intimate with the English Clergyman's family. He had six daughters, and one idle unprofitable son. His circumstances were very limited, so much so that neither sugar or butter were allowed at tea, except to strangers like myself. The third daughter (Elizabeth was her name) was perhaps one of the most beautiful girls I ever saw. Everything about her was nature and sweetness. To think that such a creature had to submit to restrictions such as I witnessed aroused all my dormant feelings of compassion, sympathy, and as a consequence, love. There was no task, no difficulty, no sacrifice great enough for her and her family. The bud of my juvenile passions now burst forth; a bud still, but showing its colours unmistakably. Suddenly I had an object to please and to love. I never confessed to her the passion which inebriated me, but doubtless, with a woman's instinct, she saw it and felt it; one evening she gave me a pasto [*paste*] impression of an engraved seal, small enough to wear as a ring. With the confidence which love inspires, I immediately held this trifling incident to be a confession on her part that she was not indifferent to me. Nay, I went further, I wrote home for permission to visit Paris. I gave several reasons for the necessity, but I did not give the real moving power, which irresistibly urged me to the journey – namely, the impossibility of getting this piece of pasto suitably mounted in Havre. It could only be done in Paris!! Romantic love I think makes a youth demented. I felt on my return, with the ring on my finger, that I had done a foolish thing; and the more so, as immediately after I received my recall home.

In the course of my life, I have often been desperately in love; I must however confess that at each repetition the "couleur de rose" lost in intensity: the generous incitement love imparts to do well and to do right, and to overcome obstacles, gradually by repetition loses in strength until at last it acquires a sort of prudential character bordering on calculation, if not entirely on reason.

I landed at Southampton, sick of the sea and sick of that horrid stench of rum, brandy and bottled porter, which disgraces so many of our English packet ships; sick also of the coarse, swearing, brutally uncivil set of fellows who, on this occasion, and on so many others, were my companions in the state cabin.

I remember well my first sensations as the mail coach which conveyed me to London, an outside passenger on the coach box, rattled over the stones of Southampton on to the smooth macadamised roads of which England may well be proud. That swift, rumbling, drum-like vibration, indicating the perfection of the vehicle, of the horses, and of the coachman. There is nothing on the continent that can be compared to it. It exhilarates whilst it composes; it predisposes you to a favourable view of yourself, of your travelling companions, of your reminiscences, of your connections, and of everything you pass on the road.

En route, they changed horses at an inn, where JC glimpsed a young lady walking out of a white gate. He was so struck by her that for a moment he thought of leaving the coach and staying at the inn. He commented: 'It is some consolation to me after such a glaring proof of fickleness and inconstancy, that Elizabeth Dampierre was shortly married to a rich Indian Nawob, whom she accompanied to Calcutta.'

❧ *Homecoming*

I remember well my arrival at home. It was one evening of the winter. The family then lived at No. 8 Norfolk Street, Manchester. I brought my luggage with me in a hackney or stand coach, great lumbering things in those days, damp and smelling of musty straw. The family was assembled in the library, tea was on the table, lights at the piano; and a young lady rather handsome in features was accompanying my brother Thomas who was playing some English or Irish melody of easy execution on the flute. I thought, on entering the room, that I never saw a more ravishing sight. My father, mother, my four brothers, my little sister, who was then some eight or nine years of age, were all assembled in that room.

A blazing fire gave a cheerful brightness to the whole scene. To a young man who had spent the last four years in the companionship of a huge black stove, and of a small triangular brick fireplace sans fender, such a curtained, carpeted scene as this may well make an impression never to be forgotten. On my appearance, as the servant threw open the door, there was a moment's pause, and then the "Why it's James" burst from my Mother and several others, and in an instant all was "welcome", "how are you my boy" and I was in my good old Father's embraces. The next moment was one of observation of cut and general appearance. My brother Thomas, who never lost an opportunity, was the first to notice my peculiarly Frenchified looks, the short square cut of my coat, for the swallow tail with buttons was at that time the 'go' in Lancashire – also my long, curly, rough head of hair through which from habit, peculiarly French, I ever and anon passed my fingers to give it, I suppose, the 'grazia' of a stack of hay. This giggling certainly discomposed me, but when I opened my lips to order the servant to pay the coach, and withdraw from it my "nécessaire" as I felt quite "dérangé and wished to make myself decent", my brother roared aloud with laughter. "Good God!", he exclaimed. His sides shaking and his speech impeded by a fit of laughing, "James says he is deranged. Only think Father," shouting in his ear (my father was deaf) "he has brought with him a nécessaire and wants to make himself comfortable".

I have already stated that one result of my French education had been to imbue me with a tolerable opinion of my own superiority, and I did think that my various accomplishments in the languages, in music etc. and even my external appearance, would have commanded respect at least if not admiration from my kindred. If ever it has happened to anyone, in a dream, to fancy himself suddenly falling down a precipice; or if anyone on his exit from a vapour bath had felt the sensation which a bucket of cold water produced when dashed over his shoulders; or if a man can fancy the effect of being considered a mere 'snob' when he had made up his mind most satisfactorily that he was something prodigious, and this too from his nearest relatives, from whom at least he had a right to expect some little consideration, such a person I say may imagine the sudden revulsion from joy to anger, from excitement to mortification, from happiness to vexation, which this piece of wit at my expense produced upon me. I made no reply. I suddenly left the room. And when I returned to it, I felt too timid and too angry to enjoy that evening the affectionate welcome my parents gave me.

✥ *Set to work in Manchester*

1818: I was now entering upon what I may term the fifth phase of my life. The first being my infancy; the second my boarding school days; the third my Frankfort days and the fourth my Havre days. I was soon introduced into my Father's counting house and warehouse. His business was the shipment of cotton manufactures to various markets, where he had establishments under the management of special Agents. [*These must have been finished goods, as later in this same paragraph the text shows that the firm also undertook the cutting, bleaching, dyeing, etc.*] One of the principal ones was in Messina, under the direction of Mr Max Fischer, formerly a woollen manufacturer or shipper in Leeds, but an unsuccessful one. My eldest brother was on the point of attaining his majority, when he was to be admitted as partner into the firm. My brother John had previously returned from Frankfort where, since my quitting him, he had spent some eighteen months in Mr Aubin's office, and now I found him working at my father's ledger; an occupation ill calculated to improve his mind or talents. William, whose health was still precarious, though considerably better than when I left him, was a sort of volunteer apprentice with Mr. Sanderson, a Cotton Spinner; and Frederic had not completed his school days, or had only just finished them at Formby.

I was immediately appointed to superintend the manufactory of the Fustian [*a type of cotton cloth*] department of the firm, under the direction of a clever little fellow of the name Birch – who took pains with me; in a very short time I became a somewhat competent assistant in this branch. I was ever what may be termed a willing worker, I pulled with all my might at whatever I was yoked to. In the course of eight or nine months (and what business may not be learnt in that period, when everything is laid open, and all mystification removed) I had gone through several branches. I had obtained a generally correct idea of all the processes of cutting, bleaching, dyeing, finishing, printing; I had also gone though the process of invoice making, correspondence, checking account sales, and entering bills &c. &c. When I had completed my nineteenth year, I was judged to be a fit and proper person to be sent out to Sicily to assist Mr. Fischer and to acquire a competent practical knowledge of the business there, in the view of my returning in two or three years to manage myself that special branch of my father's business in Manchester.

My mother kept a good, I may say, a comfortable home for us all. I look back at it with pride and affection, and I remain to this day impressed with the good policy of parents, who having the means and the will, make their home a pride and a pleasure to their children. It is money well spent and far more meritoriously spent, than in the indulgences of hunting, shooting, gambling and such like amusements, in which a family, as a family, cannot participate. How much better it is for a man having children, to confine his tastes for enjoyment to those recreations which can be made common to all! My Father and my Mother had no special amusements. They spent their money freely, perhaps too freely, for I have heard my mother say that the expenditure of her family was not under £3,000 per annum at this period. But their home was a comfortable home, a happy home for us all; and though I cannot say it was a luxurious one (for carriages and horses we had not) I shall ever remember Norfolk Street with affection and respect.

   Norfolk Street in those days was not as now a street of offices and warehouses. It was inhabited by several families, with whom my parents lived on terms of neighbourly civility and kindness. Opposite lived Mr. Tomlin, a drysalter, who had several sons and handsome daughters. Higher up lived Mr. Johnson Edinsor, who had three daughters but no son; the eldest, Christiana, was about a year older than myself. She was more of an elegant girl, than a beautiful girl. At the same time she was certainly good looking, well formed, highly accomplished (for no expense had been spared on her education in London), intelligent and well informed. She played on the harp and sang sweetly. Edinsor had made his fortune in cotton dealing, and at the period I allude to, passed as a man of some £50,000.

About two pages have been cut from the following account of JC's love for Christiana and his thoughts on Love in general.

I hardly think it is possible for a lad of nineteen or twenty <u>not</u> to be in love with some one. He must have some object on which he may exercise the craving of his affections. It is nature that speaks aloud; without such an object he may be a dutiful, an affectionate son; but the noblest and highest aspirations are wanting: aspirations which prompt him to exertions. How beautifully, it seems to me, has nature arranged all things. Love in youth prompts exertion, and exertion is necessary to create a position sufficient for the wants of a family. It required but a short time to extinguish all remembrances of Stanius, Elizabeth Dampierre and of the 'white gate'. Christiana's voice, figure and features would absorb my thoughts, whether awake or asleep. Not a doubt, but that she knew what was passing in my sentiments. Not a doubt, but that I occupied Christiana's thoughts, just as much as she did mine. I remember Mr Edinsor's butler calling to deliver a neat parcel, addressed to James Close Esquire. What could it be? Why to me? The paper contained a square lump of a sort of Toffy called in Lancashire 'Alicampaign' and certain words neatly written … I instinctively felt that I had been the object of her attention and thought … after a day spent in enquiry I called to beseech an explanation … how can I forget Chirstiana's smile, and the hearty laugh of her cousin Miss Hughes, when the latter assured me it was nothing but a piece of mischief on her part. But there was something in it, for I was already in <u>flames</u>. Ah! Women, how well nature has provided you with the power of penetration. I proposed and was accepted. I obtained from her the usual lock of hair and her miniature, which was well done by a first rate artist. I sent her mine from London, done by one of those wretched impostors in Cheapside who charge five guineas for a daub. My poor brother John had in silence also felt the power of Christiana's charms. He also proposed but I had preceded him.

It was about this period that my brother Frederic professed a desire to enter the army, much against the wishes of my Mother. General Lyon, on my Father's application, wrote to the Horse Guards, and by return obtained for him a Commission of Ensign in a Regiment on the point of embarkation for India. A fine opportunity it was! But my Mother's entreaties prevailed, and an exchange into the 86th Regiment, then quartered in Ireland, was obtained without difficulty. Would he had gone to India! It is a great error in parents to allow their intelligence to be guided by their affections. Fred was the youngest son, his Mother's pet child! She could not make up her mind to part with him. His tragical fate in 1826 has already been related. [*Summarised in the Family History section.*]

During the few months I was in Manchester, I became a somewhat zealous churchman. It was not the custom of my parents to encourage family prayers in the morning and evening, the whole household attending, as is now somewhat the 'fashion' to do, especially among the wealthier classes. I am of the same way of thinking as my parents. These prayers in most instances are a mere form; annoying to many, irksome to the parents and to the younger members. It is a mere piece of show and vanity to collect the servants in a file, and headed by the housekeeper and butler, march them into the lower end of the dining room or hall, according to their rank or pay. My zeal as a churchman only extended to my attending St. Mary's Church twice every Sunday for some two or three months, to hear the sermons of a clergyman (formerly a gambler and a man of the turf), which sermons struck me, at this early period of my life, as containing something rational and logical, which experience has since taught me, are rare qualities in Clergymen of all sorts. With the departure of this preacher my 'zeal' departed also; I feel content that it took no deeper root in me.

❧ *Messina*

It was in the summer of 1819 that my four Brothers accompanied me to the coach which was to convey me from my home, and from every thing that was dear to me – we never met again all together! It was arranged that I should take patterns and prices and proceed through Belgium, Germany, Switzerland, Italy, and from Naples embark for Messina. I was well provided with letters. The business part of my mission proved rather a failure in regard to Belgium and Germany. But in Frankfort I met with a travelling companion in the person of Captain James Grey of the Royal Artillery, for whose suggestions and enlightened hints during our journey to Naples I shall ever feel grateful. We parted there, I to Messina, he to Otranto and Corfu. I have never seen or heard from him since. It was on this visit to Naples that I became acquainted with the family of the Meuricoffres, an acquaintance which during the course of nearly forty years has never been interrupted, and which has long since ripened into affectionate intimacy and friendship.

I remember well my passage in a Spironara to Messina, I believe it was in the month of August. I was the only passenger; amongst other provisions I had a bale of snow, with plenty of sugar and lemons. It took me four days to Messina. We arrived in the evening after sunset, and anchored for the night at a place half way between the faro [*lighthouse*] and Messina. I shall not readily forget the impression that evening made on me. In those days, I had imagined Sicily to be still the island where the gods and goddesses dwelled. It was a moonlight night, but the rough ravined mountains which spring from the edge of the channel were in the shade, and but dimly visible. A light here and there twinkled from some imaginary fairy palace, and the sounds of the ghitarro and of song, and merriment lasted till late at night. There was a perfume too, which the land breeze wafted from the shore, which I inhaled with extreme delight after the onions and strong cheese in which Sicilian mariners delight, and which gives a peculiarly unpleasant smell to the vessel and to everything on board. I mention these impressions though partaking somewhat of the poetical, because they stand out in prominent relief on my memory. Besides, I was at the time supremely happy and contented. I was not alone in the world. I loved and was loved. Christiana's portrait was never out of my hands. During my journey it was ever under my pillow; and once (only once) I forgot it; and though not addicted to blushing,

I did feel a flush come over me when the maid servant of the hotel at Cologne laughingly presented it to me.

I was kindly received by Mr. and Mrs. Fischer and their three daughters, and lodged in their house. Old Fischer was an extraordinary man, bordering on his seventieth year, very diminutive, very passionate, very head strong and very impracticable. He would sometimes threaten to shoot himself, cut his throat and 'jouer la comédie' before his assembled family. In many other respects he was but an indifferent character – I do not think he was so highly respected as he might have been in Messina. He was a Swiss by birth. Mrs. Fischer was an English lady, and entitled to every regard. The daughters were none of them pretty, but all talented, foreignised and great talkers. I immediately obtained an Italian master. I attended to the sale room, and counting house. In a very few weeks I felt at home, when news came from Palermo that our agent Lorenzo Bruno had gambled away a sum of £2–3,000 of our money. Green as I was, I was immediately sent to take charge of our stock, and such Bills and moneys as I could save from the wreck of our Agent. I remained some months in Palermo, took a house, furnished it, and paid the utmost attention to the business, which I greatly increased and consolidated. I had only one clerk, named Stellario Cesarco; a rum little fellow, but very active and co-operating. He lived in the same house with me. I was fortunate enough to engage a married couple – the wife an Irish woman, the husband cook and man of all work – as my sole servants. It was surprising how soon I learned the language sufficiently to enable me to transact business with my customers, even without the aid of a master. Doubtless the few lessons I took in Frankfort assisted me greatly.

I returned to Messina to give an account of my stewardship. I found Mr. Fischer greatly excited in consequence of a correspondence from his bookkeeper, an Englishman named Williams, who had been discharged. This man accused Fischer of robbing his correspondents in the prices made for goods sold for their account. I received in consequence instructions to look into the matter. I went through all the sales effected during many years. It was a laborious job, and took me some weeks. It resulted in the satisfactory exculpation of Fischer. It was immediately after this event, namely in 1820, that Fischer made up his mind to retire from the management of the concern. I accordingly received instructions to assume the same. I requested the Manchester house to send me an assistant, recommending to their notice Mr. John Nicholls, whom I had known in Frankfort and subsequently in Manchester. The choice was excellent in some respects. He was honest, steady and prudent, but he lacked in breadth of mind to manage such a business. He lacked in resource and gumption. In the meantime I returned to Palermo to place matters there on a permanent footing, and to receive the stock which Fischer had to hand over to me formally. I also besought the Manchester house to send me my brother John, as I considered that his abilities would be more suitably employed as head of the Palermo branch, than as a mere bookkeeper in Manchester. I then returned to Messina, where I took a small but comfortable house and a sufficient store. In the meantime Mr. Nicholls joined me.

I need not detail the various and incessant efforts I made during a couple of years. It was my ambition that the affairs confided to my management should in no ways suffer by the change Mr. Fischer's sudden retirement effected. The severe application and the manner in which I based my mental and physical powers proved too much for my strength. During two or three months I fell into a desponding stupid state, seldom speaking, and exceedingly drowsy. I would sit for hours by the fireside, saying and doing nothing. My kind friends Mr. and Mrs. Joseph Oates did all they could to rouse me; but in vain until one day Mr. Thomas Dawson, brother of Jonathan Dawson of Manchester, called on me, and upbraided me with faintheartedness and want of courage. The next morning I was up at my usual hour of five o'clock, looking over my ledger, journal, cashbook and in a very few days the business was wholly mine again.

❧ *Farewell to Christiana*

I think it was in 1822 when my brother John Close came out. Just before his arrival, I received a letter from Christiana Edinsor putting and end to the connection we had formed, and which had kept my spirits up under many difficulties. The reason she assigned was 'real or fancied slights from my Mother and my family'. This was a sore trial. I showed her letter to Nicholls who endeavoured to console me in every way he could. But I would not be consoled; I made up my mind to return to Manchester to look into this strange affair myself, for by this time I had acquired habits of independence and command; I could not brook being crossed in a matter so dear to my happiness and, as I made it out, to my honour. No sooner therefore did John make his appearance in Messina and had been installed ten days in my armchair and at my desk, than I took my passage on board a Genoese sailing ship for Genoa, thinking that fortune would favour me with a rapid passage. I well remember my brother John's remonstrances at being so soon 'deserted by me in a strange place'. I felt however that by throwing him on his resources during a couple of months he would acquire more rapidly those habits of command and self reliance, without which no business can be vigorously conducted. It is necessary that a man should make some mistakes, and that in his own conscience he should feel them and 'fry' for them, if his experience is to be worth anything. Not, that I know, dear John ever made any mistake, except that of being too prudent. Any how he had Nicholls near him, and I had a right to think that between the two matters could not go far wrong during my absence.

My passage was unfortunate. Bad weather forced the ship to take refuge in Gaeta. I had been sick and frightened, for numbers of ships perished during that storm. My family had learned of my departure but where was I? At Gaeta I wrote to Naples for credits, money &c. and on receiving them started by the courier for Rome, Florence, Milan, Paris &c. Mount Cenis was now blocked up by snow for carriages and I had to sledge it. I did not permit myself to remain a single night on the road. I reached Manchester as soon as a letter could do. The coach stopped in the Bridgewater Hotel Court. I left my portmanteau there, and after shaving and making myself presentable I walked to Norfolk Street, and ringing the bell of Mr. Edinsor's house I requested to see Christiana. I was doubtless somewhat excited. The length of my journey, no stopping, but onwards; as I approached the object of my thoughts I did feel bewildered, for I stared about me wildly when, on being admitted to the breakfast room, there were only Mr. and Mrs. Edinsor to receive me. There was no Christiana! Had I seen her then, I have no more doubt than I have in my existence, that the whole course of my subsequent life would have been changed. Of course I could not say one word to her father and mother, who received me kindly and courteously; and who I am sure must have perceived something wild and unusual in my agitated manner. I waited some time with my eyes riveted on the door hoping or expecting to see Christiana's graceful form emerge; but at last concluded that she purposely declined meeting me. I therefore took my leave, and taking a coach reached my father's residence at Chestham Hill late in the evening.

What a meeting was that! My excellent Father with uplifted hands thanking Heaven that I was safe! My Mother too, in tears of joy that I was not lost at sea as was reported and generally believed. "But why did you not write" asked my brother. So much anxiety and mourning might have been saved! It has been said, with some truth, that our defects descend into the tomb with us, whilst our good qualities arise from it. Certainly I was an instance of this truth, for I heard from more quarters than one how deeply I had been lamented. On the question being put, why I had so suddenly returned, my courage failed me. How could I after such a scene vent upon my own affectionate Mother my pent up indignation? All the fine things I had composed on my journey, all my wrathful speeches died on my lips. I only asked "Why, why, were you unkind to Christiana?" "I unkind, James? Certainly there must be some mistake." I found my parents afflicted, my brother's remarks soon made me feel that other deeper considerations occupied the attention of the family. The story was soon told. The proceedings of the Couplands in Liverpool and Jamaica were unsatisfactory; and my family's fortune was greatly involved. My brother therefore put it to me if under such circumstances I could continue the connection with Miss Edinsor, at least honourably, without confiding to her parents the uncertainties in which the house was involved, and that to confide that, which was then but a supposition, would be most unfair to my own family. The argument I thought conclusive; and Christiana's non appearance when I called led me to suppose that she had made up her mind to break off for the questionable reason alleged; or <u>perhaps</u> she may have heard something in respect to the tottering affairs of my Father's house. I considered my way as an honest man to be clear. A few days after I called again on her, and never shall I forget the interview I had with her. She seemed to have expected my call, for she received me as if anxious to forget the past and again be to me what she was before she wrote the letter, for she asked me why, why did you return the miniature and my letters? I sometimes think I had only half the heart of a man; that my love for Christiana was a sham, a youthful imagination without depth or reality. The interview was brief. I had made up my programme. The altered position on Christiana's mind was unheeded by me. "Christiana!" I replied, "what you have done is well done. Circumstances hereafter may prove that it is so, for your and my welfare. I have called to say this; that I have loved you with my whole soul, and to say farewell. I return immediately to Sicily." She heard, breathing with difficulty. She received our last kiss, and even now I remember the slam of the front door, and the sound of my own footsteps as I descended the steps into the street. I have only seen her once since; she was then the wife of a Birmingham Banker, immensely wealthy, and the mother of two daughters. I was a widower and the father of one child, my Henry. She had altered into the matron. That she had long thought of me I know; and her image as she was when I last saw her as Christiana Edinsor long haunted my dreams. Through the whole of my life I have retained an affectionate remembrance of her form and features; and I have shown it by my attachment to her widowed mother who in after days used to call me her son.

James Close's autobiography ends at this point.

❧ *Two family firms*

*J*AMES CLOSE'S father's firm dealt in cotton goods. The period described in JC's early life coincided with the Lancashire cotton boom – 50,000 tons of raw cotton were imported in 1815 and 100,000 tons in 1825, much of them for re-export as finished products. In 1820 half of all UK exports were in cotton goods and yarn. Manchester was known as 'Cottonopolis'.

Yet at the tail end of this cotton-based prosperity his father's firm declined and JC founded his own firm on the Continent. These events were connected with further disagreements with his elder brother Thomas. They are related below, drawing on further extracts from JC's autobiography.

The various references in James Close's two documents to his father's firm tell us that on the retirement of his fellow partners Mr Barlow and Mr Wittemberg, father John had taken control of the firm and renamed it John Close & Co., with Solomon Rimhold, previously a clerk, as the only other partner. It specialised in cotton goods and shipped them to agents or branches in Cologne and Heligoland. About the period of JC's birth (1799), Maximilian Fischer was sent out to establish a branch house in Sicily.

The choice of Heligoland needs some explanation. The tiny island was, according to the following quotation from Napier's *War in the Peninsula*, a useful base for trading with the blockaded Continent: 'Napoleon's Continental system was so efficient that the British Government was driven to encourage and protect illicit trading to the detriment of mercantile morality.' This comment was inappropriate. Even from Sicily many firms were able to smuggle goods into Napoleon's none-too-efficient blockade, via Spain, the Adriatic ports or Turkey, according to where the war was not being waged at the time and where things were comparatively quiet. Some British houses managed to continue to operate in Naples throughout the occupation, and may have helped with the smuggling into the peninsula. Since the idea of the blockade was to impoverish Britain to the point of surrender, attempts to evade it were surely acceptable.

So with possible backdoor access to the blockaded Continent, John Close's firm had prospered during the war. The first set-back after it ended had been the rise in the value of the pound sterling in 1815, which as usual hit all exporters. JC attributed the strong pound to 'the cessation of subsidies to our Continental allies or to the resumption of cash payments by the Bank of England'. Much more serious for the firm, according to JC, was the return in 1818 of his brother Thomas from his two-year tour of duty in Naples and Sicily. He then 'took a leading part in the management of the house and was made a partner on completing his twenty-first year'. He made it his particular concern to help out the failing ventures of Thomas Coupland, Aunt Betsy's husband. JC wrote: 'It was at this period, that with a view to assisting my cousins Coupland, and to giving a new direction to the business of the house, an arrangement was entered into with their incipient houses in Jamaica and Liverpool which led to the total ruin of my Father's house in 1826.' Expanding on this in his autobiography, he wrote:

> My eldest brother's attention was to be more especially directed to the new branch of business in Jamaica and Liverpool he was establishing, under the guidance of my cousins Thos. and John Coupland, those very children on whose ponies we used to race in years gone by, but who like myself had now attained man's estate, and whom, as relatives and able men, it appeared just and right to encourage. I have heard Mr. Rimhold say that when the war with Napoleon was brought to a close, the capital of the firm was not much short of £70,000. I have reason to believe that this statement was over-rated. I am certain however that at this period the credit of the house was unquestionably good and that the firm was considered to be one of the most respectable in Manchester, both in regard to business and also to its social standing.

It is little wonder that any money invested in Coupland's ventures would never be seen again, when it is recollected that of his three sons, Thomas committed suicide, Henry went bankrupt in Liverpool and John 'died in a garret of a loathsome disease'; while their sister's husband emigrated to Canada and 'shot himself or got shot'. Yet if JC had taken a broader view, he would not have loaded his brother with all the blame for the collapse of his father's firm. 1826 was a bad year for many banks. L. H. Grindon, in *The Troubles of 1826*, wrote that 'no fewer than sixty-three provincial banks, or about one in every ten banks then existing, being compelled at this dreadful period to succumb for ever … Manchester suffered severely.' John Close & Co. may not have been a bank, but credit must have been tight and any temporary difficulties would not have been easy to resolve: many businesses failed.

After the disaster of 1826, JC's father ceased to play an active part in the firm; but it was not altogether dead:

> … in 1827 my eldest brother Thomas married Miss Ellen Smith of Nottingham, a lady of some fortune … He retired to Nottingham, placed £5,000 of his wife's

fortune in the reconstructed firm, and leaving the management of the house in Manchester to Mr. S. Rimhold, on an annual allowance, became a sleeping partner with 3/8ths of the profit. In 1831 my brother retired, in consequence of dissensions with me in respect of future division of profits. In 1832 my father died of disease of the kidneys, brought on by change of climate and system of living [*He had recently returned from a post-retirement five-year stay in Italy.*], and doubtless aggravated by the dissensions between his two sons. It is impossible for me to look back to this distressing period without feeling the bitterest regret. How much misery would have been spared to me and to the Family, if my brother Thomas and myself had acted in a spirit of liberality towards each other, instead of jealousy!

According to Anne Eaden (a granddaughter of JC, who prepared an unpublished version of the Journals), JC had helped the post-1826 UK firm to get back on its feet, but how and when is not mentioned. Had he not done so, it is difficult to see how he could have had much claim to a share of the profits.

JC had written in his Family History that Thomas exacted deference as the eldest son, had never forgiven his father for appointing JC and not himself as executor and that the two of them had not spoken for twenty years. The tension between the two brothers was also seen on the occasion in the History of my own Life, when JC, aged twenty-three, returned to the family house in Manchester after having been away for four years. That very afternoon he was mocked by Thomas for his Frenchified ways. This episode showed that JC himself was not faultless, in that he was too quick to take offence and full of *amour propre* – as he himself engagingly recognised. Soon after this, another such incident had further embittered relations between James and Thomas. While in Le Havre and in love with the Rev. Dampierre's daughter, JC had rashly promised to find a place in one of the London houses for Dampierre's ne'er-do-well son. So on his return from France to England, before going home to Manchester, he had called on one of his father's friends in London, a Mr Prendergast of the East India company, to ask if he had at his disposal a writership or directorship. The sequel came a fortnight later:

> ... a parcel from Mr. Prendergast brought me the writership I had solicited (name in blank for me to fill up), much to the surprise of my Father and Brother to whom I had said nothing on the subject. On being questioned I stated the promise I had made, and my joy at being also able to perform it. [*By an unfortunate co-incidence*] a few days before this event occurred, Mr. John Hardman, one of my Father's oldest friends, had asked him to use his influence in procuring

a situation for one of *his* sons. ... There can be no doubt that Mr. Prendergast, in obliging me in this matter, did it not for love of my ugly mug, but because I was the son of my father. And it might moreover be said that I was expending my father's influence on behalf of a party whose habits and attainments were altogether unworthy of the favour.

While his father hesitated to disappoint and perhaps humiliate his son, his brother did not:

My brother Tom's impetuosity, and the habit he had unfortunately fallen into of considering his younger brothers as persons not entitled to a will, a voice or wish of their own, carried the day. The appointment was abruptly taken from me and sent forthwith to Mr. Hardman, and I was left to make the best excuse in my power to young Dampierre, who in reply sent me a letter so injudicious and taunting that not only did I at that moment reconcile myself to the somewhat harsh measure my brother had taken, but I resolved neither to answer the letter nor to give myself further trouble about him. This incident, combined with my brother's making me his butt on my arrival, did not tend to produce in me a state of mind towards him likely to lead to that affectionate regard which such near relatives ought to entertain for each other.

I will just add that young Dampierre later joined the transport which was to convey him to India, and was drowned on his passage out by falling overboard. Thus ended my romantic love for Elizabeth Dampierre.

As the breaking off of JC's later engagement to Christiana was partially caused by the impending collapse of John Close & Co. and to the extent that Thomas had been responsible for this, JC may have held him also responsible for the loss of his fiancée. Certainly it is clear that he was always going to run his own affairs and could never have worked in a subordinate position to his brother. Happily their permanent geographical separation seems to have healed the rift, as by 1858 they were in amicable correspondence.

It has been seen that in 1819, the year after brother Thomas's return from Italy, JC was sent out to Messina. A year after his arrival, Fischer, who had been there since 1799, retired. 'Thus I found myself at the early age of twenty encharged with the sole management of this branch of my father's business. In 1921 my brother John was at my request sent out to assist me.'

It had been assumed that after a couple of years JC would, like brother Thomas, return to Manchester and John Close & Co. But within two years he had re-established control in Palermo, brought out brother John to help him and changed the name of the Italian business to *James* Close & Co. This firm was further strengthened with the opening of a Naples office in 1824. (Some kind of correspondent's office in Naples, in his father's name, probably existed before 1824: as has been seen, brother Thomas went out there just before his return to England in 1819, and JC had spent some time there when he first left England, on his way to Messina.) JC controlled all the James Close and Co branches from Naples, while brother John was based in Messina. Not only had JC got away from his brother Thomas's influence, but he had also, by establishing a separate firm, escaped ruinous involvement in the 1826 collapse of the business at home.

JC was never to work again in England. Staying on in Sicily was partly fortuitous, as Fischer had quickly taken advantage of his arrival and obvious abilities to retire; and JC had had no option but to stay in Sicily until things had been sorted out. But apart from that and the need to be independent, his further education in Germany and his business training in Le Havre had given him a taste for living on the Continent and a cosmopolitan outlook that he was never to lose. His business life in Europe was nearly as peripatetic as that of today's tycoons, despite the lack of air travel.

❧ *Note on business in Sicily*

*T*HAT JC's father had two offices in Sicily is not surprising. Following the American war of Independence and the exclusion of English goods from the United States in 1790, England had been searching for other markets. She successfully exported to the Continent of Europe, and as far as textiles were concerned, had done particularly well in the German states and the Italian peninsula. Before the war with France, England had been predominant in trade with the Kingdom of the Two Sicilies, and there had been a prosperous community of English merchants in Naples; but during that war, from 1806 onwards, the Italian peninsula from Naples southwards had been ruled by Napoleon's brother Joseph and from 1808 by his brother-in-law Joachim Murat. The Bourbon Court along with many British merchants had moved to Sicily. British traders in the island had already been doing well, but following this new influx, exports from Sicily increased fourfold. As a result of Napoleon's blockade, Sicily became the only country in Europe with which England could trade openly.

Nelson had his fleet there and the influence of the English was strong. A constitutional parliament was established under their aegis. Moreover Messina with its central position in the Mediterranean was an important entrepôt for trade and ideally placed for merchants, who made a living by getting commission on the cargo ships they chartered. Also, Messina was a free port – any ship could dock there without paying harbour fees. So traders around the Mediterranean would use it: cargoes from the Levant, for example, would be taken to Messina for the merchants to organise reshipment. While most of the British merchants operated from Messina, the boom in trade also benefited the capital and by 1811 there were ten of them established in Palermo.

Sometimes the ships bringing freight into the Mediterranean would have to deliver it to one port, but sail to another to get a cargo for the return journey. Another advantage of Sicily was that besides having an abundance of fruit and wine, she offered sulphur, and this was becoming her main export. It was used in England for the manufacture of industrial machinery. It helped solve the problem of the return journey. Fruit and wine were seasonal: sulphur was always available. It was exported from Palermo in such quantities that Sicily's balance of trade with the UK was in surplus.

CHAPTER II

1824–58: The Intervening Years

J AMES CLOSE'S autobiography ends with the breaking off of his engagement
to Christiana in 1824 and he does not speak to us again until his account of the
family cruise to Venice in 1858. He leaves no writing – not even letters – about the
greater part of his working life, so little is known about his private thoughts and
motivations.

His business affairs however were closely bound up with the political turmoil
during these years, as while he had dealings with the King and was *persona grata*
at Court, his brother-in-law Giuseppe Romano was regarded as a dangerous liberal
and *his* brother, Don Liborio Romano, whom Ferdinand II imprisoned, was to be
an important player in the change of regime in 1860. So a review of the political
upheavals during this period and of the role of the Romanos will provide the background to JC's working career. Some account of that work, in the absence of any
record from his own pen, can be given from research in the Neapolitan archives.

First, that which is known about his family life during this period can quickly be
told. JC must have acquired a home in Naples not long after opening an office there
in 1824, as after the collapse of the Manchester firm, his parents and sister Paulina,
refugees from the 1826 troubles, came there to live with him. In his family history,
JC writes:

> In 1827 my father, mother and sister joined me in Naples, where they soon for-
> got the mortifications they left behind in Manchester. Between myself in Naples
> and brother John in Messina, my parents spent five years in the enjoyment of
> as much happiness as an united family, moderate prosperity, and good health
> could confer.

When later on the family packed up to leave Naples, there are references in the
Journal to clearing the house. At least until 1859 this was at 20 Via Ascensione, a
grand street in the middle of the city, leading directly down to the sea. (See plate 9.)
A photograph shows this house to be large and imposing, but they could not have
had all of it, as Anne's sister Mrs Burd wrote that during her visit there she was put
up 'in a flat under Mr Close's … The houses have flat roofs which form most agreeable terraces. Mr Close has one which I am sure I shall often enjoy.'

In late 1831 JC's parents and sister returned to England, but father John Close died the following year. JC felt that 'because of the reverses of John and myself', he could no longer afford the upkeep of the family house in Manchester; so mother and Paulina returned to Naples.

⚜ *Marriages*

*J*AMES CLOSE remained a bachelor for ten years after opening the Naples branch. Perhaps after the two failed engagements already described, he was cautious about trying again. He was travelling about and doubtless continued to be smitten as frequently as he was in his youth. He had written: 'in the course of my life I have often been desperately in love', although 'at each repetition the *couleur de rose* lost in intensity'. In 1834 however he married Henrietta Gaskell, daughter of a Wigan solicitor. It was a happy marriage, but in 1836 she died giving birth to their only child, Henry Gaskell Close.

Another ten years elapsed before JC married again. His second marriage was to one of the daughters of his old friend, the prominent banker Samuel Brooks of Manchester. Samuel's father had started a calico business in 1792 jointly with his friend Roger Cunliffe, who went on to fund religious and educational projects in his neighbourhood. Through a process not uncommon at the time, the firm gradually got into the banking business and became Cunliffe Brooks & Co. But it was Samuel who really established the wealth and reputation of the firm. In *Manchester Banks and Bankers* by L. H. Grindon (also the author of *The Troubles of 1826*) it says: 'Speculation was rife as to how much money "Old Stink o' Brass" had left. Some said up to two and a half million pounds.' Samuel Brooks was one of the richest commoners in the country, according to a contemporary issue of the *Manchester Guardian.* Grindon tells us that 'the engineer Brunel had once swallowed half a sovereign whilst playing with his children, and John Brooks (Samuel's brother) had advised "they should send for our Sam: he'll get it if anybody can".' Yet Samuel did not hoard his money. In his only recorded public speech he said, "Money is like muck, of no use unless well spread."

Samuel Brooks's wife had died in 1842 leaving him with a large family to care for. Anne, born in 1821, was the second of five daughters. In 1844 she was suffering from bronchitis and needed to escape from the cold and damp of a Manchester winter. Her anxious father thought it would be an excellent idea for her to go out to Naples, where she could enjoy a better climate in the care of James Close. The Brookses and the Closes were family friends; to take such a step seemed the most natural thing in the world and so Anne, together with her younger sister Alice, was sent on what was to prove a most fateful journey. Great was Samuel Brooks's consternation when the unforeseen happened: his beautiful young daughter and her host, a widower twenty-two years her senior, fell in love and sought his consent to their marriage. Letters passed between Naples and Manchester. James Close's letter to Samuel Brooks must have been a difficult one to write in the circumstances; it is not known how he put his case or what was the reply from Samuel Brooks, but the two men remained friends. A letter from Anne to her father, however, has survived, dated January 1845. It shows how hesitant her father must have been in giving his consent and her anxiety to reassure him as to the suitability of the proposed match:

My dear Papa,

Nearly three weeks have passed without my hearing from you, this gives me much uneasiness for if my prospects had given you pleasure you would not have kept me in suspense. I know that your only thought is for my welfare – let me assure you most solemnly, that I firmly believe I secure my happiness by uniting myself to Mr. Close. I cannot give you too many assurances, your silence alone makes me unhappy. I would not willingly be the cause of one moment's anxiety to you and yet I know I have occasioned you painful thoughts for although you have not written I am sure you often think of me. Of course no arrangements can be made until we receive your letter to Mr. C. but should William [*Anne's brother*] & Jane come here, I should like them to spend five or six weeks with us before the marriage takes place, in order that they may have some knowledge of Mr. Close before he enters our family. I am quite sure he would at once gain their esteem and love.

I mentioned in my last letter Mr. Gaskell [*Henry Gaskell, brother of JC's first wife Henrietta, and future husband of Alice Brooks*] Do not take any notice or tell anyone what I am going to say, but he certainly pays Alice very marked attention. I dare not say a word in his favour for fear it should have a contrary effect – but on the whole I think she rather likes him. He is a most amiable kind hearted man, and Mr Close has the highest opinion of him. I am sure she would not better secure her happiness than by marrying him. Do not then be surprised if in a little time, you should receive communication of a similar nature to those we made – but I will let you know how

things go on. Alice unites with me in kind love to you and, believe me dear
Papa
   Your affectionate daughter
   Anne Brooks

In the end Samuel Brooks gave in to his daughter's pleadings and, whatever misgivings he may have had, particularly about the twenty-two-year age gap, he gave his consent. James Close and Anne Brooks were married at the British Embassy in Naples on 15th April 1846: the bridegroom was forty-six and the bride twenty-four. All Samuel Brooks's doubts were to be dispelled, for the marriage could not have been happier or more successful: James Close found in Anne Brooks all that he could have hoped or wished for in a wife, while she in turn proved to be fully justified in her firm belief that her happiness lay in uniting herself to Mr. Close. Ten years later she wrote: 'My marriage has been beyond the most romantic expectations of my girlhood. Never have I known a void of the heart.' The portraits of JC and Anne reproduced in the colour plates were painted six years after the marriage.

The wedding day was a happy one too for the son of JC's first marriage, Henry Gaskell Close, bringing as it did a warmly loving and much-loved stepmother into his life who, over the next thirteen years, provided him with eight half-brothers and sisters. When, as presaged in Anne's letter to her father, her younger sister Alice Brooks married Henrietta's brother Henry, all the Closes, Brookses and Gaskells became related – in some cases doubly so. Henrietta Close's memory remained green, and JC used to say that, with Henrietta his first wife on one side of him, and Anne his second wife on the other, St. Peter would never have the heart to lock him out of heaven.

Anne would be spending half her life at sea, managing a growing band of children, their tutors and the family servants, with responsibility for all domestic arrangements – food, medication, sanitation, where everyone would sleep, where the children would have their lessons, and so on. Whenever JC was away on business, the ship's captain would report to her, as she assumed ultimate responsibility for the ship and the ship's company. Monumental calm was required, and this she had. It is described in a passage from the February 1975 issue of *Blackwood's Magazine* by one of her granddaughters, Ruth Eaden (sister of Anne):

Granny Close, who had an unshakable faith in her maker, was a woman of unruffled calm and resource. Well she needed to be, with a troop of small children on board, a husband who had gout in both feet, and she herself martyred by a chronic sea-sickness that forced her to retire to her cabin if the *Sibilla* so much as curtsied in a mild sea. It was she, untrained, who dealt with all the first-aid work abroad. There were no doctors within call, there was no wireless, and the drugs of today were in the distant future. She had a fund of inner strength and common sense, and she never lost a case. Her skill was stretched to the full when little Will, still at the low-necked frock and petticoat stage then in fashion for toddlers, escaped from nursery supervision and made his way down to the galley to see what was cooking for the crew's dinner. It was during his investigations that he succeeded in tipping a cauldron full of boiling macaroni down the front of his frock. The terrible chest burns that resulted were dressed with olive oil and a piece of clean linen under a thick layer of cotton wool, and then bandaged. Once young Will's burns had healed he suffered no ill effects, the word 'complex' not then having been coined.

Only once did Anne appear to lose her calming influence and self control – when she spotted one of her sons doing gymnastics at the top of the rigging. When he had been coaxed down, she fainted.

The links between the Closes and the Brookses remained strong and all Anne's children were christened with Brooks as a middle name. When JC's eldest son John Brooks Close also married a Brooks (and became a director of Cunliffe Brooks & Co.), he changed his name to John Close-Brooks – as a result of which some of the many descendants of the family today are named Close-Brooks as a surname, while others remain just Close.

The Romanos

A MORE STRONGLY disputed marriage took place in the same year as JC's marriage to Anne. Paulina, his sister, married an Italian. She had after all been living in Naples, with one short break, for eighteen years. By this time she was getting on, and proposing to marry into a well-known Italian family, the Romanos. Yet marrying into the local community was not acceptable to the 'colony' of English. The vice-consul in Messina, William Barker, who married an Italian, was accused of acting against the British interests and of becoming 'Sicilian' in mentality. Raleigh Trevelyan, in his book *Princes under the Volcano*, wrote that 'the British, as usual abroad, kept their distance from the natives, intermarrying among themselves and keeping rigidly to their roast beef on Sunday tradition.' JC was implacable in his opposition to the Romano marriage, as can be seen from these further extracts from his family history:

> The romantic notions she acquired at school of love and matrimony exercised a prejudicial influence over her prospects in life. She played her cards to her own disadvantage and married late in life (aged 36) a Neapolitan advocate, Joseph [*Giuseppe*] Romano, a man of good provincial family and of respectable standing in Naples, but of little fortune beyond his professional earnings. This marriage was concocted by my sister without consulting me. She drew my mother to her side, and though I refused my sanction, I could offer no effective resistance to the joint representations of both. After great difficulties, she being a Protestant, they were married in London. Although the conduct of Romano both as a husband and as a member of society has been unexceptionable, I am not certain if this marriage has answered in every particular my sister's expectations. I know it did not my mother's. I utterly object to marriages between English girls and Italians. Their education and habits form a fearful contrast with ours. However, if the assurances my sister's husband and relatives held out in respect to fortune have proved delusive, and she is compelled to observe the strictest economy in her domestic arrangements (notwithstanding her own income of from £250 to £300), I am bound to acknowledge that hitherto he has shown himself to be a temperate and moderate man; industrious in his profession, anxious to get on, and devoted to his home and children. My sister has borne three children: Mary, John and Thomas, and she sets no bounds to her affection for them. The weak feature in my sister's character is want of judgment to direct an overflowing heart and to give point to her buoyant sensibilities. To me she has ever been an entirely affectionate sister, and I believe there never was a person, who showed a kindly feeling towards her, who could complain of her not having met it, and cordially. [*After the marriage JC's mother moved in with the Romanos.*]
>
> The Romano family is from Patu, a village in the Province of Lecce, where the family has been settled for some 300 years. They have estates there, which yield very little. The family professes extreme liberal principles. It has suffered much from persecution.

JC later claimed that 'The Romano family had distinguished itself during the last three-quarters of a century by constant opposition to the Bourbon Dynasty. Most of its members of the last and present generation have suffered persecution and imprisonment for their conduct.'

The Romanos were said to have come from Russia. Their name had been

Romanoff, but the last two letters had been lost. The original immigrant Roman-offs were two brothers, one of them, the ancestor of Giuseppe and Liborio, being a bishop of the Greek Orthodox Church. They had landed near Otranto, the near-est port on the heel of Italy to the other side of the Adriatic. The Greek Orthodox religion had been practised for centuries, and for a long time the Greek language could be heard in this corner of Italy. The Romano family estate at Patu, referred to in JC's account, was near the town of Gallipoli in the Gulf of Taranto.

Both Paulina's husband Giuseppe (always referred to as Joseph by JC) and Don Liborio, his more forceful and flamboyant brother, were lawyers. Although JC had been full of foreboding about his sister's marriage, in time Anne Close did much to soften his antipathy to his brother-in-law, who eventually earned the grudging tributes quoted above. Later, after the fall of the Bourbons, Don Giuseppe was to be the MP for Gallipoli and his brother Don Liborio a Minister of State in the new regime. JC's comment on that was: 'Time will show the results of this political elevation in respect of both brothers. I expect no good from it to either, and should the Bourbons return, both must leave the country.'

🐎 *Business in Naples*

A useful source for this section, and the only source for the next, 'JC at work', has been Barbara Dawes's *British Merchants in Naples, 1820–1880*, published in Italy in 1991.

*A*FTER THE DEFEAT of Napoleon, Naples again became the capital of the Bourbon Kingdom and King Ferdinand's court left Sicily, together with most of the diplomatic and commercial communities. There had been a colony of Eng-lish merchants in the city since the seventeenth century. Now their return was welcomed and their numbers increased. JC set up his own Naples firm in 1824. It was estimated in *The Gentlemen's Magazine* that 400 English families were living there at the time.

However welcome the return of the exiles, the favourable treatment accorded to the English and Scottish firms ever since the Treaty of Utrecht in 1713 was not reinstituted. That Treaty, ending the War of the Spanish Succession, had granted to the recently created Great Britain both monopolies and free access to many mar-kets world-wide, including The Two Sicilies. Now import duties on British goods were reimposed. This was in part due to an understandable need to encourage the growth of local industry, but to the government in London this seemed like ingratitude. Some lesser privileges were granted to British ships in 1817, but this was partly in return for the British navy keeping Italian ports and off-shore trade safe from Barbary pirates. Disputes and friction on these matters rumbled on until the middle of the century and legal imbroglios were increasingly time consuming and financially damaging. The merchants never hesitated to raise contentious issues with their local Consul General, whose job it was to raise their complaints with the local authorities. If that did not work, the Consul would bring in the British Minister at the Legation (Lady Hamilton's husband), who would approach the Italian Foreign Secretary. If that did not settle it, Hamilton would report the issue to the Foreign Office in London, which in turn would sometimes get the complaint raised in the House of Commons. As will be seen, this cumbersome procedure was sometimes short-circuited, and it is surprising how often trading matters were referred to the Foreign Secretary in London or to King Ferdinand in Naples.

Naples was a good market for British goods, but the problem of finding a return cargo was worse there than in Sicily, as Neapolitan exports were comparatively paltry. In the post war period they consisted of such items as liquorice, cream of tartar, sumac and leather gloves. Often the ships had to leave the city loaded with nothing more than ballast, and find a cargo elsewhere. Triangular journeys, a to b, b to c and c back to a, each time with a different cargo, were common, and exercised the organising skills of the merchants. Where opportunities arose they were taken, and merchants would charter ships from any country to sail to any port.

International banks did not exist at this time, and the merchants were responsible for organising the finance. Invoices were usually paid with credit or with bills of exchange, and bills proffered by the British were the most reliable. Consequently merchants found themselves acting as bankers, and that is how JC later became one of the bankers to the King.

During the 1830's, when Ferdinand began building his own merchant navy and when he introduced further protectionist measures, the disputes with the merchants grew more serious and the weaker ones closed down, or left for other states such as Venice. Those that were left pulled the strings leading to the House of Commons as hard as they could, and very often succeeded in overturning a decision by the Neapolitan officials. Ultimately England had the whip hand, as was demonstrated when in July 1838 King Ferdinand tried to award a monopoly on the export of sulphur to the French. Palmerston (Foreign Secretary at the time) blockaded the Bay of Naples with warships. Ferdinand not only had to abandon the French monopoly but also had to agree to compensation for the English merchants. This startling show of force must have been one of Palmerston's first acts of 'gun-boat diplomacy'. A factor behind Ferdinand's capitulation was his fear that the English might side with the Sicilian revolutionaries in their struggle for independence from Bourbon rule.

A treaty resolving these disputes was finally agreed in 1845. It was not favourable to the Neapolitans. British exports flooded in, and although the privileges granted were later extended to other countries as well, England acquired a near-monopoly of the carrying trade in the Mediterranean. Many workers in Naples trying to build up home-based industries had to be sacked. Local textile factories in particular were badly hit. But this relief for the English came too late for many of the eighteen merchant houses that had done business in Naples in the 1820's. Most of them had succumbed to the pressures brought about by the long-running trade battle, with retaliatory protectionist measures being introduced by both sides. Only three English houses of the original eighteen listed in the twenties were still in business. Those three survivors (together with a number of newcomers) emerged from the struggle stronger than ever, as they had been able to take on some of the business of the failed firms. One of these survivors was James Close and Co.

✺ *JC at work*

*W*HEN James Close and Co first set up in Naples it was not of course one of the larger British firms. In 1827 the Neapolitan authorities produced a document listing British merchants according to size. The bigger ones were taxed more, but were also more credit-worthy. The figures were supplied by the firms themselves and may not have been altogether reliable, but since there were advantages as well as disadvantages to being among the larger firms, the figures may have approximated to the truth. JC's firm, 'Giacomo Close & Co', is ranked tenth out of twenty-four British firms. Not bad, considering JC had only opened his office there in 1824.

The first incident involving JC mentioned by Dawes occurred in 1827 and related to Naples, Messina and Palermo. As Dawes refers to 'Close', it is not clear whether she refers to JC himself or to his brother John, who at that date was running the Sicilian end of the business. The passage begins:

In 1827 a cargo of cotton textile goods arrived in Naples from Liverpool on the brig *Juno* for the merchant Close, part of which was unloaded at Naples and part of which was to be taken to Messina and consigned to Close's branch there. At Naples the Manifesto was presented to the Customs and handed over to the official interpreter for translation (the British having the right by decree of 1818 to present their declarations in English).

At Messina the Customs refused to accept *cotoni* (for cottons), which they argued should have been described as *tessuti di cotoni* (cotton textiles) – a higher duty was payable on made up cloth and clothing. They delayed the ship for fourteen days and imposed a heavy fine. The penalty charge was withdrawn after reference to the main Customs office in Palermo, but the delay had been costly to the firm and Close sought compensation from the Messina Customs. He refused to press his case through the local Court, as he felt sure they would rule in favour of the Sicilians. Instead he appealed directly to the British Minister in Sicily, through whose intervention he won his damages.

The above incident has been related in detail as it is typical of the sort of hassle that constantly arose. In 1833 JC was barred from landing a cargo of iron because Naples was suffering a bout of cholera and strict quarantine regulations were in force. When he finally landed it, he found that during the waiting period there had been a hike in the duties payable. He said he would take the iron on to Messina unless he was absolved from paying at the higher rate; and this threat was enough to win his argument.

Another difficult area was the regulation that imports that were useful to Neapolitan industries and could not be made locally were duty free. But how to determine whether or not they could be made in the Kingdom? In 1844 JC imported machine parts for converting carbon fossil to coke and the Director of Customs gave his consent to exemption. Yet the Finance Minister insisted on a more detailed examination of the possibilities of the machine parts being made in the Kingdom, and the owner of a big Neapolitan foundry was asked to make a report on the matter. In the end JC prevailed and no duty was paid. In a similar case in 1852, he wrote directly to the King, suggesting that the import duty on anchors should be abolished, as there was no local production and they were needed by the Neapolitan Merchant Navy. In this case, he did not get his way.

A more high profile case, which JC eventually lost, involved two Foreign Secretaries and was the subject of a lively debate in the House of Commons. In 1838 it was announced that the export of corn from the Kingdom would be banned from the end of the year. On behalf of an English grain merchant, Gower, JC had ordered 26,000 quarters of corn to be delivered before the end of December. He had already bought this and started to charter the ships, when a royal decree brought forward the date of the start of the ban by one month. As a result, the price of corn in Naples fell sharply and JC was left with an unexportable heap of corn. The Neapolitan authorities agreed to pay him the cost price for some of it, but most remained in his hands until the ban was lifted several months later. Then, when it reached England, Gower had missed the market and had to stock unsaleable corn to the value of £8,783.

JC decided to bring the matter up with the Manchester Chamber of Commerce, which had a powerful lobby in the House of Commons. The House debated it and decided in JC's favour: Foreign Secretary Palmerston declared that the Neapolitan government had the right to impose export bans, but not at the expense of British merchants. Yet still the Neapolitans refused to accept JC's claim and the dispute dragged on for years. Several administrations later Lord Aberdeen (Foreign Secretary under Peel), while admitting the justice of the claim, said that the only way to enforce it would be an outright declaration of war on Naples.

The merchants did not specialise in the kind of freight they carried and JC handled as wide a range of goods as any. He did, however, manage to be the Kingdom's main importer of coal. Manchester, near to both coal mines and the port of Liverpool was a good base for the export of that product and JC, with so many Manchester contacts, was well placed to pick up the trade. In the 1840s coal was increasingly in demand in the Italian peninsula to fuel the gradual introduction of a steam-powered navy, to power railway building projects and for conversion to coke, needed for the newly introduced gas lighting in town streets.

In addition to a contract to supply the Navy with coal, in 1844 JC won a huge contract to supply it with mixed iron products, deliverable over a number of years. This was particularly profitable in that the imports were exempt from duty. In 1846 JC shipped not only coal and metal parts for Ferdinand's new navy, but also 112 trees and 1,203 planks.

Another product he often shipped was marsala, which had been stocked by English warships since the days of Nelson. He benefited from its growing popularity in England, trading with the famous Sicilian firm of Ingham & Whitaker.

The final destinations of ships chartered by JC to sail from Naples were not always known, which required some adaptability. In 1841 he chartered *I Quatri Fratelli* to collect a cargo of olive oil in Gallipoli and Bari, and to take it to Falmouth, where the captain would receive instructions to sail on to one of eleven specified ports, ranging from Liverpool to St Petersburg.

These incidents all describe JC's work as a shipping merchant. The carrier trade alone, however, constituted but one part of his business activities. According to Barbara Dawes, whose book covered all British merchants in Naples, JC was 'by far the most enterprising and dynamic'.

The first dated diversification is in 1833, when JC set up a type foundry, to which was added (later) a printing press. Also in 1833 he acquired another factory, for processing madder. In 1838, sensitive to the requirement that local industries must be fostered, he organised a joint stock company for the manufacture of cotton textiles – after all, he had been trained in Manchester on every aspect of that industry. This got as far as receiving the seal of approval from the King, but JC did not take it further as one of the many conditions imposed was that the government should have the right to control the company.

JC embarked on a series of purchases and new ventures. He bought a depot for the storage of olive oil and came to own some of the warehouses he used. He began to acquire a number of ships. Apparently only smaller ships were suitable for carrying coal and with his regular trade in that business, he must have thought it expedient to build up his own specialised fleet.

Not all JC's projects succeeded. At the end of the 1830s he negotiated with the Archbishop of Salerno for a lease on a very large piece of land along the river Irno. This included country as well as built-up areas and JC planned to use it for market gardens, factories and water-powered mills, which would help him control the price of grinding corn. Two consultative bodies rejected the plans, not confident that JC would use the land in the best interests of the locals. One of them defined JC as 'an adventurer who will tomorrow deprive us of the high honour of his presence'. Nonetheless the King finally assented to the project but with so many strings attached that JC withdrew. A few years later, in 1845, JC attempted a second bid for a large area of land, this time near Castellammare. This too failed through local opposition.

Concerned about the smuggling of sugar and other foodstuffs into the Kingdom, JC prepared detailed proposals for diminishing this, including the building of a sugar refinery in Naples. None of these plans received sufficient support. Undeterred, JC's next venture was to present the Government with plans for a railway connecting Naples with Gaeta and Puglia. 24 million ducats would have to be raised, in exchange for which shareholders would get a guaranteed 6 per cent per annum. He suggested that the sum could be used immediately by the Government to write off the National Debt, which would enable them to reduce the rate of interest they were paying on Government bonds. Perhaps less surprisingly, this proposal too was rejected.

JC's most successful enterprise, however, was the inauguration in 1839 of the first coastal steamer service on the Western Coast of The Two Sicilies. He supplied these vessels from England – and it is clear that they were primitive. Mrs Sarah Burd, Anne's eldest sister, on one of her first visits to the Closes in Naples, risked the journey on one of the new steamers, which was being delivered. The terrible pitching and tossing she experienced on that voyage made her so appallingly seasick that on her return journey she travelled overland in her own carriage, with her two boys and their ponies. The pole of their carriage broke while they were crossing the Alps and the party had to wait in a shepherd's hut until it was repaired. "At least it didn't rock and roll", she said. Nonetheless, for a time the steamers were useful as a quick way of delivering mail and transporting coastal trade.

When in the 1850s a regular steamship run between England and Naples was started by P & O, the novelty of JC's steam-powered vessels began to fade.

Throughout this period, JC was consolidating his banking activities, which took an increasing proportion of his time. Success depended largely on mutual trust not only between the English merchants in Naples, but also between them and other Neapolitan Banks. As a rule, that trust was there. During one dispute over the non-payment of money, JC won his case due to the support not only of his English competitors, but also of Neapolitan merchants, and some from other countries as well.

This summary of JC's business career, impersonal as it is, suggests boundless energy; an open-mindedness that made him ready to seize any opportunity and an indomitable toughness in standing up for his rights when necessary.

❧ *Political and social background*

FOLLOWING THE END of the Napoleonic wars and the Congress of Vienna, Austria was the dominant power on the Continent and Italy, as a nation, did not exist. The peninsula was divided into the Papal States, with the Pope as temporal ruler, and independent duchies and Kingdoms. The largest of these was the Kingdom of the Two Sicilies, made up of Sicily and the 'leg' of Italy to the south of the papal states.

James Close's long residence in Naples covered the full reigns of the last two Bourbon kings, Ferdinand II (1830–59) and Francis II (1859–60). Neither did much to contradict the old saying that the Bourbons never forgot anything and never learned anything. Both believed unquestioningly that they were divinely appointed to rule, a philosophy that led to absolute monarchy. Ferdinand told his brother-in-law King Louis-Philippe of France that he did his subjects' thinking for them. Yet this supreme self-belief contrasted oddly with the insecure political situation. Periodic uprisings by his subjects showed that many of them, much of the time, were discontent. After Waterloo the Kingdom had no army to speak of, and Austria had assumed the role of military protector, not only when Napoleon was driven from the Kingdom, but also in 1820–21, when Austrian troops quelled a revolt in Naples. Ferdinand took on the task of building up his army, but even with later insurgencies, he had to rely on Swiss Guards to keep them down. His navy and his merchant fleet at the end of the war were insignificant, and at first he had to rely on British ships for both protection and commerce. This protection had been given during the war, in exchange for a promise from the Bourbon King that he would not make a separate peace with Napoleon. Now it could in theory be withdrawn.

The start of the Ferdinand II's reign in 1830 had been more glorious. Naples, the capital, was still regarded as one of the most brilliant and cosmopolitan capital cities in Europe, with its distinguished international colony and foreign visitors, the operas and plays at the famous San Carlo Theatre, the magnificent balls and receptions and the beautiful shops, all enhanced by the superb natural setting of the city and the climate with which it was blessed.

To add a lively touch to this scintillating scene Naples was also an international naval station, now remembered in this country for its earlier association with Nelson and Lady Hamilton. On the reverse side of the coin was the abysmal poverty in which the least fortunate lived; the squalor, corruption, venality and lack of justice that were taken for granted as part of Neapolitan life.

The young King Ferdinand was at first better liked than his forebears. His exuberant and extrovert personality, cheerful bonhomie, sense of showmanship and, until later marred by corpulence, his good looks made him a popular figure, while his genuine attempts at reform gave hope for a more liberal regime. He had the deep superstitious fear of the Evil Eye common to all Neapolitans, while his religious fanaticism equalled, even surpassed, their own: for example, every officer and soldier in the Army wore an amulet and carried a sacred image in his equipment, while St. Ignatius Loyola, the Army's patron saint, was granted the rank of Field Marshal, his pay being made over by the King to the appropriate Order, the Society of Jesus. The Army enjoyed Ferdinand's special favour: as the years passed his sense of mistrust of all around him and his feelings of insecurity led him to rely more and more on his Army and the Swiss regiments to crush any opposition among his subjects.

The King's marriage in 1832 proved popular. The choice fell on Maria Cristina, youngest of the four daughters of the late King Victor Emanuel of Sardinia. She had set her heart on taking the veil, but was persuaded that her piety and prayers would be of more effect in Court circles than in the anonymous seclusion of a convent, and that it was the will of God that she should be a comfort to Ferdinand. The marriage was a success but did not last, as Cristina died aged thirty-six at the birth of their son Francis. [*It was the same year as that in which James Close's first wife also died in childbirth.*] Although she had been Queen for so short a time, Maria Cristina's piety did have a marked effect on the Neapolitan Court, while her dedicated concern for the poor won her the wholehearted love and admiration of her husband's subjects. One of Francis's numerous nicknames was to be 'Son of the Saint'.

It was expected that Ferdinand would marry again, and this he did in 1837. His second wife was the twenty-year-old Archduchess Maria Theresa, daughter of the Archduke Charles of Austria, who bore him ten children. Maria Theresa however had the disadvantage of being seen as a representative of the powerful and dominating Austrian Empire; a fear that was justified since the Austrian influence was increased noticeably. She was also in the daunting position of having followed the revered Queen Maria Cristina, whom she had no hope of replacing in the hearts of her husband's people. She did her duty conscientiously by her stepson but she disliked Francis, wanting the succession for her own children, and later plotted to have him set aside as heir to the throne in favour of her eldest son.

❧ *1848: Reform and repression*

THIS WAS THE YEAR of insurgency throughout Europe and the first and most determined uprising was in Sicily, where not just reforms, but total independence from the Bourbon kingdom was the aim. There had already been a revolt there in 1820 (not mentioned in JC's autobiography, although he was there at the time and Palermo had been bombarded), but on 12th January 1848 began a revolution which by the end of the month had ousted royalist troops from all of the island except Messina. Ferdinand dealt with this promptly, subjecting Palermo to a naval bombardment and in 1849, when Messina too fell to the rebels, bombarding that as well. This earned him the sobriquet King Bomba and the reputation of a tyrant in France and England.

Shortly after the Sicilian rebellion, fighting broke out in Naples itself. JC may have witnessed the fighting, and the circumstances will be described in the next section.

An uprising in Paris, in February 1848, forced Ferdinand's brother-in-law King Louis-Philippe to go into exile. In March the people of Milan rose against their Austrian rulers and succeeded in expelling Austrian troops from their city within five days. In the same month there were riots in Vienna, leading to the downfall of Metternich. In Venice, the lawyer Manon succeeded in expelling the Austrians and setting up a republic. In November Pope Pius IX's Minister Rossi was assassinated in the streets of Rome. Although *Pio Nono* had set out in 1846 to create a more liberal regime in the papal states and in March 1848 had appointed, for the first time, a Ministry composed chiefly of laymen, he was forced to flee Rome and take refuge in Gaeta. For Ferdinand, 1848 ended with an attempt in Naples by one of his own soldiers to shoot him.

Many other European countries were affected by similar risings, but enough has been said to show that Ferdinand was not the only monarch to find that his throne was at risk and that if he wanted to hold on to it, firm action was necessary. At first he had attempted to combine repression with concession and had already in January issued an edict that formulated a constitution for his Kingdom, which he swore to uphold. Although this had been rejected by the Sicilians, such a move became top of the list of demands of the rioters elsewhere. During the year constitutions were also granted in Tuscany, in Vienna and in Turin, where King Charles Albert, ruler of Piedmont, Genoa, Sardinia, Nice and Savoy, had felt pressurised to follow suit (but unlike Ferdinand's, the Turin constitution survived as the basic constitution of Italy until *after* the second world war). They were seen as a guarantee of the basic rights of the peasants and other workers, a check on the privileges of the aristocracy and a move towards the achievements of Great Britain, where the first steps towards a democratic electoral system had already been taken and where the powers of the monarch were already restricted.

Yet within little more than a year not only had the Sicilian revolt been crushed with the capture of Palermo by royalist troops, but so had most of the newly formed republican governments elsewhere. The Austrian army reoccupied Venice and, with the aid of a French army, forces loyal to the Pope regained Rome, expelling the republican forces led by Garibaldi.

As early as May 1848 Swiss guards clashed with rioters in the streets of Naples, leading to many deaths. Thus ended the first tentative steps towards constitutional government. Ferdinand claimed that he had been acting under duress and although he did not revoke his proposed constitution, he made no further effort to put it into force. As time passed, hopes of a more liberal system of government faded. Without a constitution, ministers had no real power: it rested with the King whether any decisions they might come to were implemented. In March 1849 the Neapolitan Parliament was dissolved. The invasion of Sicily was in August. After fighting which shocked British and French representatives by its brutality, the island reverted to Bourbon rule.

Ferdinand's chief preoccupation was with the continuation of his dynasty. He had little to do with the aristocracy, who maintained their own life-style; he despised the intellectuals and feared and mistrusted the middle classes, from the ranks of which liberal elements were drawn. He had an aversion to Naples, particularly after the attempt on his life. He came into it as little as possible and spent most of his days in the great 2,000-room palace at Caserta, modelled on Versailles. Here he enjoyed a near-bourgeois family life with his Queen and children.

⚜ *James Close, Cavaliere and Royalist*

*I*N this revolutionary year of 1848 JC's office was probably in the thick of the troubles. We know from Neapolitan official records that some time between 1846 and 1853 he moved his office from Strada Medina to the Palazzo Cirella. This overlooked a Square which, according to the two contemporary etchings (plates 2 and 3), was the eye of the revolutionary storm. Both show hundreds of citizens packing the Square and leaning out of windows and both have the Palazzo Cirella clearly in the background. In the first, dated February 1848, the crowd is wildly rejoicing, having heard King Ferdinand's announcement that a constitution would be granted. The other is dated three months later, and shows a battalion of Swiss Guards shooting into the crowd.

That JC may have witnessed the fighting from the windows of his new offices is borne out by Miss Wilson, a friend of the Brooks family. With Anne's sister Mrs

Burd, she was on a nine-month stay with the Closes in 1849–50. In her diary she wrote:

> Mr Close had the opportunity of noticing all during the revolutions in 1848, and he says it was the fight on 15th May that saved the King. He had the *Tancredi* steamer ready to take him away at a moment's notice, he could not depend on his soldiers and they were ready to fraternise with the people, but in a lucky moment for his kingship and a most unlucky one for those who had hopes in the prospect of liberty for Naples, the people fired upon the soldiers and so exasperated them to the attack. Mr Close does not believe there were many above a hundred killed.
>
> The period to which they gave the name of the Constitution lasted from January to May 1848 and during that time there was a species of liberty, the King making promises which he never meant to fulfil. There was to be a Chamber of Deputies and the representatives were chosen and the day fixed for the King to open the Parliament, but on that very day the conflict between the soldiers and the National Guards took place, and it is the general opinion that the King brought it about and caused the barricades to be raised to suit his own purposes.

JC was at the midpoint of his career. By the time of his first marriage in 1834, he was already well established as a leading member of the English community in Naples. The astonishing range of his business activities did not prevent him from playing his part in the community as well. He was deeply interested in public health and was also involved in planning the drainage system and waterworks for the city of Naples. Early on he had attempted (without success) to open a school in Naples for the teaching of sacred music. He also joined in efforts to persuade the King to allow the English to build their own church, but the Catholic fervour of the Bourbons was such that the project was out of the question while they were still in power. When Garibaldi later agreed to its being built, it was the first Protestant Church in Southern Italy and JC and Henry each paid for a stained glass window, in memory of their mothers. (The stained glass windows were shattered in World War II.)

JC's royal connections began by acting as a banker to King Ferdinand II. Soon his business relations with the King went beyond the financial. He might have been expected to react against the savage and prolonged naval bombardments of Palermo and Messina, as these were the two towns where James Close & Co had branches; but JC does not appear to have objected: as has been seen, he even put a steamer on standby in case the King needed to make a rapid getaway.

Merchants based in Naples mostly supported the King, while those based in Sicily backed the rebels – but not all of them. According to Raleigh Trevelyan, Joseph Whitaker, one of the most successful in Sicily, was glad that the revolution ultimately failed, saying, "We shall now return to peace and tranquillity after 16 months of misrule with all its evils." There was a crisis of confidence in Naples when the King demanded a forced loan from the merchants to help pay the costs of putting down the rebellion. Some of them, with the backing of Palmerston, refused. Others quitted Naples for Sicily. The demand was withdrawn, and those merchants still in Naples continued to support the King.

Why did JC support such repression? It is true he had been acting as one of the King's bankers, but it was not just a question of maintaining a good client relationship. JC was in any case a royalist. His political views seem to have been similar to those of his father, whom he described as a 'Church, King and State man; an upholder of the constituted authorities, a conservative'. Ferdinand had started as a popular King and had shown signs of becoming less despotic than his predecessors. JC supported him for this and perhaps because, like most of the ruling class in England and throughout Europe, he had in mind the horrors of the French Revolution (still within living memory) and would support any measures to prevent similar uprisings.

Ferdinand II was not ungrateful. Wishing to update his fleet, he acquired from JC two of his coastal steamers, *Dieppe* and *Brighton*, offering in exchange two schooners from the Neapolitan navy: his royal yacht *Sibilla* and the *Sphinx*. Two such luxurious ships in exchange for coastal steamers may seem today a good bargain for JC; but in exchanging all-sail schooners for steam-powered vessels, Ferdinand was modernising. Moreover the steamers were probably bigger, if less elegant, than the schooners. They were noisy and smoky, but did not have to wait for a fair wind. The *Sibilla,* on the other hand, was ideally suited to JC and his large family, and he used it for much of every year until his death. Both parties were happy with the deal and JC became accepted in court circles. He felt things were going his way and his business prospered. He was created a *cavaliere*, the equivalent of a knighthood in Great Britain. He recorded his sorrow that his brother John (who had died of consumption in 1842, aged forty-four) was not there to share in his success.

Yet soon after the crisis of 1848 JC came perilously near losing his favoured position when his brother-in-law's brother, Don Liborio, was arrested. Miss Wilson provides the startling details:

> *Monday 11th Feb. 1850* This day has been rendered remarkable by having our thoughts turned to a most unjust act of the Government. Don Liborio Romano was arrested in the middle of the night. Soldiers and emissaries of the police surrounded his house and took him out of his bed to prison. No reason was given for the arrest, but as the chief of the band who arrested him took a pleasure in the work, he told him that another company had gone at the same time to the Palazzo di Salza to arrest his brother [*Giovanni*], and this was a lie for nothing of the kind took place. This affair causes much distress to Mrs Romano, partly on Don Liborio's account, but much more in apprehension for her husband, who of the two took the most decided part against the Government in 1848.
>
> Mr Close went to the Minister of Police, not to interfere on Don Liborio's account, but to give his word for Mr. Romano that he was engaged in no secret societies. Mrs Romano is however very uneasy, for she knows the Italians are not to be trusted. She was here tonight, and Mr Romano slept here to make her feel more comfortable, but Mr Close thinks it would be the best for him to go on as usual, without appearing to shun notice or have anything to fear. ... Mrs Romano is very free in giving her opinions against the Government and the King, [*which she expresses with*] much energy in her manner. Mr Close thinks her imprudent, for it is no uncommon thing here, in case of private spite, for persons to be denounced to the Government for what they say or do.

From now on Ferdinand became increasingly repressive, filling his prisons with political opponents. Perhaps he saw further repression as the only means of saving his throne. He conducted government like the worst of police states and JC became increasingly disenchanted both with the King and with Naples.

Ferdinand's repression caused concern abroad and in 1850 Alexander Baillie Cochrane, Conservative MP for Bridport, visited Naples 'in search of truth'. The British Ambassador, Temple, because he was the brother of the reforming Lord Palmerston, did not enjoy the confidence of the Neapolitan court; so Cochrane chose instead to seek information from James Close, whom he described in his book *Young Italy* as 'universally respected and beloved and well able to form a judgment'. JC gave as his opinion that the Neapolitans were not fit for a constitution, but that the King, whom he believed to be an honourable man, having granted a constitution, as a man of honour was bound to uphold it. He advised Cochrane: 'If you should chance to see the King and he speaks to you of political subjects, the points to insist on are the frequent arrests, the infamous judicial system, the petitions supposed to be originated by the Court against the Constitution and the miserable state of the prisons.'

Later Cochrane did have the opportunity of speaking to the King at an interview given at the palace of Caserta. He came away impressed by Ferdinand's evident concern for the lot of the political prisoners, and comforted by his reassurances. However, it turned out that his outspokenness had done more harm than good. Cochrane wrote:

> The result of this interview was that in a few days the political prisoners were separated from the general mass. Some few, I believe, were released. … So far, so well; but to my very deep regret, I have heard from Naples that the political prisoners have been only removed to a much worse place, that their communications with their families have been still more restricted; that the few who were released were men quite unimportant, and would have been discharged at any rate; and what does give countenance to several other reports is that within the last few weeks, I see by the papers that the Constitution has been virtually abolished.

Paulina's husband would have shared the fate of Don Liborio but for JC's protection. Don Liborio's only crime, in common with that of most of the other prisoners, was to have given support to the Constitution the King had sworn to uphold.

At this time two Presbyterian ministers on their way to the Holy Land were arrested on their arrival in Naples. They were thrown into prison. They had introductions to James Close. He found that a red, white and blue pen wiper, discovered when their luggage was examined by Customs, had been taken for a revolutionary emblem!

Cochrane had been able to visit political prisoners who were being held indefinitely while they were awaiting trial together with criminals in unspeakable conditions, some of them unaware of the charges against them. Gladstone, who had himself visited the political prisoners and attended trumped up trials, wrote to Lord Aberdeen:

> The effect of all this is total inversion of all the moral and social laws. Law, instead of being respected, is odious.
>
> Force and not affection is the foundation of Government. There is no association, but a violent antagonism, between the idea of freedom and that of order. The governing power, which teaches itself that it is the image of God upon earth,

is clothed, in the view of the overwhelming majority of the thinking public, with all the vices for its attributes. I have seen and heard the strong and true expression used 'This is the negation of God erected into a system of Government – *E la negazzione di Dio eretta a sistema di governo.*'

Gladstone's letters to Lord Aberdeen were discussed and endorsed by Palmerston in the House of Commons. Other countries were also expressing disapproval. After the bombardment of Palermo, Thiers had expressed horror in the French Chamber of Deputies that any government could perpetrate such an act against its own people; and in 1856 both England and France broke off diplomatic relations with King Ferdinand, after he had ignored their requests to modify his absolutist regime.

Anne Close, in a letter to her father in May 1851, summed up the situation from a more domestic point of view:

> We are very quiet in Naples; but the Government is very strict and apparently unnecessarily severe. No person can remove without giving notice to the police. Passports are required for any distance greater than twelve miles and the period of their stay written in the passport; no Neapolitan allowed to visit England during the Exhibition [*the Great Exhibition of 1851 in London*]; there are one or two exceptions but the permission was gained with difficulty; and no printing establishment but on a ground floor and the doors to be always open. Mr Romano [*Don Liborio*] is still in prison, but hopes to be soon let out; should any disturbances take place in France or on the Continent he is likely to remain there for some time. James saw the King last week and he has gone again to Caserta today with Mr Guppy. They were to have a private interview with the King.

These were the conditions under which the Closes lived for the remainder of their time in Naples. In another letter to her father, written in 1852, Anne wrote:

> The King is seldom in Naples – he was reported ill and we hear out of his mind, which we do not believe. He is fortifying Gaeta, which is situated on the sea-side near the Roman frontier, and provisioning it for a six-month siege.

❧ *Friends and acquaintances*

*A*FTER JC's marriage to Anne Close in 1845 his social life may have taken a turn for the better – at least more is known about it. From 1849–50, for nine months, the Closes accommodated, in a flat below theirs, Anne's sister Mrs Burd together with her four children and her companion, Miss Wilson. There is a super-fluity of information about this period, as Miss Wilson kept a diary, which runs to fifty-three pages. It will be remembered that Mrs Burd had already made the journey from England at least once, returning by pony over the Alps. This time she and her party again came by sea, accompanied by JC himself in one of his best steamers, the *Dieppe*. Storms on the four-day stretch from Plymouth to Lisbon caused sickness all round.

One of JC's friends was Charles Turner, another merchant with roots in Manchester. His firm and JC's had both withstood the difficult years of the wrangling over import duties: like Giacomo Close & Co, Carlo Turner & Co was one of the three English firms that had survived from 1827 through to 1850. The two must have been good friends: the following parody of a day in the life of Anne Close, although written by Turner, is written as if by Anne:

> *Friday 15th May 1850* Uncomfortable. Up at six after a restless night occa-sioned by the fatigues of our excursion to Caserta yesterday, with my sister and husband and all her children; first, with the object of visiting the King, then of our seeing all that is worthy in the vicinity; and afterwards, having presided at a dinner at home and been to the Opera in the evening. Settled various accounts with the butler and the cook, being middle month day. Made breakfast for all my own family and my sister's children, embarked with both families at 8 o'clock on board the *Dieppe* [*later in the year acquired by the King*] for an excursion to Ischia, rather dismayed at the appearance of the weather, but it favoured us for a couple of hours; started from the mole at 9, steamed completely round Pro-cida, got into a rough sea off Ischia, which disinclined us for further proceed-ings [*Anne suffered from seasickness*], but my husband wishing it, we cheerfully continued and coasted all round Ischia, suffering greatly from the effects of a rough sea and contrary wind for a few hours, till we landed at 1 o'clock at Baja, where we enjoyed an hour or two, rambling all the morning, visiting the temples and antiquities, and partook of a champagne luncheon. Re-embarked at 3 and returned to Naples rolling and suffering all the way.
>
> Had only time to dress for dinner on reaching home, and hastened to a large dinner party in town, to meet the American commodore, officers and friends; after which to a concert at Mrs Romano's and repaired to bed at 12, fearing from prudential reasons, my expecting an enlargement to our family six weeks hence, to remain out at a late hour, especially as tomorrow we have to prepare for a picnic with the Commodore with 20 friends and must return home to receive a dozen for a quiet dinner and go to the French play in the evening, which can

be easily accomplished as the following day will be Sunday and a day of rest, on which we shall only go to the two Church services, take our usual drive and have our usual family circle of 20 to dinner and a few musical friends in the evening to finish the week and talk over our projected tour to Malta, Tunis, Athens and Constantinople and neighbouring places, to fill up the time until my return and confinement.

Tongue in cheek maybe, but Turner's description of 15th May is almost identical with an account of 15th *March* by Miss Wilson, who describes a very similar journey, with Turner on board. The same sick-making waves going round Procida and Ischia; the same tour of classical sites at Baia. On their return, they did have an evening dinner party to attend, followed by a musical evening at the Romanos. Mrs Burd's sense of self-preservation led her to try to get out of these last two engagements, but she was overruled by JC, as Miss Wilson relates:

The coming in to Naples was quite beautiful, and we arrived at about half past 4 o'clock. It was very necessary to be early, for Mr and Mrs Close and Mrs Burd had to dress for a dinner party and after that they were engaged to a musical party at the Romanos. It was certainly too much for one day, but it was the Naples way of doing things, and not at all too much for Mr Close. Mrs Burd had been hoping all along to escape the dinner party, and on our way home in the carriage she gave a hint to that effect to Mr Close; but he would not notice it, she had no good reason to offer, but at last a bright idea came to her. When she was nearly dressed she looked in the glass and discovered that she was sunburnt, so she sent me upstairs to tell Mr Close that she really was not fit to go. He however could see no objection to a sunburnt face, but thought it rather a recommendation. He would take no denial, so Mrs Burd was obliged to go.

Clearly Anne did have a heavy social round, particularly in view of the fact that she was expecting her third child in six weeks' time. (John, her first son, was born a few weeks later and Charles Turner was his godfather.)

Another friend at this time was Mrs Westropp. She appears later, in the Journals, when the family was based in Antibes. The ten years between then and now she spent in India, writing up her experiences in her own Journal. She also wrote notes on days spent with the Closes in the Naples area soon after their marriage. In early August 1852 she and Anne steamed round Capri in Mr C's steamer *St. Winifred*. They bathed from it in the deep waters off the island. In June 1853 she sailed with both of them to Ponza, which she describes as a penal settlement: of the total population of four thousand, 1,600 prisoners were detained there. The crowds at the quay pressed round, mainly to catch a glimpse of JC's Negro servant. Calling at Zannone in the same group of islands, she tells us that it was only a mile in circumference and uninhabited. (JC later tried to buy the island from the King.) 'JC is a great man here', she wrote. 'He owns the steamer that affords means of communication with the outer world.' On the same expedition Mrs Westropp added 'Mr C. wanted to take one of Nero's baths, which would be efficacious for gout and rheumatism' – so we know that already in the early fifties he was stricken with these infirmities. In July she too went with the Closes on a seasick-making tour of Ischia in the *St Winifred.*

Meanwhile JC remained a royalist, even with Don Liborio in prison. Yet he became increasingly disgusted with the King's repressive behaviour. For ten more years, JC continued as a successful merchant, while still seeing a great deal of his sister and left wing in-laws, whose children played and knocked about with their Close cousins. His doubts about Paulina marrying Giuseppe mellowed, but did not disappear. An idea of his grand acquaintances can be had from this extract from a letter from Anne to her father Samuel Brooks:

> We have a dinner party today, Sir William Temple, Lord and Lady Overston, Lord and Lady Napier, Madame and George Meuricoffre, Prince and Princess Ischitella (he is the present Minister of War and served under the great Napoleon), and Charles Turner. Paolo is to do his best and I am sure he will give us a good dinner.

John's godfather Charles Turner is only mentioned as an afterthought. The Meuricoffres were their best friends, Temple was the British ambassador. Napier was a subordinate who sometimes acted as his *chargé d'affaires* and was also an authority on the Neapolitan school of painting. Prince Ischitella had also been on the staff of Joachim Murat, King of Naples from 1808. (Paolo – see plate 12 – was chef and remained with the family until Anne's death in 1876.) Into this letter JC had slipped a note for his father-in-law saying that King Ferdinand's brother was about to visit Manchester and would be calling on him (Samuel Brooks) as he (JC) had given his royal acquaintance a letter of introduction. He asked Samuel Brooks to be helpful in any way he could.

An even grander occasion was held on board the *Dieppe,* and shows that JC's

steamers were no mere packet boats, and had probably improved since their introduction in 1839. Here are excerpts from Miss Wilson's description of JC's party:

> ***8th March 1850*** Amidst all the pleasures, this day's have certainly been the
> greatest. Again on the steamer, lovely day, and sailing close to the most beauti-
> ful coast in the world. Mr Close gave a grand entertainment, and no fewer than
> 120 guests sat down to dinner. There were English, French, Swiss, American and
> Italian officers and all the ambassadors of foreign nations at Naples. First there
> was Mr Temple, the brother of Lord Palmerston, but he did not seem to me at all
> a good representative of an Englishman. He is a little shabby looking man with
> a red scorbutic face, as if he drank to excess, and he is very quiet and reserved,
> having nothing of the ease and affability of manner that one naturally expects;
> yet I do not think he wants sense. I, however, was more interested in the Spanish
> minister at Rome, Martinez della Rosa, because I was told that he is the author
> of plays which rank high in Spanish literature, and also that he was noted for his
> eloquent speeches in favour of Italian liberty.
>
> The steamer had been newly painted for the occasion and every part was beau-
> tifully clean. Mr Close soon gave the order to start and we all felt very happy in
> the brightest of anticipations. We had just had time to look at each other, when
> there came a shower of the dirtiest blackest rain, pouring through the awning in
> immense drops. Alas for the bonnets and the velvets and the satins! There was a
> general run from one side of the boat to the other, for the drops only fell through
> the awning in parts, but the wise ones followed the example of Mrs Burd [*once
> again careful about her own comforts*] and sought speedy shelter below. She
> looked once at the gathering drops and once at the cabin door and she was out
> of sight in an instant.

When later in September JC lost the *Dieppe* for the *Sibilla*, he was at first down-
cast. Miss Wilson recorded:

> Mr Close brought word at dinner, with a countenance full of grief, that the
> steamer was no longer in his possession, but had been made over to the King.
> … it is satisfaction to think they will not be degraded in their use. The *Dieppe* is
> destined for the King's own use, and the *Brighton* is attached to the Neapolitan
> fleet.

The Closes were constantly entertaining, both at their town apartments in the
Via Ascensione and now on board *Sibilla*. Friends and friends of friends, or anyone who came with an introduction, could be sure of instant hospitality and help

or advice if needed. Outside Naples, JC made a point of getting to know the local mayor or any other kindred spirit in every port of call, and the first thing he would do when revisiting would be to renew any friendships he had struck up. The Closes' greatest friends, however, were the Meuricoffres, and they do need some introduction. He (Tell) was a Swiss banker, she (Harriet – see plate 4) was English and the sister of Josephine Butler, a social reformer well known at the time. JC had first come across them when he stopped off in Naples on his way to Messina in 1819. Now they were a leading family in Neapolitan society. Tell also had been created a *Cavaliere* and also had financial dealings with the King. As Protestants, they were a ready source of godparents to the Close children. They lived in the Villa Meuricoffre at Capodimonte. This couple will appear frequently in the Journals. JC wrote in 1859: 'There is not a single resident family here (except the Meuricoffres) that I would choose to be connected with by marriage.' As will be seen from her work in 1860, Harriet's social conscience was every bit a strong as that of her sister Josephine.

❧ *The Sibilla and her early voyages*

JAMES CLOSE once boasted that there was not a single port of any substance on the Continent that he had not visited. From this it can be deduced that his business activities had been widespread in Europe and that sail had been his preferred method of transport. From 1850 onwards, these voyages were on board the *Sibilla*.

Like the two steamers for which the *Sibilla* and her sister-ship were exchanged, she was British-built. She weighed approximately 140 tons, had been a fast sailing schooner of the Neapolitan navy and later had been used as the royal state yacht. In this latter capacity she was replaced by one of the two steamers, the *Dieppe*, now renamed by King Ferdinand the *Freccia* (Arrow). It is not known when the *Sibilla* was built, but she is on record as having been used on a royal occasion in 1790. Until the advent of King Victor Emmanuel, she sailed under the red-white-and-green tricolour in common use by the independent states of the Italian peninsula. Her new burgee was the gold device on red of the Royal Victoria Yacht Club, of which JC was a member.

The *Sibilla* was exchanged for the steamers in 1850 (the very year when Don Liborio was jailed!). JC had her refitted in Portsmouth: her two brass cannon were removed and she was redesigned as a family home, using material from another of his coastal steamers, which had been broken up. By early 1851 the work was completed and the ship was restocked with food – by Fortnum & Mason, who supplied over 200 tins of anything from milk to lobsters, as well as boxes of dried fruit, four hams, a flitch of bacon, Stilton cheese and various bottles. The whole lot cost £40 2s. 6d. (See Appendix II for full list.) The quality of F & M's tin must have been exceptional, as the last of the salmon was not eaten until fifteen years later, when it was judged to be excellent.

List of provisions from JC's pocket book

Although the *Sibilla* no longer belonged to the Royal Family, its members felt free to borrow her back. Anne records in a letter to her father in June 1852:

> … our plans have been upset by the King's brother asking James to lend him the *Sibilla* for two months. James was not able to refuse him and today he went on board and set sail for Sovieto. We watched her from the terrace until she anchored and took in sail.

The *Sibilla* sailed under the command of two captains. One was responsible for the crew; he recruited them and like them, was engaged for the duration of each voyage only. The other, Luigi ('Louis') Panzera, was permanently employed. Although Panzera was JC's secretary as well as being the second captain, his duties and responsibilities were far wider than these titles suggest, as will be seen. A man of many abilities – he frequently extracted a child's tooth and in an emergency he even undertook minor surgery – he was invaluable to the Close family. JC himself, however, took command and gave orders whenever he felt the situation called for it.

The crew, consisting of twelve sailors, a steward, a cook and his assistant were, being Neapolitan, by nature fond of children and Anne Close describes their kindness to her young family when writing to her father in 1852:

> The sailors are so good to the children dragging them about on a piece of carpet up and down deck, carrying them on their shoulders, making balls, fish-hooks or boats, dancing the Tarantella. Even Johnny does not roar so much on board.

JC was always concerned for the welfare of those employed on his ship, including the spiritual side. He took pleasure in standing on deck, hat in hand, in the evening to listen to the murmur of the crew as they recited Vespers, and upbraided the members of one crew for being slovenly in appearance when they went ashore to hear Mass on Sunday and were not wearing their best outfits.

The *Sibilla* was a second home and held in great affection: the Closes saw it as part of the family. JC, left in charge of the rest of the children at Toulon in 1863 while his wife took John, James and Thomas to visit Samuel Brooks in Manchester, wrote in the Journal: 'When Mama is away the soul of the ship is gone.'

JC was always at great pains to make sure that the *Sibilla* should never give the impression of being a luxury yacht, and with good reason. Pretentiousness, idle pleasure and unnecessary expenditure were all alien to him, and he was fully aware of the pitfalls of being taken for a rich English yachtsman when he put into port. The sails were patched in different colours, which he regarded as being 'ship-shape and nonsnobby' and his daughter complained in vain about 'our miserable flags'. Nevertheless he was undeniably English, owned a yacht and had the title of *Cavaliere* or *Chevalier*, and so was liable to be classed automatically as a *milord*. This label persisted even after his death, when an obituary notice in a local French newspaper mistakenly endowed the *Sibilla* with an auxiliary engine and a chapel and credited 'milord' with having his own private chaplain on board.

How many voyages the *Sibilla* made in earlier years before those recorded in the Journals is not known, but in his 1859 letter to his brother (see '1859: Future Plans' in Chapter III) he claimed that there were few Mediterranean ports that *the family* had not seen, and he emphasised the educational value of this, which shows that the 1861 family cruise was by no means the first. There is little information about these earlier journeys. One pre-Journals voyage in the *Sibilla* was in 1851, when Anne was pregnant with her fourth child, and it was decided that business should be combined with family affairs and that the baby should be born at the home of Samuel Brooks, Whalley House, Manchester. Preparations were therefore made for James and Anne and their three children to sail for England in time for the birth. Their departure was delayed for various reasons, as explained in a letter from Anne to her father dated 20th May 1851:

> We are nearly ready for starting, the day is not fixed but it will be some time next week. It is difficult to get the papers in order – James is a member of the Royal Victoria Yacht Club but this government only acknowledges ships of War, or merchant vessels; and under the latter description we must sail. Our Captain, Maresca, has delayed us – he was the one who was so ill on our trip to Constantinople – he demanded an increase of salary, and being refused, left the ship with fifteen of the sailors he had engaged.
>
> Should I not find myself well on our journey we should put in at Gibraltar, or Lisbon, according to circumstances, but I hope to arrive safely in England. The present plan is to sail for Southampton. James will take me to London, where we remain, if we have time, two days. We think of sending the *Sybil* [*sic*] with the children round to Liverpool, so if anyone would like a sail there's the opportunity. These are our plans and we shall know best what to decide when we arrive.

All went well, and James Brooks Close was born at his grandfather's home on 30th July 1851, the only one of Anne Close's children not born in Naples.

An account of another pre-Journals voyage (exact date unknown) is given by Ruth Eaden, again in her *Blackwood's Magazine* article:

> For some unexplained reason JC was not on board when the *Sibilla*, with her usual complement of children, was running off the coast of Morocco. She had crammed on every stitch of canvas she could carry and was making all haste on account of the pirates that infested those waters. A stiff breeze had kicked up a bit of sea, and Granny [*Anne Close*] was in her cabin. A strict look-out was being kept by the watch, and it was not long before he sang out "Ship astern!". She was a big black Corsair, and she was fast overhauling the *Sibilla* when Granny came on deck and took command.
>
> In the saloon the yacht carried one of those now almost obsolete shiny black horsehair sofas, with raised and equally shiny round ends. At Granny's orders she was brought on deck, manned three aside and run out, Navy fashion, to the stern, with both round ends facing seawards. The bluff worked. The Corsair's captain had no wish to engage a ship carrying cannon. He shortened sail and fell astern. No doubt Granny ordered a double issue of Chianti for the crew that evening.

This story is not all that improbable, as pirates were at the time still encountered operating from the coasts of North Africa, and even a few years later, in the Journals, fear of pirates still comes into decisions on the most advisable routes to take. Moreover the same story is told from another source – although different in detail, clearly some such event did take place. Etta Close, the daughter of Henry, JC's son by his first wife, records in her *Excursions and some Adventures*:

> My father remembered well being chased by Barbary pirates. In those days a steam yacht was unknown; and the wind dropping, the pirate got dangerously near. There was consternation on the yacht, for there were no guns on board, only a few muzzle-loading muskets. However, somebody had an inspiration. The legs of the dining-saloon table were of mahogany, large and solid and bound with brass. These were taken off and pushed through the port-holes, and the pirates, taking them for guns, sheered off and disappeared.

In Anne Close's May 1951 letter to her father about her coming to England, there is a reference to an earlier voyage to Constantinople. It may be that the city was a regular port of call, as a description of another expedition there in 1856, when the Crimean War was drawing to its close, is given in letters from Anne to her husband. She, left in charge in Naples during one of her husband's absences on business, had been summoned to take the *Sibilla* to Constantinople to meet him there. She was accompanied by her five children, the youngest, Frederic, still requiring a wet nurse. On his different route to Constantinople, JC had been caught in a terrible storm following a hurricane on 14th November 1855, that had caused immense damage to the Allies by land and sea. The ship on which he was travelling, the *Sebeto,* touched a sandbank, but her sister ship, the *Tevere,* was lost. Anne, anxiously awaiting news, wrote to him on 25th January 1856:

> My dear Husband,
>
> We are looking forward and not without anxiety to the news we may have of you, by tomorrow's post. We have heard of the wreck of the *Tevere* and many other vessels, which has by no means tranquillised us with regard to your safety – I console myself by arguing, that according to the rules of chance, the *Tevere* being lost, the *Sebeto* ought to escape unhurt.

The letter continues with an account of the doings and health of all their children and an evening with her sister-in-law Paulina, when they listened to a Mr Owen reading extracts from an American book on Spiritualism:

> ... the book affirms as a fact 'that we are not separated by death from those we have loved on earth but that during our life they are ever around us ministering to us, and that by the purity of our lives we may be reunited with them' ... how consoling a doctrine it would be to me – that your spirit would influence me in all my actions (for I cannot do without thee, Jimmie, thy spirit must guide me whether it be in the body or out of it) should our last farewell on board *Sebeto* be a long one.
>
>   As you expressly desired me to have nothing to do with mesmerism, I won't say a word about rappings and spirit conversations – of which the book abounds. Paulina has received an invitation to Sir William Temple's ball, it came late, after everyone had received theirs, and Paulina got fidgety.

On 29th February Anne wrote again to her husband:

> My answer to your invitation to join you at Constantinople is that we are to be on board on Tuesday the fourth of March and start for Castellan on Thursday – return to Naples on Saturday – and after receiving your letter, fairly start to join you, provided always that your next letter does not express a wish to the contrary. I have been looking over with Panzera the list made out of provisions, for a voyage of two and a half, or three months duration: we wait Saturday's or

rather Sunday's post (for I generally get your letter after Church) before purchasing them.

The boats are in order, and all the painting done – the ropes are only half tarred, the wet weather putting a stop to the work – Panzera says that they can finish the remainder on the voyage.

… Don't be alarmed, however, should we be longer than you anticipate on the voyage, for you know by experience that we are fond of Port in rough weather, and we shall look before we leap on coming on Cape Papero, to avoid passing such another night, as the one that name reminds us of.

We get on board some days before starting to accustom ourselves to the motion, remembering your advice on the subject.

My only difficulty with regard to arrangements has been my baby Fred. Don Martino said it would be running a risk to wean him, he has come on so well, since I changed his nurse. He looks delicate tho' healthy – he is full of life constantly in motion with lungs that speak plainly of his health. I much fear that this noisy exhibition of health so often repeated by five out of your six children will drive you distracted – and you will be wishing us all away again. I sent the wet nurse on a trial trip, with Panzera in one of the sailing boats to Castellan. She did not suffer – and yesterday she went with Donna Maria in the country to ask her husband's permission, which he very willingly gave, so all anxiety about baby is over.

The little pigs are all paid for and I have used the money for house expenses. There was an offer for fifty ducats for the Pig which of course we refused. [*Samuel Brooks had exported breeding stock for the Closes.*]

Charles Turner proposes that I should put off until April our starting and meet you in Malta – I should not like to go to Malta without the certainty that you would be there to meet me. Write to Paulina, she observed that her name was not mentioned in your last letter and Don Peppino was disappointed not to have a letter in answer to his – he is full of hope about the banking business. In writing to him, spare the character of the Italians. Pugh gave us a sermon of more than an hour on the [*Florence*] Nightingale funds. He did her cause great harm, and created ill will, by his injudicious remarks – Lady Strachey wants to know from you the truth of the reports about Miss Nightingale having become a Roman Catholic.

With the *Sibilla* nearing her destination, there was a final letter from Anne showing that, before reaching Constantinople, she sailed up to Sebastopol at the tail end of the Crimean War:

Keu Kioi, Sunday 30th March 1856

My Dear Husband,

We anchored here last evening having made some twenty miles, this is slow work – the wind today is blowing hard right in our teeth. We were invited by Dr Wells to attend Service and dine with him; the children were all dressed and the Nurse ready, when it came on to rain – so we had to undress, which was a disappointment to the children as they had seen some Highlanders on shore, and their curiosity had been excited.

We have been on shore, and were introduced to Mrs. Wells, a young and pleasing person, and dined with her and some eight other ladies with their husbands all holding some post connected with the Hospital. I sat next to Mr. Brunton the engineer – he was formerly with Brunel. The unmarried officers dine at six. We returned on board at four o'c and tomorrow if the weather will permit the children are to go on shore for half an hour – there is no making head against such a wind and we may be detained days here, and therefore, if we can get a tug at a reasonable price will engage her. [*A battleship eventually gave the Sibilla a tow.*] The Forts are firing on both sides, we conclude peace is declared! [*It was declared in April.*] I hope to arrive before this letter, I sent you a long letter yesterday from this place, but the land post is not always regular, and the latter may be detained a week at Gallipoli, so to make sure, I have written these few lines, you ought to get the other tomorrow. We are all in good health; buy some trifles for the children – bonbons if nothing else. I hope to find you well my dear husband and believe me

Ever your affectionate wife
Anne Close

The *Sibilla* was the first non-combatant ship to enter the port of Sebastopol after the siege, and James Close was presented with the key of the Citadel to mark the occasion.

It was while Anne Close was shopping in Constantinople, the *Sibilla* having finally arrived, that the three-year-old William was lost. The children had been following their mother, but William failed to follow her with them into one of the shops, and when she rushed out into the street to look for him he had vanished. The British Fleet was in the Porte and detachments of sailors were landed to search for him. He had been picked up by a Turk and taken to a village in the hills where a fair was being held, and there a stranger noticed the child because he was repeating, "Sibilla! Sibilla!"

CHAPTER III

1858–61: *James Close back in Focus*

🐚 *1858: Shipwreck*

> *Our plans being all arranged we entered Gallipoli at dusk but what was our surprise when the first object which presented itself was my poor "Sibilla" laying on her side stranded on the rocks, and a heavy sea dashing at her broadside as if trying to dash her to pieces She had broken both chains during the storm of the preceeding night and had drifted on the rock,*

*I*N SEPTEMBER 1858 JC took his family on a cruise in the Adriatic. He describes it in a letter he wrote to his wife's aunt early in 1859. He only did so because Anne, with her sea-sickness and pregnancy, was in too delicate a condition to write it herself. Nevertheless having read the letter, she had the foresight to copy it into her commonplace book – not all of it, as the description of the voyage breaks off abruptly. It is the only retrospective account of any of the cruises; it describes the hazards attached and at last we have another chance to look at events through the eyes of JC himself. The attenuated letter runs to twenty-six pages of typescript, most of which is given below.

The children on board and their ages were Margaret (12), Grace (10), John (8), James (7), William (5), Frederic (4) and Annie (eighteen months). Henry, JC's son by his first wife Henrietta, was a student at Cambridge at the time. The letter was to the Rev. Sandford Adamson and his wife. He was the vicar of Padiham near Burnley in Lancashire. She was Samuel Brooks's sister.

My dear Uncle and Aunt Adamson,

First of all, Annie and I join in hearty wishes that the young year may surpass the old one in health and happiness to you both. She has deputed me to write you an entertaining letter. "Remember", says Annie [*JC, confusingly, often refers to Anne as Annie*], "that at this season the snow is on the ground at Padiham, that Aunt cannot leave her comfortable fireside, that a letter from abroad is, of itself, an event in this quiet and peaceful home. Since she cannot peep in upon us here, try your best, dear, to bring us all to Padiham."

   We left Naples in September last, of course with all our little ones with us; this time (for once) without a wet nurse! Annie and myself, our seven children, a Swiss under-governess, a Swiss governess and an Italian maid of <u>all</u> work, but who can do little or <u>nothing</u>. Thus we are twelve, living in the so termed <u>State</u> cabins of the *Sibilla*. Our crew consists of the first and second captains, twelve seamen, a cook and cook's adjutant. In all twenty eight souls.

At this point JC embarks on a three-page justification for having a yacht at all, making out that it was in many ways an economy. He makes a good case for this, comparing his costs with those of running a gentleman's carriage, with liveries, repairs, tolls, groom, coachman and a pair or three horses in London.

   Again before getting on with a factual and perhaps more 'entertaining' account of the voyage, JC sets out on a further justification of his unusual method of bringing up his children; but enough of that has already been seen earlier in this book. He then claims that their life on board was less dangerous than life on shore. How he could argue this in view of the perils and disasters that befell them and are described in the very same letter is hard to understand.

Now what do I get from the extra that I spend? First of all I see the world, and mind you not selfishly, as sportsmen, gamblers and drunkards enjoy themselves. My whole family participates with me, and that they enjoy as much or more than I do. They have visited every principal place in the Mediterranean with the comforts of a home around them. The constant change of air and scene and the sea breezes have established their constitutions, and until the last two months kept them clear from disease. In the next place, being on board our floating home, Annie and I have emancipated ourselves from many social trammels which on shore leave us no leisure and diminish our desire to attend personally to our children. On board we have no other occupation. Each child lives within arm's reach of us. We educate them. I think it a great privilege to be able to say that we entrust them to none. The vices of other children cannot reach them on board. So far from life being dull for ourselves and children it is a chain of end-less variety and instruction. Finally what shall I say of the enjoyment our yacht-ing life affords to Annie and myself? In what other situation can we ever be nearer or more constantly with each other. Not a pleasure, not an anxiety, not a thought, not an act that is not common property! On board the *Sibilla* we are 'King and Queen'. Wherever we land we are received with courtesy and respect, for, as I said before, to the many a yacht means wealth and a respectable social position.

As to 'the dangers of the seas to gentlemen who live at home at ease', doubtless they appear to be great. To my mind, however, fox-hunting, shooting, racing and such like amusements present in reality greater dangers. A yacht is unlike a merchant-ship, packet, or a Ship of War in this: she need not go to sea in bad weather, and she can turn into any port should bad weather come on. A yacht is usually well found, well manned and never burthened with cargo beyond her trim. I have never seen any statistics of sea life, but from what I can judge of it during the last seven years I cannot persuade myself that it is more dangerous to life than living on shore. I should say that my children, placed in a crowded school and kept in doors at study some eight or ten hours a day and in play hours exposed to the chances of cricket, fighting, boating and other similar recrea-tions, would have less chance of life and health than those which my present yachting life affords them. After this defence of my folly I will tire your patience no longer with the subject.

Our voyage to Trieste and Venice was in every respect pleasant. Always in sight of land and a smooth sea, our lessons and occupations going on as regularly as on shore, Annie compared it to "seeing the world without moving from her armchair". I dare say our children are more backward in reading and spelling than any of their cousins. Nor can I pretend that our yachting life tends to a high refinement of manners in children. I am however one of those (as yet few) persons who believe that it is not desirable that children should be taught 'pretty manners' until seven or eight years old. I am satisfied if my children acquire 'good habits', not so much by precept as by example, and in like manner to be natural in all their ways.

Artificial manners are a stepping stone to affectation, and affectation is the half-way-house to falsehood and hypocrisy. If children of this age be surrounded by an atmosphere of truth, plain-dealing, cleanliness and order, I believe that these qualities are the substratum upon which all that is gentlemanly or lady-like must rest, and without which 'artificial polish' is mere tinsel. From eight to fourteen I wish my children to learn the useful practical 'arts'.

After more on education, JC at last starts his account of the voyage.

In sailing up the Adriatic we called for one evening at the island of Lisa [*an island off the Dalmatian coast, now known as Vis*]. It possesses a beautiful port. During the war it was occupied by the English. Its forts and batteries still retain the original English names. We landed and of course were a 'sight': English children are seldom seen in number in the Mediterranean. Ours are invariably dressed alike [*in sailor suits*]. Can you imagine, in an out of the way place, a ship sailing into the harbour having the appearance of a ship of war, the forts saluting her with their flags, the people rushing down to the beach. A boat is lowered. Four neatly dressed sailors jump into it, and handle their oars. The companion is lowered, a child is handed down, then another and another until seven are counted. Then the governesses, then Mrs. Close and finally the great 'Milord' himself descends. A few short strokes bring us to the landing place. A dense crowd of men, women and children press forward but give way as our party lands. The women count the children; some say 'all boys', some 'all girls'. A space is made and 'my lord' heads the procession through a double line of curious but respectful people. We reach the square or principal street or market place. I observe a red-legged Priest, a tall handsome fellow with a three cornered hat and crimson band, surrounded by some of the 'respectables'. I take off my hat to the 'cloth'. The group graciously returns the salute. I advance a step as if to ask a question. The red legs are already in motion and before I can say a word I am most civilly welcomed to the island. I ask the way, <u>any</u> way, and the three cornered hat is restored to its place with a kindly offer to be our guide and conductor. No end of questions. As we pass with our new friend the Rector or Archdeacon the crowds respectfully lower their caps. The children burst into runs and frolics and peels of joyous laughter, 'Milord' and the Priest bring up the rear with becoming gravity, immersed in economy, political and ecclesiastical enquiries. Our walk over, the boat awaits us. I ask the great man to honour our tea-table. He is delighted with our comfortable home, enjoys a cup of black coffee, sips a few drops of Maraschino, listens to our usual 'evening hymn' [*Glory to Thee, my God, this night*] and 'God Save the Queen', and soon after dark steps into the boat well lit with lanthorns and returns on shore delighted with us, with the ship and with himself.

... At Trieste we set out for a walk along the seaside. We entered some beautiful gardens. They were public gardens. We followed the crowd and, turning a point on the shore beheld the Austrian squadron in line. The yards were manned, steam was up, some event was evidently expected. We all sat down on the trunk of a fallen tree. I enquired of a man who was standing by in Italian (for such is the language spoken in Trieste) what was to be the upshot of this naval exhibition. He looked at me and my family with a smile and answered me in perfect English; I was surprised, for his dress was any thing but English, or denoting an educated man. But such is the fashion now a days with English travellers on the continent; they affect an inferior class of dress. I invited him to a seat on our log, and after the Archduke Maximilian [*brother of Franz Josef, Emperor of Austria*] had reviewed his fleet and the last ship had sailed he joined our party on our walk homewards. I asked him on board, and the next day to dinner. I found him to be a particularly well informed and unaffected man. He was on his way to Vienna and Constantinople by the Danube and Black Sea. He is since returned to London and I have received from him the kindest letter imaginable, hoping if I came there I would not fail to give him a call.

We were intensely interested with Venice. It is different to all other places. Few who have seen it can form an accurate idea of it. Its origin in the year four or five hundred, as a retreat from the barbarities of the Huns and Goths. Its situation on a vast shallow lake which as the tide falls (only two feet) exhibits a lake of mud save where channels have formed themselves by the retreating waters; its canal streets; its magnificent square; its peculiar architecture; its singular Cathedral of nine hundred years standing; its brilliant history of fourteen centuries; its long line of a hundred and twenty three Doges; its sudden fall and occupation by Napoleon in 1798 – all these circumstances render Venice unique amongst the cities of Europe.

Constantinople alone is a competitor in this species of interest. I hardly can say to which I should give the preference – they are in every respect so widely different. The children were most amused with the pigeons which crowd the square of St. Mark. An old maiden lady left them a legacy of corn to be supplied every day at two o'clock at a certain window. The children begged to feed the pigeons, so Annie had a huge cornucopia of corn supplied to each child. Our visit to the horrid prisons in the ducal palace, now no longer used as such, had a powerful effect on the children. The *Sibilla* was moored exactly opposite the Pope's palace and the famous Bridge of Sighs. Of all these things and of the celebrated paintings by Tintoretto and Titian we obtained beautiful photographs, as indeed we do of all the places we visit when we can get them.

It was a splendid day (16 Oct) when we took our last view of Venice as we sailed rapidly down the channel to Malamocca, and then through two long moles into the open sea. We next visited Ancona where we were wind-bound three days. Wherever we landed we received the utmost attention and respect from the

Neapolitan consuls. They called on us, and placed guides and boats and any assistance we required at our disposal.

The appearance of our six children [*Annie being too young*] in the theatre of Ancona will not soon be forgotten. We took two boxes. The cost of both was ten shillings! In Italian theatres all the boxes are private; I mean the whole theatre is partitioned into small boxes like the Italian Opera in London. Another feature in these theatres is the order and propriety which are observed there. I consider an English theatre to be a scandal to our civilisation, a blot on our manners. At the Ancona theatre, a handsome large theatre, three of our children sat in front of each box all dressed alike in white – an English looking set of children, especially when set off by the dark, sallow, tawdry dressed children of the Italians. Do what they will, the Italians cannot make their children look decent. They load them with finery, bedizen them with parasols and hoops, ornament them with lace and jewelry, and starch and glove and shoe them like dolls copied from the latest fashions. But with all that they never look like gentlemen's children. Their little minds are engrossed in their dress. It was something new to the people of Ancona to see my little Freddy jump on a chair and coolly seat himself on the velvet balcony, exhibiting his bare legs and asking Mama why he could not sit there? The people when the theatre was over waited in the hall to see us go out. The bare legs of the children amused them exceedingly.

We would not allow ourselves to be tempted to visit the celebrated house of the Madonna of San Loreto [*said to have been the home of Our Lady in Nazareth and to have been brought to Loreto by angels*], distant about 20 miles from Ancona. That the lower classes of the Italians should give in to these delusions does not surprise me. But that crowned heads and Princes should make pilgrimages to such a glaring imposition is beyond my comprehension. I observed in Ancona that the natives decline all intercourse with the Austrian Garrison. And yet the Neapolitan consul, the Chevalier d'Auria, assured me that the conduct of the Austrians, both officers and men, was most exemplary and forbearing.

We sailed from Ancona and after three days of baffling winds we put into the port of Molfetta [*next to Bari*] in the kingdom of Naples. After Trieste, Venice and Ancona it is surprising how much we, and even our Neapolitan sailors, were struck with the dirt and squalor of this large town. How can it be accounted for? It is situated in one of the most fertile and wealthy provinces of the kingdom. The Neapolitans are less taxed than any other people in the Peninsula. The government pays its employees to the day, the public debt of the kingdom is quoted at a higher rate than that of any other European stock except England and Holland. There is a constant and increasing demand for all the produce it can spare.

We left Molfetta for Cape Leuca [*the Southern tip of the 'heel' of Italy*]. We had long promised a visit to the relatives of my sister's husband, Mr. Romano, who resides at a small village called Patu, which is within a walk of the celebrated promontory. The weather was against our landing on an open coast so we steered for Gallipoli, the great shipping port of the well known Gallipoli oil. [*It had in earlier days been a useful supplier of olive oil for the 'return' journeys of JC's ships.*]

On the twenty ninth of October I persuaded my healthy joyous family to see the churches and curiosities of the town. In the church of the Franciscan Friars we were shown the extraordinary figures carved in wood by an artist of the town, viz. the two robbers who were crucified with our Saviour. The one on the left was called 'the bad robber' and the other on the right 'the good robber'. Certainly the artist must have had immense natural genius. I shall never forget the expression of the 'bad robber' – such a compound of mockery, malice, vexation and hard suffering I never could have imagined.

… The following morning, 1st. Nov, one of the Romanos accompanied by his brother-in-law, the Baron Maglietta, came from Patu with carriages to take us all and our three maids to the family residence. My sister and her husband met us half way. Within five miles of Patu we had a good road which had been recently constructed. The remainder of the road was the same as it was some two thousand years ago. Nature made it! With the exception of some half dozen arterial roads recently constructed in defiance of many of the rich proprietors of the soil, there is not a district or parish road in the province. No blame to the authorities. The owners of the land object to paying the expense of making them.

We spent ten happy days with my sister's family. We went over the estates which are covered with olive trees, the great produce of the soil. I was however struck with the want of energy in other branches of agriculture. I found out that the supplies of the ordinary comforts of the house had to be sent for at a distance. Meat, vegetables, fruit (except hard indigestible dried figs), milk, all mostly from Gallipoli. Butter there was none. Fish was however excellent and in fine weather abundant. I was struck too at the high price of land in the neighbourhood of the Cape. I also observed there were few or no day labourers, which fact may account for the absence of all kinds of domestic cultivation. No gardens, no dairies.

On the eleventh of November we returned to Gallipoli fully intending to visit the principal city of the Province, Lecce, or as the natives call it the Athens of the Kingdom. I had received a most cordial invitation from the Intendente or governor of the Province, Baron Sozi Carafa, an old friend of mine and of my late brother John. Another brother of the Romano family who resides at Lecce had prepared his house to receive us all.

Our plans being all arranged we entered Gallipoli at dusk, but what was our surprise when the first object which presented itself was my poor *Sibilla* laying on her side, stranded on the rocks and a heavy sea dashing at her broadside as if trying to dash her to pieces. She had broken both chains during the storm of the preceding night and had drifted on the rocks. The crew had been able to land and some few things had been got ashore. We thought ourselves fortunate that our kind friend the Baron had bespoken a lodging for us at the best Inn in the town. He conducted us there. It consisted of three rooms, which contained six beds. It was a comfortless Inn. Two or three dozen old chairs, one sofa without cushions; one of the rooms a mere passage with no glass. I tried to be cheerful. What use in fretting, but I must confess that however much I tried to appear composed I was nervous and ill prepared to make the most of our forlorn position. But I had in Anne an excellent substitute. She distributed the rooms, saw to the beds, and after a supper of eggs and macaroni spoilt by bad cheese she saw to the comfort of each child and to every member of our party. The beds were not inviting, though they proved themselves clean. It was with a plunge of necessity that I laid myself by my smiling, patient and collected wife.

The next morning I tried to be merry. I ordered up the ship's cook, his assistant and the steward. We had the rooms thoroughly swept – they had not been cleaned for months. The walls were streaming with damp and ornamented with cobwebs. I made a speech at breakfast. I would have no murmurings. I exhorted all to make the best of it. A few days of "roughing it" would be a useful experience. After breakfast we all went to see the wreck. The sea had subsided. We went on board; the children made slides down the deck, and thought it was "rare fun". After consulting with my officers each of us set about the work that was to be done: one to fish up the parted chains and anchors, another to clear the ship of water, which to our surprise was very trifling nor was any portion of our furniture or effects damaged. My duty was to organize assistance on shore for landing the ballast quickly to lighten the ship preparatory to our designs of dragging her by force into deep water.

It is on such occasions that the character of a people shows itself. When the ship went ashore, not a hand was raised or offered to save her, or the crew. An appeal was made to the captain of the port. His reply was, "how much will you pay?" When the crew landed wet to the skin no one offered them a shelter. My two Captains were obliged to keep a strict watch on the shore to prevent wreckers from pillaging the ship. It was the wish of the population that the ship should go to pieces in order to divide the spoil. Enormous prices were asked for a cable or an anchor or for boats.

The day after our arrival the Governor of the town and the other principal officers called on me, and offered every service in their power. Matters then became more easy. I soon enrolled four bands of labourers of ten men, each commanded by a corporal, and placed the whole under the orders of a ship-interpreter and him under that of my officers. I instructed the latter to order these bands of men one at a time to prevent confusion and robbery. When one band was set to work, to call for another when wanted. To count the men who came, and tick off their names; to dismiss instantly any man who was a loiterer; above all to enforce silence. By these means a strict discipline was observed. Our first operation was to fish up our chains and anchors. The first captain succeeded in a few hours in reconnecting them to the ship, hauling them taut so as to prevent her from moving further on the rocks should the sea return. In the meantime the ship had been pumped dry and a commencement made in the discharge of the ballast. We then hired a strong cable and fixed it to the stern of the ship and to a strong holding on the mole opposite.

On Saturday 13th Nov. the ballast was all out. All hands were then ordered to the windlass and to the pulleys on the hawser. During the night we moved the ship six feet; the weather continuing fine we moved her another six feet on Sunday. On Monday morning a heavy sea set in, causing the ship to bump frightfully. In the meantime portions of the false keel floated up alongside. The rudder from the commencement had been unshipped, forcing up the quarter deck and smashing it to pieces. The heaving of the ship's stern as each successive billow rolled in afforded us a last chance. The windlass and pulleys were strained to the verge of snapping. A huge billow lifted the stern, when all at once she glided with a crash into deep water. She was immediately hauled out to her anchor. All hands were ordered to the pumps. But wonderful to say, she made little or no water. In the meantime about thirty six feet of the keel of the ship floated alongside, with portions of the copper bolts, some bent and some broken, projecting from it. On the same day all the hands were discharged and our own crew returned to sleep on board.

The joy of having saved our old *Sibilla* was however damped by the events occurring in the interim at our wretched Inn. Whether my children had been affected by the air of the Province noted for its fevers or the moisture which exuded from the saline stone walls of the Inn, or whether some well-intentioned but officious neighbour had given the children some tough dried figs which are eaten in these parts in lieu of bread, I cannot say. While at Patu John had been the whole time in bed, but was convalescent again when we returned to Gallipoli. Annie [*Anne*] had been hot and feverish there, tho' not in any way to prevent her joining our excursions. Be this as it may, on the third day after our return from Gallipoli John was seized with diarrhoea which soon degenerated into typhus. Annie was also seized with asthma, cough and fever which was soon found to be intermittent. John became delirious and violent; his speech inarticulate; his lips, teeth and tongue covered with black mucus. Annie became so weak that she could scarcely speak, whilst her asthma and hard dry cough prevented her from laying down in bed. In this state of things I obtained the assistance of a doctor who immediately ordered John to be removed from Annie's bed, fearing he might expire at her side. Grace was next seized with fever. In three days her nervous system collapsed. It is now thirty one days since she has uttered a connected sentence, and during twenty five days she never said one word. She was insensible to every want: her bowels were in a state of extreme irritation, her eyes glazed, and to all appearance she was blind, dumb and deaf. James was next seized with fever, and like the others was carried into our miserable hospital room, in which an extra small bed was placed for him. Grace had also a small bed, but John and Anne lay side by side. The next victim to the adverse circumstances in which we were placed was our youngest daughter Annie. The same influence produced in her diarrhoea and fever. Our hospital being full she was carried to my room, the one without glass in the window. I slept in one bed with little Fred. Mag had charge of Annie (daughter) in another bed by my side. Finally I was seized with gout in both feet, and confined to my bed seven days.

We were fifty four days in this dungeon of a tavern, the doctor visiting us four times every day. I must admit that nothing could be more attentive or painstaking than he was. My kind and amiable friend the Baron Maglietta hardly ever left my side. I really owe him a debt which never can be paid. He worked for us like a servant. He protected us from impositions of all sorts. He had a resource for every emergency. He whiled away my solitary hours. He discussed with the doctors and myself every symptom, every prescription. He was never in the way, always at hand. He found means of procuring everything we wanted. He settled every dispute with the Knaves we had to do with in a gentle but firm manner so as to satisfy everyone. I must also add that the Governor of the town and the Receiver General of Customs and the Inspector of Police did not send to enquire or come themselves.

Whilst these sad scenes were going on at the Inn, I had given orders that the *Sibilla* should be laid down on her side to enable us to ascertain the extent of the damage to her keel and the steps to be taken to get her and us back to Naples.

I found on inquiry that there was not a single ship's carpenter in Gallipoli; no instruments or machinery adapted for shipping, no ropes or chains. For all these requisites we were obliged to beg, hire or borrow from the shipping which came into Port to load. Can any thing be more decisive as to the idleness and want of energy of this population? However we laid the *Sibilla* down on her larboard side as low as we dared. We found she had lost about two thirds of her keel in midships. Her cutwater and stern post were sound. She had enough of keel left, we judged, to enable her to steer. We thought it unnecessary to lay her down on the starboard side as from her position on the rocks larboard could not have suffered so much as the starboard. I then gave orders for the ballast to be reshipped and the vessel to be well aired and cleaned and put in order to receive us on board as soon as my sick could be removed with safety. This was soon accomplished. I next ordered the ship to go to sea on trial. I went with her and invited several ship masters to accompany us in the view of obtaining their opinions as to the ship being seaworthy – for I had already heard that eleven out of my twelve seamen were plotting to desert the ship on the plea of her being unsafe.

The trial of the *Sibilla* at sea was in every respect successful. She steered just as usual on both tacks and made no more water under canvas than at her moorings. All the masters declared she was sea worthy to go to Naples.

It is one of the peculiar features of the Neapolitans that you not only cannot trust to any declarations they may make to your face, but what is still more extraordinary they themselves don't in the least think bound to adhere to them or dishonoured by the breach of them. It is different with a written declaration. But in writing their statements they have a knack of expressing themselves so as almost always to admit of discussion as to the interpretation to be put on them. They have inherited this characteristic from their ancestry, "the Greeks". [*Although JC attributes this deviousness to the 'Neapolitans', he is probably referring here to the locals in Puglia as well as his crew. This is understandable when it is remembered that 'The Two Sicilies' were also known as 'The Kingdom of Naples'. Both Naples itself and Puglia had once been part of 'Magna Grecia'. 'Gallipoli' comes from the ancient Greek for 'beautiful city'.*] It appears to be in the blood which circulates in their veins. They cannot say the truth – there must be some reserve, something kept back. You may be aware that altho' a seaman is bound by his engagement not to abandon his ship, the latter becomes null & void by the ship becoming what is termed "not sea worthy". Before however he can leave the ship a survey of ship masters must declare her unseaworthy by certificate. [*Otherwise*] the seaman is bound by his contract to navigate her. Should he refuse to work her such refusal would be mutiny. Should he leave the ship he would be treated as a deserter. It has not clearly transpired what object my seamen had in conspiring to leave the ship.

Such was the position when I invited the masters to sign before the Captain of the Port a declaration that the *Sibilla* was in a fit state to proceed to Naples. There can be no doubt that the Captain of the Port involved himself in this question. It will turn up, I doubt not, that secretly he encouraged my seamen on their promising to divide with him any extra compensation they could extort from me, whilst to me he sent messages without end, threatening the men with imprisonment if they left the ship or refused to work.

The masters assembled at the office of the Captain of the Port. They at once declared that the *Sibilla* was in a fit state to proceed to Naples. So far so good, and here my officers wanted them to stop and sign. But some influence must have been at work for the Captain of the Port left the room that the masters might deliberate freely. They then added to their declaration these singular words "but in her present state they cannot say that she will reach her destination", and they all signed.

Annie was the first to leave her bed. John's fever left him on the twenty eighth day, and tho' reduced to a skeleton, he entered on the period of convalescence. Jemmie's fever was thrown off on the seventh day after commencing quinine, and as he had not lost much flesh he was speedily turned out of the hospital. Grace's complaint was unlike the others. Her collapse has continued until this day, 12th January, the fortieth day of her illness, tho' considerably modified for the better. Her fever has left her, the irritation of her bowels has long since disappeared, her functions are regular tho' still involuntary. Her eyes are clear, her sight is restored, she can hear but how imperfectly we can not tell, she utters occasionally a word or two, sometimes half a sentence under the excitement of mustard plasters. For hours however she remains silent, never ceasing even for an instant rubbing her face and passing her right hand over her brow to her right ear, whilst her left fingers are continually picking her frill under her chin. She eats the light food we allow her voraciously and her poor bones are beginning to acquire flesh again. It is distressing to see her little wrinkled face never once lit up with a smile since she was carried into our hospital. [*Grace recovered, but was subject thereafter to fits. The other children suffered no after-effects. Suzanne Knowles, after consulting with doctors, wrote that the fever they suffered from was probably typhoid.*]

After the trial of the *Sibilla* I had made up my mind to return to Naples in her. To prepare myself for the first favourable wind, I thought it my duty to pay a visit to the Governor of the Province of Lecce, to thank him and to excuse the promised visit of my family. On the tenth of December I accordingly took a carriage and with my kind friend the Baron reached Lecce to dinner at Mr. John [*Giovanni*] Romano's [*another brother*], who had provided most comfortably for us all in his neat and well ordered house.

Whilst at dinner the Governor called upon me and took a seat by my side. He gave me the welcome of an old friend. His conversation was frank, to the point, intelligent and business-like. I observed however on the part of Mr. Romano a timidity, a hesitation in joining in our conversation. Not only so, but what struck me most was his not offering the Governor even a glass of Champagne. This lack of civility, in his own house too, astonished me. But the Governor took not the slightest notice: on the contrary, addressing himself to Mr. Romano, he said it gave him pleasure to inform him that he had that very day received His Majesty's commands to commence the roads to Cape Leuca, one of which would pass thro' Patu, "so that I hope", added he, "you may be by the end of 1859 in carriageable reach of any part of the Province". Coffee being announced in the drawing room, Romano took courage and asked the Governor to partake, which he instantly and frankly accepted. The conversation, however, continued entirely between me and the Governor. We spoke about the Province roads he had constructed under opposition and difficulties on all sides, of the obstinacy of the landed proprietors in refusing to contribute to the expense and in refusing to admit the utility or the necessity of the roads. We also entered at length on the Orphan Asylums for Boys and Girls he had founded, also the Agricultural College he had instituted and other similar establishments. He went on to state his projects for establishing deposit and saving banks by means of which he hoped by degrees to subdue the almost invincible prejudices and apathy of the inhabitants in all matters connected with real improvement and progress. "Is it not strange," he added, "that whilst in my province the influential and wealthy land owners are for ever meddling in politics they do nothing, literally nothing, to improve their families & their estates? The fact is they want the state to do what it is their duty and interest to do for themselves. They call themselves liberals and yet they oppose every liberal project the Government offers them". As I have stated these magnanimous descendants of the Greeks have in politics, as well as in the management of their own affairs, for centuries habituated themselves to think that it is folly to work when the olive trees work for them, and in like manner the State should supply them with all sorts of conveniences.

The present Governor or Intendente of the province of Lecce, the Baron Sozi Carafa of St. Nicholas, is by universal opinion, even of the Liberals, admitted to be the most intelligent, the most considerate, the most zealous promoter of the best interests of the Province on record. He was appointed in 1849. Consequently he has been at the head of the province about ten years. He is now only thirty nine years of age. During his administration there has not been a single outbreak. He has not required the aid of a single regiment of troops during the whole of this period. At this moment there is not a soldier in the province. The only force at his disposal is about two hundred Gens d'armes and the Urbane guard, which means a few citizens armed by rotation in each parish with fowling pieces, without uniforms or discipline, under the orders of the respective Mayors or Syndics of each parish. With this small force he has managed to keep the peace, to suppress every tendency to disorder and to a certain extent to conciliate the respect of the disaffected, to whom he has not left a single well grounded grievance to serve as a rope to hold them together. This line of policy has nearly destroyed the liberal party. Individually they vent their spleen by growls and imputations of motives. But they cannot deny the fact that these roads are doubling the value of their property and that the province never was so quiet or more prosperous.

Knowing as I do the character of the natives it did not in the least astonish me to hear my brother-in-law refuse all merit to the Governor for what he had done on the grounds that a large portion of the expenditure filtered itself into the Governor's private purse. He, Mr. Romano, could give no authority for this assertion: he inferred it from the high price of four hundred pounds per mile, at which the contracts for the roads were taken by public competition. "Just double" he added, "the real cost"! He could give me no authority for this statement. It happened on the following day, on one of our excursions, that we met one of the contractors. He informed us that he was an unsuccessful candidate for fourteen miles of the road we were then travelling on. It had been knocked down at three hundred and fifty pounds per mile. He stated that it could not be done at the price, to leave a living profit. I made inquiry into the subject in Lecce, and I was informed that without placing himself in the power of all the clerks, secretaries, cashiers and engineers of the office of Public works, robbery by the Governor was impossible, at least in this direction.

The salary of the Intendente is only about five hundred pounds per annum with a house to live in. What allowance he may have in the form of rations, secretaries, etc, I know not. He is the representative of the King in his particular province.

Anne's copy of the letter ends here, and it is not known whether any further misfortunes occurred on the way back to Naples. By now JC's royalist views no longer ran to approval of the King himself, but this did not make him a liberal and he still supported the existing system of Government, as his high praise for the Governor (Intendente) of the Province (Lecce) shows. The above first-hand account of how Baron Carafa ran this Province helps to explain JC's support for the Monarchy.

✍ *1859: Future plans*

*I*N APRIL 1859, shortly after writing the letter to Padiham, JC wrote another lengthy letter, this time to his brother Thomas. In it, he asks for his brother's advice, so showing that the former animosity between them had been smoothed over. It covers the state of his business affairs, his hopes for the future, with various ideas as to where he should settle after leaving Naples. It is useful as a rationale of his actions from then until his death. Although he is the author of much of the Journals, in them he only writes of the events of each day, never of the thinking behind his decisions or of his long-term plans.

JC's mood in the letter is low – he even talks of selling the yacht. Perhaps he had not yet recovered from the family's experiences at the end of their 1858 cruise. Yet it is clear that he had good reason to worry about the future. Apart from the unstable political situation, his finances were not in good shape. In the Adriatic he had continued to behave in each port as an important visiting dignitary, but there is no record of any voyage of the *Sibilla* in 1859. He was involved in costly lawsuits and failing to collect what he was owed. He only continued to live in Naples because that was the best place to sell off his assets and collect his debts – and because Naples was so cheap!

Moreover he had suffered from one major financial set-back (the exact date of which is not known). In later life, he had come to rely to a great extent on his dealings in the financial world, and the few references in the Journals to his business activities are mostly to his study of the markets in *The Times* and to telegrams he sent giving instructions to his agents in England. He was not always successful. On one occasion, he was in the act of transmitting a large sum of money to England through an Italian bank when the bank closed its doors. The money was lost. JC was on board the *Sibilla* at the time. He was seen to take a few turns on deck before sending off a telegram – he had already begun to restore his losses. No wonder he was deeply concerned about the future of his young children.

Later JC becomes more positive and his years of cruising with his wife and children are said to be the happiest of his life. It is just possible that in this letter he had family reasons for exaggerating his poverty to Tom. Tom was childless, whereas JC had eight children to support. But more probably his financial problems had taken a dip and the gloom was therefore temporary.

JC's opening shows that he is replying to a letter from his brother.

My Dear Tom,

You ask me what I am doing in Naples? In reply, I have yet to realize my warehousing property, my schooner Sphinx, my yacht, my furniture, and I *have* to recover some still outstanding debts. In all from £1,200 to £1,400. More than that, I have to finish those wretched law suits in which the Romanos have entangled me during the last twelve or fourteen years, and from which they appear to have lost all hope of ever extricating me, without loss and humiliations to me intolerable. Strange! that they have never yet gained a single cause of mine; they never recovered for me a single Ducat of my claims as a creditor; and in almost every suit I have had to pay costs! However simple my case, the same result has ever followed. Its phases have become so embroiled by law proceedings, that I could no longer recognise my own. I have spent enormous sums of money, only to be plunged deeper and deeper in the meshes of the law. These lawsuits have poisoned my existence. I cannot see the Romanos without suffering from nervous affection. I distrust their opinions. I disbelieve their professional statements. There is not a doubt, that much of my illness, my gout, and my extreme nervousness derive from mental irritation, and the annoyance of witnessing my debtors' triumph at my expense. And there is also no doubt that unless I can make up my mind to renounce all my claims and accept any terms, and thus rid myself of this intolerable vexation, my days will be shortened, as it has already rendered Naples intolerable to me. [*Dickens's 'Bleak House' was written in the same decade as this letter, and the parallels with Jarndyce and Jarndyce are striking.*]

These lawsuits have made me disgusted with the King, whom I have not seen these last three years: with the Ministers, whom I hold to be even below contempt; with business, seeing that my property is not secure, and that the trade of Naples is demoralised to an extent of which no idea can be formed, unless by those who daily experience it. Contracts, and bills are forged in heaps. Houses of consideration (native), finding it inconvenient to meet their engagements, coolly deny their signatures, tho' certified by public notary! Defaulters on change, protecting themselves under the gambling laws. The business of imports fallen into the hands of shopkeepers, and third or fourth class native houses; the consequences of smuggling, which the Government winks at thro' its employees. The exports in general adulterated, & purchasers involved in law suits. The English houses fast decaying from fruitless efforts, and from inanition. Such, in a few words, is the present condition of trade in this Kingdom. It is very possible the approaching death of the King may lead to a change, to a more progressive government, to a purification of the courts, to the admission of foreigners to the concessions of railways and other public works, to an improved administration of the Customs, to a new Tariff of duties, and in some years or perhaps generations to an improved standard of morality amongst the population.

But at my age, and with the disgust which oppresses me, these changes offer me little or no inducement to remain in Naples in respect of business, or to desire to establish any of my sons there.

And if I look forward to the time of *my* daughters' growing up to the marriageable period of their lives, Naples appears to me of all places in the world the least eligible for me to reside in. To marry them to Neapolitans is out of the question. Sooner bury them. [*Here he reasserts that there is no Naples family he would consider as in-laws other than the Meuricoffres.*] And as to the travellers who visit Naples – Pshaw! who knows them, who and what they are?

The advantages Naples offers us are climate and economy. The former as affecting myself and my wife, the latter as securing to us our enjoyment of many luxuries and comforts, we might elsewhere be obliged to forego. Moreover Naples offers us cheap masters and good ones for the instruction of our children.

How if we went to reside in London? Our expenses? Our health? Our social habits? Masters for the children? at what cost? Myself without a regular occupation, in the midst of money making men, men of that single one idea?

How if in some retired part of Devonshire? within reach of the railway? This idea is less gloomy, but having masters for the children there is out of the question. Expense would be more moderate. I might even meet with a sociable neighbour or two. And the climate might offer some compensation for the loss of the one we are accustomed to. But would not the children be as much out of the current of success in life there, as here?

How if at Bowden in Cheshire, on one of the Estates recently bought by Mr. Brooks from the Earl of Stamford & Warrington? But Manchester proffers fewer attractions to us both than even London. Masters worse, even if obtainable at that distance. Climate colder and more rainy.

How if in Switzerland for a few years, until the boys be of an age to go to college in Germany or elsewhere, for as to sending them to any school whatever, either in England or elsewhere, our minds are fully made up to the contrary. Until they are fifteen or sixteen, none of them shall leave the paternal roof. Their natural affections, their morals, their health can no where be so well attended to, as at home. As to instruction, and the development of their intellectual powers, it will be time enough to attend to that, when they are old enough to discern clearly between what is right & what is wrong and when their affections can be weaned from home without violence. I have observed that it is time lost to teach a child before it has sense to appreciate knowledge, and to teach itself. I have observed that a child of ten years learns in a day what it requires months to teach a child of five. In Switzerland or at Baden Baden we could live with economy. The children would not lose what they already know of French and Italian. There would be society for us, on a less formal scale than in England. If we sent our boys to the German colleges we should be in the neighbourhood to watch over them. The climate would be more congenial to us.

But, you will naturally ask, to what professions do you intend to prepare your children? The question is most difficult to answer. I have no business to leave them. All my mercantile connections are gone. My eldest son has selected the Church, and I am most thankful he has done so. My mind is at rest with respect to him. As to the law, or medicine, I have not the slightest leaning that way. Remain Engineering and trade. Mr. Brooks made us a promise that John should have a place in the Bank. What if James could be made a junior partner in some London firm as a Merchant? What if William, who appears to be less mercurial than the others, could join some manufacturing Establishment in Lancashire. As to Frederic, whose abilities and elasticity are in excess, I may almost say, what of him as a civil or military Engineer?

I do not wish to infuse ambitious views into the minds of any of my children. I mean to say, that whilst I hope and expect that at home they will acquire the habits of gentlemen, they will at the same time acquire the impression that labour and industry are absolute requisites to their independence and happiness. Supposing even that at mine and Annie's death, we could leave them £80,000 or even £100,000 – what is it in the way of independence for eight or nine children? Nor can I at all rely on that; for Securities may fall, and Sam Brooks may change his intentions, or may live like his father till he be near one hundred years old – and long before then all my children must be started in their worldly career.

These considerations lead me to conclude, that it is preferable to give my younger boys a mercantile and practical education, rather than a classical one. And I consider Germany to offer better opportunities for this sort of instruction than England.

Thus you see, that the more we consider the subject, the more our inclinations, and our interests tend in the direction of Switzerland in case we make up our minds to quit Naples.

It is an ugly thought to quit this smiling, cheerful warm climate, to sell our furniture, break up old friendships, to bid adieu to the easy life that social intercourse admits of here. I fear, I dread, that once transplanted elsewhere, our reminiscences of happy years spent in Naples, of its blue sea and purple mountains, of its cloudless days, of the bustle, and of the resources it has ever afforded, I dread to say, that reminiscences would be too strong for us. Spleen, gout and rheumatism, nay my extreme nervousness, might compel me to return. 'Tis like transplanting an old tree. It may be done, but with care and much forethought.

Another plan has often been discussed between us, namely: to suspend any determination until we know where Henry will be able to obtain a living, and then settle down near him. In the meantime I may hope to realise what I have here, and settle these law suits.

Perhaps in the course of some months chance or circumstances will point out more clearly the course I ought to pursue, so as to leave no doubt.

Several of our friends who have abandoned Naples, I must observe, have lived to regret it, and to wish they had not done so.

If you on mature deliberation can suggest any thing, which you think likely to meet the doubts and difficulties I have explained, I shall feel grateful, and will give them my serious consideration.

Your affectionate brother,
James Close.

Expectations with regard to Sam Brooks were reasonably accurate. He did not live to a great age, but died five years later, leaving Anne £100,000. John did become a banker. Otherwise, JC's forecasts were not good. No more was heard of Henry's decision to go into the Church. The careers of his other sons were different from those predicted, except in the broad sense that they avoided Medicine and the Law, embraced Trade and worked hard for their living. The family did leave Naples, but not for another five years and not for Switzerland, Manchester or Devon. Far from Ferdinand's son Francis proving a better monarch, he exacerbated the situation. And there is not a hint of any awareness that the monarchy itself was in danger, still less that within a year The Two Sicilies would form part of 'Italy'.

CHAPTER IV

Change of Regime

❧ *Decline of Bourbons*

*I*N A SECOND 1859 letter to brother Thomas, written only a month later, JC realizes that the Kingdom is about to collapse:

> And Naples? A dying King! He may be dead to-day, tomorrow. His successor is 23 years old. Not a Minister, not a General of note. The Royal Family divided in opinion; all hope of help from Austria is at an end. The whole Peninsula gone over. Its Tuscan relatives run away! The Pope helpless! Without an ally! No not one! Nothing to be relied upon, save some 10–12,000 Swiss troops. For as to the Neapolitan troops, they would disband or revolt tomorrow, were it not for the Swiss troops. Now that France has declared itself for the Italians versus the Austrian influence, I consider the game is up.

After this letter, as the political crisis worsened, JC may have decided that it would be imprudent to put on paper any further comments. There is nothing further from him in writing on the political situation until 1861.

Ferdinand died on 22nd May 1859, after months of agonising pain caused by an abscess on his thigh, which spread through his body. The royal obsequies were not without their macabre moments. Harriet Meuricoffre was present and recorded them:

> The ceremony took many hours. Towards afternoon a herald entered the church and proclaimed: "The King's dinner waits"; he was accompanied by the royal cook. Another voice from the other end of the church replied: "The King will not dine today". Towards evening again a herald entered: "The King's carriage waits", and the reply came with a strange and awful sound, "The King will not leave the Church today".

The young King Francis II began his brief reign with every disadvantage, not the least of these being his own character upon which his upbringing had had a disastrous effect. Francis had none of his father's Neapolitan *joie de vivre*, while his mother's acceptance of the present situation had developed in him to a paralysing degree. After his mother's early death, he had grown up dominated by his stepmother and under the influence of the Austrian priests at the Court, and had accepted the *status quo* dutifully and without question. Until his marriage he had never been permitted to be alone, day or night, and spies reported his every word and action to the King and Queen. A crippling shyness undermined any self-confidence he might have had, and by the time he came to the throne he had taken refuge in an attitude of fundamental indifference which in time came to be reciprocated by his subjects.

Sir Henry Elliot, the new British Minister in Naples, gives a first-hand account of the new King's manner in *Some Revolutions and Diplomatic Experiences*:

> He had none of that generosity of nature which might have prompted him to appeal to his people, asking them for their support and promising to redress their grievances, at a moment when an impressionable population like the Neapolitans would have been quite ready to look kindly on their young Sovereign if they had seen a symptom of his looking kindly upon them.
>
> An entire want of sympathy or feeling for others was visible in the cold manner, unlike everything you would wish to see in a young man of twenty-three, and it was painfully exhibited before his whole Court on the day on which he received the homage of all the great people of his kingdom. He stood on a carpet in front of the throne, and as the lieges passed before him they kissed his hand, which he did not take the trouble to raise, allowing it, when they had kissed it, to fall back by his side as if it had been the hand of a doll, while he did not even look at the person who was doing homage, but peered about examining those who were coming next. One very infirm old man caught his foot in the carpet and fell flat on his face close to the feet of the King, who neither stirred to help him nor allowed a muscle of his face to move while the poor old fellow, awkwardly and with difficulty, scrambled up and passed him without a word from the King of condolence for his mishap or enquiry whether he was hurt. It afforded an insight into the King's disposition, and it must have impressed many of his subjects who witnessed the scene much as it did me, when I remarked to my neighbour that 'that young man will finish badly'.

Although internal pressures for the unification of Italy were now even greater than in the reign of his father, Francis had had no education in statecraft apart from some precepts and advice dictated to him by Ferdinand during his last illness, which he took down in a notebook to be referred to for guidance when he came to the throne. He did not lack advice from various quarters but steadfastly refused to listen to it; though later when in exile he said he might still have been on his throne if he had taken the advice of Sir Henry Elliot, offered on behalf of the British Government. As it was, Francis governed through his police spies, so that, as Harriet Meuricoffre observed, the head of police was something like a prime minister.

🐚 *1860: Garibaldi*

*I*N A LETTER to her father written early in 1860, when Francis was nearing the end of his reign, Anne Close comments:

> Whilst Manchester is thus prospering everything conspires to make Naples poorer and more wretched, our crops of corn, wine, oil and silk were failures last year, the uncertain state of politics has checked the usual influx of strangers, the severe measures of government have carried terror and distrust and suspicion into families – business is suspended, shop keepers are failing from misfortune or roguery, the priests are preaching agitation and the people in the provinces are starving. Who can say how all this will end for as yet there are no signs of change in the policy of the government. Meantime all eyes are turned to passing events in the north of Italy: James says that Tuscany and the other provinces will all end in annexation by Sardinia, that Savoy will be quietly ceded to France as most expedient to all parties, perhaps against an indemnity that there will be no war and finally that Austria, Naples and the Pope must knock under or cut their sticks. What say you?

Little wonder that JC decided that this would be a good time for the family to visit Anne's father in England. By the time the *Sibilla* left Naples the atmosphere in the city was one of tension, uncertainty and apprehension. The campaign for the unification of Italy was well under way and in August General Garibaldi, following his successes in Sicily, crossed the Straits of Messina with his volunteer force and started to make his way northwards through Calabria. No one could predict what would happen in the next few weeks.

Owing to the family's absence in Great Britain, there are no Close papers relating to the momentous events in Naples after the letter from Anne to her father quoted above. JC himself was keeping a low profile, in view of his association with the Bourbons. But he had every reason to keep the closest possible watch on what was happening. First, Don Liborio acted as the lynch-pin between the two regimes and played a major part in maintaining order in the city. Secondly, JC's friend Harriet Meuricoffre was in the thick of the drama, and played a small but worth-while part in it. While in England, he may have seen some of the reports that Harriet sent home to her parents. Her descriptions of Garibaldi and his arrival in Naples; of the conditions in which the prisoners of the old regime were kept and of the hospital where she did her best to help the wounded *garibaldini,* are vivid and informative enough to be in print and so add to the general store of knowledge about the *Risorgimento.*

The fact that JC and family returned to Naples at all may have had something to do with the success of both Romano brothers under the new regime and the continued residence there of the Meuricoffres. On his return, JC did not leave the city permanently for another three years, and he will be found helping out disbanded royalist troops *(relegati)* one day, while having tea with Garibaldi the next.

Following Ferdinand's death, his son, Francis II, could do little to save his Kingdom. Totally on his own, supported by no other power and with a cold, indifferent outlook described by Sir Henry Elliot, the young King was unfitted to deal with the crises of his brief reign or to offer an effective challenge to an opponent who was already receiving enthusiastic support from some of his subjects. When, urged to do so by his Queen, Francis revived in June the 1848 constitution that had been abandoned by his father and introduced certain reforms, it was far too late: his subjects were no longer interested. His Government was now a constitutional one with powers of its own, but its members were at odds with one another and with the generals. There was no real hope of success against the approaching forces of liberation which had landed in Sicily prior to crossing over to the mainland, and Francis's own panic reaction to the news that Garibaldi had entered Palermo was to telegraph to Rome five times in twenty-four hours for the Pope's blessing. The soldiers of the Bourbon army were brave men, but they were poorly led by officers they did not trust, and by whom they felt they had been betrayed. Some went over to the invaders, now making their way towards Naples. Others retreated or surrendered.

The *relegati,* who had been disbanded when their leaders surrendered, struggled to make their way home, utterly destitute, and for these Garibaldi, generous in victory as ever, did what he could to help from his own pocket.

On the evening that Garibaldi reached Salerno, 6th September, King Francis, in order to spare the citizens of Naples the horrors of civil war, left with the Queen for Gaeta, some forty-seven miles to the north, there to defend his crown. During the day a royal proclamation had been made outlining the King's position, declaring his intention to continue to serve his subjects' interests should destiny call him back and imploring them not to resort to violence in the city. The King had asked his Ministers to draft the proclamation: when the result was submitted to him he recognised it to be the work of Don Liborio Romano, now Minister of the Interior and Prefect of Police. Before leaving his Palace Francis bade farewell to the members of his Government, and on saying goodbye to Don Liborio, whom he had every reason to distrust, said half-jokingly: 'Watch out for your head, Don Libo!' His scheming Minister assured him that he would do his best to keep it on his shoulders, secure in the knowledge that Rear Admiral Mundy had undertaken to give him political asylum on board *H.M.S. Hannibal,* anchored in the Bay of Naples along with the naval vessels of other foreign powers and of the Neapolitan navy, in the event of the King's return.

It has never been clear whether the King really expected to return to his capital, but he took only a few of his personal treasures and not a great deal of money with him, and the Queen told her maid only to pack a few clothes for her since they would not be away for long.

In his book *H.M.S. Hannibal at Palermo and Naples during the Italian Revolution, 1856–1861* Admiral Mundy describes the royal departure:

> Shortly before 7 o'clock in the evening, the King and Queen, a few gentlemen of the Royal household, and the Ministers of Austria, Prussia, Spain, and Bavaria ... put to sea, and passing close by the *Hannibal,* proceeded on their way to Gaeta.
>
> The King in his proclamation beseeches his loving people not to let excessive zeal for his dynasty be made a pretext for disturbance. They obeyed him only too well! He left the palace of his ancestors, and drove down to the Mole amidst a vast crowd of the inhabitants, but not a tear was shed, nor was a "God bless you!" even heard. It was the desolation of indifference. Indeed, a melancholy spectacle, which it grieved me to behold.
>
> As Francis II, the last King of the Two Sicilies, left Naples for ever the command was signalled for his fleet to follow. Not a single vessel moved.

Early the next day, 7th September, Don Liborio Romano sent a telegram to Garibaldi at Salerno, in which he hailed him as the invincible Dictator and told him that Naples awaited his arrival with the utmost impatience in order to salute him as Italy's redeemer and to place all power and her own destiny in his hands. In the brief but extremely tense and potentially explosive interval between the King's departure and Garibaldi's arrival, when the slightest incident could have sparked off bloodshed and anarchy, it was Don Liborio who maintained law and order. The only effective man of power in Naples, with the police, the National Guard and the Camorra (the criminal association) at his command, he succeeded in keeping the peace and could justly claim that he had saved the city from destruction.

Garibaldi made his way by rail from Salerno to Naples that same morning. His troops were too far behind to accompany him, and he travelled with only members of his staff, plus as many friends and supporters as could cram into the train or cling on to it. He had only landed on the toe of Italy the previous month, but he must already have realized that he was safe without his troops and that the population was behind him. At Naples an expectant crowd gathered at the station in the midday heat, with Don Liborio ready to make his carefully prepared speech of welcome. This was to have been the proudest moment of his career, but alas for the vulnerability of human ambition, so easily destroyed by something entirely trivial. The train was an hour and a half late, having been delayed by the cheering and ecstatic crowds that lined the track all the way and sometimes invaded it, and when the hero of the hour finally stepped on to the platform he excused himself and retired briefly behind a railway carriage. By the time he emerged the crowd had taken over, cheering so loudly that it was impossible for Don Liborio's words to be heard, added to which he failed to make his way through the increasing mass of people to take his seat in the carriage in which Garibaldi was to make his drive into the capital.

The above account of Don Liborio's role in keeping the peace during the hand-over period has its farcical side, but the historian G. M. Trevelyan concedes the importance of the part he played. In *Garibaldi and the Making of Italy* he writes:

> Don Liborio Romano, the new Prefect of Police, was the sole exception to the rule that the Ministers had neither popularity nor influence, and he was also the exception to the rule that they were passively loyal to the King. 'Don Liborio', as he was called in these days, was a native of lower Apulia, skilled in the insinuating manners and arts of the political intrigue which the inhabitants of the region between Taranto and Brindisi are said to have inherited from their Greek ancestors. He had been an active liberal as early as 1820, and had often suffered as such at the hands of the police. But he belonged essentially to the world of Levantine intrigue, rather than to the world of European revolution. For this reason, he was able, from June to September 1860, to preserve the confidence of the inhabitants of the capital by a kind of masonic mutual understanding or sympathy of character, which a more straightforward man would have failed to establish with the Neapolitans. After his retirement he always asserted that he had taken office, not

in order to save the dynasty, which he believed to be already lost, but in order to preserve his fellow-countrymen from anarchy and civil war. This account of his motives, if a considerable allowance be made for his vanity and ambition, is accepted by the most competent and unbiased authorities which knew Naples of that day well, and they are also of opinion that at the moment of entering office he did actually achieve his purpose and save the city and perhaps the whole Kingdom from a terrible disaster.

Don Liborio had been appointed Minister of the Interior and Prefect of Police by Francis II as a belated sop to liberal pressure. Trevelyan's analysis of his devious character shows how he was able to accept such an offer from the monarch while remaining an acceptable or even popular figure with the public. Later, as recorded in JC's Family History, he was 'elected deputy to the Chamber of Representatives in Turin by eleven colleges'. He also served briefly as Councillor of the Interior for the Neapolitan provinces under King Victor Emmanuel.

Throughout the change of regime the Meuricoffres remained in Naples, although they took the precaution of entrusting some family silver temporarily to the captain of a British man-o'-war anchored in the bay. Harriet recorded the events in letters home and the following description of Garibaldi's arrival is the first extract from these letters:

It is difficult to describe the excitement. After about an hour's waiting, there came up a red shirt on a carriage-horse, with its blinkers on, to give warning that Garibaldi was coming, and then the cheering rose louder and louder as the carriage came slowly along. And there he was without a bit of state – three red shirts with their backs to the horses, himself and another man in the seat of honour, and three more in a stuck-up rumble behind; such fine old heads, with whitened beards, and all their red shirts covered with purple stains, like English hunting coats which have been through sundry squire-traps. Their earnest, calm, sunburnt faces spoke of different work from running up and down a street shouting, but what could we poor contemptible people do except shout and clap our hands? ... I was told that I would never have seen so fine a sight as Paris welcoming home her heroes last summer [*when Napoleon III's troops returned from warring against the Austrians in Lombardy*]; but this one carriagefull of weather-beaten elderly men was far grander – not the sight of a monarch who makes war for his own ambition in one way or another, but of the triumph of moral force and single-minded devotion. I wish I could convey to you an idea of how he looked, the dear old weather-beaten angel.

The response to Garibaldi's personality was overwhelming and sometimes near-idolatrous. The volunteers followed him blindly to the death. The Calabrian peasants held up their children to touch his clothing. The society ladies of Naples hero-worshipped him – and Harriet was his devoted admirer. To the Liberator himself, single-minded in his task of uniting Italy, any kind of adulation was irrelevant. He soon secured the support of the entire English community, whose first request to him was that they should be allowed to build a protestant church – something that had always been refused by the Bourbons. Not only did he agree to that, but he gave them the land on which to build it.

Garibaldi was indifferent to acclaim from any sector. When in 1864 the Duke and Duchess of Sutherland brought him to England, where he had a huge popular following, he was bored and bewildered by the lionising of London society. He felt more at home in the company of North Country miners who, as a token of their esteem, presented him with a sword for which they had subscribed at a penny a head.

Harriet, who had the double advantage of bearing the influential name of Meuricoffre and of being English, was more likely to be helped than hindered when she went out and about. She took her young sons Johnny and Freddy to Palace Square to see Garibaldi presenting colours to his soldiers:

> … we found a National Guard keeping the square, but one of them said that I might pass, as I was English … We reached the edge of the group of people around Garibaldi and the other generals. A tall national guardsman said: 'Follow me, and I will make a way for you.' Everyone seemed bent on protecting me – I think because I had my jolly little boys with me. Suddenly I found myself face to face with Garibaldi, people pressing on him from behind. I had been asked by the national guardsman if I would like to be presented to him. I said: 'No: I only wish the children to see him', but when I found myself quite facing him, and looking at each other, I held out my hand instinctively, and he shook it heartily. I said: 'May God grant you all your heart's desire for the good of Italy; Venice and all. I believe that He will'. He smiled and said: 'Thank you, thank you. You are most kind'. This was all our interview. I was quite proud of my presence of mind in making such a fine speech, quite impromptu. When I used to answer old King Bomba's remarks I felt as cool as three cucumbers, and I think I should before any man who is only a King; but I felt quite agitated in speaking to Garibaldi, because I reverence him so much.

Other society ladies were not so concerned about imposing on Garibaldi's time, and vied with each other to get a lock of his hair. Perhaps to get away from the socialising, he removed his quarters to the palace of Caserta, and invited all the ladies to visit him there at 12 o'clock on the coming Monday. Harriet described the scene:

> Garibaldi lives in a great palace, but takes only three modest little rooms, reached by a pokey side stair. He was in a narrow room with his little white bed down in the corner. He left his writing and came forward and shook hands heartily with us all. He has a cheerful, simple way of saluting everyone – not that high society knack of appearing to be intensely listening, and anxious for your answers, when you know you will fade utterly out of that person's memory in five minutes. ... He gave his mind as completely to the work of writing the little things we asked him for, as he could have done if it had been a plan of attack. We all sat down. First, Mrs Strange told him that Queen Victoria had expressed a desire that he would send her his photograph, and that he should write his name under it. He said in very innocent, clear English: 'But do you really think her Majesty would like me to do that?'

There were many sick, wounded and disabled soldiers to be cared for in Naples. G. M. Trevelyan had this to say about their treatment:

> The Neapolitans did little or nothing to make life more comfortable for their deliverers. Those of the wounded who were sent back to the Capital fared worse than those left at the front, for the usual peculation and carelessness of the hospital officials and the consequent dirt and absence of necessaries were not remedied on behalf of the *Garibaldini*, except to some degree by British help in the form of materials and money from England and personal service by some of our countrywomen in Naples.

Two of the women from the international community who played a part in caring for the wounded *Garibaldini* were Harriet Meuricoffre and her sister-in-law Sophie. A ward at the Sant'Apostoli Hospital was given up to Sophie Meuricoffre entirely: Harriet, who was her assistant, provides first-hand evidence for Trevelyan's accusations in a letter to her father on 8th October 1860:

> I am impressed with the courage of the men in bearing pain; I think the courage required in battle is a trifle compared with it. Sophie only spoke to some; the others showed their native courtesy in scarcely giving her a sign of recognition as she passed, lest they should seem to put themselves forward, although their faces beamed with pleasure. There is a boy who had had a large ball which went

slantwise through both shoulders and back. He showed me the ball – thimble-shaped, as large as a small wine-glass, but solid. He is obliged to sit curled up forwards night and day. Another whom I was struck with was a young Lombard gentleman, serving in the ranks, very beautiful, like the St. Michael of the Louvre, with reddish hair flowing back in wavy curls from the smooth white forehead. He is mortally wounded, I fear. His fine chestnut eyes are glassy and vacant.

Money has been given most liberally, but it gets shamefully thrown away, through the incorrigible thieving propensities of the Neapolitan officials. Baskets full of provisions come in at one door and go out at the other, and are resold; and the money goes into the pockets of the hospital staff.

Garibaldi visited the hospital. There was a cry outside that he was coming, and all the officials rushed with brooms and swept, and the Governor sidled up to Sophie and hoped that she had found the broth better in the last few days. He went over all in the first and second sala. Sophie's is the second. Presently the General came in. A swarm of doctors and attendants surrounded him, praising themselves and craving his notice, so that one could not hear what he said. But he did not fail to speak to each one of the fifty-two men. As soon as it was known he was coming all the men began to sit up in their beds and shout 'Papa nostro'.

Following the entry of Garibaldi into Naples the four great castles dominating the city were evacuated by their Bourbon garrisons. Before leaving for Gaeta King Francis had ordered them to remain neutral and avoid bloodshed: his orders had been obeyed and his troops were allowed to leave without molestation. In October Harriet was one of a party taken on a conducted tour of the castle of St. Elmo. This massive fortress-prison was built on a rock, three sides of it shelving steeply down to the sea and the fourth merging into the hill behind. At the top of it, enclosed by huge walls, was a large barrack square with guns and mortars and mounds of shells. From here the whole of Naples lay like a map spread out. Below were three grim storeys, down to which Harriet and her party were led by the light of a lantern to see the hut-like cells in which prisoners of the regime had been kept in solitary confinement in unspeakable conditions, sometimes for years: in one of them was a bed of stone with a pillow of stone. Harriet describes what she saw:

They have been cleaned out and white-washed, but the stench is still overpowering; imagine what is was when inhabited by people who were never let out, who had no mattresses, and had to wear their clothes night and day!

There was one cell still worse than the others. A little winding staircase led up to it. Even with the door wide open you could not see the person at your elbow. I had heard and read all about the prisons, as you will read this; but, standing there, it came upon me as it had never done before, as a new sense, what it would be to have that door shut upon one. Even when it was open, the darkness seemed to weigh like a year of midnight on my chest, and to crush the breath out. I don't think I should have the courage to try to keep alive there; I should lie down on that plank bed and never move again. A man was kept sixteen years in that hole! In that moment the last spark of pity I had felt for the Bourbons died out of me, and I could have clapped my hands for joy to think that it was over.

But these are not the worst prisons. They are dry; there are others by the sea which drip night and day; and a gentleman who was with us had been informed by one of the released prisoners of the torture invented by his jailer – to pour on him, through an opening at the top, cold water at any time, night or day. There were names and dates inscribed on the rock – one of a Spanish nobleman 200 years ago. Some told of very long imprisonments: it seemed as if the very rocks were impregnated with sighs and tears, and groans, and they weighed and crushed one's heart with misery.

But there is more to tell, very horrible and mysterious. In the middle of this large cave there was a great round hole, with a low parapet enclosing it; and, looking down into it, we saw another hall cut into the rock, like that in which we stood – larger because of not being filled with the cells, and very deep – lighted by a slanting shaft to the opening of the upper one. They told us that this was the place in which they used to put a number of prisoners, whom they wanted to get rid of, and shoot them from above.

It will be remembered that Pope Pius IX had fled to the castle at Gaeta back in 1848. In 1852, Anne had written to her father saying that Ferdinand 'is fortifying Gaeta, which is situated on the sea-side near the Roman frontier, and provisioning it for a six-month siege'. Francis II and his much diminished entourage soon made use of his father's preparations. The fortress, defended by troops still loyal to the Bourbons, was besieged by the forces of Garibaldi and the newly proclaimed King Victor Emmanuel II of Italy. The siege dragged on for months; bombardment and typhoid took their toll of the garrison and food became scarce. Having appealed in vain to the sovereigns of Europe for aid, Francis determined to fight on alone, showing a sudden and unexpected spirit of resolution and courage in the face of hopeless odds. The end came when a powder magazine exploded within the walls of the fortress, and the capitulation was signed on 13th February 1861. The King and Queen joined the rest of the royal family in Rome.

The *Risorgimento* had long been at work, but it was not until 1860, with the proclamation of Victor Emmanuel II as King of Italy, that the new nation began to emerge. The new King entered Naples with his Piedmontese army on 8th October, and on 15th of that month Garibaldi 'presented' the Two Sicilies to Vittorio Emmanuele. Italy was to remain a Kingdom until 1946, when Umberto II abdicated following a plebiscite.

1861: Getting away from Naples

IN JULY 1861 James Close gave his views on current affairs in a third letter to his brother Thomas in Nottingham:

> Since last I wrote to you events have progressed in Italy. France has recognised Victor Emmanuel as de facto King of Italy. I doubt not that other provinces will do the same. Cavour is dead, a heavy loss. But he has got the ship of state within sight of port, speaking politically; his loss is not irreparable. Riscasoli has taken his place and if he will follow in Cavour's steps in respect of Rome, the Pope, and Venice, all will go right.
>
> The Pope's temporal days seem to be counted. It is impossible that he can hold on longer against the wishes of subjects. The contest has become ridiculous, his subjects laugh at him, at his Monsignors, Signori, and Eminenzos. They play hide and seek with his Zouaves and Gens d'Armes.
>
> Napoleon III has no intention to preserve the Temporal, and does not care a pin for the Spiritual power of the Pope. In Naples from bad to worse the change has as yet brought no fruition. Everything seems going down. Neglect, immorality or incapacity, meet you at every turn. Surely Cavour was no administrator. They are now voting about eighty millions of Pounds Sterling for railroads and the country has not the means or the energy to construct ordinary carriage roads and when their railroads are made it will be years before the traffic pays the annual expense of working them. The Italians are poets, singers and dancers, but not men of business.

This letter continues with a brief review of the political situation in other continental countries. In the course of it JC imparts the news that his brother-in-law, 'Joe' Romano, had been elected deputy for Gallipoli. His comment on that achievement was 'I fear it will not bring grist to the mill'.

A week after writing the letter, James Close and all his family set sail in the *Sibilla* for Toulon, not to return until December. He was not to leave Naples finally until 1864, but from now on he had prolonged holiday cruises with his family every year, and his business activities seem to have been less frenetic. Some of his work consisted of managing his money, using the new facility of telegrams. Most British merchants were content to stay on under the new regime, and new ones arrived. But while some of those had been able to hand on the business from father to son, JC's children by Anne were still too young, and Henry may have been disinclined to take it on.

As ever, there is no word from him as to why he chose this particular time for a prolonged absence, but the tumultuous conditions he describes must have played their part. Also, although in many ways reluctant to leave Naples, he was already nearing retirement age, was in poor health and perhaps felt left behind by improvements such as the telegraph and the faster steamships, which by now were replacing sail. He may already have had it in mind to find a more peaceful and less revolutionary place to live in for the rest of his life.

Whatever the motivation, the voyage to Toulon turned out to be the first of four such prolonged cruises, all of which are described in the Journals.

CHAPTER V

1861–5: The Journals

✿ Introduction

THE JOURNALS kept by the Close family, whether on board the *Sibilla* or at home in Naples and later in Antibes, cover the period 1861 to 1865, the last entry being dated three days before James Close's sudden death. Initially JC made all the entries, always writing in the third person, on behalf of the whole family, and referring to himself as 'Papa'. When he was too unwell to write, or away on business, Anne would take over. Later, as they became old enough, the children would be encouraged to make the entries and later still it was mandatory for one or other of them to do so every day. JC saw it as part of their education to observe and notice things, which they had to do in order to write about them. Early efforts have not been included, but later, as their descriptive powers increased or when they write of significant events not recorded elsewhere, some of the children's entries have been kept. JC continued to write his own entries whenever he wanted to make a point or describe a particular scene.

When JC was incapacitated, it was usually because of his gout. He suffered great pain from this, in various parts of his body, and sometimes endured violent stomach pains as well. He did not complain about it but it must have exacerbated his already fiery temper, as did the tossing of the ship and the noise made by so many boisterous children. When at its worst, it must have blighted the enjoyment of the voyages for the rest of the family. There are near daily comments in the Journals as to whether these maladies were better or worse and except for major crises, these have been cut; but they were an ever-present consideration in the minds of those on board.

JC's method of educating his children was an original experiment remote from the usual Victorian approach, and arose directly out of his reaction to his own schooldays. He believed that children should be brought up and educated at home, close to their parents: it was a perversion of natural instincts to send them away to

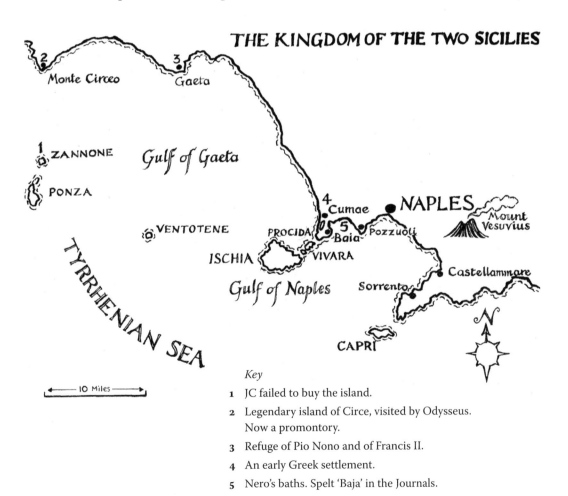

THE KINGDOM OF THE TWO SICILIES

Key

1   JC failed to buy the island.
2   Legendary island of Circe, visited by Odysseus. Now a promontory.
3   Refuge of Pio Nono and of Francis II.
4   An early Greek settlement.
5   Nero's baths. Spelt 'Baja' in the Journals.

school. Corporal punishment was out, and discipline was maintained by example, by admonishment and by a system of 'tickets' (sometimes referred to as 'numbers') which had a cash value, and which were awarded for something well done and deducted for misbehaviour. JC acted as bank and each child knew how much was in his or her account. They were expected to pay for their own pleasures out of what they had earned. It was theirs to spend as they wished – and so they learnt early to appreciate the value of money.

Hired tutors taught them at regular hours throughout the cruises. JC and Anne also took many of the lessons. Henry, now adult, would stand in when needed. The curriculum was geared to what would be of practical value. Latin and Greek were not included. French governesses were engaged to live on board and a German tutor also survived some months. Italian was taught by JC and Neapolitan Italian was picked up from the Neapolitan crew. French too was taught and to some extent acquired from their on-shore visits along the French coast, particularly from JC's French friends in Toulon. Music played an important part and a music mistress normally joined the cruises. The family sang the harmonies of the hymns on Sundays, while both Margaret and John, Anne's two eldest, accompanied on the piano. The children became experts in seamanship and swimming, and gymnasts from clambering about the rigging. Deprived of modern medicines and anaesthesia, they developed a robust attitude to danger and pain, and were given a freedom to run around the schooner and even dive into the sea in a way that would horrify any parent today.

Granddaughter Anne Eaden wrote these paragraphs in her introduction to her edited version of the Journals:

> James Close intended that his children should receive an education designed not only to nourish their minds but form their characters and prepare them for hardships and trials that might befall them in later life. Courage, endurance, cheerfulness, consideration for others and many other qualities were inculcated by their common life on board.
>
> The experiment could hardly have succeeded as it did but for the characters of James Close and his wife. There was a considerable difference in their ages but they both loved the sea, they loved to be together and they loved to have their children round them. Moreover, they provided a perfect foil for each other. James Close possessed great resilience and force of character, a high moral sense (even bordering at times on sententiousness), boundless enthusiasms for any project that caught his imagination and an innate authority.

Anne Close was the ideal partner. Through births, illnesses, accidents, storms and the many dangers incident to the presence of small children on a sailing yacht, she retained her calm cheerfulness and quiet capability. She must have been a delightful companion too, young enough to enter into all the fun. Water battles were popular. Opposing crews in an open boat endeavoured to throw each other into the sea. Anne sat at the stern. It was against the rules for her to be thrown overboard, but it was allowed to throw buckets of water over her. She cared little for appearances.

There is no record of any Journal being kept before 1861, but as it starts so abruptly in that year, it is possible that some sort of log was always made, in which case the only novelty for 1861 is that from that date it was more carefully preserved. There is however a little information about the last pre-Journals voyage, which was in 1860 during the upheavals in Naples, when the Closes went to England to visit Anne's father. Even on this comparatively routine voyage, the *Sibilla* lost her fore-topyard in heavy seas and contrary winds off Cape St. Vincent and had to back and anchor in the roads of Lagos, South West Portugal. Fortunately, among the twenty or so other vessels waiting for a change of wind, there was a Neapolitan ship with a spare fore-topyard for sale. Anne, always calm in a crisis, on this occasion seems to have been impervious to it altogether. Waiting for a favourable wind and writing to her father from Portugal on 12th August, she describes her youngest child Thomas, then only thirteen months old:

> We are all well. Baby, who was a miserable bit of a baby, hardly able to stand when we started, has wonderfully benefited by the pure sea breeze – he cuts his teeth with difficulty, and consequently screams and cries – more than is agreeable.

It was nothing to the Closes that their babies had to learn to stand and toddle on board a sailing boat, sometimes in a storm: as a result, they became as much at home at sea as on land.

The Journals that follow represent a third change of viewpoint in this narrative. Chapter I was an ageing man's own account of his forebears and of his youth; Chapters II, III and IV mostly an impersonal overview of political developments, together with an account of JC's business activities. Now there is a change down to first gear, with a day to day account of life at sea, written as a kind of collective diary.

At the start of the 1861 cruise Henry Gaskell Close was 26. The ages of Anne's children were Margaret 15, Grace 13, John 11, James 9, William 8, Frederick 6,

Annie 4 and Thomas just two. As the years went by, the difference in the ages of Annie and Tom became less marked, and they became inseparable playmates. The four boys banded together until the last year of the Journals, when there are signs of John pulling away into adulthood.

The excerpts that have been selected represent about a quarter of the full Journals. Editorial cuts are numerous. Spelling and punctuation have been modernised but outdated words and forms of expression have not, except occasionally for the sake of clarity. Extracts are in-set. In 1861 all are by JC himself.

1861: Naples – Nice – Toulon – Naples

WHILE THE CRUISES recorded in the Journals were partly designed to widen the horizons of the children, they were also an opportunity for JC to keep up his business contacts abroad, and they always included Toulon, where one of these contacts was a banker (whose name is sometimes spelt Flameng, sometimes Flemang and sometimes Flamin). Moreover in Toulon it was easy to find a berth and he knew the port authorities. The routes taken between there and Naples varied each year.

The first few entries, as written by JC, are given here in full:

Monday 15th July We got under way at seven o'clock a.m. There was a slight breeze from the land, which soon subsided into a dead calm. The boat was lowered, and four men towed the *Sibilla* out of the harbour. The wind then set in from the S. and soon carried us round Cape Misenum. Baby hurt his head by falling on the chain. It was bandaged with arnica, and was not much the worse after an hour or two. The milk was badly corked. Papa was angry, and ordered it to be boiled all over again. The bath was filled yesterday with snow and our milk, butter, cheese and fresh meat put in it to keep.

  p.m. We have made little progress since morning, the wind having veered to the W. We had the awnings up fore and aft, which made it pleasant. The sea has been as smooth as glass. We dined at two o'c. At seven o'c the ship did scarcely move, so Papa allowed us to have a swim in the clear beautiful blue sea. We were a little afraid at first, for one of the sailors told us there were sharks. But Papa said it was all nonsense. Whilst bathing a gentle breeze sprung up. Johnny was alarmed at the current of water, and was soon ordered out. Mag [*Margaret*] and Jemmy [*James*] swam bravely. The wind is now off the land, and promises progress during the night.

Tuesday 16th July The night was beautiful. A wind from the land, gentle but steady, enabled us to set our sails. There was not the slightest perceptible motion. After the usual dew at sunset, the air became dry. The moon was in its first quarter. The comet, scarcely visible, was passed from the Great Bear. Grace got up at half past two in the morning, washed and dressed herself. When she came on deck, the watch officer thought she was walking in her sleep. We are now within ten miles of **Ponza**. John declared himself unfit for his music at six o'c, on the plea of a cough, for which Papa sent him a cup of Linseed water with three drops of bitter sedative. He has not been heard to cough since. Mama not well and in bed. [*She suffered from seasickness.*]

Wednesday 17th July We had scarcely finished writing yesterday, when a strong gale from the West suddenly burst upon us, as we were quietly moving under full sail with a gentle breeze from the S. In a moment the ship was laid on her side, rushing through the foaming waters at great speed. The ship, under shortened sail, beat up to windward with the greatest ease, and the second tack brought us safely inside the port of Ponza. The ship was soon moored alongside the Quai, some hundreds of spectators watching us from every side of the little port. Our old friend the Parroco [*parish priest*] was the first to welcome us. At 7 o'c we went in the launch across the bay to call upon our friend Giovanni; and after a pleasant walk to the beach by moonlight, we returned to the *Sibilla* to tea.

Thursday 18th July Giovanni came on board first thing this morning. ... General Ambrosio paid us a visit, and dined with us, bringing with him his friend Capt. Celentano. Although friends, they fought against each other at Capua – Ambrosio for the King, and Celentano for Garibaldi. Several exiles, called here 'relegati', brought petitions to Papa for assistance. All of them disbanded soldiers of King Francis. After enquiries, Papa sent money to some, and clothing to others. [*The conflict had split many friends and even families, as in Lampedusa's The Leopard; but such differences were soon forgiven. Similarly, JC continued to count the Meuricoffres as his best friends, even though he had been a monarchist, while they had become enthusiastic supporters of Garibaldi.*] After tea Papa wrote a letter to Aunt Romano enclosing the Journal copied by John, for which he earned 100 numbers. Flies plague us.

Friday 19th July Henry went off early to photograph. He took several views, especially Fort Bentinck, the rocks behind the baths of Pontius Pilate, and a view of the port from the Summer house of Ambrosio – he was not successful in all. Photography seems to be attended with many uncertainties. [*Henry took his photography seriously and at nearly every port of call took himself off in search of suitable scenes.*]

The wind having subsided our moorings were cast off. The *Sibilla* swung round in the port on her anchor. Instead of sailing round Zannone, the ship's head was put towards the last group of small rocks which in several places show themselves in the space which separates Zannone from Ponza. The idea of passing over this reef alarmed us all, particularly Mama. A man was sent aloft to look out for shallows, which are easily seen in the blue Mediterranean by their white appearance. We were soon through, and several miles of sailing saved. The wind here became contrary. The *Sibilla* had to beat. Her first tack was to Mount Circe [*Monte Circeo*], described by the ancients as a beautiful woman, enticing mariners to her embraces, in order to devour them.

Saturday 20th July Since we turned our backs on Mount Circe on Thursday evening, we have had beautiful weather. The whole of yesterday the *Sibilla* remained opposite Porto d'Anzio, called "Antium" by the ancient Romans. Antium was the birthplace of the great Coriolanus. The Emperor Nero in later times constructed a magnificent military port there, of which the remains are still visible, contrasting strangely with the small shallow port built by the Popes in one corner of its ruins. Many fishing boats passed us during the day. They fish in pairs, dragging a net between them. This coast is lowland, and the sea shallow and sandy for some miles seawards.

Monday 22nd July Yesterday (Sunday) morning we found ourselves opposite Cape Argentario in the midst of the small Islands (once inhabited) of which Giglio seems the principal. The coast of Corsica was in sight, and the Islands of Elba and Monte Cristo in the distance. A dark cloud had been gathering in the West; from which flashes of lightning and peals of thunder proceeded. Gradually it extended over half of the horizon, bringing with it gusts of wind and showers. We took in sail to be prepared, but it passed over without inconvenience. At half past ten we went down to prayers. We sang two Psalms, and chanted two Canticles. We had no lecture but Papa read his prayer instead. Mama was in bed. We had turkey and a ham for dinner, with pease pudding, haricots and tomato sauce and roll dumpling with wine sauce. Oranges and fresh almonds for dessert. Our stock of cherries, pears, figs, plums, and apricots was finished and so was our snow, so that we had to drink tepid water. At sunset the crew assembled in the bows, and said Vespers and when they had finished, we sung the "Evening hymn", finishing as usual with "God Save the Queen". This morning (Monday) we have passed Monte Cristo. The weather still calm.

Tuesday 23rd July No wind, and a blazing sun. Without our awnings, the heat would have been unbearable. We got up early to our music; Zéline took us to French at half past seven, we breakfasted at 8 o'c, Zéline took us to our "calculs" (arithmetic) at 9.30, Papa to our journal at 10 o'c, Mama to reading at noon, Zéline again to dictation until one o'clock. We dined at 2 o'c, and in the afternoon had a music lesson from Margaret, and Margaret one from Papa. At sunset the evening hymn, then tea, and then to bed. *Sibilla* is now entering the port of **Bastia** [*North East Corsica*].

Wednesday 24th July The *Sibilla* is moored in the outer port. In the evening Papa and Mama went in the boat to see the Penningtons at their country house distant about two miles along the coast, on the top of a hill. They found Mr. Pennington disabled by paralysis. Mrs. Pennington in good health, but careworn and anxious. The walk was too much for Papa. His foot became inflamed and painful. He could not sleep, and this morning he cannot walk. There are some extensive iron works near Bastia belonging to a Mr. Jackson. The iron ore comes from Elba.

Thursday 25th July A little boy upset Henry's photographing machine, and broke it. Mr. F. Ballero, the Italian consul, spent a couple of hours on board with his son and daughter. Vito, the cook, went to market in the morning early and returned with a good supply of meat, fruit and vegetables, very inferior to those of Naples, which is the cheapest and most abundant market in the Mediterranean. We saw some divers fixing large bottles filled with gunpowder on the rocks under the water in the port. In the evening they set fire to the powder which blows the rocks to pieces and makes great commotion under the water. Lion [*the dog*] stole a joint of veal, and jumped overboard with it; but frightened by the clatter of the cook, he let it go, and it sunk to the bottom. Lion thought he had done a clever trick, for on returning on board, he seemed to laugh at the Cook, as everyone else did, for the cook was in a great rage. Lion is a great favourite, he is a fine noble fellow. He swims and dives, and would fetch any of us out of the sea, if we fell in. We got under way at seven o'c this morning, with a gentle breeze and a calm sea. The coast of Corsica, with its high mountains, studded with villages, looks beautiful.

With her husband incapacitated by gout, Anne Close took over the Journal temporarily.

Friday 26th July We are now in sight of the mountains of Nice which we are fast approaching. A seven knot breeze laid the ship so far on her side that the water spurted up occasionally through the scuppers. It was amusing to see Lion watching for the spurts and springing upon them, and regaling his zeal with a mouthful of salt water from time to time.

Saturday 27th July Yesterday afternoon, a breeze from the W. stiffening, we found we could scarcely make Nice, so it was determined that we should enter Port Maurizio for the night; in a few minutes we were off its mouth, but the warning of a pilot, who came to us, made us back our sails until he came on board; he then took us in, but just as the *Sibilla* was between the moles she stuck fast, the pilot from ignorance or perhaps because he was no pilot at all, had mistaken the draft of the ship. The *Sibilla* took the ground at her stern and luckily for us, heeled round so that when she became fixed her bows looked seaward; a couple of lines were thrown out to the hauling stumps on each side, the people of the town civilly hauling on one side and the windlass on the other, in a few minutes the *Sibilla* was again afloat without hurt or damage.

Sunday 28th July Yesterday was one of the unpleasantest days of our sea life, namely, no wind and a heavy swell, the ship rolling, the sails flapping, doors jamming, and every body out of sorts. This morning we found ourselves safely moored in the harbour of **Nice**.

For the next three days the family explored Nice. The descriptions of the town would have been of interest to readers in England, to whom copies of the Journal were sent, but have been omitted here because they are not very different from those to be found in modern guide books. Henry was in charge of the expeditions. The Tuesday was James's tenth birthday and was declared a holiday. 'The children had been wild in getting rid of their prize money; trumpery bows and arrows and John bought home a straw hat used by the peasantry.'

Thursday 1st August Yesterday Papa was on deck for an hour or two. He laughed at the freaks and habits of the French crew in the steamer alongside of us. They danced the chassés, the polkas, the waltzes, with the affected sublimity of the *grand ton*, and many other antics, which showed their high spirits and at the same time their perfect sobriety. In the evening they sang for us, displaying excellent voices and some knowledge of music. The steamer is kept in beautiful order, and the men cleanly and well clothed.

For the next three days Anne is preoccupied with a crisis in JC's worsening condition. She writes to his brother Tom about it. A doctor is summoned. 'This morning at 5 o'clock Papa was again attacked with fever. He felt cold and trembled in every limb for near an hour, after which he experienced burning heat.'

Monday 5th August The English have built a handsome new church at a considerable expense at Nice, but it has not yet been opened for services.

Some amusement was occasioned in the little port where we were moored by an unfortunate teal, which was hunted by several boats and which, when they approached to strike it, immediately dived beyond their reach. One of our men was bathing, and as the bird dived, he dived also and caught it under the water, to the disgust of the crowd, who wished to destroy it. He brought it on board and afterwards the children took it in the dinghy to sea and there liberated it.

The ironic style is probably Henry's. By Friday JC was sufficiently recovered to resume entries himself.

Friday 9th August This morning early the chain was got in and the *Sibilla* floated in the centre of the port. As soon as the breeze of the morning set in, our sails were set, and we sailed imperceptibly through the narrow channel in to deep sea water, opposite the town, and there lay to, that is, our sails were so placed that the force of the wind was neutralized, the ship moving neither backwards nor forwards, until the cook who had been to market rejoined us with a two days supply of fresh provisions. We then set sail and coasted several miles in the direction of Antibes. We then turned to seaward on the opposite tack, so as to clear the Cape. It was very pleasant, for the breeze was heightened by the ship's movement, and the cool ventilating temperature with the varying beauty of the scenery was refreshing in the highest degree to us all.

Saturday 10th August This morning we sighted **Hyères**, but the wind failed and it was evening before we anchored in that roadstead. We found there four French line of battle ships. We anchored near to an American three-master loading salt which is produced in large quantities at Hyères by evaporation of sea water. We could see large heaps of salt on the sea shore.

Sunday 11th August John went with Capt. Mazella to the town of Hyères, distant about four miles, and brought back some beautiful fruit, peaches, nectarines and a melon. Henry caught a bucket full of fish early in the morning. The evenings at Hyères were not only delightful but were remarkable by the number and splendour of the meteors which seemed to play across the heavens.

Monday 12th August At eleven o'c we sailed for **Toulon** with a fine 8 Knot breeze, passing in the middle of Islands, the views changing every instant. We anchored in Toulon Roads at 2 o'c. On passing the Guardship we were hailed, and ordered to send a boat with our papers alongside. We cast anchor alongside the Imperial (paddle) Steamer, the *Queen Hortense*. Henry and Mag went through the town in the evening, and reported unfavourably of the streets and of the scarcity of respectable people. We are surrounded by ships of war at anchor, and by others in ordinary painted lead colour. Opposite to us is a building divided into five compartments, roofed in, but open to the port in the form of arches. In this building five men of war can be constructed all at once. Toulon is surrounded by bold lofty mountains.

Tuesday 13th August The weather continues to be beautiful. Panzera on shore to obtain samples and prices of sugar, coffee and other supplies for ship's use, also of the wines grown in the neighbourhood, such as Cassis and Lamargue which are good, pure and cheap. We are quite out of clean linen, and no washerwoman has come as yet, so that it seems clear that the *Sibilla* must remain here some days.

Wednesday 14th August The washerwoman comes at last and has taken away three weeks' consumption of linen, to be returned on Monday or Tuesday next. Great preparations for celebrating the Emperor's birthday tomorrow.

Thursday 15th August The morning was ushered in by a salute of 100 guns from the forts. The men of war in the harbour fired a salute at 8 a.m. and dressed ship: we followed their example in putting out the French flag at the main mast. About ten there was a general review of the troops; at eleven there were boat races and other games in the harbour; and at 2 p.m. more games. At sunset a salute from the ships and fireworks in the evening.

Friday 23rd August Henry fished in the morning early, successfully, for breakfast. In the afternoon he took us all to gather blackberries for preserving. It is a favourite preserve of Papa's. We brought home a good basket.

For the next six weeks JC is in continual torment from his gout, and most of the entries are about his symptoms and the visits of doctors. When he begins to get better, he is well enough to make his presence felt:

Wednesday 4th September Papa's gout continues to break out in fresh places. He paints each place with nitrate of silver, which burns the skin and turns it black. He was angry at dinner because it was not cooked to his liking. The veal was dark and coarse with much bone. The crust of the pie was soft and doughy. The cucumber was cut carelessly and thick.

John's foot painful. [*It had gone septic after he cut it when bathing.*] Panzera pared the skin of the heel gradually down with a razor, so that the gathering became visible. He then quickly gave it a gash and a mass of thick matter gushed out. John yelled loudly, but was instantly relieved and can now walk with ease.

The rest of the family enjoyed the summer – not a holiday, because lessons continued on board, with *Sibilla* switching her mooring between Toulon and, more often, St Mandrier, a peninsula jutting out into the sea at the South end of the bay. Only on one occasion did JC's system of education nearly fail, possibly due to irascibility caused by gout:

Friday 13th September Today was an unpleasant one for every one on board. Papa has observed, for some weeks past, an indisposition to attend to the daily lessons. A habit had obtained of crying over lessons, and of speaking in a complaining, quarrelsome tone, as if it were a hardship to learn or to be taught. Papa, therefore, ordered the entire system of tickets to be suspended; he threatened to cane those who did not learn their lessons; and concluded by giving us notice that, since he could not govern us by gentle and compensatory means, he would in future have recourse to stronger and forcible means.

As might be expected, some members of the crew also became restive. Panzera, the permanent of the two captains and much trusted family factotum, spent an unauthorised night ashore after a visit to French sailors moored nearby. The cook too got into trouble:

Sunday 22nd September Our cook and his adjutant left the ship early this morning, in consequence of a box on the ear from Papa and quarrels with Zéline. Left thus suddenly in the lurch, every one on board lent a willing hand. Henry peeled potatoes and boiled them splendidly, taking care to steam them well, all the while shaking them up to prevent them burning. Panzera turned out the fry and Mazella the roast, while Antonio provided the rice pudding. It was a jolly affair and our dinner excellent.

Monday 23rd September The cook and his man Friday returned to their work on board at 2 o'clock, and looked foolish enough. The Italian consul sent them back with a flea in their ears.

When lessons were over, there were educational tours of such institutions as the seamen's hospital, which could accommodate 1,600, and the arsenal:

Thursday 3rd October Mr. Conte, the Imperial *procureur général*, whom we knew at St. Mandrier, took us through the Toulon Imperial Arsenal. We visited first the Museum, then the ropery, then the template works, then the metal warehouse, bronze foundry, the electro tinning process for preventing chains, nails and sheets from rusting. We passed by the coal deposits and visited the abattoir, where the animals are killed for the use of the Marine, and entered the iron foundry. [*After lunch*] we visited the Emperor's private steam yacht the *Aigle*, which is beautifully fitted out. We were presented on board to Admiral Dupuis, who received us with kindness. We then saw the vast timber stores, and entered the saw mills, and finished by climbing into the inside of a large line-of-battle ship which was being built in one of the five sheds erected for the purpose. We were greatly pleased with all we saw but very tired.

It is not known how many of the children went on this expedition, which would surely have tired anybody. Other such educational visits included one to La Seyne, on the upper end of one of the creeks in the bay of Toulon, where Lt. Armstrong took them to see a private shipbuilder employing 3,000 workers. Among many ships under construction was 'a large iron-coated frigate, built of iron plates, covered with thick wooden planking, and made ball-proof by outside blocks of iron four inches thick being bolted on to the wood and iron'. Another trip, 'an excursion by carriage to the Fortress of Lamalgue where Abdul Kadur the great Arab chief was confined' was cancelled because of high winds.

On the same day as the visit to the Arsenal:

Papa and Mama and Margaret went for an hour to the Theatre with Mr Armstrong. It is small, ill ventilated and unworthy of a city like Toulon. A new theatre is being built. Mr Flamin kindly placed his box at their disposal.

Lt. Armstrong was an officer in the French navy who had become friends with the Closes in Constantinople. They spent a number of evenings with him this summer in Toulon. Flamin, the banker, lived both in Toulon and in a country house 1½ miles out of town, which the whole family visited on 29th September:

Mr Flamin came to meet us as we entered his pretty garden, which is surrounded by green fields, well wooded and artificially irrigated. He introduced us to Mme Flamin and to his married daughter; also to the Italian Consul, Signor Bapo and his wife. Each family brought its young branches so that children were in good number. We were treated to some beautiful fruit, pears, grapes, figs, walnuts with biscuits and wine. We then played blind man's buff.

Most of the family needed medical attention from time to time, and that same morning it had been John's turn:

> John had a loose tooth pulled out by Panzera. He cries and roars and we all laugh at him. He won't believe that tears and screams don't lessen the pain.

Living on the boat at the entrance to Toulon, the toing and froing of naval ships was a continual diversion:

> **Friday 6th September** Two Italian war steamers went out this morning, after repairing in Toulon. A few hours after their departure they both returned, having fouled each other at sea. The large ship had her bows broken in, and the small ship lost her masts.

Shopping expeditions lasted the whole day – not surprising when on one of them *all* the children were fitted with a new pair of shoes. On the same day 'Papa bought a supply of Porcelaine plates and dishes for use in Naples, being good and cheap. Also a quantity of Table wine, Orgeat, Absynth, and bitter wine called Vermout' – plus a long list of foodstuffs. On 25th September JC and Anne went on their own to Marseilles for the day, returning with seven dozen white porcelain cups and saucers of beautiful quality; soap, vinegar and two pots of toothpowder and five tooth brushes.

Departure from Toulon was delayed as the health of Anne's father had deteriorated, and a summons for her to go back to England was expected. By 5th October, however, came the first hint that JC thought they need wait no longer and was planning to return to Naples:

> Crossed over to St Mandrier in the morning. Papa read prayers, and instead of a lecture, read a prayer composed by himself. We then accompanied him on a walk round the creek, speaking a civil word to each villager whom we met, who appeared to be sorry at our approaching departure.

On the 7th (Monday) it was settled that they would depart 'this week', but the following extracts show to what extent they were at the mercy of the weather:

> **8th October** Before sunrise the men were getting up the anchor and setting sail for Toulon, where we arrived at 7 o'clock. Some of us did not know we had left St. Mandrier. The weather is bad and unfavourable for Naples. Captain Mazella says that being October, this wind may keep us here for some time. Papa has given orders for the provisions of the ship to be completed, the water tanks to be filled and everything to be got ready to sail on Thursday.

Friday 11th The wind continues to blow from the South East, quite contrary to our route to Naples.

Monday 14th The boxes of vinegar, mustard, olives, dates and prunes are at last arrived from Marseilles. So there is nothing now to prevent our sailing, as soon as the wind is fair. Being our last day in Toulon, Mama expressed a wish to visit Cape Brun, to enjoy once more the walk on the sea side called the 'Sentier des Douaniers' and which in point of variety and beauty cannot well be surpassed.

Wednesday 16th The weather is beautiful and seems settled, but contrary for Naples. Papa however this morning gave orders for the ship to be got under weigh or way, having determined to sail for Port Mahon, Algiers or Ajaccio as the wind might serve when out at sea. But before the boats were hauled up, the wind got up so high that Panzera came into the cabin to recommend delay, which of course Papa concurred in. It would seem that we are not to leave Toulon for the present. [*For the full entry on these adverse winds, see the facsimile opposite.*]

However, the wind did change, the very next day. As soon as fresh food stores had been brought aboard:

The *Sibilla* was under way, and sailing swiftly out of the bay of Toulon under a leading wind. Many other vessels did the same, but we were the first. We counted sixteen ships under sail. We soon left them all behind.

JC's original intention seems to have been to make straight back for Naples and home, but again and again the weather intervened. The following extracts show that at every stage of the voyage, their route was determined by the wind:

Friday 18th October The wind fell during the night, and changed to the SE, so that our bows have been for some time in the direction of Genoa, instead of Cape Corsica. A dead calm the whole day. The helm without power and the ship carried round and round by the currents; but at sunset a slight breeze enabled the ship to get round – and we progressed at a modest rate.

19th October The calm returned at 10 o'c last night and still continues. The night was however splendid,. The moon at its full.

20th October The weather has changed. Until noon we had a stiff breeze from the East with a rising sea. After consultation Papa gave orders to put back into Nice, which was at no great distance. At one o'c the wind fell and with it the sea, so that we remain as we were, surrounded by a fleet of about 30 sail in the same position.

At last we sailed but the wind being

October contrary and a heavy sea outside, we

1861 again anchored at S.ᵗ Mandrier. In the evening we all took a walk on the sea side passing the walls of the battery—

Wednesday. The weather is beautiful and seems

16.ᵗʰ settled, but contrary for Naples. Mama wrote last night to uncle William for news of Grandpapa's health to be addressed to Toulon. Papa however this morning gave orders for the ship to be got under weigh or way having determined to sail to Port Mahon, Algiers or Ajuccio in Sardinia, as the wind might serve
"when out at sea. But before the boats were hauled up, the wind got up so high that Panyora came into the cabin to recommend delay which of coarse Papa concurred in. It would almost seem that we are not to leave Toulon for the present. However no one seems to be distressed at the delay John has been in bed three days of a cold and Papa is again complaining of pains in his back and loins He refused his dinner to day, and retired early to bed Mama sent round for fresh laid eggs to the village to serve instead of milk on our voyage The milk we got at Toulon

By evening they were able to leave the coast of Nice and Genoa, under an overcast sky 'not at all promising'. The navigation was not good as in the morning the two captains found they were on the wrong side of Cape Corsica:

> We were now beating under the lee of the island in the hope of weathering Cape Corsica before sunset – a doubtful case! The mistake of our captains has cost us a day, and no-one can tell how many more to come. We are on our preserved provisions, our fresh being finished. We cleared Cape Corsica in the afternoon, and sighted Bastia Light at 8 o'clock. Papa gave orders to enter the harbour, and at midnight all was snug and at rest on board.
>
> *Tuesday 22nd October* It was a lucky hit to get into port, for a furious storm burst for the at 2 o'c this morning, and continues. The rain poured down in torrents, the first we have seen since leaving Naples of any consequence. The wind is SE, precisely contrary for Naples.
>
> *23rd October* Mama bought 1,000 cigars and presented 50 to each seaman. She has reserved a couple of hundred for presents in Naples. There is no duty on tobacco in Corsica.
>
> *24th October* After lessons Mama took us to the public baths, where we had a most comfortable scrubbing, herself and Zéline included, at the rate of 7d per bath.
>
> *Friday 25th October* The wind having veered to the North, and the sky being clear, Papa gave orders for our departure. The Pilot however expressed his incapacity to get us out of the port until the sea went down. Meantime fresh provisions were brought on board and the ship's papers got ready. Mr. Taberie having kindly consented to allow his steamer to tow us out, at 5 o'c all was ready, and the steamer moved on. But on turning the elbow of the port, it was found that the steamer would not steer. So she let us go, not caring for our dilemma, and saved herself. We had a sea in front; to leeward the new mole and the rocks which protect it; and a slight breeze barely sufficient to fill our sails blowing from the Island on to the mole. The way the ship was under when cast off took us half way up the channel; but now the *Sibilla* began to edge away to leeward. Every sail was rapidly set which could give us a lift. The Pilot's boat was urged on to tow our head round from the danger. Our second boat was lowered to lend assistance in the same direction. Still the *Sibilla*'s stern neared more and more the rocks which were foaming with the surf. Masts and boards were collected at the stern, to assist in keeping it off. The landspeople flocked to the dangerous point with

poles and what was at hand to thrust us off – our bows were out of the harbour, but our stern was within 2 or 3 yards of the point. Every one on board had his own sensations. The men worked like Tigers. Henry had a hand on every rope. Papa sighed for his ship, foreseeing a terrific bill for repairs. Mama's smile never left her countenance. Every one shouted to the boats to pull for their lives. At this moment a puff of wind, a friendly Zephyr filled our sails. The *Sibilla* moved gently forwards. The danger was passed, and all on board breathed. We were soon at sea. The pilot's boat pulled alongside the companion, and with an 'all's well that ends well', he jumped into his boat. We are now sailing at 8 knots an hour, with every appearance of continuance.

Two days' sailing in rough weather brought the *Sibilla* to the channel of Procida, a small island between Ischia and the mainland, close to Naples. However they lingered on the boat for some weeks before moving to their house in Naples, mooring first at **Baja** (today spelt Baia), where they stayed until 13th November; and then at the island of Ischia. The chief attraction of Baja was the natural steam baths:

Monday 28th October The land was illuminated with the rays of the sun, and seemed to welcome us back to Naples. At one o'clock our anchor was dropped at Baja. Lessons having ended Papa and Mama made the whole lot of us (except baby, whom Mama refused to let go) go with him, to have a "sweating" in Nero's Bath [*where Nero is supposed to have murdered his mother Agrippina*] First to go in was a procession of us four naked lads under Papa's leadership. We felt like tallow candles in an oven. After rubbing us well, he dismissed us one after the other. Mama was ready with a bucket of cold water to throw over each of us. A pleasant operation, very! But Papa says it keeps us clear of Scarlatina, Measles and Fevers. The second division consisted of Mama, three sisters and Maria, the nursemaid. Papa remained in the dark hole 50 minutes!

Visits to these baths were almost daily and the crew were also permitted to use them. Time spent at this small port would have been less but for a strong Sirocco, 'the only wind against which Baja is unprotected'. Other ships were stranded there for the same reason and one three-masted schooner fouled *Sibilla's* anchor chains. Archaeological and geological instruction was provided by Henry, who led the family on walks to the Temple of Venus and to Cumae (one of the oldest Greek settlements in Italy); and by 'geological phenomena such as extinct volcanoes, craters, lava, lapilli (stone fragments ejected from volcanoes) and tufo. At every step we stumbled on the tessellated ruins of ancient villas, baths and temples, some of them converted into wine presses and stores, others used for cowhouses or pig-sties'. As they passed from one estate to another, the farmers would show them their wine cellars and make them taste the different qualities.

Lessons continued as usual every morning, and physical labour was also part of the curriculum as the whole family was put to work building their own mole for *Sibilla*. JC could not walk, but he could wield a spade and a pickaxe, while Mama carried the stones. An additional pastime was catching rats on the boat: Papa offered a reward of 4d for each corpse.

The nearest they came to any real trouble was on 4th November, when both parents, James and Grace took a coach to Naples for the day:

> They left Naples at 5 o'c in the evening. By the time they reached Pozzuoli it was dark. The coachman had neglected to prepare the lamps. On passing the foot of Monte Nuovo neither the coachman nor the horses could distinguish the road. They first dragged the carriage up the side of the bank. The carriage was nearly over. Papa got out and brought the horses into the road. He then walked on a few paces telling the coachman to follow him. But scarcely had the carriage moved a few paces, when the wheels sunk on the side next the sea, and stuck fast. The horses could not drag it out. The harness broke, the reins got entangled, it began to rain, and the carriage was in momentary danger of turning on its side down the hill. At last Papa set out in search of help. There is a coast guard station some 400 yards from the spot where the accident occurred. Luckily two soldiers were inside sleeping on their pallets. Papa roused them up, and they willingly pre-pared a lanthorn and followed him. They put their shoulders to the forewheel Papa and Mama put theirs to the hind wheel, the Coachman after arranging the harness as best he could, mounted his box. Grace up to her neck in the brush-wood held the lanthorn. After repeated efforts the carriage was extricated; but again involved in a hole or ditch on the opposite side. At last the middle of the road was attained. The soldiers marched in advance with the light, the horses followed, and we arrived at 8 o'c at Donna Rosa's where our seamen had been waiting two hours for us. The delay had produced anxiety and perplexity on board. The roads near Naples are not safe from banditti, and in this idea prepa-rations were being made to arm and land the men, despatching them in search of us. Fortunately we arrived in time to save all this trouble, and best of all to sit down to an excellent dinner, of which we stood greatly in need.

> *Wednesday 6th November*   After breakfast we all worked at the little mole where the boat lands us. Papa worked with both spade and pickaxe. Mama carried

stones, Henry was chief builder, John and James brought stones from the beach in the dinghy. Margaret placed the stones and worked with spade and pickaxe; Grace took to excavating the old Roman ruins near us in search of treasures in broken pottery, and old coins. Will and Fred were enchanted to fancy themselves helping, whilst wading up to their knees in the sea. Finally Annie and baby were busy as bees in the dirt, digging, rooting, messing, picking and doing everything which ought not to be done. And thus a happy day has been spent. A shrill whistle brought us on board for dinner at 4 o'c.

When they finally left Baia, it was not for Naples, but for **Ischia**, the island just off the bay.

Wednesday 13th November Our harbour is an extinct crater. A few years ago it had no communication with the sea, from which it was separated by an narrow strip of sand and lapilli. In the centre of the lake there is a small island, being the summit of the cone formed by the ejection of burning material, when the volcano was active. This little island has been cased in masonry, and furnished with half a dozen stone stumps for the convenience of shipping. It is to this little island that the *Sibilla* is moored, with bows looking towards the sea through the entrance to the port. Nothing can be more picturesque than the *Sibilla* so moored; and nothing more picturesque than the scenery from the *Sibilla*. There is nothing like it in the Mediterranean. On the height which commands the entrance in front of the light house, King Ferdinand has built a pagoda in the Chinese style, and planted shrubberies and flowering trees round the greater part of the port. He has also built a pretty church of Grecian architecture opposite the entrance, which gives the port a classic character.

Thursday 14th November There has been some movement on board the *Sibilla* in preparing and inventing rat traps. The weather again threatens from the SE. The evening was however beautiful, the weather mild and balmy. The moon in her full. We are still wearing our summer clothing, and last night Mama and Papa were seated on deck without hats or shawls, whilst Henry and Mag were enjoying a moonlight row in the dinghy.

Friday 15th November Papa has great difficulty in walking. Nor can he ride far on donkey back without inconvenience. We got him with Henry's help up to the telegraph, from the foot of which the best view is obtainable. On arrival there the good people of the hamlet immediately brought us chairs. Whilst admiring the view Johnny joined us with an arm chair suspended on poles and carried by two stout men. We put Papa in the chair, and set off for a long walk up the mountain called Monte Rotaro. The great interest of the excursion is the magnificent prospect of the Islands, of Monte Procida, Cape Misenum, and of the whole of the Bay of Naples.

Another expedition the next day took the family to a different viewpoint. Clearly it had been a favourite spot for JC for much of his life:

> It was to this terrace that Papa immediately proceeded, and there remained gazing, as if to re-feed his memory with impressions and reminiscences extending over a period of nearly forty years. It was a point from which at one flash every incident during that period might be reviewed. From that terrace, it seemed as if his memory took wing to review the sea of events which have marked each period of his chequered life since he first stood there at 25 years of age! "I little thought in those days that I should review this scene surrounded by nine children. The sun of my life was then rising; it is now setting. Still the scene is glorious! If hope no longer gilds it, reminiscences increase its interest."

Food plays a prominent part in the Journals. This one extract shows that the family did not go hungry, at least at breakfast:

> ***Sunday 17th November*** Papa joked Mama this morning at what he called overfeeding us. A can of milk and a piece of bread was his allowance at our age. But we began this morning by a plate of water porridge with milk and sugar. After that we had a dish of kidneys 'sauté au vin de Marsala'. Then came a dish of cutlets and a large dish of fried potatoes, brown and crisp, which we ate like bread. Then came a dish of stewed prunes. Then we had coffee and tea. Hot and cold milk. Fresh bread and toasted bread. Butter and marmalade, also a tin of Nantes sardines in oil. Now although all these things were on the table, we did not eat them all, and Papa forgets that instead of dining at 1 o'clock, as we used to do, we dine at 5 or 6 oc. after a walk of some miles.

> ***Tuesday 19th November*** Mama received a letter this morning from Aunt Alice, telling her that Grandpa wished to see her and Margaret. We return to Naples tomorrow in consequence.

On the Wednesday the wind blew hard into the port and they could not leave, but the next day:

> At 4½ a.m. the *Sibilla* weighed anchor and with a gentle breeze from the W. sailed out of Port Ischia. It is decided that Henry accompanies Mama and Mag to England. The *Sibilla* is to winter in Port Ischia. Her rigging to be overhauled.

Her ballast to be landed. Her hold to be filled with water to the flooring; pumped out; ventilated; dried; and whitewashed with quicklime. She is to be given a new divan in the cabin, divided into three parts. The gig is to be masted. The mattresses are to be redone. The sofa in the nursery to be repaired. The paint below to be washed where necessary.

We anchored at St. Lucia at 2 o'c. Not a cloud in the sky nor the slightest motion in the ship during our passage. How beautiful Pausillippo seemed as we glided past its shores. So bright, so smiling! Each well-known villa as we passed it seemed to welcome us.

Paulina and Giuseppe Romano, together with their three children, visited them on board to welcome them back to **Naples**, as did various friends including Mr Turner and the Meuricoffres. The final entry reads:

Thus ended our excursion in the *Sibilla* in 1861. Barring Papa's illness, the four months we have spent on the *Sibilla* have been four months of enjoyment and happiness to us all.

🐚 *1861–2: Vesuvius*

W ITHIN A WEEK of landing in Naples, Anne left for England, accompanied by Henry and Margaret. Being left to cope with the remaining seven children, JC hired a new Governess, Miss Molteno, and saw to it that strict discipline was maintained. As before, lessons took up every morning, with the exception of Sundays. After Grace and John had both been ill, for them at least, according to one chilling entry, 'the cold bath and pianoforte practisings at six o'clock in the morning by candle light have not yet been resumed'.

JC's family duties during this motherless period in Naples kept him busy. As a way of keeping Anne in touch, he made Grace, John and James take it in turns to make a neat copy (out of 'school' hours) of his Journal entries for posting on to her in England. Their old family friends are not properly introduced to future readers and so cannot be described here. The last entry is for 17th January, after when there are no more entries until the next cruise begins in May.

After the morning's work, riding lessons for the boys took up part of the rest of the day (see plate 11). They had a good teacher, and John and James soon learned to 'sit on their horses fearlessly and well'. Gymnastics for both the girls and the boys were also arranged. Otherwise, pastimes were mainly exchanging visits with friends, walking and expeditions to see the sights.

There were plenty of exchanges of visits with the Romanos – not all of them successful:

> *27th November* Aunt and Uncle Romano spent the evening with Papa, but both fell asleep.

> *5th December* Aunt Paulina and her three children took tea with us. The boys were noisy and rough, and Papa scolded us all. James was fined 50 numbers for helping two Romanos to use, break, and throw about the apartment the new pens Papa had carefully put into the two inkstands only half an hour before.

> *12th December* John and Tom Romano spent the afternoon with us. Papa ordered Marie to be with us, to prevent the furniture being broken.

At the Romanos they met Charles Bradlaugh, who later became notorious for his frequent expulsions from Parliament on the grounds that he refused to swear on the Bible. He was a freethinker, but not irreligious:

> *28th November* Mr Bradlaugh was there. He speaks and writes Hebrew like a Jew. He has the old testament at his finger tips. He cast up for us the 7,000 years since the day Adam was created.

Don Liborio was also in Naples:

> *6th January* Liborio Romano was stopped two evenings ago by three thieves in the Vicco Freddo just after dark, and robbed of three piastres. People laugh at Liborio, ascribing the visitation to his friends the 'Camorristi'.

Sunday service was an important feature of the week, although 'Papa does not seem to think much of Mr Maitland's manner of reading or preaching. The former has the evangelical ding-dong whine, and the latter is heavy and dull.' The children were well trained in singing and together provided a mini choir:

> *1st December* We went to church in our white shirts and trousers. We occupied a whole bench in the gallery before the organ. We sang the Canticles and one psalm.

> *7th December* Holmes [*music teacher*] came in while we were at dinner to tell papa that the Psalms to be sung tomorrow were changed. Thus all our practising during the week was lost. So papa said we should have service at home, although the Bishop of Gibraltar was at church.

Descriptions of the eruptions of Vesuvius during this period are so detailed that they could even be of interest to vulcanologists. They are given here in full:

8th December We remarked an unusual mass of thick dark cloud rising apparently out of the sea between Naples and Castellammare, to a prodigious height.

9th December The cloud we remarked yesterday afternoon turns out to be an explosive eruption of Vesuvius! It burst out at a point between Resina and Torre del Greco on the flank of the mountain, not more than a mile or so from the high road, amongst the vineyards and close to a convent. Scarcely a house in Torre del Greco that is not injured by the repeated earthquakes, which shook the neighbourhood, and dislocated the pavement of the road, during the explosions. The inhabitants of Torre have fled in dismay. The lava has taken a direction above Torre and should it overflow the valley, Torre will be buried. Numbers of English went in the night to witness the grand sight. Today the eruption has extended to the crater on the summit, which throws up fire every two or three seconds. But it seems the flow of fire has ceased from the lower crater.

10th December Last evening after dinner Papa took us all in the yellow chariot to St. Lucia to witness the eruptions. But the lower crater was dark and seemingly extinct; that on the summit of Vesuvius threw up fire in showers every half minute or so. Dr. Sim advised Papa not to go to the Torre as the dust was overpowering, some 8 or 10 inches deep, and there was nothing to see but crowds of disappointed people returning home on foot, in cittadinis [*carriages*] (for which large payments were exacted) and in any conveyance they could secure.

11th December The whole of the 22,000 inhabitants of Torre del Greco have abandoned their homes, 7 to 8,000 are fled to Castellammare and 6,000 to Torre dell'Annunciata. They fill the squares and portoni [*doorways*] and staircases. There is much wretchedness. The mountain is quieter. Several houses in Torre fell in yesterday. The ground and pavements of the roads exhibit cracks of several inches in width. The weather continues to be dry and cold. The wind from the NE.

17th December [*Written by John.*] Vesuvius has been tolerably quiet these several days, but today it emits an incredible quantity of smoke which rolls itself in huge dark masses, forming fantastic figures high in the air extending over the bay to Capri, and letting fall a 'rain' of dust into the sea. A subscription is being got up in Naples for the houseless inhabitants of Torre del Greco. But God only knows if one Ducat of it will ever reach its destination. The want of honesty and social confidence has choked charity itself in this country. Papa has given nothing. [*Not necessarily meanness. Undoubtedly Harriet Meuricoffre would have told him about what had happened to food and other donations given to the hospital where only a year earlier she had been working for the Garibaldini.*]

18th December It appears by the statement of the Director of the Observatory of Vesuvius that Torre del Greco and its neighbourhood have risen about five feet during the recent eruption. Not in consequence of lava or cinders or ashes, but from the interior upheaving of the ground. This phenomenon explains at last the long vexed question of the Temple of Serapis at Pozzuoli [*which is known to have fallen as well as risen in historical times*].

21st December Vesuvius is quiet again. It seems that Mrs. Whyte and her daughters, led on by curiosity to examine closely one of the cracks or chasms in the neighbourhood, if not in Torre itself, inhaled so much carbonic acid gas as to fall down insensible. She had to be dragged away, and well dosed with salvolatile and other restoratives. Her daughters were also seriously affected.

23rd December The wind brought the smoke and a rain of ashes over Naples. The trees and plants became grey, as if covered with dirty snow.

27th December Vesuvius sent up volumes of smoke charged apparently with ashes, which fell in the direction of Castellammare.

29th December When we got up this morning, we found the terraces and balconies covered with red brown ash from Vesuvius.

Despite what happened to Mrs Whyte, JC took the whole family, together with Miss Molteno and Zéline (nursery governess), to inspect the damage at Torre del Greco. Most of the houses had been destroyed but those still standing, although cracked, were being propped up and repaired. It was necessary to clamber over the rubble to get along the street.

1st January 1862 A slight odour of carbonic acid struck us as singular. We descended to the Madre Chiesa, one side of which, including the sacristy, was rent in many places, as if struck by lightning. Workmen were busy in propping and securing the immense building from further damage. A number of donkeys loaded with lime and stones were waiting patiently in the sacristy to be unloaded. Descending towards the sea, the fumes of carbonic acid became stronger. … In the interior of some of the still standing houses our lungs became affected with the carbonic effluvia. We got out of breath as if after a fatiguing effort.

The sea was boiling up, to the distance of some hundred feet from the shore, by the escape of enormous quantities of gas from the bottom. In like manner the water in the wells was bubbling and boiling, and the gas emitted up the shafts took away instantly the power of breathing. The ground we trod on emitted gas, which being heavier than atmospheric air, remained grovelling, as if it were, on the surface, ready to stifle all those who were unable to keep their heads above it. People went about with half lemons applied to their noses. The inhabitants had time to save their lives and their furniture. The working class has lost nothing beyond a few days labour. The sufferers are the owners of houses, most of which will have to be rebuilt.

On returning to the carriages the guide who had conducted us made an impudent demand on papa's purse. Papa's fists were into his mug in a minute. We got back to Naples at 4 o'c.

11th January On getting up Papa observed that the Manilla straw carpet at his bedside had been burned. On making enquiry, Fred immediately stood up and said he had done it, in trying to light the night light. His manly candour saved him from a severe punishment. At breakfast Papa stated that Someone had burned paper in the closet, and had burned the seat! He alluded to Frederic's truthfulness, and hoped that if any of his children had done it, they would in like manner stand up and state it. Not one of us stood up, and each in turn personally denied all knowledge of the fact. Thus the matter rests for the moment.

JC's volatility may have been aggravated not only by the fumes, but also by the prolonged absence of his wife. He had hoped she would have returned from England by Christmas. Yet when she finally did return, he succumbed to another fit of temper:

Mama's return. (16th January) All the house stirring at 6 o'clock. Papa started at 7 o'c to meet Mama at the Immacolatella. At 8½ the carriage returned, and down we all went to meet Mama in the courtyard. No Mama! The steamer was not in. At 10 o'clock we discovered a large steamer rounding Pausillippo Point. Again Papa started to meet her. It was the Genoa liner, and Papa soon returned. At 3 o'c another steamer rounded Pausillippo, and this time it was the *Hermes* with Mama, Harry and Mag all right. On landing Papa had a tremendous flare up with the boat men and porters, who wanted Dollars instead of Carlines. It came to blows, and Papa was terribly excited. Antonio was left to settle the dispute before the commissary by paying the tariff price of three francs in all. We were all delighted to have Mama back again. Dinner table looked as usual, when the whole family was once more united.

🐚 *1862: Toulon – Switzerland – Cagliari – Naples*

T**HE NEXT** Journal entry is not until May. For three months of the 1862 cruise the parents were away in either Baden Baden or Manchester. After their departure, at first John (12) tried his hand at a few Journal entries, but soon handed over to others. Henry and the governess, Miss Rose Molteno, both contributed, but the majority of the entries were by Grace (14). She gives a good account of their daily lives and obviously enjoyed the task; but in the absence of JC and Anne, life was quiet and repetitive, and nearly all her entries have been omitted.

The main events of the sailing year were:

7 May – 13 June	*Sibilla* taken out of winter quarters, restocked and spruced up. Many short trips to islands in the vicinity, but main voyage delayed probably by JC's severe bouts of pain.
12 June	Sail to Toulon via Corsica and Elba
27 June	Arrive Toulon
8 July	JC and Anne leave for Baden Baden for a cure, together with sixteen-year-old Margaret, who was going to finish her education in Geneva.
August	JC and Anne, while still in Baden Baden, get summons to see Samuel Brooks in Manchester, so they arrange for family to come from Toulon to stay near Rolle in Switzerland while they are away.
October	Re-united family returns from Rolle to Toulon and, after delay waiting for wind to change, sail back to Naples via Sardinia.

Wednesday 7th May The *Sibilla* left Port Ischia, where she had wintered, and anchored off the villa. She is commanded by Don Alessandro Jojema. Louis Panzera sails this time as second in command; of the former crew we have Nostruomo, Maestro Raffaelo, Pepe and Antonio. The remainder are new men. A likely lot, stout and seemingly able.   Papa

Thursday 8th May Papa visited the *Sibilla* and found her in excellent order. He provided the saloon with new divans and cushions. To prepare a yacht with all the comforts and necessaries of a reasonable existence requires prevision and thought. The sails and rigging are first overhauled carefully. The hull and deck repaired and caulked and repainted. The interior washed and painted. Bedding washed and kept aired. Furniture strengthened or replaced. Lamps and lanterns carefully examined and the broken substituted by new ones. Kitchen utensils re-tinned. Seamen's clothing counted, the ragged removed and new shirts and trousers substituted, black silk ribands with the word '*Sibilla*' distributed for their hats, oil case hats and woollen caps supplied.   Papa

Friday 9th May Mama busy packing and selecting clothing for us eight children, with cloaks, shawls, carpets, paper, pens, ink and schoolbooks.   Papa

10th May The old dark chariot, once an elegant £350 carriage, now used as baggage van, was brought out from the recesses of the coach house, the horses put to, and the work of removal on board commenced.   Papa

By the end of that day all were on board and as a sirocco seemed probable the next day, that night JC set sail for Castellammare, on the other side of the bay, that night. On Sunday they enjoyed that town's celebration of its feast day. On Monday:

Ship's provisions for five months were brought on board. Biscuits, macaroni, cheese, hams, lard, potatoes, salted sardines, lamp and eating oil and other condiments. But neither wine nor spirits, for the crew denies themselves these superfluities.   Papa

Although they had stocked up, the ship did not yet leave for Toulon. JC's symptoms, which included abdominal pains, suggest other maladies besides gout, but nothing specific was diagnosed. The usual remedy was brandy mixed with chloroform, to be taken a teaspoon a time. Here is just one of the many entries on the subject:

Saturday 17th May Papa got up. But he had no relish for breakfast. Towards noon the fever returned with violent shiverings, thirst and vomiting. With some difficulty Henry and the servants got him to bed at the house [*which they had revisited to pay bills and check that all had been properly cleared up*]. Dr Sim declared it to be 'intermittent' fever. The shiverings ceased at 6 o'clock and at 3 o'c they were succeeded by the usual perspirations. Quinine was administered in hourly doses.   Papa

JC was soon on his feet again, but he then thought it time to make a will – an exercise which took him nearly a fortnight. Meanwhile the family continued to live on *Sibilla*, cruising from island to island at night, with visits on shore during the day.

Tuesday 20th May Tom fell headlong through the skylight onto the floor of the main cabin. He fell between two armchairs which broke his fall and saved him from injury. The King embarked at midnight. The English ships of war saluted, and illuminated with Bengal lights. [*This was Vittorio Emmanuele II, King of those parts of Italy that had united so far.*]   Papa

Thursday 22nd May Mama, Grace and Margaret rowed themselves round the lighthouse in the gig, to a cave where the girls had a delightful bath, leaving Mama to keep the boat off the rocks. The water is clear, sheltered from the sun and from the gaze of the public.   Mama

While waiting to start on the main journey, the children toured the neighbouring islands. The following entry was written by Anne:

Sunday 25th May The children repeated their catechism with Mama, after which Papa read service. At 11 o'c we went in the Gig with Henry to sea. We only caught two fish in two hours. We returned on board, where some of the children continued to fish with better luck. Mama and the girls took their usual bath; in the evening we went with Papa and Mama to Casa-Micciola and walked up a ravine which led to a little cottage. As we ascended the owner, his wife, and children came out to meet us and invited us to remain in their garden. He spoke to Papa, showed us his cherry trees and vineyards. Papa bought 60 pounds of beautiful, large ripe cherries which he divided between the cabin and forecastle.
                                                                        Mama

Thursday 27th May We sailed to an island called Vivara, situated between Ischia and Procida and which no doubt was thrown up by a volcano. The bay on one side forms a fine crater, two sides of which have fallen in. The island is distant a gunshot from Procida. The summit is cultivated and the slopes are covered with flowers, herbs, ivy, myrtle and broom. What a volcanic region the bay of Naples must have been, especially on the Ischia and Baja side! Volcanoes and craters are to be seen everywhere, and the very stones the houses are built of have been thrown from the bowels of the earth. Sometimes the lava lies in strata, the heaviest on the top dark and grey, with a soft yellow tufa underneath. Sometimes the contrary happens. Vivara rises sheer out of the sea, which from its great depth, close to the island, has the appearance of ink.   Mama

Other entries by Anne describe visits to Capri and the Blue Grotto, Sorrento, and:

Saturday 7th June On getting up we found the *Sibilla* quietly at anchor off the town of Procida. After dinner Papa and Mamma, Grace, John, Fred and Annie went across the channel to visit Monte Procida. Papa came home astonished at the fertility and beauty of this mountain. We sat down to repose ourselves at a cottage by the roadside or rather pathside, for no wheeled carriage has ever yet been seen or used in this district. The cottagers brought us chairs, water and excellent wine – the real Falernian. We then visited Captain Alessandro Jojema's house. He is a native of Monte Procida. He married two sisters. Has three daughters by his first wife, and a son by his second, who was the elder sister.

Mama

After a round of farewells, they finally set sail for the main voyage on 12th June:

The ship is in great confusion, everybody hurrying to and fro. The cook getting his provisions stowed in the gig (which is turned into a fruit and vegetable store room, because the wind ventilates and preserves them). Every thing denotes our departure from Naples. Dr Sim came on board to wish us farewell and at last, up anchor, up sails, and the *Sibilla* moved forwards as if glad to leave Naples and all its bustle.

Mama

Rolling seas and adverse winds make progress slow. Most adults in the party suffered from seasickness, for which Anne 'administered a teaspoonful of brandy saturated in chloroform'. The cook was too ill to provide meals. As they were nearing Cape Corsica, a gale set in which forced them to turn tail and dock at Ferrajo in **Elba**. They noted the reconditioned fortifications organised by Napoleon during his exile. They walked in the afternoon, resting in a flour-mill, driven by an English engine made in Glasgow. 'We had a hard and wet pull to get back on board for the wind had become a sort of hurricane, with lightning and a fierce sea outside. Did we not enjoy our tea with fresh bread and butter and milk from the town when we thought of Cape Corsica and the raging storm outside.'

18th June Papa entered the Municipal school or gymnasium, where the youth of all classes are taught elementary knowledge. The expense is paid out of Municipal funds. Each branch has its separate room and professor. Corporal punishment is unknown. Boys not conforming to the rules are dismissed.   Mama

Tuesday 19th June In the afternoon we went (the whole kit of us) into the town to show ourselves, and see others. As usual we made a sensation in the neat pretty town. People crowded round us and the balconies were filled. On returning home, we observed that the two and twenty vessels which had taken refuge were making ready for sailing by daylight. [*The children then swam from the boat.*] It is a sight interesting to Pa and Ma to see us jump into the sea from the bulwarks and shrouds, diving, swimming and playing with the water. Annie is the boldest considering her age [*five*]. She swims however with a cord round her waist.

Mama

Friday 20th June We landed at the quai, where we found four charabancs waiting to take us to San Martino, better known as Napoleon's Hermitage. A nicely macadamized winding road leads to it among vines & sloping hills. It skirts the port for about a mile and passes over a short causeway, on either side of which are salt pits, or large squares of shallow land prepared for receiving the sea water, to the depth of a few inches which the sun evaporates, leaving the salt in the dry bottom. By repeating the operation several more times a large mass of salt is collected, ready for being shipped or refined. The distance to San Martino is about two miles rising up a beautiful valley. The "hermitage" has the appearance of the country house of an English gentleman of moderate income. It rises two storeys in front, but being built against the hill it has only one storey behind. Napoleon modernised its interior, which is comfortably divided into about a dozen rooms which were occupied by himself, his mother, one of his sisters & two or three of his generals. The house itself has not been changed, but the grounds which surround it, & the shady walk (Napoleon's favourite resort) which leads up a ravine to a spring of water, have been replanted and beautified by Prince Demidoff, the husband of the Princess Matilda (Napoleon's cousin). This wealthy nobleman has spared no expense in preserving this beautiful reminiscence of the Great Man's exile at Elba. He has extended the terrace in front of the house (tho' without disturbing the Gardens & trees planted by Napoleon himself) by building underneath a splendid museum of granite, which he has enriched with paintings, statues, and works of art, all bearing upon & connected with the Emperor & his family of Kings & Queens. [*This museum was later destroyed by a landslide.*] The whole is completed in princely style, & as the Keeper told us, at the expense of 5 millions of francs. Papa thinks the taste & judgement shown throughout are undeniable. It is the curiosity of the Island, & as years & ages roll on this most beautiful site, if permitted to exist, will become an object of deep interest to all those who will view Napoleon's life & career as the starting point in a new system of world government.

Mama

On 21st June a fair wind blew, and the party could at last leave Elba. But they soon ran into another storm. Anne's full description of the transition from calm to storm follows:

Well out of the harbour the wind fell and we were almost becalmed. It seems to be blowing hard outside the cape, for we have overtaken a ship closely reefed and laying to. 10 pm off the light of cape Corso. The wind upon us, before we had finished reefing, with every indication of a heavy sea ahead. The sensation on the nerves of a ship straining against or (in sea language) sailing close to a stiff gale is remarkable. Every rope sail and timber seem to brace themselves to the effort – one would say the ship had a nervous system like ourselves. …

… The ship falls off; as her head goes round the tension diminishes, the vibration ceases, the nervous excitement subsides and in a few moments the lungs seem to draw, the heart ceases to throb; and by the time we have fairly turned tail on the wind a complete silence supersedes the moaning, whistling, and the splashing of the waves, smiles and conversation succeed to serious looks and half suppressed fears.   Mama

The *Sibilla* had turned into a small roadstead on the wrong (east) side of Cape Corso to shelter from the continuing storm. There they had to wait, sheltered by the high mountains of **Corsica**, for a further three days before making further progress.

Monday 23rd June The same wind blowing as strong as ever. Margaret, John and James during a lull imprudently went ashore in the dinghy. They had no sailor with them. In returning, they hoisted the sail, and were caught by one of those fearful gusts. Papa was much excited, as the cutter was ashore and the gig hoisted up. Fortunately they steered well, took in sail in a seamanlike manner and ran alongside the gangway without accident. But Papa was very angry.

Mama

The next day the *Sibilla* was able to clear Cape Corso but was further delayed by lack of wind. Life was far from idle. For every meal there were fourteen round the table in the 'state cabin'. Lessons included arithmetic, spelling and geography. 'Although the sails may sleep for days and nights', wrote Anne, 'we are always employed and hard at work. John and James begin at four o'c in the morning. The children have profited from their gymnastic lessons and climbed up a single rope to the main crosstrees sixty feet from the deck by way of exercise'. When the next rough weather comes she writes: 'the squall has burst upon us. We are scudding on bare poles accompanied by a multitude of fishes whose silvery scales reflect the flashes of the lightning.'

Finally they reached the coast of France, sailing along the coast within sight of

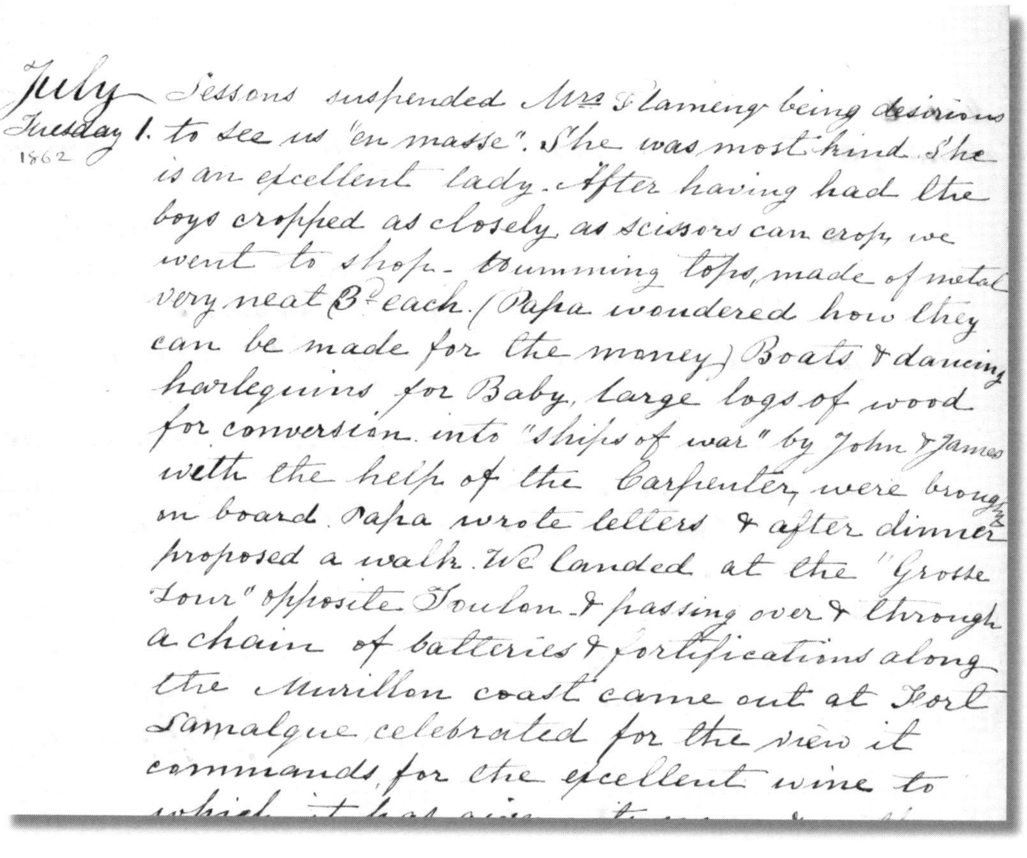

[handwritten manuscript]

July
Tuesday 1.
1862

Lessons suspended Mrs Flaming being desirous to see us "en masse". She was most kind. She is an excellent lady. After having had the boys cropped as closely as scissors can crop, we went to shop – humming tops, made of metal very neat 3d each. (Papa wondered how they can be made for the money) Boats & dancing harlequins for Baby, large logs of wood for conversion into "ships of war" by John & James with the help of the Carpenter, were brought on board. Papa wrote letters & after dinner proposed a walk. We landed at the "Grosse Tour" opposite Toulon & passing over & through a chain of batteries & fortifications along the Murillon coast came out at Fort Lamalgue celebrated for the view it commands, for the excellent wine to which it has given ...

Nice, Antibes, Cannes (where Napoleon landed and where Lord Brougham lives), Hyères – and **Toulon**, where they berthed as usual by the 'galley slave prison ship'. Here they soon resumed the patterns set in previous summers, renewing friendships and, for JC, business contacts.

On 8th July JC and Anne left for Baden Baden, where he was to 'take the water'. They took with them Margaret, dropping her off at Geneva. They left Rose Molteno, senior governess, in charge of the children, with Henry, from now described in some of the entries as The Admiral, in overall charge. They continued to live on board, but mostly they used a berth at St. Mandrier, the picturesque peninsula across the bay. Lessons continued as usual, but the afternoons left time to go ashore on expeditions, swim, sail, go for adventurous walks, visit other ships in the harbour and enjoy a comparatively normal summer holiday. Until:

> ***Monday 8th September*** [*Anchored at Toulon.*] We went on with our lessons until 1 o'c when just as we were finishing our Italian lessons, Henry, who had been on shore, entered with a letter and a certain important look on his countenance and said: 'Come all and listen for I have some thing that concerns every body on board.' They [*the parents*] had had a pressing invitation from Grandpapa to spend some days with him in England. They had sent a refusal, if it were to see only the Exhibition, but, if he still wished to have them, we were all to start immediately for **Switzerland** and remain there until they had paid their visit to England and could come and join us. Oh what a commotion and excitement. All day we could settle to nothing. Grace

Plainly the invitation was not just to see the Exhibition, for after a two-day wait, a telegram arriving confirming the original instructions. Packing and other arrangements took three days, but meanwhile Grace recorded another drama:

> ***Thursday 11th September*** The awful event to be recorded was the tremendous storm which began at 4 o'c in the morning. The crash was tremendous. All [came up to] the saloon and nursery and lo, *Sibilla* was struck. Injury done in the kitchen where the fluid entered, fortunately a bucket of water stood there and perhaps saved our lives. Injury done to the mast and sails. The smell of sulphur was so strong and suffocating. Grace

It took a further two days to leave the boat and get on the train, partly because thirteen boxes had to be taken ashore to the Customs house, and there was no-one there to check them. Finally the whole party squeezed into two first class compartments and left for Geneva on the morning of the 14th. They got out at Marseilles for a comfort stop and on their return found some of their seats had been taken by strangers. A few stops later they were quizzed by the guard as to their ages, as a result of which Henry had to pay more for the tickets. Strangely, they next detrained to take a carriage to a hotel for the night. Rising at 4 o'clock, they boarded another train, but because of further delay with the tickets, did not even have time for a cup of coffee. 'Reached Geneva at twelve o'c very tired and exhausted', wrote Grace. From there they took another train to Rolle, where 'dear Papa met us, looking well'.

Rolle is on the northern shore of Lake Geneva and was just within walking distance of the Benedictine Convent, where the children were to stay. The convent was near a house owned by their parents' friend Georges Meuricoffre, brother of Tell. Lessons started again the next morning, and that afternoon the parents left for Manchester. For the next month, in the afternoons the children played by or sailed on the lake, visited nearby chateaux and enjoyed what was for them a very different summer holiday. Henry organised a major project to keep them busy: they were to help him build a mole for their boat and dig a canal that would link it to the lake (see plate 7). Grace wrote a lengthy entry for every day. During this time she describes Henry as Head Cook. On 5th October he provided them with potatoes and chestnuts cooked in a pot over a fire of dry sticks. The first course was boiled potatoes and chestnuts mashed together; the second course potatoes roasted alone, the third chestnuts roasted alone and the fourth, bonbons.

> *Tuesday 14th October* A splendid day for our picnic after all. Before breakfast Margaret suddenly made her appearance with an order from Henry to proceed immediately to the lake. Off we scampered and were all photographed at the works. We arrived at the Signal de Bougie at about 3½, the sentimental portion of the party admiring the lovely view, the others with more sense making immediate preparations for cooking macaroni, Henry cordon bleu, Margaret second in command. Grace

Papa and Mama returned on 18th October, in time for a dinner, which 'Papa and Mama thought very meagre after Manchester fare'.

> *Saturday 25th October* A beautiful day, luckily for us. Great bustle, getting boxes corded up. The last accounts were paid. A huge wagon with two horses drove into the yard, and Antonio began to carry boxes down. They numbered twenty-three, besides eight bundles or cases, which we carried in our hand. Then

came a carriage for Papa, Mama, Zéline and the little ones. The boys went on foot with the wagon. Farewell to Rolle and to beautiful lake Geneva. The carriage passed the party on foot, and reached the station where we found Antonio and the luggage. We occupied 15 places on the train.   John

So ended the summer holiday. By 27th October they were back on board the *Sibilla*. Most of the entries to be quoted for the rest of the year are JC's. As before, many of them concern ships:

Tuesday 28th October A boisterous wind. The sea must have been high outside. An English ship, the *Launceston*, bound for New York, put in having sprung a leak. In the bay she fouled a French steamer of war, which ran into her midships. Her mizzen top mast was carried away by the shock, her main top yard was broken in two, and the ship's waist was pressed in about six inches. She was towed into shallow water near the *Sibilla*.   Papa

Friday 31st October Weather continues bad. One of the ships near us dragged her anchor and swung upon our bowsprit. The two Captains Billingsgated each other. No damage done to either ship. Papa made up our prize money accounts. After paying F.170 for John's watch, F.85 for Grace's and F.65 for James's, our respective accounts stand thus, including presents received in England and Mr Turner's legacy of £5 to his Godson John.

A list follows showing the number of points each had earned, and their value in sterling. This ranged from £8 15s. for John to £1 for William.

John's watch is a gold hunting watch, the other two are silver; all have been paid for out of earnings. But John considers his watch to be Mr Turner's legacy and intends to have it inscribed *in memory of my excellent godfather, Charles Turner, Esq. Banker. Naples.* Papa is much pleased at the idea.   Papa

Saturday 1st November In the evening Papa, Mama, Grace, John, and James went to see the new Theatre. Mr. Flameng gave them his box. The theatre is pretty, the corridors and stairs paved with marble. We saw a French drama by Dumas.

Weather better. Papa and Mama went on shore to take leave of our friends. Ship's provisions came on board. Tanks were filled. Bills were paid. Capt. Chastenay told us a story about French politeness. The Marquis of Devonshire [*whose yacht had also been moored at Toulon*] proposed to the French Admiral a race between his gig and the Admiral's. His daughter volunteered to steer his yacht's gig, and of course her boat won the race. The next day the Admiral proposed another race, both boats to be steered by men. The poor Marquis was beaten with ease!   Papa

A letter on 5th November announcing the birth of two more cousins caused JC to make an analysis showing that he and Anne had between them a total of fifty-one brothers, sisters and first cousins, and a further twenty uncles, aunts and parents.

The next day the weather was fine and JC ordered fresh provisions to be brought in and set sail. By sunset they were at sea and out of sight of Toulon. Two days later a heavy sea made them change course and head for Sardinia. Two more days of being able to make no more than nine miles an hour brought them to the capital, **Cagliari:**

Monday 10th November Fine weather, but no wind. Entered Cagliari Bay in the afternoon. We returned to our lessons, and every one became cheerful & lively. After such a storm our ideas of the pleasure of trying to sail across the Mediterranean have suffered a change.   Papa

Tuesday 11th November We anchored off Cagliari this morning at sun rise. A glorious morning! Cagliari, the capital of Sardinia, stood before us rising amphitheatre-like from the water's edge at the head of a long bay with distended arms on either side to the summit of a hill crowned by its citadel. It looked bright and beautiful. It said to us after the last three days of storm and tempest, here you will find repose & welcome. Our sufferings were soon forgotten, and, when the signal to prepare for landing after lessons were over came, clean shirts and gowns and bonnets sprung out of their hiding places, the very dogs leaping and jumping for joy. We landed at the quai of the health office. We entered the city gate. Alas! how different is sad reality to the gilding of imagination! This city of the Phoenicians, Greeks, Carthaginians, Romans, Vandals, Moors, Pisans and Genoese, who have held it in succession, is a poor, poverty stricken, ill built place, showing neither progress nor life. We ascended its streets, and traversed it from one side through to the other. Priests and monks swarmed, but both churches & convents seemed dilapidated and wretched. The carts drawn by puny oxen were the same the Romans used. The wheels (one pair only) of one solid piece without spokes and diminutive in size. Mere wheelbarrows or chariots. But the drivers and porters gave the scene a classic cast by their handsome Greek costumes, which seem to have never changed since the foundation of the colony. We returned on board tired & disappointed, tho' amused at the novelty of the scene in these piping times of general improvement. Meantime the clouds

had gathered in the west, the wind blew in gusts, the rain pattered on the deck
and the bright vision had veiled itself again in darkness & tempest.   Papa

Storms were to hold the party for five more unscheduled days in Cagliari. As usual,
JC busied himself by visiting every kind of establishment and local industry, taking
his family with him for instruction and recording in the Journal what went on and
how things worked. On Wednesday they visited a church and convent outside the
town, where the superior told them of the two miracles of the Holy Virgin that had
occurred in the vicinity. He went on to explain that the object of his Order was the
redemption of Christian slaves from the Barbaresque powers of Africa. (The last
raids by Barbary pirates were less than ten years earlier.) He related that in former
years there had been an Englishman called Albion Serafio in their community, who
was martyred by the Pasha for daring to preach the Gospel to his Mohammedan
subjects. Worse than the Barbary pirates, said the priest, was the constitutional
government of Victor Emmanuel, which had seized their estates and limited the
continuance of the Order to the lives of its present members, with a miserable
allowance of fifteen pence per diem to each.

  On Thursday they climbed up to the Citadel and viewed the Roman theatre
hewn out of the rock, dining afterwards with the English Consul. On Friday they
looked round the Cathedral 'rich in marbles and ornaments, but to modern tastes
inconceivably confused and ugly'. On Saturday they walked to the lime kilns, dis-
cussing with the owner how they worked; and on Sunday the salt pans, again with
a detailed description of the method of operation.

  After such conscientious and educational sightseeing, a rainstorm on the way
back to the *Sibilla* provided a welcome diversion:

Mama tucked Tom and Anne under her silk dress. Raffaella turned her cotton
gown over her and Grace's heads. All was useless! Parasols, dresses were like
so many gutters. Johnny was our steersman, and faced the huge drops without
winking. Willy had crept under the bench, but the gutters drove him forth. It was
glorious fun! Who has not felt the queer sensation of a stream of water silently
working its way through a pocket hole, then through this and then through that,
until the cool refreshing element reaches the warm quick precisely where least
wanted and least expected! Each of the company went through the exhilarat-
ing process under shouts of laughter. As the draggle-tailed procession crossed
the deck and disappeared below, it seemed as if so many weeping willows had
acquired the power of motion.   Papa

Monday 17th November At ten o'clock we set out to see the Museum and University [*which*] has a public library open to all with paper and writing materials gratis.   Papa

On Tuesday, on the way back from 'the great lake' they walked by a cliff which was 'a honey comb of caves which in ancient times were houses and tombs'. It was another three days before the wind was in the right direction for their yacht to set sail. Events while waiting included a visit by Prince Umberto, Crown Prince of Italy, to Cagliari, for which the *Sibilla* was dressed up in grand 'gala' – but 'the people murmur against him'. Their dog, Lion, had a fight with a horse. 'The horse bit him as he passed; Lion instantly sprung at the horse's throat, and forced him on his haunches.'

At last, on 22nd November, conditions were right for sailing to Naples. Panzera was sent on shore to get enough fresh provisions to last four days, which included a hundredweight of sea biscuit for the crew. They then set sail and by sunset were out of sight of Sardinia.

Sunday 23rd November We breakfasted late. Papa blew up the crew, for not doing honour to the day by shaving and putting on their best suits. At noon we had service, and No. 2 of papa's lectures on the omnipresence and omnipotence of God.

We dined at our usual hour, 5 o'clock, on macaroni à la tomate, stewed celery, and two brace of red-legged partridges (excellent). We had an apple and rice pudding. Papa treated us all with a glass of beautiful wine called Marcobrunner Auslese, which he bought at Frankfort. We were all able to sit down to dinner. No one was sick.   Papa

The next day, when they had hoped would see journey's end, they found they had only got as far as the Ponza islands, some fifteen miles north of Ischia. The weather worsened and it was decided that they should make for the port of **Ponza**, which they reached by sunset.

Tuesday 25th November A dreadful day! The wind during the night continued to rise from the S.E. and the morning broke under the influence of a furious tempest. Though in a safe port we had to strengthen our moorings with our strongest cables. The gusts were so sudden and powerful that it was difficult to stand and walk on the deck. The sea outside was furious. It leaped up the sides of the rocks opposite, foaming with rage. The swell reached the port, the *Sibilla* rolled, so that when Papa proposed to take us up the hill to the light house to view the sea, we were glad and thankful. Mama, Grace and Zéline left their bonnets behind, not to have them blown away or inside out, and went hooded. It was a grand sight! It seemed as if the sea, at times so calm, gentle, and smiling, had worked itself into a passion! It showed its white foaming teeth over its whole surface. It came on in rolling billows. It dashed itself over the island-rocks below, boiling, roaring and sweeping past them in headlong fury on to the coast opposite, whose dark caverns fringed themselves scornfully with the silvery shreds of each receding outburst of the furious waters. Towards evening the wind changed to the South and the violence of the elements abated. Several ships sought refuge, and seemed grateful to be at rest. The Governor, General Aiaca, with his staff called on Papa. Many changes have been made since our last visit. Our friend Tricoli was in prison. The Parroco had been turned out of his house and for a few days put under arrest. Our friend Giovanni had opened a draper's shop in the town, and seemed to be less of a farmer. He sent us a basket of Indian figs [*prickly pears*], which we fell upon like thirsty wolves, and devoured with delight.

Papa

Wednesday 26th November Mama and Papa, who had returned the General's call, then took us for a walk through the tunnels. We met many exiles, who presented petitions for money. They are sent here by sentence of the authorities, some for petty theft, others for cutting and maiming, others for insulting the authorities, and some for being 'camorristi', so called because they form a sect for thieving purposes – in short a thieving club – which boasts of thousands of members amongst the lower classes of the Neapolitans, who after all have only carried out to its consequences the thieving propensities of their superiors.

Papa

By 29th November the family was back in Baia, and that is the day of the last entry for the 1862 cruise.

ᴤ *1863: Genoa – Toulon*

THE *Sibilla* did not leave Naples this year until August, and there are no Journals until then. Strangely, JC's initial entries are in Italian.

Movements for the rest of the year were:

15 August	Set sail for business visit to Genoa.
19–23 August	Forced stop at Port'Ercole.
28 August	Arrive Genoa, having lingered in Elba four days.
18–29 September	JC and Grace collect Margaret from Miss Maunder's school in Geneva.
3 October	Anne, John, James and young Thomas leave Genoa for Manchester.
7 October	Rest of family leave Genoa on *Sibilla*, arriving at Toulon three days later.

Later in October Henry arrives from Cambridge, together with his friend Mr Blakiston, who makes his appearance in the Journals for the first time this year.

7 November	Anne's party returns, bringing with them Charles Gaskell, her sister Alice's son, who suffered from asthma.
3 December	*Sibilla* leaves for Naples.

Saturday 15th August As always happens, the day of departure is a day of intense activity. Everyone tries to remember whether they have forgotten something or somebody. Provisions for five, ten or fifteen days, as God sends the voyage; the washing to come and the laundry; accounts to be settled; the official instructions and letters, but above everything else the ceremonial visits of various officials, who believe it would show a want of due respect not to present themselves in the last crowded moments before departure. It all makes one's head spin.

   But the weather was magnificent. The sea tranquil. If we had not seen the lights of Santa Lucia and the dark walls of Castel del'Uovo slowly fading into the distance we could hardly have believed that we were not still anchored in the roadstead of Santa Lucia.   Papa

Monday 17th August The names of those on board the *Sibilla* are as follows:

Mr and Mrs Close with seven children, namely: Grace, John, James, William. Frederic, Anne and Thomas

Mlle Clair Naudin – music teacher

Mlle Anna Staudenmeier – Nursery Governess

Graziella Monte – Nursery Maid

Arnold Feldman – Preceptor

Louis Panzera – Secretary and Ship Captain

Antonio Mannasterioli – Steward

Giovanni Coronia – Cook

Errigo Coronia – Undercook, together adding up to 17 persons

The crew consists of Captain Giuseppe Caflero, together with 13 sailors; in all 14 people. Even without Henry and Margaret, there are 31 souls on board, without counting the two dogs, Lion and Jesse.

In the afternoon we found ourselves beating past **Mount Circe** [*half way between Naples and Rome*], and as the sea was calm and the wind light, at Mama's request the cutter was lowered and we all, except Papa, went ashore. We landed near an old ruinous building which a man told us was at one time the Pope's palace. Mount Circe stands out from the coast, a lofty and beautiful landmark for navigators in the Tyrrhenian Sea.   Papa

The weather held and it was hot: 'certain savoury smells of meat boiling in Marsala wine and spices indicate the effect of the heat on some parts of our supplies'.

Wednesday 19th August A heavy roll set in from the N. West early. Barometer falling. No wind. Ship rolling, sails flapping and most of them taken in. Lessons impossible – chloroform and brandy in request amongst the womenkind. The cook frightened out of his wits, very sick, and making his will in favour of Antonio and sundry of the seamen.

We hoped to work our way under the lee of Giglio, but the sea was rising, and the sensation of beating against wind and sea is far from pleasant. Papa ordered the ship to run into **Port Hercules** for shelter. How pleasant the sensation of sailing suddenly into a calm sea! How singular to hear the silent people begin to chatter, and smile. How soon the prostrate and dead rise to life and action again.
                                                                                    Papa

Thursday 20th August The boys, Mr Feldman, Mr Panzera and the cook start at 5 am on foot for Orbetello, a good hour's walk. Orbetello is a clean, well to do town, built in the centre of a lake, which is famous for eels. They brought some back, also some fresh beef.

That evening a boatload from *Sibilla* visited the main town. A striking description of its topography has been omitted, although at the time it might well have constituted the best available guide for tourists. JC tried to garner some information on the town's history, but even the priest did not know when the town was built, nor how old the church was. Much of it was deserted. They walked up to the fort at the top of the town:

> There were barracks inside for a regiment of soldiers, with a chapel, etc, but now falling into ruins. The fort was garrisoned by a man, two women, two donkeys and a goat. The business of this community was to attend to the light house. The town contains 600 or 700 inhabitants, who seem to have neither trade not profession – except some 20 to 30 fishing boats, and these were chiefly Procedani. [*Even at Toulon the previous year they had found that most of the fishermen came from Procida.*] Papa

> *Friday 21st August* A stormy night, which made us thankful to be in port. At four o'c in the morning our anchor came home. A struggle on deck, a few words rapidly uttered, and down went another anchor. Papa was on deck in a minute, but only found the usual guard pacing as if nothing had happened. But the *Sibilla* was only two ships' length from the rocks.
>   [*Later that day, on their own, JC and Anne were waiting in a fishermen's village opposite the town for a boat to bring them back.*] The inhabitants soon collected about them, some fifty children with their mothers. Papa enquired where the school was. There was none. So Papa advised the villagers to unite their efforts, to assist each other for the common good, and to trust to their own good sense and not to Government. Papa

The weather the next day enabled them to leave Port'Ercole and a day's sail took them to **Elba**, where they tied up at Porto Longone, in order to visit the iron mines, two miles' walk away. JC was greatly interested in such matters, but at the same time this was clearly part of his grand scheme to give his children a practical education.

> *Sunday 23rd August* They [*the mines*] are quarries of ironstone which seem to have been formed in large boulders, and buried in loose earth. When dug out they are red from oxide, but when broken they show a brilliant grey crystallization,

sparkling and uniform. The ore contains from 60 to 80% of metal. [*For JC on the way back*] Panzera had rigged up a portantino chair on two oars, to be carried by two men like a sedan chair. [*They sailed that evening.*] Just as the anchor was leaving the bottom of the sea, a man missing was reported, viz. the cook's boy. The dinghy was again lowered with Panzera, who found our man in a tavern drinking wine with two soldiers. Panzera soon collared him, and brought him on board in a shower of cuffs and kicks from everyone.   Papa

Overnight they sailed round the island to Portoferraio, for another look at Napoleon's villa at San Martino. They remained in Elba for four days, JC's opinion being that 'there was no bay or port in the Mediterranean, except for Port Ischia, which was so well adapted, so agreeable, and so convenient for a family'. On the second day there the whole family 'inspected a peculiar formation of limestone rock, which contains an endless quantity of diminutive fern plants, petrified'. On the third day their departure was aborted on account of bad weather and then the stay was extended yet again, because Grace had successfully pleaded for an expedition to Rio, across the mountains on the East side of the island. This set off at sunrise, on four horses and an ass, not returning until 5 p.m. By 6.30 that evening the *Sibilla* had left Elba and was on her way to **Genoa**.

> *Friday 28th August* The children woke Papa and Mama early – "Genoa in sight". It seems to extend itself miles along the coast. Houses of six or seven stories, built like blocks. A church steeple rises from every group of houses. What glorious lines of mountains rising up behind each other, till lost in the distant mists! The anchor is dropped in the port. It rains – a bore! We haul to our moorings under the wall of the town in the line of packet steamers and opposite the railway station. We are besmoked, besteamed and bewhistled out of our senses.
>
> Papa

A bundle of papers and letters for JC was brought on board. Although he lived on the boat along with the rest of the family, this was a business visit for him and the rest of the family were often left to their own devices. The *Sibilla* was moored in the noisy port, which it was not to leave until 3rd October. Even although inside the mole, rough seas outside would cause a swell, making Anne seasick. She did her best to keep the children occupied:

> *Wednesday 2nd September* We went with Mama to visit some of the famous palaces, Balbi Serra, Brignole. All very fine, very expensive and very uncomfortable. What have we to do with old pictures, gilded furniture, musty rooms, fine

columns and grand staircases? We wonder if ever anyone dines in them, or if anyone ever dances in them? They looked so cold, so deserted and so stingy of creature comforts. The Genoese seem to be all misers. Streets narrow, shops dark and discouraging. We were glad to get back to the *Sibilla*!   Papa

3rd September Papa and Mama and Anny took a walk on the old mole against which we are moored. They came upon a slip for careening steamers [*turning them on their side for cleaning or repair*] and saw the original mole and lighthouse of the good old times when Genoa was a republic under the Dorias, the rival and enemy of Venice, her sister republic. The vessels in those days [*that took part in the sea fights*] were triremes, moved by three banks of oars. They were called Galleys, the rowers were slaves, and were chained to their oars, Hence the word Galley Slave, in use to this day to denominate criminals condemned to forced or hard labour. The old Doria palace is still in existence, facing the entrance into the port.   Papa

In these unaccustomed, towny conditions, discipline among the children was becoming lax. Instead of filing into meals on the beat of the second gong, in order of seniority, brushed and spruced up, they were arriving late and untidy – sometimes even unwashed. At dinner Papa delivered a long and pompous blast, with the peroration: 'Whereas I have of late observed that either from neglect or indifference or from slovenly disregard of so excellent an arrangement, several of you remain absent when Grace is said and dinner commenced, and whereas your late appearance at table, climbing over the sofas into the back seats, squeezing yourselves into spaces, and squabbling for elbow room disturbs the harmony of the family meeting.' And so on. After three more whereases in the same sentence, he ends up with 'This is to give notice that from this day, whoever shall be found absent, or in negligent toilette at the moment when I shall take my seat at the bottom of the table shall be fined ten numbers.'

JC admired the 'wealth and nobility of Genoa, and the number of noble looking palaces, which adorn the mountain sides and the valleys', but he was scornful of the city and its inhabitants in other respects:

Monday 7th September Papa made us observe the peculiar architecture of the older palaces and houses, which is certainly handsome and striking as regards the entrances and staircases. As to the interiors, they are forbidden to strangers. The Genoese never invite anyone. In their domestic arrangements they are notoriously inhospitable. In like manner the civil department of the town seems to think that the art of civil administration is to obstruct, and not to facilitate communication. The streets are dark and narrow, regular rat-holes. There are only two or three landing places in the circuit of the entire port. The gates are all closed at sunset except one, and that is closed at midnight. The style of architecture and the illiberal habits of the place remind us of the Moorish Byzantine Harems. The business of the Genoese seems to be to get money, to economise it and to hoard it.   Papa

Lessons continued every day, usually from six in the morning until 3 p.m., with an hour's break for dinner. One of the tasks JC now set the children was the translation of the daily entries in the Journal into Italian. More and more, however, he was intent on training them in financial matters. His own work seems to have become largely that of buying and selling stock by telegram. On 9th September he sold stock in Turkish Lire and asked John to calculate what he would get in sterling for 10,000 of them. 'Papa generally tells us all about these Telegrams, and his operations.'

This still left time for more boisterous activities:

> *Thursday 17th September* After firing exercise was over [*they had musket drill*] the boys stripped for a sea fight, which consisted in challenging the steward Antonio to throw water over each other. The four boys embarked in the cutter, Antonio in the Gig. Antonio had decidedly the best of it.   Papa

On 18th September JC and Grace left for Geneva, to collect Margaret (now seventeen) from Miss Maunder's school.

> *Saturday 19th September* Mr Strettle called, hoping to have seen Papa. He returned with us on shore. We landed at the gate of the Arsenal at which place Fiesque (the rival of Doria in 1549), when embarking to command his fleet, was accidentally drowned while stepping into his boat, dressed in full armour. We visited the Dorian palace, which must have been a grand place 300 years ago, with its marble terraces and gardens extending to the sea; now however the town has encroached, nay surrounded it, the road and railroad cut through the gardens close to the house. There is a striking portrait of Andrea Doria as an old man, over the bed in which he died.   Mama

> *Wednesday 23rd September* Mama took us all on shore again at 12 o'c. We visited the Palazzo Reale, which formerly belonged to the Durazzo family. It was

sold in 1842 to Charles Albert. [*King of Sardinia 1798–1849, he abdicated 1849 in favour of his son Victor Emmanuel II.*] The rooms are full of pictures, the best of which have been taken to Turin and placed in the royal gallery. On leaving the palace James said he was hungry. We all seconded James's proposal but Mama said there were two more palaces to be 'done' and that as today was the last day, she would take us sightseeing – we must have patience. We crossed the Strada Balli and entered by a flight of marble steps the Court of the Durazzo Palace. The staircase is magnificent, the finest in Genoa. John and Fred have it impressed on their minds for they lost 50 numbers for scampering up and down it as fast as they could. Lastly we visited the Pallavicini Palace, which contains many old pictures of great value. We boys availed ourselves of comfortable chairs in each room and waited patiently for Mama, consoling ourselves that there were no more palaces to be done.   Mama

Thursday 24th September The weather continued stormy and rainy. John, who had made himself independent of the rain by the purchase (with his own money) of a suit of waterproof oiled sailcloth, regular tar's costume, sallied forth with Panzera to purchase ditto for James. The time is spent after lessons by William, Fred and Annie in arranging a 'hunt'. Mama, Mr Feldman and Meyer drew the horses and their riders, dogs and the fox; Will and Fred paint them and cut them out.   Mama

It rained nearly all the time in JC's absence. On 28th September, the day before his return, the monotony was relieved by another sea fight:

After lessons Mama offered a prize of ten francs to us four boys, if we could upset the Gig and right it again without help. Of course we instantly stripped for the exploit. We found it impossible to capsize her by our weight or by sheer strength, so with the assistance of buckets we filled her with water, and sunk her as far as she would sink. Then, mounting her side, over she went, carrying us all four with her into the sea. We then got onto her keel, and with our joint weight on one side, over she went again righting herself. We soon bailed out the water, and earned our half Napoleon with great applause.   Mama

Next day, after meeting JC and his two daughters at the station, they welcomed him back on board in nautical fashion:

We went through our musket drill, firing several rounds. At a sign from Papa we four boys sprung up the main mast, and each seizing a rope we climbed up, hands over head to the crosstrees, thence Fred passed to the shrouds and so down by the ratlings. Jim came down by the main stay, John and Will descended by the same ropes they ascended.   Papa

Friday 2nd October Mama packing and preparing for starting tomorrow for Manchester with John, James and Tom. A Joint Stock Company, Limited, projected by us, for the purchase of a boat. Prospectus prepared by Mama and John – Capital 300 francs. Managers John and James, Secretary Panzera. Shareholders rag, tag and bobtail, amongst whom, of course, Papa for f.40, or two shares. The whole amount was enthusiastically subscribed in a few minutes and the list closed.   Papa

The Manchester party, which consisted of Anne, John, James and Thomas, left on 3rd October. No reason is given in the Journals, so it was probably just to give Anne's father the chance to see some of his grandchildren. JC was forlorn – 'the soul of the ship' had gone; and so was Annie, who missed her playmate Tom. However the *Sibilla* was soon due to leave Genoa for Toulon.

On 5th October 'Miss Close [*Margaret*] made her first appearance at drill, musket in hand; she fired several rounds, and bids fair to excel as a soldier!' On the next day JC went on one more visit to satisfy his curiosity about things mechanical, taking Will and Fred with him:

Tuesday 6th October We went to visit a new auxiliary merchant ship built for the Buenos Ayres trade, the first of the kind built in Italy. The engine is 30 horse power, bought for a trifle from a shipwrecked English ship. The timber of the ship was a cargo of African 'timber' rejected by the Arsenal at Spezia. The ship is 650 tons, and will carry 300 emigrants. Cost about £10,000. The owner is the Captain. [*More technical details.*]   Papa

Next day at 6.30 p.m. the *Sibilla* left Genoa for **Toulon**. They made good progress that night and the next day, and no-one doubted that they would arrive by the evening of the 8th. But:

At four o'clock orders were given to reef; our flying sails were taken in and the ship make snug against what the clouds on the coast seemed to be preparing for us. Sickness became more general. A heavy sea set in. The skylights were secured. A flash of lightning brought out our conductors. Down came the rain – a torrent. The wind dropped and the billows were in possession of the ship. Not pleasant as flash succeeded flash, and down below silence became more general. Poor Lion whined for admittance, and being a spoiled dog, obtained it.   Papa

Although Hyères lighthouse was in sight, they had to spend the night rolling about on board, with much sickness, before entering Toulon harbour at 8 a.m. next morning, 'rolling and flapping to the last'.

They soon received visits from their many French friends, including the family of Miss Naudin, the music teacher. But the rain continued so relentlessly that no expedition ashore was arranged until the 14th. Then they were put out by a passage in the local newspaper that had just appeared: 'The *Sibilla* arrived here on Friday, from stress of weather. She belongs to a very rich Englishman, le Chevalier Close, who travels in her every year.' JC's comment was 'Tant pis pour nous, for that means double charges in the shops.' Nonetheless they all went ashore, shopping and renewing contacts, with Papa flaunting his long white beard. (Margaret accused him of being vain about it.)

The *Sibilla* was being smartened up in anticipation of the return of Henry and his friend from Cambridge. In order to counter the impression of JC as a plutocratic yachtsman, the sails were just being patched and mended. The repainting caused some inconvenience:

> **Saturday 17th October** The *Sibilla* is in a state of siege, for no-one, at least with crinolines, can get on deck without the risk of getting white or black. Lion bit Will's hand rather seriously. He does not like being tied up, but it was necessary as he rubs himself against the paint if let loose. He bit Margaret also.   Margaret

For much of the rest of this visit to Toulon, JC was confined to his cabin, being too incapacitated to do much else. He spent his time writing – sometimes on his sermons, sometimes on a treatise on what should be done about the Neapolitan cloacks (i.e. sewers – the Latin word cloacae was still in use). He read to Margaret bits of his autobiography, and she herself took over most of the Journal entries. Her style is more discursive than JC's and as little happened between now and the family's departure at the end of November, most of them have been omitted. Yet she rose to the occasion for a major event. Here is some of her description of a visit to an English warship moored alongside:

> **Sunday 18th October** Beautiful morning! Bright sunshine! The ships of war looking their best. Cutters and Admirals Gigs crossing the harbour in every direction. Bands playing, a most lovely sight. At breakfast a message from the *Revenge* invited us to prayers at 10½ o'c. We were soon alongside. On reaching the upper deck Papa took off his hat, as is usual with well-bred seamen, to the

I Portrait of James Close by Edouard Dubufe (1852)

II Portrait of Anne Close by Edouard Dubufe (1852)

1 Four Close brothers in sailor suits.
Clockwise from top left: James, John, William, Fred

2 11th February 1848. A constitution is proclaimed in Piazza Ferdinando, Naples.
JC's office was in Palazzo Cirella, the tall building on the right.

3 15th May 1848. Despotism is restored.

4 *Left:* Boon companions Annie and Tom. Too young for lessons, they were 'the licensed idlers'.
Top right: Henry Gaskell Close, with Lion, in 1863
Below right: Mrs Harriet Meuricoffre

5 The family and *Sibilla*'s crew. JC and Anne are just discernible at the back.
Photograph by Henry, 1857.

6 Baia. The Temple of Venus, near the landing place for Nero's Baths.
From left: John, James, Margaret, Grace and two sailors. Photograph by Henry, 1861

7 Henry's photograph by Lake Geneva in October 1862, showing the children at the end of the canal they built for their boat. William is on the left; the three in a line are, from the top down, Grace, Annie and James; then Margaret (kneeling), Fred and, to the right Tom is fishing; on the far right, John. In the dark dress is Mrs Georges Meuricoffre.

8 A bearded JC in discussion with Henry, with Mr Blakiston sitting nervously between them

9 The Palazzo Reale in Naples with hill of St Elmo in the background, photographed by Henry Close (James Close's apartment was nearby)

10 *Top:* Margaret with Grace in a cart
Bottom left: Margaret in 1863
Bottom right: Grace in 1866

11 *Top:* John and James at riding school in Naples
Bottom left: John at Cambridge
Bottom right: William at Cambridge

12 *Top left:* JC's sister Paulina Romano

Bottom left: Paolo the cook

Above: Luigi Panzera, secretary and ship's captain

13 James Close senior, 1862

14 *Above:* Anne in later life

Right: Anne's brother, Sir William Cunliffe Brooks, MP, in a cartoon by Spy (Sir Leslie Ward), well known for his portraits of celebrities

15 Château Antipolis, as far as it had got at JC's death

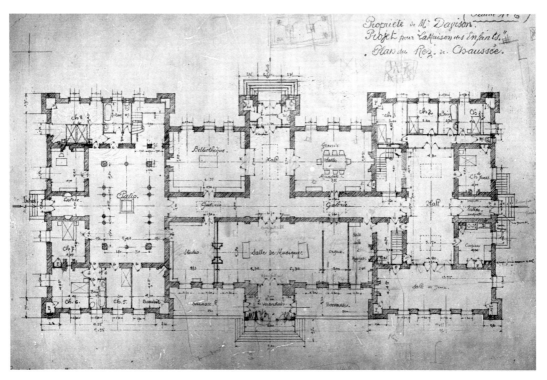

16 *Above:* Ground floor plan of Château Antipolis as it was in 1914

Below: Antipolis transformed into La Résidence du Cap, from the hotel's 1953 brochure

17 Villa Closebrooks, the widow's more modest home not far from Antipolis

18 House party at Villa Closebrooks in 1873. Anne was not bereft of company in her last years.

19 In this enlargement of a section of the previous photograph, a youthful William stands at the top, above his mother, who is talking to her brother Sir William Cunliffe Brooks, MP. In front of the open door and next to her mother is Margaret, and below her are Emily Brooks (Anne's niece) and John, who were soon to be married.

20 *Above:* The children with Sambo the pony
Below: JC's brother Thomas on his shooting pony

21 *Left:* The office, formerly in Quorn, now in Kingsley, from which the Close brothers sold land (by permission of Plymouth County Museum)

Below left: Fred with arm in sling, after falling from his horse at Uncle William's. He died later the same year.

Below right: An older James, taken in Chicago

22 Preparing a track in the rock face for the White Pass & Yukon Railway. Tunnel Mountain, c. 1898
(Harry Barley. Negative UW274732)

23 The summit of White Pass on 20th March 1899. Even after completion, the line sometimes had to be cleared of snow.

(Eric Hegg. Negative Hegg 6904)

24 William, John and James in old age, with John's son Arthur on the left. Arthur died young in the Great War. His widow continued to live in their Suffolk home until 1990, when she died aged 99. The house then passed to Arthur's great nephew Jonathan Close-Brooks, whose family still live there.

III *Sibilla* in a storm, by an unknown artist

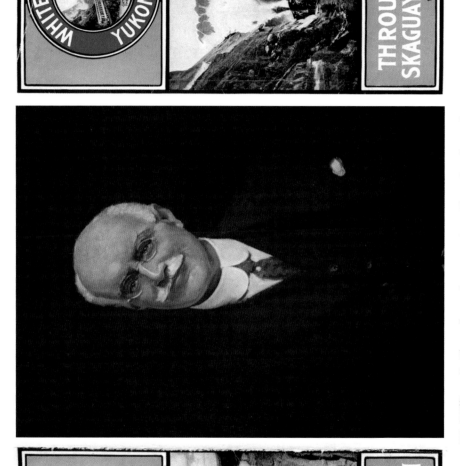

IV William B. Close, from the portrait at Close Brothers plc,
flanked by images from the 1905 brochure of the White Pass and Yukon Railway

whole crew, ship, guns, tackle, and officer on watch at the gangway. Miss Close [*in Anne's absence, Margaret was the senior female member of the party*] led the way, escorted by an officer. We followed in procession through files of Blue Coats on one side and Red Coats on the other, arrayed for Sunday inspection before divine service. [*After a visit to the wardroom*] Captain Foley invited us to service on the main deck, and handed us to our places, near to Admiral Yelverton. From the point we occupied on the larboard side, with a huge 42 pounder for our nearest neighbour looking towards the ship's bows, lines and lines of Bluecoats closely packed on benches, with their honest open well-shaved countenances, open throats and carefully negligently knotted ties, prayer book in hand, presented themselves. On the starboard side, the same lines of Red Coats combed, shaved, pipe clayed and cravatted, extended themselves forward à perte de vue. Every man in his proper place is the motto on board a Battleship. In front of the men and facing them sat the Admiral and Captain, in isolated state with flags for kneeling cushions. As the Admiral entered all rose, and after politely bowing to our party, he took his seat near the Captain. The Chaplain in his surplice mounts his low reading desk. We all rise and the service commences with 'I will arise and go to my father', sung by the whole ship's company. In the midst of guns, muskets, pistols, boarding pikes, cutlasses, balls and bombshells, to pray for deliverance from battle, murder and from sudden death! But who thinks of logic on board a man of war?

The sermon was on 'Faith'. Clear doubtless to everyone present, but Papa said incomprehensible to him. The benediction given, we all mounted to the upper deck, the crew piped to dinner. Admiral Yelverton introduced himself, invited us into his cabin, took Annie in his arms, and seemed to bury in her the thoughts of his own daughter, whose portrait he immediately presented to Margaret. He had married the Marchioness of Hastings, now dead.   Papa

The other two major events, also described in full, were two royal visits to the busy Toulon port:

Thursday 22nd October We are in summer again! At 3 o'c a salute from the French and English ships informed us that the French fleet had arrived, consisting of four line of battleships. We suppose they are here to honour the Greek King. [*George I of Greece was brother of Alexandra. She had married the Prince of Wales, later Edward VII, in March that year.*]   Margaret

Saturday 24th October By the extra number of boats passing to and fro we were convinced something was going to happen, especially as the Greek King was leaving for Athens. Suddenly the three-decker *Ville de Paris* fired two guns which were followed by a salute from 10 to 15 ships. At the same time yards were manned and ships dressed. A grand sight! George I [*aged 18*] had made his first public appearance as King. [*He was assassinated in 1913.*] Half the day was passed in saluting this poor boy as he visited the different ships of war, cheered by the sailors.

Margaret

That evening Henry and his friend Mr Blakiston arrived. 'Lion knows Henry and nearly knocked him down.'

> *Thursday 29th October* Early this morning the Empress Eugénie arrived in the Imperial Steam Yacht, the *Aigle*. The whole roadstead was in movement. All the ships were dressed, and the yards manned. A treble salute of 101 guns from every ship welcomed her arrival, with shouts of 'Vive l'Empereur!'.

She visited many ships, including the three-decker *Ville de Paris* and an iron-clad, the *Gloire*. She visited the Arsenal, inviting a large number of dignitaries to dinner.

> At two o'clock the new Iron Clad ship, the *Provence*, was launched, the Empress placing herself in a prominent position on the bridge of her Yacht. Flags, bands of music and innumerable boats filled with well dressed people of both sexes. Covered Loges were erected on each side of the shed for the accommodation of the Elite. Towards seven o'clock a rocket from the Admiral's ship gave a signal, and immediately all the ships opened fire to give the Empress the representation of a naval combat by night.

Papa

Every ship was illuminated, sometimes with Bengal lights on the crosstrees and bulwarks of the ships. And so it went on until 8 p.m., when the Empress had a train to catch. Her departing boat was followed by a procession illuminated in many colours. 'The whole thing was well managed. The French can do these things wonderfully', wrote JC.

> *Saturday 31st October* This morning Henry, Blakiston and Panzera with Annie and the two boys went in the cutter to the Seyne, to enquire if the *Sibilla* could be put on a slip to have her coppers [*sheathing on the hull*] examined and cleaned. All the slips were engaged for a month to come.
>   Papa was not well today. He was drowsy and his limbs ached. In the evening we had a performance of theatricals to amuse him. Grace of course was the Queen. Will and Fred, dressed like monkeys, were her sentinels, being armed

with muskets. Annie sat on the throne near the Queen and looked charmingly. A fight between the sentinels, and being both killed, the Queen dies also. The drama in four acts was succeeded by a ballet. The musicians were myself and Mag, a shipwhistle being her instrument. Henry was bass, with a huge water funnel. Blakiston played on the gong and a paper cone. Feldman performed solos on the speaking trumpet. The din was incredible and the actors repeatedly called out. The ballet music was creditably performed by the musical box. After the performance was over, the elder branches except Papa took a moonlight sail in the cutter.   Papa

Saturday 7th November Mama has at last returned on board. The difference is already felt in several ways. We are all delighted.   Henry

Anne brought with her not only John, James and toddler Thomas, but also nephew Charlie Gaskell. His mother was Anne's sister Alice, and his father was the brother of JC's first wife Henrietta. About the same age as John, he suffered severely from asthma and it was hoped that the sunny Mediterranean and the sea breezes would help him. He had a bad attack the very next morning, so Margaret and James took all the other children off in the gig, leaving John to look after him. With nine children and Blakiston, tutors and governesses, the party that sat round the table at each meal now numbered seventeen.

JC had worried about the condition of the coppers of the *Sibilla*, since she was grounded on the rocks earlier in the autumn. On 31st October a party headed by Henry and Panzera had been to enquire if she could be put on a slip to have her coppers examined and cleaned. All the slips were engaged for a month to come. On 12th November JC tried again:

Papa went to the Admiral and Préfet to obtain permission to dock the *Sibilla*. He walked with difficulty and by intervals. After much talking and walking

backwards and forwards from one office to another, he succeeded, and the ship
goes in on Monday.   Henry

This meant that alternative accommodation would have to be found and on
Saturday Henry went to **Hyères** and booked rooms at the Hotel d'Orient, as well
as a diligence to take them there. The family was accustomed neither to packing
nor to travelling by land. They left on Sunday 15th November and the weather did
not help:

> Margaret, Will, John and James with Mr Feldman [*tutor*] climbed onto the top,
> although the rain had begun to descend. But having each a mackintosh, they
> seemed to enjoy the idea of defying the weather. It rained a good part of the day,
> and we could see but little.   Margaret

They may have missed seeing the scenery between Hyères and Toulon then, but
later they described it as one of the most beautiful areas to walk in the Mediterranean. Later that evening Margaret's Journal entry records:

> Papa had retired to Charlie's room to soothe himself by the side of a snug little
> fire. To make sure that Charlie's pillow was dry and comfortable he placed it
> before the fire and gradually fell asleep. He was awoke by a scream from Mama,
> who found the end of the pillow frizzling in the fire and the burning feathers
> filling the apartment with that horrid smell! Not much damage, but Papa won't
> forgive himself.   Margaret

Later in the week Charlie, who had been improving, had another bad asthma
attack. This was treated by their Galvanic Machine, which appears to have soothed
him with some kind of vibrations. (Galvanic was the contemporary term for elec-
tric, from the name of the 18th-century physiologist Luigi Galvani.) Otherwise
there were no major incidents and everyone seems to have enjoyed the five-day
break on dry land, during which lessons had been suspended and the sun had
shone.

Preparations to leave for Naples had begun on 24th November, but this departure was not until 3rd December. The reason for the delay is not clear, but it was
probably a mixture of his continuing bouts of pain and the weather.

> ***Thursday 3rd December*** Papa gave orders to weigh and sail for Naples. Wind
> westerly, warm, bright and pleasant. The whole ship a bustle, every thing being
> cleared on board. Panzera on shore for fresh provisions, Post Office etc. Naudin
> off to say adieu to her parents. Staudenmeyer to get back her linen wet or dry.

Henry, Blakiston and Feldman to post the last letters. Meanwhile the anchor up and with a single Jib we glided out of the Rade. Off the round tower the boat rejoined us, sails were set and off we went rejoicing at the fine weather, fine breeze, smooth sea and prospect of a pleasant passage. We passed the islands of Hyères, made out the familiar scenes of a week ago, dined and laughed till sundown sailing all the while nine or ten knots an hour, without a motion.

Margaret

But:

As we left the land and opened into the dreaded Gulf of Lyons the wind and sea assumed more serious dimensions. Sail by sail was taken in to ease the ship, until at last only one topsail remained and that was close reefed.   Henry

Friday 4th December Early Corsica was sighted. Suddenly from the Gulf of Genoa a hurricane from the North surprised us. Cape Corse was on our lee and must be weathered. "Shall we weather the Cape, Mr Panzera? What if we do not?" "Why Sir, we must hope to run the *Sibilla* ashore in a soft place between some of those dark rocks. If we do, we may thank the forty pounds you spent in cleaning her coppers." "Look at the foretop mast. It will go Panzera." "No it won't Sir. A good stick." "How it bends. Can't you relieve it a little?" "Not an inch Sir. Our lives depend on the topsail and that spar." "The cutter is full of water." "Stove her in with a handspike" was the quick reply. [*After much anxiety and dramatic lightning, it was at last decided it was safe to turn South.*] Poggia! Poggia! [*Italian for Starboard*] Instantly at that magic word the *Sibilla* heeled round and the terrific strain ceased, the very nerves of the ship relaxed. We were running down with the wind along the east coast of Corsica as daylight broke upon us.

Margaret and Henry

Both the dinghy and the cutter had been wrecked. They left Corsica by noon and found anchorage off Elba, having made 240 miles in twenty-four hours. They thought they would be in Naples by 2 o'clock, but just as they approached Cape Argentario, which covers Port'Ercole, the wind changed to the East. Three days later they had still been unable to get anywhere near Naples, so JC appeared from his cabin, and ordered the ship to bear down into **Ponza**. Everyone was called up to see the curious island. The port was crowded with ships which likewise had been successful in finding refuge.

There was no word about continuing the journey until 10th December, when they set sail not for Naples, but for **Ischia**.

⚘ *1863–4: Ischia*

*D*URING THESE EIGHT MONTHS in the Naples area, the family flat in Via Ascensione was not used, even when from mid-December they were moored for a month at the *Arsenale,* in the middle of the town. A possible explanation is that JC and Anne no longer felt so at home in a republic, where society had switched its allegiance. Perhaps some of their royalist friends had left, and they entertained less. Or more simply they did not intend from the beginning to stay long in the middle of town, and it was not therefore worth the trouble of opening up the home. They had now been living on the boat since August 1863, and as it turned out, would continue to do so at least until late in 1865.

In January they sailed to Ischia, which was to be their base until August. It had the ideal harbour for mooring the *Sibilla*: it was a circular crater lake 1½ km across, the seaward side of which had been deliberately pierced to allow access to ships in 1854. We know from the 1863 Journals that JC had a fondness for the island and that he had visited it during his earlier business career. He may well have had something to do with turning the crater into a harbour – pure speculation, but it is difficult to imagine him not getting involved. Now he was stricken by gout most of the time, was not conducting business on the scale of earlier years and perhaps thought that the *Sibilla*, moored in this sheltered harbour, was an ideal retirement spot, close enough to see his Naples friends as often as he wanted, but away from the bustle of the city.

On 7th June they received a telegram with the long-expected news that Anne's father, Samuel Brooks, had died that morning. Anne had known he was terminally ill but, so long cut off from her parents and other relations in England, took time to get over the news.

When JC is away or too ill with his gout, the Journals are taken over by his wife and increasingly by Henry, Margaret and James. James is down to earth and succinct, Margaret more discursive, Henry supercilious and jokey. As before, there has to be an entry for each day, most of which have been omitted. Those selected show the family's remarkable range of activities and the energy and confidence with which they are pursued.

When the *Sibilla* finally arrived in the Naples area in mid-December 1863, there was no rush to go to the town itself. Two days at the island of Ponza and a week at

Ischia were followed by a return three-day visit to Nero's Baths and the volcanic curiosities of Baia, which was only cut short by the ship getting grounded. After a disturbing number of bumps at breakfast time, it was established that, although *Sibilla* had been carefully moored, she was now stuck fast:

> *Saturday 19th December* But now for getting her off! She must have dragged her anchor during the night. We put ropes out to different ships and endeavoured to drag her off by main force; but that not succeeding, all children and Mama and the maids were sent on shore, to clear the ship. The ballast was taken out of the hold and put on one side of the bows, in deep water, so as to cause the stern to rise. They then ran an anchor out and by hauling on that and a rope run out to a neighbouring ship, we got her off. Papa is afraid some of the copper may have been rubbed off.   Henry

> *Saturday 20th December* Having seen that the rudder had not suffered from yesterday's bumping, Papa gave orders for the anchor to be weighed. We arrived at the Arsenal at 5 o'c. We were stopped by the guardship at the entrance, but after much fuss and bother we were allowed to moor ourselves in our old berth.
>   Margaret

The ship then docked at the Naples Arsenal until 19th January. Christmas was celebrated on board. Old friends and the Romanos were visited and were in turn entertained on the boat. It was not a cheerful time. 'It poured all day. The *Sibilla* is worse than ever on a rainy day in the Arsenal. 'It is difficult to get on shore without getting wet, and we are quite out of the way of everybody', wrote Margaret.

> *Thursday 24th December* A holiday. Grand preparations for tomorrow. Everybody has a secret of his own on these occasions, and we are afraid to speak for fear of letting out something we should not. Mama on shore all day with Margaret, Grace and Charlie. We boys went to Lago d'Agnano to get evergreens to adorn the ship. We came home loaded heavily and with innumerable scratches, but that was all the better fun.   Written by Margaret for the boys

> *25th December 1863* A glorious sunrise and nipping north-east wind to illuminate this happy day, when men seem inclined to forget and to forgive and to wish to be at peace with the world. At daybreak we were all on the move to assist Henry and Mr Blakiston in the preparations for a merry Xmas day, of which Papa was to know nothing. Our first move after quitting our berths was to sing the excellent Christmas carol *Christians awake, salute the happy morn*, which sounds better at sunrise than midday. After that, Papa and Mama being in bed,

we went to work; hammering, fixing, inventing and arranging the deck destined to be our scene of action. At breakfast papa growled about the noises and the trampling overhead and ended by declaring himself a 'guest' at his own table and sulkily after service (no sermon, luckily) went ashore with Mama to return visits. Mama filled her pockets with dollars to make the usual presents of one to each of our sailors and servants on shore as well as on board. Meantime our work went on with redoubled vigour, everyone lending a hand.

Papa returned and quietly read his newspaper below until the Romanos came on board with Dr Sim and Miss Vogelsang and the bell tinkled us all to our seats at the dinner table on deck. The tables mounted on empty water barrels formed three sides of a square. They were handsomely adorned with flowers and all kinds of fruit. The deck was carefully covered in by the awnings and lined with the ship's flags of all colours tastefully arranged. Behind Papa's seat at the centre of the table was a transparency with the words A Merry Christmas.

A capital dinner, flanked by Papa's best wines and six and twenty merry countenances could not fail to get up Papa's steam, who soon was as merry as ourselves. Champagne came with the capons. The health of 'all friends round the table' 'Grandpapa', 'Uncles', 'Aunts and Cousins' by cartloads, amidst rounds of cheers from us youngsters on whom the good things had already had a most joyous effect.

Tables cleared, began the games, bobbing at suspended pears, ducking for apples, snapdragon [*etc.*] finishing with a tree loaded with presents for everyone present, big and little, old and young, master and servant, even to old Lion, who joined in all the fun and was not forgotten at the tree. In descending to our berths Will exclaimed 'Ah Mama, I have never spent so happy a day'. Even Papa said he never thought 'the thing' could have been so well got up 'without his help'! Dear Charlie was neither the last nor the least in the fun. Asthma was forgotten and he was as blithe as the rest.

Bill of fare. Mock turtle soup. Eels stewed in wine. Lamb cutlets with green peas. Capons with salad. Plum pudding and mince tarts. Hurrah for Papa and Mama, Henry and Jack Blakiston! May your shadows never be less!

Margaret and Henry

Saturday 26th December Freddy in bed this morning. Oh! Oh! Effects of plum pudding and champagne.

Henry and Margaret

New Year's Day 1864 A rainy, cold, windy stormy day. At breakfast one of the boys rushed into the cabin crying "A ship on the rocks: quick! Come and see it!" And there it was! A three master being dashed on the rocks by the furious waves.

We could only see her masts, but that was enough to inspire us with horror and compassion. Each wave drew her off and then as she struck, her masts and rigging quivered as if in pain. Although it was raining hard we went on shore to have a better view of her from Mr Turner's house; but we were too late, as she had already gone down and only her topmasts with the tattered remains of her sails and her Russian flag were to be seen. Her crew remained on board to the last. She was laden with pig iron and coals and that accounts for her sinking so soon.

That evening they went on shore to dine with Aunt Paulina and spirits rose:

The health of everyone round the table was drunk amid rounds of cheer. After dinner, games of every description, winding up with Sir Roger de Coverley and other dances which Mr. Haring [*the new tutor*] kindly played for us. Tom [*now aged four*] sat at the children's table and being away from Mama, helped himself freely to Champagne. After dinner he managed to get to Mama's knees where he fell asleep. We got Papa to dance and really he made us all feel ashamed of ourselves. He stepped out beautifully and skipped about as if he had never known what gout was.

Henry

The weather then became startlingly cold:

Saturday 2nd January The weather changed in the afternoon and became cold and damp. And at 7 o'c a storm broke over us. Down came the rain and the hail and the wind. All the boys rushed on deck to make balls of hail which they brought downstairs making themselves and everything around them wet.

Margaret

Sunday 3rd January Oh! How cold! We are surely not in sunny Italy. Look at Vesuvius, his crown white and a broad streak of snow down his side. Mama has lived many years in Naples, and she says she never saw snow like that on Vesuvius and Monte St. Angelo.

Notwithstanding the North wind that pierced to the very bone, the Pompeian party set out by train, well wrapped up in furs and cloaks. They were caught in a snowstorm while at Pompeii, which was something quite extraordinary.

Margaret

Monday 4th January All the Neapolitans look as if they were frozen and are the very picture of misery, while the English come out looking as if they were in their element. The weather does not suit Papa, who remains in Mama's room the whole day. His head wrapped up in a hood, his shoulders in a cloak, his hands in

> *1804* Papa, who remains in Mama's room the whole day. His head wrapped up in a hood, his shoulders in a cloak, his hands in woolen gloves, & his feet in a fur footbag. He cannot bear the cold & longs for the sun. How happy we are to be in port. We hear of so many shipwrecks & we can snap our fingers at the wind which is whistling through the rigging. Listening to it alone makes us feel cold & shivery—

woollen gloves, and his feet in a fur footbag. He cannot bear the cold and longs for the sun.

Margaret

Thursday 7th January We all revolted because Mama insisted on our taking a cold bath every morning. It is really awful, for the water is kept upstairs all night and then we have to throw a jug full over our shoulders. The sensation of cold water trickling down from the nape of our neck to the ankles is beyond description. However, Mama kept her ground, and we undergo the operation every morning on getting out of bed.

Margaret

Friday 15th January The weather is as obstinate as ever, and we shall soon skate if it goes on. Our friends say it is impossible to see us for it is quite out of the question to visit us on board in such weather.

John

Sunday 17th January The water on deck was frozen three or four inches thick.

James

Monday 18th January We are afraid this cold weather will kill many Neapolitans. The water in most of the public fountains is frozen and never has there been such cold in Naples.

James

Three incidents had meanwhile distracted the family from the deep freeze. The first shows how the Camorra, the Neapolitan version of the mafia, were treated in those days. The second was Henry's escape to Egypt, and the third Fred's arrest by the army.

Tuesday 5th January This morning a large war steamer or transport embarked a considerable number of that class of criminals known as the 'Camorrista', drones or parasites, who have formed associations for the express purpose of living on the industrious classes. This class is largely disseminated in the country. It seems to indicate one of the results of Jesuitism. Their principle is to exact rewards for not doing injury, which indicates a low standard of morals. The ship was moored alongside of us. On the mole a number of the wives and children of these prisoners assembled to bid adieu for some years to their husbands and fathers, who were being transported to Ponza or to Tremita [*an island penal colony in the Adriatic*]. Their screams, howlings and lamentations reminded Henry of the bewailings in Eastern countries over the dead.   James

Wednesday 6th January Henry and Mr. Blakiston left for Alexandria in the large ship the *Tripoli*, one of Cunard's boats. Some of us envy them; everything on board looks so comfortable. They have taken our servant Antonio with them. Henry has long been preparing for this trip and his photographic apparatus has been put together with great care.   James

Monday 11th January Papa and Mama on shore all day Papa returning a few hours before Mama. John, Will and Fred took tea with the Miss Plowdens. On going out of the arsenal gate, Fred was arrested by the soldier on watch who had taken him for one of the little sailor boys belonging to the ships of war. Fred's astonishment was great and he could only say in Italian Why! Why! Mr Feldman soon came up, but of course the soldier had seen his mistake for Fred does not <u>look</u> like an Italian boy!   Margaret

Tuesday 19th January We left the Arsenal at 11 o'c for Castellammare, sailing briskly with a favourable wind. We were about half way, when a gale came down from the mountains right in our teeth. We were rolling and tossing so unpleasantly that Papa ordered the ship to be turned. We had scarcely gone 100 yards when our jib was torn to shivers; we had just taken in its tattered remains when the flying jib comes down with a crash. To prevent further calls upon Papa's purse strings, he ordered Panzera to run with the wind and in a couple of hours the *Sibilla* was anchored quietly in her old resting place, the pretty port of Ischia. We are glad to be there again.   James

The party thus seems to have arrived in Ischia by chance, but there they remained – until August. Lessons were an important part of the routine, on every day except Sunday. Rooms were hired on shore so that classes could be conducted 'without the disturbing noise of the piano'. They usually lasted from 10 o'clock to 1.30 and so took up a major part of the day. Sunday was a 'holyday', when best clothes had to be worn, not only by the Close family, but also by the crew. While the latter went on shore for mass, a family service would be held on board and JC would himself deliver the sermon, on subjects such as The Benevolence of God, the Omnipotence of God, the Omniscience of God, etc. Another series was on the History of the Jews:

> **Sunday 13th March** Our usual service at 11 o'c. Papa's lecture was No.10 on the changes and phases the Jewish nation passed through, from the time of the patriarchs to the advent of our Saviour, a period of 1,600 years. He gave a sketch of the religious beliefs of the Egyptians, Chaldeans, Hebrew Patriarchs, Greeks and Romans, and the chaos in religion and politics and languages which existed in Jerusalem at the time Christ commenced his ministry.   Papa

These sermons lasted about twenty-five minutes and were sometimes in French; rather surprisingly, since this year JC had started off the Journal in Italian – and his second language, he maintained, was German. Psalms and Hymns would be sung. References to these services, as well as notes on JC's own devotional thoughts, appear throughout the Journals and are an ever-present background to the children's education.

The following highlights of the family's stay in Ischia are on a subject-by-subject basis, not chronological.

The Bath Chair Expeditions

16th January Mama went to the house where she saw the unpacking of Papa's Bath Chair. [*She seems to have visited the flat twice in this period, mainly to make inventories.*] She is very much pleased with it, but Papa declares he will never put his foot in it, that he will not be made an invalid of. Mama on the contrary says he will like it so much that he will never be without it.   James

27th January Lessons over, lunch accomplished (we all helped Papa to finish his stewed kidneys), Mama's proposal for an excursion to the crater near Barrano was carried by acclamation. The Bath Chair and three donkeys were soon in readiness, and fifteen souls landed at the steps of the little Church of Port Ischia. In a few minutes Papa was settled in the chair: a double rope was strapped to the front, and six little ponies yoked themselves to it, neighing, snorting and pawing the ground with impatience for the start. We soon ascended to the aqueduct, thence descended towards Barrano – rough stony roads were no obstacle The cottagers came forth to see the Carnival fun! Some accompanied us; all were glad and pleased. The crater was attained in a couple of hours. A curiosity! A giant bastion! We returned by the new unfinished road across the great stream of lava – the three donkey drivers shouldering the chair across the impassable part. And so we returned at sunset to a cheerful happy dinner table, which we all enjoy when Papa is well enough to tell his stories, and when his gout has left him.   Papa

29th January [*Three of the children take their pony Sambo, which two days earlier had been shipped over from Naples, on a trek to buy stamps.*] The road crosses the stream of lava thrown up by the last eruption 450 years ago; the stream, which in some places reaches the sea shore, is half a mile wide. Mr. Meuricoffre's house *La Mandra* is built at the foot of the lava: he has purchased a slice of this 'lava land', a mile in length, planted it with pines and other trees, and made a carriage drive right through it. His example has been followed – the whole stream has been bought by various proprietors and is in various stages of cultivation.   Mama

On another expedition, Sambo was yoked to the Bath chair:

10th February All being ready, we landed after lunch. Papa gave the word and off we went, to the amusement of the village. The Palace garden gate being opened, Papa went up the hill to the Palace. Unyoking Sambo, he tried the descent without using the Shoe. A dangerous experiment, for the Chair rushed down with increasing violence, until it became unmanageable. Down it flew and rushing though the Gates into the road, lodged itself against some young trees and the opposite wall – most luckily without damage.   Papa

Occasionally JC would use Sambo, originally bought for the children, as a substitute for the Bath Chair. Anne Eaden described the scene:

JC was tall and spare and Sambo, a glutton for food, was as round as the proverbial pippin. On their expeditions ashore during summertime, both wore straw hats against the Mediterranean sun. The pony's model had ear-holes bound with coloured braid, and a parti-coloured pom-pom was stitched to the high, cone-shaped crown. JC's hat, though large, was more conventional.

Afloat, the pony was stabled in a padded loose-box against bruising and was fitted with a padded sling to enable him to keep his feet in rough weather.

❧ *Gardening*

20th February Directly after lessons and even before lunch was over we all went on shore to hire a piece of ground. We found a suitable spot for 5 francs a month. We have planted potatoes, but Margaret and Mama say they will not be ripe before we go. However, potatoes are very necessary in a garden and we shall plant other things as well.　　　　　　　　　　　　　　　　　Mama

30th April We have had new potatoes during the last ten days. John brought in the first dish from the children's garden, planted by themselves. Papa was delighted to see them. Fred had the impudence to ask him to celebrate the auspicious day of New Potatoes by giving us a holyday. It was no go.　　　Papa

❧ *Mending the roads*

Just three of a number of entries on the subject of road-mending are given below.

Sunday 20th March After dinner we boated to Casamicciola and walked through the village and half way to Furia on the upper road. As usual, the village boys and girls accompanied us, gathering flowers and heaping the bath chair with them. Papa told them he liked services better than flowers, and telling <u>us</u> to clear the road of the stones and volcanic embers which obstructed it, the village boys and girls seized the hint, running before, collecting the stones and making the way straight and smooth. Whereupon Papa gave them a couple of francs to be divided among them according to the activity and goodwill they displayed.
　　　　　　　　　　　　　　　　　　　　　　　　　　　　　Papa

26th March This day had been fixed upon by Papa some days since for carrying out an idea of his which has greatly excited our curiosity and interest. By the shameful neglect of the parish authorities of the island the roads from Port Ischia in every direction are encumbered with large stones and cinders thrown out of the vineyards by the proprietors as the readiest way of clearing their land, and partly also by the rains carrying them down from the mountains, converting the roads into water courses. The movements of the Bath Chair were seriously impeded. It was in vain that Papa applied to the *Sindaci* to repair and remove the obstacles. So he made up his mind to do it himself – hoping that the sight of himself and the whole of his family working on the high road would make a noise in the island and shame the inhabitants to a better disposition to do something for the common benefit. Having made his arrangements beforehand, he left the *Sibilla* at 6 o'c in the morning, followed by <u>all</u> of us children and Charles.

Mama, the three women, Mr Davenport and six seamen were under orders to join us at 9 o'c after breakfasting on board, and to bring with them our breakfast. On landing we found four donkeys with panniers, spades and picks, Pasquelino, his brother and six boys from the village waiting for us, also Sambo and the Bath Chair. Papa ordered each of us five boys to select one of the village boys as an assistant, to stick to him and make him work. Papa mounted his chair with Tom as postilion, and Grace for his guide, and after two words of instruction to the group, started at walking pace, surrounded by his little army of stone-gatherers, some collecting them into heaps, others piling the big stones on the tops of the walls on each side or filling the panniers and leading the donkeys to places where the panniers could be kicked or tipped over and emptied of their contents. It was an animated scene, for everyone worked with a will. The weather was sunny and beautiful. Before 9 o'c we had cleared a good mile of every stone which encumbered the road, so that when Mama came up with her party and with the seamen as a reinforcement, she was surprised at our progress. She brought with her the breakfast bell, the tinkling of which sounded like a harmony in our famished ears. Work was knocked off for half an hour. Hot coffee and milk with eggs and ham and bread were served out in a wood close by, old Sambo and Lion being of the party. The donkey-men and boys had loaves of bread distributed to them, and we were then soon ready for our second 'pull'. Papa now sent the women and us boys forward to clear the road, he bringing up the rear, pulling up projecting stones, filling up the holes and the crevasses with men armed with shovels and picks. The work was heavy, for the road was almost impassable. Many cartloads of stones were removed, the inhabitants stopped to look at the busy group and the countrywomen, on passing Papa seated in his chair and as busy as any of us in directing our movements and sometimes indulging in the luxury of removing a stone which had been left behind, approached him with a "Dio vi lo rende per il bene che ci fate." [*God reward you for the good you are doing us.*]

By one o'clock another half mile was finished. Papa knocked off work. A huge marmite of macaroni had been preparing in a cottage for the donkey men and boys; and our dinner of capons and a roast leg of mutton with potatoes in their jackets with sundry bottles of wine came up from the ship and under Mama's management were disposed on the side of a rock of lava commanding a splendid view of the sea and the mainland. Papa now laid himself full length on the grass; he began to show signs of fatigue – but the lovely scene, the good humour which prevailed and the leg of capon, washed down by a tumbler of excellent Ischia wine (2½d. a bottle) restored him. Our six seamen were now ordered up, and it is satisfactory to think that whatever might have remained of the capons, mutton and wine was not wasted. The hour was up however and we still had a mile of road to clear. By six o'clock all was accomplished and the party returned by detachments, Papa bringing up the rear. On reaching the port Papa assembled the donkey-men and boys round his chair, classified them into good, middling and lazy workers, paid them each according to his merit, and for once received the thanks of every one.

Papa

By mid-April a two-mile stretch of road had been properly repaired, enabling JC to use it without difficulty in his Bath Chair:

3rd May The hammering of the caulkers over our heads was too much for any of us. It caused books and boxes to jump out of the shelves! So Papa said he would give us a holyday. By a holyday he meant a good twelve-hours hard labour at road mending. This time it was a serious affair. John [*now aged 14*] was put in command at six o'clock in the morning. The first use he made of his momentary power was to engage 48 men, women and children, in short all the tag and rag that presented themselves and were willing. When Papa joined us (John, James, William and Frederic), he was stunned with the bustle and noise. He first placed ten of them under John. Then ten under Jim, and ten more under William, sending them on a distance before each other, with orders when they had finished their section of 100 yards to pass each other and set to work at a similar distance. Fred [*aged 9*] had five men assigned to him. Papa remained with the rest in the rear, finishing up and filling and smoothing the road. He complimented us on our steady work. He says that we and Grace were the busy working bees of the hive, Mama and all the rest of the party were drones. They did nothing but join in the picnic dinner, and perch themselves under the shade of the trees to enjoy the scene. After dinner papa received a kick from a passing mule on the calf of his leg, which was more serious than we thought. However he was lifted on Sambo again and remained with the 'forces' until the rain and the setting sun stopped further work. The drones had long before returned on board. When Papa reached the port he had to be helped from the pony and almost carried on board, where he went to bed immediately – he had been badly bruised. John had fallen from a mule, landing on his 'seat of honour'. Tho' we teased him, it was no joke to him: he went lame, but still stuck to his work to the last. As to Grace, Papa says she is a brick, and Fred is sure one of these days to be Commander in Chief somewhere. The caulkers finished the deck this afternoon.

Papa

❧ *Shooting*

Musketry and the use of other firearms had for some time been part of the boys' training:

21st and 22nd January John and James's guns arrived with a few parcels from England. Papa says that he will not let them shoot at every little bird that they see.   James

26th January John, James, Charlie, Mr. Feldman [*a tutor*] and Panzera went off after lunch with their guns in the hope of finding a woodcock – they returned empty handed. Mr. Feldman's gun burst while in the act of shooting: he escaped most fortunately with only a slight bruise on the forehead and the loss of one eyelash and one eyebrow.   Mama

28th January Mr Feldman's eye being inflamed from the gun accident, Mama put two leeches on his temple.   Mama

9th February Mr Feldman is leaving for Naples on account of a boil or gathering on his forehead, a consequence of the bursting of the gun.   Mama

Tuesday 12th July Mr. Wreford, *The Times* correspondent, with Ricciotti, the youngest son of Garibaldi, called to see Papa. They went with him to see us practice pistol shooting. Margaret shot into the bull's eye twice.   John

❧ *Hardihood*

Living on a boat was hazardous, and the children were bold, adventurous and indifferent to danger. It is not surprising that they often suffered accidents, almost on a daily basis; but even with the primitive medicines of the time, they always recovered. Injury and pain were born without fuss.

22nd March Annie [*now seven*] feeds Sambo, who follows her about like a dog. She enjoys a canter, but Sambo in his hurry to get back home forgot who he had on his back, and changed his canter into a gallop. Annie stuck on valiantly until Sambo was suddenly brought to a stand by some soldiers – whereupon Annie was jerked to the ground, without being hurt, however.   Mama

23rd March Tom got a ducking near the canal. He lost his balance and went in head first. He gained his feet in a minute and as the water was not deep, he helped himself out and was sent on board laughing at the excellent joke.
                                                                                     Papa

24th March James fell from the studding sail boom slap into the sea, amidst the jeers and laughter of the crew.   Papa

6th July James in bathing near the *Sibilla* dived down to the bottom 14 feet deep. John, not liking to be beaten, took a header and dived down, and to the astonishment of all, brought up some mud.   John

8th July Annie fell down some three months ago on the root of a fallen tree. She scratched her leg, but Mama did not think her much hurt. Since then she has complained of a pain in her leg. Dr Sim when he saw it thought there must be some foreign substance under the skin, but Mama assured him that the skin had not been broken. Mama while changing the poultice this evening saw a black point protruding and pulled out a splinter more than half and inch long.
                                                                                     William

The last entry quoted above was one of the first by William, now aged eleven. As will be seen in a later chapters, he did not waste his early training in keeping a diary.

❧ *Garibaldi, princes, brigands and Pompeii*

The next entry shows how quickly JC, along with the rest of Neapolitan society, had come to terms with the enabler of the new regime. Since Garibaldi's entry into Naples in 1860, he had attempted to march on Rome at the head of a volunteer force. In contrast with his arrival at Naples, he met with resistance, and to prevent fellow-countrymen fighting each other he forbade his men to return fire and surrendered. As they walked down the hill, Garibaldi was shot in the foot. Imprisoned, he was later released and paid a visit to England, where he was fêted. It is unfortunate that there is no better report of his conversation with JC than that recorded below:

Sunday 19th June A day to be noted in the history of our monotonous life in Ischia. Early we had notice of the arrival of the Duke of Sutherland's yacht outside the harbour, Panzera being sent for to pilot her in. At ten o'clock she appeared outside the entrance, and cautiously advancing she entered and down went the anchor within thirty yards of the *Sibilla*. We saw nothing like a Duke or a Duchess on board. Passengers certainly, but of a riffey raffey looking sort. Blakiston saw something red, dirty red, but certainly not a lady. Panzera at last returned and told us that General Garibaldi was on board and had come for the waters of Ischia.

[*Later, after prayers and a sermon from JC on the life of Christ ...*] a message from Garibaldi took Papa on board, where he remained talking with him at least an hour on all sorts of subjects, but chiefly Denmark, United States and the state of Italy. Garibaldi said his leg was troublesome; the wound had re-opened and his doctors had recommended 20 days of the mineral waters of Casamicciola. Papa sent him *The Times* and half a dozen of the latest Naples papers as well as a fine dish of strawberries.

The Duke and Duchess of Sutherland were friends and great admirers of Garibaldi. When he had made his triumphal visit to England in April they were his London hosts, and subsequently brought him home to the Mediterranean. Presumably they had lent him their steam yacht *Ondine* for his stay in Ischia.

Also on this same Sunday two young Russian princes – Prince Georg and Prince Serge, the sons of the reigning Duke of Leuchtenberg – with whom the boys had become friendly, came to dine:

The eldest took his seat by Papa's side as a matter of rank, and amused him with anecdotes of the Emperor of Russia and the Emperor Napoleon III, who had shown them all attention in Paris. Amongst other things he assured Papa that he knew his cousin, the Prince hereditary of Russia, well, and could answer for the untruth of the report of his marriage with the sister of the Princess of Wales. He was not surprised that Napoleon had had a ducking in his pond at Fontainbleau, for he had seen him in his punt sail across it with an umbrella for a sail. He spoke of his mother the Grand Duchess, calling her 'Mama', saying that she was an admirer of the talents of Napoleon. He asked Jim if he still liked the Poles. "To be sure I do" said Jim. "Do you (poking him in the ribs several times)? I hate them." Jim answered "If I were to die for it, I would still say I like the Poles." When he rose from his place, the prince went up to Mama and with a graceful bow thanked her for the excellent dinner.   Papa

Tuesday 5th July At 9 o'c the Duke of Sutherland's yacht steamed out. It is going to take Garibaldi's son Menotti to Caprera. [*Menotti, like his father, had also been wounded in the battle of Aspromonte. Caprera was Garibaldi's island home off the east coast of Sardinia.*]   Grace

15th July [*Mama had taken a party across the bay of Naples to shop at Castel-lammare.*] Provisions were shipped to last the sailors four months, principally biscuits and macaroni. Castellammare is a dirty, noisy town, filled with dirty looking sailors. But when the town is once left behind the place is pretty. The hills are dotted over with houses, many of which are hired by the merchants of Naples for the season, for as the railway arrives here at all hours, when their work is over they come to spend their evenings with their families. But the brigands have kept many away. They told us that it is not safe to go farther than Quisisana (the King's Palace); so it is impossible to take any donkey rides in the beautiful woods. Mama took us all in the boat along the coast towards Sorrento. She landed to walk on the high road, but we all said we should be taken, for it was only about a month ago that 10 carriages were stopped and all the people taken up into the mountains, and all this done in the middle of the day by a band of 100 badly armed cowards who might have been put to flight by a few determined soldiers.

Margaret

Sunday 17th July [*Still in Castellammare, they discussed what time of day it would be best to visit Pompeii.*] It was decided that it would be cooler to visit Pompeii under a midday sun, when it would be ventilated by the sea breeze, than in the early morning, or coming without any breeze to disturb the calmness of the sweltering dogday heat. So after a short service, Papa having excused us his usual lecture, we landed in two boats, and mounted three carriages, each drawn by three horses abreast.

We first visited the amphitheatre, then returned in the carriages to the town of ancient Pompeii. Papa was our Cicerone: and being well enough to walk, in few words he explained the marvels of this surprising memorial of 2,000 years ago. The public baths recently discovered surprised us by their extent, and by the completeness of the arrangements. These baths and the general construction of the houses prove how much more water was valued in those days than in these.

We lunched in the circular bath. Seated on the marble flags, with the step inside for our food to rest upon, we occupied the whole circle. We then inspected the groups of relations recently discovered, which are almost perfect. Also the models taken in gypsum of two other groups showing their forms, dresses and the positions in which father, mother and daughter died of heat and suffocation. It is a piteous sight.

Emerging from the Herculaean Gate and descending the Street of the Tombs, we were glad to regain our carriages.

Papa

❦ *Normal pastimes*

A typical week is described in the following six entries, written by various children:

Sunday 12th June We had prayers at 11 o'c. After dinner Papa took us to

Casamicciola to visit the Baron de Nyvenhein and the two Princes of Leuchtenberg and Colonel de Blitz. Mama has not taken a walk since Grandpapa's death.

John

Monday 13th June Mr. Blakiston had a bite from Lion and fainted. After dinner
Mama took Mr and Mrs Zumpt from Berlin in the boat to Casamicciola. Henry
and Mr Feldman are busy with photographs.

William

Wednesday 15th June In the evening instead of taking our usual walk Margaret
undertook to make some strawberry jam. It ought to have been done in 20 minutes, but having put too much sugar into it, we let it boil one hour and a half. We
then poured it into the pots, though it was too liquid.

Charles Gaskell

Thursday 16th June After dinner John and James had a sail in the two boats.
Papa now always writes on deck, being too warm downstairs. The flies are a
positive nuisance, they sometimes drive Papa out of the ship.

Grace

Friday 17th June After dinner Henry, Blakiston and Margaret, with the former's
revolver, went where the girls take their bath to shoot at a target. Margaret shoots
very well.

John

Saturday 18th June At 5 o'c we sent on board the Italian steamer to know if Mr
and Mrs Auguste Meuricoffre had arrived and being answered in the affirmative,
we accompanied Papa in the gig to the Mandra [*their Ischia house*] to visit them.
We spent an hour in their garden under the trees and returned to the ship with
them in their ten-oared boat. They took tea with us, after which we mounted on
deck to enjoy the cool breeze and splendid moonlight.

James

Monday 4th July In the afternoon Charley and John visited the castle of Ischia
with Panzera and Captain Clark, the Captain of the steam Yacht *Undine*. We
went to the top of the castle and had a most beautiful view of the island; we
returned at about 8 o'c just in time for tea. Captain Clark came on board just as
we had finished and soon after we heard a rush and then a bang and saw a rocket
shoot into the air. We went on deck and soon after many rockets and fire-works
were sent up from the *Undine*, then the whole of the ship was illumined with
red, white and blue lights. All up the masts and out at the bowsprit men were
holding the lights, then they all struck up with 'God save the Queen', which we
joined in from the *Sibilla*. Then we gave them three cheers which answered and
re-answered by us. We were then invited by Captain Clark to see the sailors
dance the hornpipe and various other dances and in the intervals they gave us
songs. We were all very much delighted, particularly as they wound up with

dressing up as Irish and knocking each other about. At last we said goodnight to all of them, for it was past 11 o'c.   Charles

Friday 29th July After tea Mama, Margaret, Henry and Miss Coventry [*a lunch-time guest*] embarked in the gig to take her home, but as soon as they pushed off, a furious gale arose, they went to the lighthouse to see if they could go, but it was impossible, the sea was too rough. Miss Coventry remained a prisoner, a bed was made in Charles's cabin, he sleeping on deck. All the boys usually sleep on deck, they bring their mattresses on deck and lay in the stern in a row, they find it too hot down below.   Grace

9th August We did our lessons on deck with Henry as usual. We start for Toulon this evening; it was a quiet night with scarcely a breath of air when we weighed anchor and glided away.   Charles

There is no earlier reference to the departure, but in effect this was JC's farewell to Naples. He had lived and worked there from the age of twenty. He was prepared to return to Naples as usual later in the year, but nevertheless planned to spend part of the coming cruise house-hunting in France. Was France considered a better retirement home than Italy? Unlikely, in view of JC's known attachment to Ischia. More probably it was that political and social factors made him increasingly uneasy living anywhere in the vicinity of Naples, and as his business was running down, he no longer needed to be there to run it.

JC's concerns about Naples were well expressed in his 1859 letter to Thomas. The English had helped The Two Sicilies in the Napoleonic wars by destroying the French fleet in the Battle of the Nile and they were well received by the Bourbon Court. The Cavaliere and his wife took part in this social scene. Now, with the situation in other parts of the peninsula still unsettled, enemies of the Bourbons were extending their influence and many of his old friends had departed. Further fighting in adjacent States was predicted and later JC maintained that the situation would be extremely volatile when Napoleon III withdrew his troops from Rome. 'It was a good time to leave Italy', he said.

1864: *Toulon and eastwards*

THE ROUND OF FAREWELLS before the 1864 late summer cruise was more assiduous than usual and included visits to or from friends not hitherto mentioned. This was just as well, as the Closes were not to return to Naples until the following April, and then it was only to clear up and close down the apartment, pack, and make the arrangements for the transportation of all their possessions elsewhere.

One monument to the Closes that was left behind was the family vault in the Protestant Cemetery. There were the tombs of JC's first wife Henrietta, who died in 1836 aged twenty-six; brother John, who died in 1842, aged forty-four, and JC's mother Mary, who died in 1849, aged seventy-eight. JC had had the vault adorned with stone carvings by Tito Angelini, the best known Neapolitan sculptor of the day, whose carvings can still be seen in many Neapolitan churches.

The year had been marked for Anne by the death of her father, Samuel Brooks. The Cunliffe Brooks Bank was now run by her brother, William Cunliffe Brooks, who from 1869 to 1880 was to be a Member of Parliament, and who later became a baronet. William had no sons of his own and was later generous in offering positions in the bank to his sister Anne's sons. He lived on a country estate in Cheshire, which his nephews and nieces would often visit.

This year the intention was to sail directly for Toulon.

Thursday 11th August In getting up, we felt the ship rolling and near Zannone. Papa ordered the captains to go into port at **Ponza**. The wind was right in our teeth so it was difficult to get in. Panzera took the rudder and the Captain was on the bows telling him when to tack. We anchored at 11 o'c. After dinner we hired two boats (as the gig and dinghy are getting painted) to fish. We caught one fish, wind blowing hard. Giovanni and the Parroco sent us two baskets of Indian figs [*prickly pears*] which we relished.   John

Friday 12th August The Parroco came on board with some friends. Papa bought a great many Indian figs to supply us with fruit for the journey. At night it blew hard, and we felt glad to be safely moored in a safe port.

The day did not pass without our recalling the hopes and dutiful wishes which with hip-hips and loud hurrahs and champagne we have for so many years commemorated. It is Grandpa's birthday! Grandpa, Whalley House, the deer, the gardens, the swinging gate! In a word, the <u>home</u> we felt we had in Manchester. All gone, like a dream never again to be a reality. It seems as if our best and biggest anchor had come home, a main stay had snapped, our mooring block had disapeared. Dear Mama feels it deeply, clings to Papa and thinks of Whalley House.   Papa

Saturday 13th August After dinner the children went out fishing and got a great many fish and Papa and Mama went to the Parroco. It blew again in the afternoon. The children have got the pricks of the Indian figs into their hands and Annie has eaten too many, she does not like to look at them now.   Will

Having left Ponza, they had a relatively uneventful trip. On the 15th they 'passed the Roman coast and could make out the dome of St Peter's with the help of the glass'. The next day there was no wind, so JC 'ordered a sail to be put into the sea in order that the boys might take a bath in this beautiful blue sea'. When Hyères came in sight, the improvement in Charlie's health since they were there last year was noted: 'Is that the boy who looked so pale and delicate and when the sun was shining brightly, was allowed to take a short walk on the esplanade? Why, Mama, there he is without a hat, his breast bare and no shoes or stockings on, and the sun has gone down this hour!'

They reached **Toulon** on Sunday 21st August.

Sunday 21st August At three in the afternoon we sailed past the 'Guard Ship', which is at the entrance of Toulon harbour. We are now anchored in our old berth near to the large hulk which serves as a prison for the galley slaves. Some five hundred are shut up there for the night and during the day they work in the Arsenal. There are many large war iron clad steamers in the port. The Emperor's steam yacht, the *Aigle*, is lying near to us – she looks in perfect order.
Charles

Thursday 25th August Permission was given to moor the *Sibilla* to one of the buoys, and as the terrible wind of yesterday had subsided, the men were set to work to get the anchor up. It was not to be. It has fastened itself on to the great anchor of the Hulk and broken away from the windlass. At Papa's request Admiral Viscount de Chavannes sent us a lighter manned by sixty forces [*men?*]. They soon grappled both anchors, raised them both, then hooking on to the great one, slackened off ours, which fell to the bottom clear and was soon brought alongside the *Sibilla* and slung to her bows. When the work was over, one of the galley slaves came on board to offer on sale some of their knick-knackeries. Of course we all bought.
Charles

Divers' suits were at a primitive stage of development:

Friday 26th August Fears being entertained that the *Sibilla* had sustained damage under her keel when she drifted on a sunken rock in the bay of Baja last year, Captain Chasteney kindly undertook to send a government diver to examine her. Accordingly, shortly before dinner a tug steamer brought a lighter along-side. When properly secured, one of her men was dressed in a complete suit of waterproofs. On his shoulders was placed a heavy piece of iron plating resem-bling somewhat in shape a breastplate of olden days; onto this was screwed a large iron helmet with three large glass eyes, the centre one being fixed from the outside so that it could be fitted on at the last minute and the man deprived of fresh air for the shortest time possible. To the back of the helmet was screwed a long flexible pipe, the other end of which communicated with an air pump. There was also an outlet for the bad air to escape. His feet were placed in large shoes, with leaden soles; two heavy lumps of lead were then secured, one on his back the other on his chest. When thus equipped, the directions as to what part of the ship's bottom he was to examining were given to him, his mouthpiece was screwed in, and he descended into the water as far as his waist. [*By means of a rope passed under the ship he was able in three four-minute dives to ascertain that all was sound.*]

Margaret

Lessons continued in harbour as regularly as at sea. A typical morning is described:

Monday 29th August On one side under the long awning, a long narrow table posed on cross legs covered with a well-worn black oil case, with inkstands run-ning down the centre, and well covered with books, papers, rulers and copy books is presided over by brother Henry, grave as a judge, scaring away nonsense not only by his looks, but worse than looks, by fines, readings in a loud voice and by algebra. Margaret, Grace, Charlie, John, James and Will formed his class and filled the sides of the table. Mama takes Fred and Annie to their reading and spelling on the opposite side. Papa with his writing desk near the helm absorbed in newspapers, correspondence and accounts. Down in the cabin Mlle Naudin flourishing on the piano, as much as to say "Who's turn is it? I am waiting". At 11 o'c Henry gives the boys half an hour's drill with muskets by way of headrests. He then abdicates his chair in favour of Margaret, who professor-like gives us an hour's exercise in French and Italian, reading and dictation. The morning's work concluded by a sum in arithmetic set us by Papa.

When the weather is fine and the sea is blue and clear we wash away our school impressions by a plunge headlong from the bulwarks. All of us swim, girls as well as boys; even Tom plunges in with the rest and paddles his way, puffing and serious, to the companion. Dinner bell rings at two, and in a few minutes we are dressed and each at his place at table.

Papa

Tuesday 30th August We had just finished breakfast when Viscount de Chavannes, Port Admiral, came on board and invited us to take tea with him tonight. We accepted the invitation. The boys with Henry fished on the buoy. At 7 o'c we went on shore to the Viscount's and spent a very pleasant evening at the prefecture. It is a large house built in the French style of 50 or 60 years ago, situated at one side of the square *Champ de Bataille.* Two rows of Plane trees line the square. A band of music plays from 8 to 10 every morning. All Toulon seems to turn out to listen to the music and breathe the fresh air.   James

On his return from a seven day visit to Hyères with Margaret and Charlie, JC wrote in the Journal:

Wednesday 21st September I am not satisfied with the manner in which this Journal is kept. Instead of exercising your minds and your memories, you seem to fancy that a mere dry statement of some occurrence of the day is sufficient. Some of you are old enough to show an interest in the daily proceedings of our yachting life, to take an account of what is passing generally – in short, to recollect matter worth being recorded. I must insist on some painstaking.   Papa

The great majority of all Journal entries from August 1864 until it ends in 1865 are by one or other of the children. As JC had commented earlier, Grace's were the best. The others are not as feeble as he makes out, but too often all the authors were scraping around for something to say, as one day was not sufficiently different from another. This explains the large time gaps throughout this section between the entries selected.

Thursday 29th September The *Sibilla* had hauled to a buoy opposite the Imperial Building yard. A crowd of spectators had assembled there to see the launch of an iron clad 240-gun frigate called *La Savoie.* [*Italy had ceded Savoy and Nice by treaty to France in 1860.*] Papa with John and Grace had accompanied Commander de Chastenet to see the arrangements, the knocking away the timbers, the blessing the ship with holy water. They then took their seats next the Admiral Préfet, M. de Chabannet. At 11½ o'c the Admiral gave the order and in a few minutes the *Savoie* glided smoothly into her element amidst the shouts of the multitude, music playing and flags innumerable. On she sped in the direction of the *Sibilla.* The prefect said 'she will be on her'. 'No fear', I replied; 'the *Sibilla* will slacken off'. I had scarcely said the word when she moved from the buoy and fell back so as to be in perfect safety.

    At six o'c Uncle and Aunt descended into de Chastenet's ten-oared gig, called here a *Balenière*. After presenting each of us with a gold piece of £20 and after an affectionate farewell from Papa and Mama, Margaret, whose things had been packed in the morning, followed them, having received her Father and Mother's blessing. Henry accompanied them to the station. There still being half an hour, Mama after tea put on her shawl and bonnet, ordered a boat, and presented herself just in time at the station to give them a last farewell. They left at 8 o'c in the evening.

Papa

The following entries, up to 9th October, are comparatively uneventful, but depict a typical week at Toulon:

Friday 30th September The piano recommenced at six, and our lessons followed their usual course. The wind was very high and we were obliged to have a sail put, to keep the wind from blowing our papers and books into the sea whilst we were working. Poor little Annie had not been at all well today. She has a very swollen face which Mama thinks arises from her having caught cold; she has been very good and patient, but has suffered much pain and was obliged to stay in bed; Mama made her hold her cheek over a jug of boiling water which has lessened the pain and soothed her to sleep.

Charles

Saturday 1st October At 7 o'c a Roman ship of war entered the port, we think she has come in to be repaired. At dinner Papa gave us an interesting lecture on the Pope's life. [*Pope Pius IX, or Pio Nono*]. After dinner Mama, Grace, Miss Esner and Henry went to St Mandrier, but as soon as they reached La Grosse Tour, Mama dared not face the wind and sea, so we turned tail and came on board, whereupon Henry and Grace took a walk round the walls of the town. In the afternoon the boys landed at the Murillon and at the Champs de Mars had a famous game of football. In the evening, to keep the boys quiet, Henry proposed a game of vingt et un, which the boys agreed to most willingly. Annie passed a very bad night and Mama was obliged to stop by her bedside. She is suffering greatly, but we are astonished to see how patiently she endures it. Little Thomas misses her greatly, for they are always together and never leave each other, he sits on her bed and tries to amuse her.

Grace

Monday 3rd October When John and James got up at 5 o'c they hardly could see, so they ordered a carcelle [*lamp*]. It was raining cats and dogs. We did no lessons for these reasons. 1. The piano is in the drawing room where we write when we cannot write upstairs, and that is going and making a terrible noise. 2. Fred shouting to Annie or bawling out 'Mama, Mama, tell Johnny not to talk to me', then after a space he again calls out 'Mama, Annie won't play nicely.'

3. It is horribly dark tho' it is 12 o'c. as the awnings have been lowered on both sides so that it makes the drawing room dark. 4. Annie [*now recovered*] and Tom shouting, laughing and running up and down the rooms, so that if any stranger were to come on board he would be pretty soon frightened out of the ship. At 4 o'c it cleared. In the evening we had a game of vingt et un pour passer le temps.

James

Tuesday 4th October Nothing but rain and wind. Today is a Spanish Feast and the Spanish man-of-war was dressed with flags. She fired three salutes during the day.

William

Thursday 6th October The same weather consisting of wind and rain. Henry's time is up for giving us lessons and we all regret it. It is not often you find a brother who will teach his younger brothers and sisters. We received a telegram from the tutor that announces that he will be here tomorrow.

Grace

Friday 7th October Professor Meibauer arrived at 7 o'c. He had been to Hyères and finding that we were not there, he returned. Papa and Mama were on shore the whole morning buying provisions and store room supplies, preparative to our sailing from Toulon. At 1 o'c Papa sent a telegram to London for money in Billets de Banque.

Grace and Papa

Saturday 8th October We were able to have a good stare at our new tutor. He seems mild, considerate and patient. Rather gentlemanly; he speaks English fairly, but slow. We had a holiday, so we took him for a sail in the gig. We clubbed together and took a couple of boxes to see a French comedy. There was much excitement all day as we were <u>all</u> going. It was dark when we shoved off, we in our monkey jackets as the evenings are growing cold. Grace had on a red shawl. We were well stared at in the theatre. Between the acts we drew the whole house.

Papa

Sunday 9th October Papa received a sealed letter before breakfast. It contained the Billets de Banque he had telegraphed for on Friday. It is wonderful. Whilst at breakfast we heard the roar of cannon at a distance outside the port. We soon found it was the French fleet returning from Tunis, and engaged in a sham attack on the batteries of the Murillon before entering the port. Papa ordered out the cutter, and in a few minutes we clambered up the hill amidst the batteries, and were spectators of the beautiful scene. The day was magnificent. The ships were all steamers; iron plated and wooden ships assorted. They seemed to fight in circles, sailing round, discharging broadsides and sometimes rolling fire at the forts.

Papa

Friday 14th October At noon we received a note from M. Thomas Andrieux from on board the *Eldorado* transport ship inviting us to see a live crocodile and other wild animals just arrived from Egypt and which were to be sent by rail this evening to the *Jardin des Plantes* at Paris. Papa went with us. As we descended the companion to the ship's deck the scene was most extraordinary. Twelve hundred passengers, chiefly sick soldiers returning from China, were making preparations to land. Boxes and parcels and sailors and passengers, mostly unshaven and unwashed, crowded the deck. It was difficult for us to thread our way, nor could we have done so, had the habitual politeness of the French not made way for us. The first animal was a gentle Llama, which licked our hands. Then a huge stork, then a bare-headed vulture tearing the entrails of some animal, then some anxious domestic poultry. On the opposite side lay the crocodile, about seven feet in length, in a wood trough, half filled with water broad enough to hold it. It could not turn or move and remained still, as if it were dead. Near it in a case was an African rat, as big as a rabbit. Alongside two white storks from the Nile was a large cage containing a splendid full-grown but young 'royal tiger', with a middle sized dog for its companion. Strange to say the dog was master. They had been brought up together as cubs, but the dog had attained maturity while the tiger was still a cub in disposition and yielded to the dog.

  Of the passengers, six had died on the passage from Alexandria and there were twenty more who M. Andrieux said would scarcely survive their removal to the hospital. We remarked several Chinese passengers in their peculiar round, hand-basin calico hats, excellent for the sun and for rainy weather.   Papa

After two months based in Toulon, orders were given on 14th October 'for sailing after the arrival of the two o'clock mail'. No explanation is given, nor any indication of their plans. It emerges that they were to sail east, along the southern coast of France. On the day of departure:

Panzera bought three days' supply of fresh provisions. At four we let go the rope which held us to the buoy, and accompanied by Commander de Chastenet, we threaded our way through the ships of war. We gave him a salute of three cheers, and proceeded on our voyage to Cannes.   Papa

Sunday 16th October At sunrise we found we had still made little progress. We were becalmed in the bay of Hyères. After dinner, we all came on deck. The sky without a cloud. Sunset. The near and distant lighthouses. The moon rising as the sun left us. The crew singing in chorus and dancing to the music of a harmonium. Even Papa made a step or two to show that if he chose he could still beat us all at waltzing.   Papa

Monday 17th October A little wind, but favourable. The view was magnificent as we cut through the blue sea. We were all delighted to see green in the mountains, so long wished for during our stay in Toulon. Lessons were given up and books put away. The boys joined the sailors in pulling the ropes and we glided slowly into the bay, until we entered the port of **Cannes**.   Grace

Henry went ashore and returned with letters, newspapers and some buns, advising the rest of the party to stay on board, as the wind was blowing so hard that it had filled the town with dust. Nonetheless JC and Anne had a stroll through it in the evening. Next day a new timetable for lessons was laid down, with JC taking part by giving an hour's tuition every morning in English, French or Italian, and by lecturing on the history of the islands opposite the town from Roman times onwards.

Tuesday 18th October After dinner we were ordered to dress cleanly for our first walk in the neighbourhood. It abounds in beautiful villas, some fitted up for hotels, some for private lodging houses. We walked along the high road to the West. It is agreeably undulated, lined on both sides with English-looking villas and gardens. We passed the French evangelical chapel and further on, on the brow of a hill, the English chapel in the gothic style, neat and pretty. Further on we came to an iron gate with a straight avenue of olive and orange trees leading to a handsome colonnaded villa. It was Lord Brougham's! [*Lord Brougham (1778–1868) was the founder of Cannes as a resort for the English. He also espoused a number of causes, such as the Reform Bill and the abolition of slavery. He founded London University and defended Queen Caroline during her trial.*] We walked up to the balustraded terrace in front. A young girl asked if we would like to see the inside. An elderly female steward showed us the library and the receiving room, which was comfortably fitted, but not richly. There were two pictures: one of Cannes as it <u>was</u>, when Lord Brougham first made it his residence, the other as it is <u>now</u>. The people say that Lord Brougham <u>made</u> Cannes. Further along the road on the side of the sea, we came to another villa built by a wealthy sugar refiner of Marseilles. A beautiful specimen of house architecture, superior far to Lord Brougham's. The house and garden kept in perfect order. The owner has nine children and twenty-seven grandchildren, who occupy the villa during the winter season. The owner himself, a M. Ronsvalle, only stays a month in it every year. Lord Brougham's grounds seemed neglected, weedy and in poor order. The Frenchman's were all that even an Englishman could desire.   John and Papa

Three days of rain followed, confining the family to the ship. Charlie's entry for Friday was 'A wet day'. JC wrote on Saturday that he was too prolix in his account of yesterday's proceedings. He might have spared time by just writing 'Wet'. In his own hand he added 'Is that all Charley? Think again! Charley! Charley! It is Margaret's birthday!'

It was not until Sunday that the rain stopped. The family went ashore for Service

> ... in the pretty gothic chapel on the road to Toulon, named Christ Church, built and fitted at the expense of Mr Woolfield, who after Lord Brougham has done so much to beautify and popularise Cannes. This chapel is simple, but entirely comfortable. The seats were all free to the first comers; our party being large (in all fifteen) took possession of three open-sided pews opposite the reading desk. To our surprise the chapel was nearly filled.   Papa

Everything about this first proper tour of the town appealed to JC. Not just the Woolfields, not just the chapel, the service (even the thanksgiving for the recent rain!) and the music, but much of the rest of the town as well.

The Woolfield family were later to become great friends of the Closes, replacing the Meuricoffres in that capacity. According to the Close family papers, Woolfield was responsible as much as Brougham for the growth of Cannes and the attraction of the English to that resort during the season (i.e. winter). Today the credit for developing Cannes from a fishing village goes to Brougham, who had bought a tract of land there in 1838. But it was Thomas Woolfield who had obtained permission from the French government to build, at his own expense, an Anglican Church on his own land. He also built houses nearby for selling and letting; he was a knowledgeable gardener and fruit grower and introduced many new species to the area; and he had a croquet lawn for the game recently introduced to the area by Queen Victoria's youngest son. In 1876 he converted the lawn into the first tennis court in Cannes.

After dinner on the same Sunday the family explored another area of the town and it is clear that, even though he had his full entourage with him, JC was already house-hunting:

> Having procured a horse for Papa, we all set off for a walk to the East side of

Cannes on the road to Antibes, which skirts the sea shore, opposite the islands. No end of excellent and well built villas; well fitted and furnished, of all sizes and styles, though chiefly of balustraded Italian architecture, like Kiddington Hall [*home of Anne's sister Alice Gaskell*]. The prices vary from f.5,000 to f.10,000 <u>for the season</u>, say from 1st November to the end of May, and an additional quarter of the price if for the whole year.   Papa

Monday 24th October After dinner we all went to see a house, which is just being finished, and situated on the west side of Cannes. After seeing it, Papa called on the Rev. Rolfe, who said that the west side of Cannes was drier and more healthy than the east side, being higher. Many of the villas on the road to Antibes are built on low marshy land, cold and wet in winter, tho' pleasant enough in the spring.   Grace

Rain again spoilt the next few days, although there was quite a bit of socialising with the family of one of the priests and with the Woolfield family, where a Miss Grey, who already happened to know Charlie, was staying.

Tuesday 25th October Wet. No visit to the islands, no holiday! Excepting for lucky Charlie, who marched off after breakfast to spend the morning with Miss Grey! Papa and Mama started off to call on Mr Woolfield, but a heavy shower drove them back. After dinner Mama proposed a walk, inviting those who had mackintoshes or waterproofs to join her. [*They all got soaked.*]   Mama

Thursday 27th October A fine day at last. At breakfast Mama proposed a walk to the village Le Cannet, about three miles distant; we were glad to have a holiday. Henry told James (who is his adjutant) to get the camera, sticks and triangle for he said he would accompany us and photograph. Charlie went off to Miss Grey. In the road Henry took two photographs of Cannet, one of a bridge and some ruins, which we thought picturesque; half a dozen of us grouped ourselves so as to be taken.   James

On Monday 31st October the entry starts: 'A fine morning, slight breeze – just enough to carry us out of port. Charlie went on shore to fetch Miss Grey, who is accompanying us to **Antibes**'. As usual, no hint of any planning behind this move is given, but the inference is that any houses seen had not been satisfactory, that the initial favourable impression of Cannes had been dampened and that they were now going to look elsewhere.

Tuesday 1st November When we got up we found ourselves anchored safely at

Antibes. The port is a very safe one. The town is strongly fortified. After breakfast Papa gave us a holiday. We visited the town and walked a mile to the Antibes
lighthouse which is situated on a high land jutting seawards from whence you
can see Nice and the islands of Lérins, or the islands of St. Honorat, on one of
which the Iron Mask was detained a prisoner eighteen years.   James

In a later account of the events that were to follow, JC claims that after visiting the
lighthouse, orders were given for sailing to Naples, but that bad weather detained
them until the 8th.

On 4th November JC went ashore to get provisions, which were running low. It
had not been thought, according to Grace's entry for that day, that 'we should stop
such a long time on our road to Naples'. On the same day he had been to look at a
house – but of that, no more is written. It can be seen from the Journals that for
some time JC has been on the lookout for a house to buy – casually to begin with
and then more and more intensively. At the start of this search, he certainly did
not have Antibes in mind, but since he had been constrained to stay there by the
weather, he did continue his search there.

Tuesday 8th November Papa and Mama accompanied by Henry with his photographic machine went to the bay of Juan to see a house. Papa was not pleased
with it. In the afternoon Panzera announced that a grand carriage was waiting
to convey Papa to see a house near Antibes; they returned in the evening. Grace

This obscure and minimalist entry by Grace (then aged sixteen) is the first indication of the development that would change all their lives. Also on 8th November
the crew had been ordered to prepare *Sibilla* for her return trip to Naples. Panzera
had been ashore to stock up and other crew members had been collecting from
the town laundry and other items left for repair. The village became aware that
the Closes were about to depart. But the mysterious 'grand carriage' was to keep
Sibilla and the family at Antibes for a long while yet.

CHAPTER VI

Antipolis

❧ The deal

G RACE'S ENTRY the next day, 9th November 1864, is more informative than that
quoted at the end of the previous chapter, although she herself was unaware of
the machinations behind the events she describes:

> Soon after Papa had given us our lesson the carriage of the Comte de Fersen
> came to fetch Papa and Mama to see a property – he was enchanted with the
> place. It seems that Lord Brougham had come here, and was going to buy a prop-
> erty, but could not agree the price, so he finally took up his residence in Cannes.
> In the afternoon one of the proprietors with his wife and daughters called on
> Papa. In the evening a great crowd had collected astern – nobody knew what it
> was. The city band began to strike up on the quay – a rumour had got abroad
> that Papa had bought a piece of land and was intending to build upon it, and
> that they were thanking him for being the first English family who were going to
> reside here. The proprietors were envious of Cannes, and wanted Antibes to be
> like it. Papa at the end addressed a speech to the *Chef de la musique* and to those
> who had collected on the quay.

The family had been moored at the town of Antibes since 1st November. Continuous rain had kept them mostly on the boat, although the boys had run around
the ramparts of the famous *Fort Carré*. In other ports JC would have renewed
friendships or at least called on the officials he had met on previous visits, but
this was his first time in Antibes. Perhaps he was waiting for somebody to call on
him. Only once did the whole family visit the town – on 6th November. By 8th
November they had decided to leave. How JC and Anne were persuaded to change
their minds about returning to Naples within the space of a few hours would be a
mystery if we had only the Journals to go by, but fortunately the answer is provided
by two other sources. One is a half-mocking article written and published two
years later in *Phare du Littoral* (Lighthouse of the Coast) by V.-Eugène Gautier.
It is headed *Comment on devient parrain d'une ville* (how to become the spon-
sor – or godfather – of a town), and deals with the episode from the point of view
of the *antibois* citizens. The other source is by JC himself and written well before

Gautier's piece – some time early in 1865. It is a more concise account of the proceedings and is much the same story, except that it is told from his point of view – so we have it from both sides.

First, most of Gautier's article is given below. The translator of the high-flown style is Suzanne Knowles. He begins by detailing the arrival of the family at the beginning of the month. He lists the names of the parents and children, mentions JC's dealings with the Bourbons but exonerates him from being tarred with their brush, saying that 'the Chevalier was by temperament dedicated to the splendour and welfare of towns, and even more so to the welfare of the poor'. Then:

> **The ascent of Notre Dame** The *Sibilla* had just left the port of Cannes. During their excursions round the Mediterranean coast, from Naples to Toulon and Marseilles, and vice-versa, the Close family had been struck by one particular place, and that was the Cap de la Garoupe. The more often this point was greeted from the open sea, the more it aroused the curiosity of its admirers. Finally it was decided to make a climbing expedition.
>
> Under the porch of Notre-Dame the chevalier expressed himself overwhelmed by the view of the eternal snows, of the high Alpine peaks and by the enticing girdle formed by the spurs of the Alpes Maritimes.
>
> Nothing escaped him: the majesty of the sea, the picturesque charm of the Golfe Juan, the inspired irregularity [*la sublime bizarrerie*] of the Estorils, the originality of the Cap de la Garoupe, the splendours of the steep slopes of Eze and Monaco, the picturesque distant silhouettes of Menton and Bordighiera.
>
> The excursion having proved interesting and steady bad weather having set in, the *Sibilla* remained at anchor.
>
> During the days of this enforced stay Mr Close's children came ashore several times to play in the ditches of the ramparts, but the crew, commanded by Capt. Louis Panzera and those who were employed on the yacht were only in contact with the townspeople for the purpose of buying provisions. This reserve, this incognito on the part of the Close family, meant that the citizens of Antibes had no choice but to show an equal reserve, however much they longed to offer a warm welcome to their guests from the sea.
>
> **A musical gesture** Nevertheless, on Sunday 6th November they relented slightly. The Philharmonic Society was due to give a concert in the Place de la Colonne between two and four in the afternoon. A programme was sent on board the *Sibilla*. This delicate little attention won over the Chevalier, he came ashore with all his family to hear the harmonious performance given by this gifted group of musicians led by M. Baptistin Roubion.

The population of Antibes was filled with admiration at the sight of this handsome old gentleman with his thick white hair and long beard blowing in the breeze. They were even more charmed by the sight of Mrs Close's face, serene with kindness and beaming with intelligence. And what a joy to see these beautiful lively children, good and straightforward, so attractive, forming a motley crowd around their parents: half of them were in sailor suits and the others in ordinary clothes.

The English family attended the whole of the concert, showing signs of the greatest pleasure, and left amid every mark of respect and deference. Mr Close, who spoke French correctly, paid the highest compliments to the Philharmonic Society, which for some years now has represented the civilization and hospitality of Antibes.

The order to set sail At last on Tuesday 8th November the sun rose brilliantly in a clear sky. With imminent departure in view, certain members of the crew visited the town to buy provisions, at the same time collecting all the goods that had been left locally for repair or cleaning.

These preparations for departure made quite an impression: there was a sense of sadness and discouragement among those who on the Sunday had been so taken by the sight of the Close family at the concert. Some maintained that if only they had performed the duties of hospitality and the customary marks of *antibois* deference more courteously and adroitly, it would have been easy to keep the well-to-do visitors. Others, going a good deal further, went so far as to say that the municipality was at fault for being such a stickler for etiquette and for respecting a reserve which the chevalier himself would have been only too happy to have broken. It was due to the natural delicacy of all good *antibois* in the presence of foreigners, with whose customs they were not completely familiar.

A good idea Joseph Raboutat exclaimed to anyone who would listen to him: "We have beautiful land to sell; we invite foreign visitors to come to Antibes by means of publicity, and yet there is not a rogue in the place who makes any attempt to go and see them and make them an offer! Françoise the washerwoman lamented the fact that she had lost good customers. M. and Mme Hugues and their young ladies, clever people, always so thoughtful, so obliging to foreigners, lamented everyone's ineffectiveness and inactivity.

"Do you know what ought to be done?" exclaimed Mme Bontemps, suddenly inspired. Her husband had just returned from Cannes, where he had gathered all sorts of information about the Close family.

"What?" chorused the despondent group around her.

"Well, the plan will be to send the family a polite invitation to have a look at our neighbourhood and to see all over the Cap."

"Too late!" cried a despondent doubter.

"No it's not too late!" replied Mme Bontemps heatedly. "I had it from a reliable source that the Close family, apparently wishing to settle in this part of the world, had been exploring Cannes and the surrounding countryside with a view to buying land. Our own neighbourhood is just a beautiful as Cannes: why don't we press Mr Close, who is also an Englishman, to do for Antibes what Lord Brougham has achieved for Cannes?"

Mme Bontemps' eloquence carried even the least hopeful, the most undecided, the timid. They went to find M. Paul Bernard [*manager of the Land Association Company*], but he was out, and so M. Giraud, the café proprietor, was appointed messenger in his place.

Before approaching the Closes, Giraud looked for someone more important than himself to go with him, and eventually persuaded M. Drevet, an architect, to do so. To add still more weight, they added Paul Bernard's name to Drevet's visiting card. They then went down to the quay, and signalled to the *Sibilla* that they wanted to deliver an envelope. A boat was sent to fetch them and at the foot of the ladder up to the deck, JC signalled to them to come up to the bridge, but either they were too humble to do so, or they preferred to leave the Closes to study the proposals set out in the note. They returned to their friends in the Place de la Colonne. Within half an hour a reply to the invitation had been received by Paul Bernard at the Château Salé. Giraud and Drevet had gone there to explain it:

The barouche that proved irresistible M. Giraud had hardly said ten words before M. Bernard understood the value of the idea that had been brought to his notice. "M. Fersen's carriage [*that which had been sent on 6th November: Count Fersen, its owner, was President of the Land Association*] has been sent out empty for a drive: go and look out for its return", he said to M. Giraud. "When it comes, tell the coachman to go and wait in the porch opposite the *Sibilla*'s moorings. In the meantime M. Drevet will set up an exhibition of his plans on all the available tables and stands in the chateau."

Just as M. Giraud was leaving the carriage in question turned up, the barouche was given a quick cleaning, the coachman put on his best livery, M. Giraud sent for his best black suit and his gloves and they arrived at the port.

The Close family was at dinner. The captain of the *Sibilla* was given to understand that the carriage was for Mr Close. It would seem that M. Giraud's telegraphy was very effective since, having briefly consulted his family, Mr Close came to this conclusion: "It must be some great noble who has sent us his aristocratic equipage and lackeys; we can do no other than respond to this chivalrous gesture".

What led Mr Close to suppose that this was indeed a gallant gesture on the part of some local notables was the fact that this time no name had been sent on board. It was only M. Giraud's animated gestures that convinced and decided the English family. Was it to offer the Château Salé to rent? Was it just simply good manners? Such were the questions they asked themselves. It was not long before Mr and Mrs Close came ashore and took their seats in M. le Comte Fersen's beautiful équipage. Maître Giraud opened and closed the carriage door with a fine flourish and took his seat beside the coachman, making a very pleasant impression on the Close family. Never had the Chevalier seen a footman, bearded, so smart, so polite, so respectful!

Reception at the Château Salé The carriage set off at a gentle pace along the road to the Château Salé. The first person the Close family encountered was M. Paul Bernard, who led the wealthy foreigners to the first floor, where they cast their eyes on the plans and drawings with which the tables were covered. "We are told that you recently visited various parts of the town and district of Cannes with a view to residing there with your family. Our intention in getting you here is to ask you to have a good look at the Cap d'Antibes and the surrounding countryside before leaving port." M. Bernard went on to explain how the Society of United Landowners was organised, then with great eloquence explained the advantages of the properties available. In particular, he drew Mr and Mrs Close's attention to the fabulously low prices of these in comparison with what they had been asked to pay at Cannes for a property neither better nor worse situated. He hinted that even better terms could be obtained if the Close family were prepared to back Count Fersen's plans and efforts.

Mrs Close, sharply questioned by her husband, and entreated to do so by M. Bernard, decided to postpone setting sail for Naples.

Exploring the Cape The next day every part of the Cape was visited. Captivated by the beauty of this enchanting peninsula, Mr and Mrs Close negotiated for the purchase of 176,000 square metres of land, which they had outlined in pencil on the map.

It was now that one of the most praiseworthy acts in M. Bernard's whole career took place. In outlining the boundaries of his domain Mr Close had included ground belonging to a number of other people, some of them members of the Society of United Landowners, some not; in short, there were people not unwilling to make a large profit from the sale of uncultivated land included in the area which Mr Close now wished to buy. It was then that M. Paul Bernard, by pleading, bargaining and appealing to the public interest finally succeeded in obtaining everyone's consent.

One more antibois family The contract was not signed until the 8th December. That day an *antibois*, whose name I withhold, exclaimed, using the colourful language of an old sea dog, "We have caught that fine big salmon James Close in our net. We have landed him." This might at first appear to have been an unseemly remark but we have been re-assured by Mr James Close himself, who enjoyed recalling it and bringing it up in conversation. Instead of saying; "I am ready to put my name to these proposals" he laughed, indicating that he hoped the salmon was cooked to their satisfaction. The day that the contract was signed was a day of rejoicing for Antibes. There were banquets, toasts, songs in every corner of the town. Spontaneous expressions of gratitude and appreciation broke out in the most polite and affectionate way. The air was full of rejoicing and schemes for the future. The Philharmonic Society performed again. In short, 8th December was a glorious date for Antibes.

And that is how Mr Close became the godfather of Antibes, after having lived in Naples for forty-five years. Why, a year later, did the hand of fate plunge into mourning this population, who were so happy to have such a powerful protector whose vast intelligence encompassed all its needs and who concerned himself always with its prosperity and future?

Here is JC's version of these events, which he called 'rough notes':

On the first of November 1864 the yacht *Sibilla* entered for the first time the port of Antibes. After visiting the lighthouse, orders were given for sailing to Naples. Bad weather detained us until the 8th November, when orders were given to provision the ship. On that day a M. Drevet, a Parisian architect, sent his card on board.

After dinner a hansom carriage drove up to the stern of the *Sibilla*. The coachman was in livery. The footman in black. We were invited to visit the Château Salé and the carriage was there to convey us. No name was given and the object could only be surmised by us. Perhaps to hire the Château, perhaps a mere civility. Mrs Close and I deliberated. We finally decided to accept. The Laquais touched his hat, opened the carriage door and mounted the box. The fiery horses drove through the town and in a few minutes, passing through a pretty garden, we pulled up at the Château Salé.

A gentleman met us at the door and politely invited us to walk up stairs. We followed, glancing right and left at the accommodations of the house as we ascended and on the first floor entered a large room. There we found several gentlemen with a table covered with maps. The gentleman who met us below now addressed us. [*Here Paul Bernard delivered the speech already quoted by Gautier.*] In consequence of these representations we consented to defer our departure and to view these lands, which we did on the following day.

The result has been that on 8th December, after many deliberations, and frequent visits to the Cape, we signed the contract in the presence of notary Chauvin of Grasse and notary Beranger of Antibes, whereby in the name of Anne Close, we became proprietors of 176 [*thousand*] square metres of land at the Cape. A map is annexed to the contract.

The land was measured by the engineer M. Bestgen of the Association. It was measured twice over and compared with the official measurements of the documents, from which it differs but slightly and that in our favour. [*This is about 43½ acres, big enough to have a road built across it, an avenue of trees and several houses and gardens in addition to the Close mansion. The exact area purchased is marked on the map shown opposite.*]

The price for the land is at the rate of 25 centimes per square metre, rough and smooth. To which must be added however five more centimes per metre, which I spontaneously offered as a contribution to the completion of the road to and at the Cape [*the road from Antibes town to the Cap organised by Fersen.*]

The purchase of this estate greatly excited and rejoiced the town of Antibes, as it looks upon this first sale to an English 'settler' as an era in its hopes of progress. We received congratulations from all sides, were serenaded by the amateur music band of the town and expressions of goodwill and kind welcome from all quarters were gratifying to us all.

As this Journal is intended to transmit to my children an exact history of the incidents and proceedings of this estate and of the cost of erecting a house and of the improvements we contemplate in the value of the property, it may not be uninteresting to record the incident which led to our availing ourselves of the handsome équipage and to our visit to the Château Salé. For it is to this visit that we owe the great change we contemplate in our removal from Naples to establish our domicile in France.

During the ten days which elapsed from our entry into the port to the day we went to the Château Salé we had received no visit either from the mayor of

Antibes nor from any of its inhabitants. Being strangers and knowing no-one, we had no claim to any such civility. When the weather permitted, the whole family visited the town, its fortifications and environs. Doubtless so numerous a family of children in their sailors' attire, myself with my white beard, and the general regularity, health and harmony amongst us impressed the inhabitants that we were 'well-to-do' in the world and respectable.

Now there is a shop in Antibes managed by an active and I believe very respectable man of the name of Hugues with his wife, two daughters and son in law. It is a provision shop and greengrocers. He undertakes to supply yachts and private families with their daily requirements and I take this opportunity of saying he does it well, obligingly and fairly.

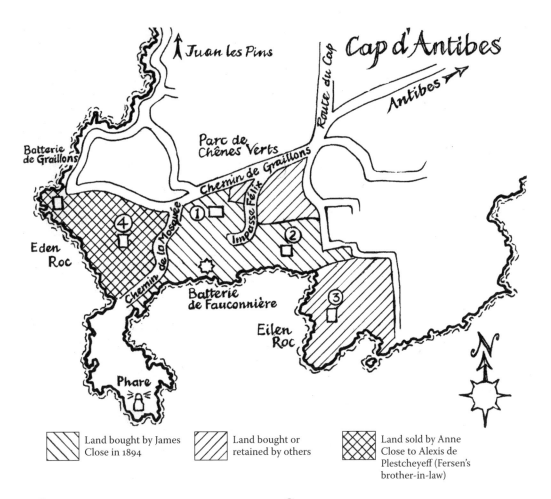

Land bought by James Close in 1894

Land bought or retained by others

Land sold by Anne Close to Alexis de Plestcheyeff (Fersen's brother-in-law)

① Château Antipolis (later Résidence du Cap)
② Villa Closebrooks
③ Villa Loudon
④ Villa Soleil (later Grand Hotel du Cap)

It was Hugues's son-in-law, M. Bontemps, who then learnt in Cannes of the Closes' house-hunting plans; and Mme Bontemps who planned the charade that followed – all much as described by Gautier and not therefore reproduced here. JC's account ends:

> Each had his part to play. M. Paul Bernard had to collect the proprietors, the architect to prepare the maps and the plans, the coffee house keeper undertook to be *Laquais* And so prepared, that fine "salmon" James Close was caught and netted and landed at Antibes. And thus it happened that after 45 years residence at Naples he is become a Proprietor at Antibes.

Until the end of 1865 the story is once again told from the Journals, either with extracts quoted or by summaries. First will be given all the entries concerning the building of JC's ideal retirement home. In the middle of this will come an account of the family's last visit to Naples and Ischia, saying goodbye to their friends and closing down the flat. At the end of the chapter will come all the entries on the off-site activities of the family, both before and after the Naples interlude, from the time they first arrived in Antibes.

🦅 *Construction*

FROM THE EVIDENCE of these two documents, it seems that although at some point the *antibois* plotters had hoped to sell JC the Château Salé, which had been rejected by Lord Brougham, the Closes had decided to buy instead a large area of land and to develop it from scratch. JC made his major decisions jointly with Anne, not only because they enjoyed working together, but also because most of the purchase price must have been paid with Anne's inheritance: this is borne out by the fact that Anne and not JC was registered as the buyer. They decided to name the main building on this plot 'Antipolis', the Greek name for the settlement there in the fifth century BC. The project was on such a scale that within a year two hundred men were working on it. JC involved himself closely with every aspect of the construction and was in overall command. Antipolis is henceforth the main centre of his interests. During the construction process, the family base was the *Sibilla,* moored near the *Fort Carré* in Antibes, while the building site was on the tip of the Cap, some six kilometres away. JC visited it every day, by sea, on horse, on pony or – occasionally – on foot.

Below are such extracts as can be gleaned from the Journals on both the bargaining stage and on the construction process, often written by one of the children.

Thursday 10th November We landed at 'Antipolis', a second Cannes (in imagination) – at present there is not a house to be seen. Papa showed us the place he would select to build a house if he were to live here, that is in front of the Gulf Juan: a splendid view, more magnificent than the Bay of Naples.   John, written by Anne

Sunday 13 November At 11 o'c we started off to Antipolis, Papa, Mama, Annie and Tom in a carriage and the rest walking. Papa walked about to try to find a site to build a house, he thinks he has settled on a suitable spot.   Charles

Sunday 20 November Papa put stakes to mark the ground.   John

21 November The architect was on the ground measuring the land. Mr Woolfield from Cannes shortly joined us. He said Papa's proposed purchase was a good one. He has been living in Cannes these 20 years and has increased his fortune very considerably by his land purchases.   James

29th November On Papa's return [*from a visit to the Estate*] he gave orders to get up anchor. During dinner we heard the sailors singing whilst drawing up the anchor, which we liked, for it is always a sign that the ship is returning home, and that they will soon see their families. Papa gave us the news that there were doubts about concluding the bargain for the land, because the owners could not agree, and that in two days we might be on our way to Naples. [*Later that day the Sibilla sailed out of the port and, becalmed, they admired the sun setting on the Alpes Maritimes.*] At sunset the wind failed us just in the mouth of the port. Our friends the fishermen of Antibes sent out three of their boats to tow us in. The town is most anxious to secure us. [*Was this near-departure an elaborate ploy by JC to force the hand of the landowners?*]   Grace

Thursday 8th December Papa and all the proprietors have signed the contract of the land on the Cape; and Papa has bought it. [*In fact the purchase was in Anne's name.*]   Charles

December 9th On the day following the signature of the contract, we thought it 'the right thing' to write a polite letter to the Mayor of Antibes communicating the fact and sending him f.500 to be distributed to the necessitous of the town. Count Fersen, being too ill to leave his room, wrote to congratulate me, as did several others.   Papa

The role of Count Paul de Fersen in the opening up of the Cap d'Antibes to the outside world is underplayed in the Journals, and nowhere is there any explanation as to who he was. A Russian aristocrat, he had been *aide de camp* to Tsar Alexander II. (His father, an admirer of Marie Antoinette, had helped to arrange the escape of the French King and Queen during the revolution, but although in disguise, the pair were recognized on the way out of the country and taken back to Paris to be guillotined.) Just as other Russian aristocrats had played a part in opening up Nice to visitors, so Fersen, arriving in Antibes in 1863 (only a year before JC), planned to do the same for Antibes. He moved into the magnificent *Château Reynarde*, which had three tiers of balconies and balustraded steps leading down to the street. Later demolished, it was just to the North of the *Chemin des Combes,* in what is now a busy part of the town.

Aged only thirty-five, Fersen saw that now was the time to open up the town and the Cap. Until 1860 Antibes had guarded the point where the frontier of France had met the sea; but in that year the border had been moved East to its present position. The batteries of guns all round the coast of the peninsula and the heavy ramparts hemming in the town no longer served any useful strategic purpose: it was the time to build more welcoming features for newcomers. Within a year of his arrival Fersen had organised an Association of Landowners and persuaded them to agree to build and help pay for a vastly improved road from the town to the tip of the Cap. They also bought up plots of land on either side of it, with a view to selling them to new arrivals. Within another year most of this anticipatory road – five kilometres of it – had been completed, much of it financed by Fersen himself. (As has been seen, JC also made a contribution.) The cost of the road was 80,000 francs, but by 1868 2.5 million francs had been brought in by the sale of the adjacent plots.

Nothing could have suited Fersen's plans better than the arrival of the Close family, and it is extraordinary that the Association waited so long with the *Sibilla* at anchor outside the town before any contact was made. As will be seen, Fersen met JC only a few times. He was already ill with tuberculosis when the Close family arrived and he died in April of the following year.

Just as the Journals minimise the part played by Fersen in the development of the Cap, so does the current literature of *Service Archives Documentation* play down the role of JC. The contemporary street namers probably got it right, as the *Rue James Close* is of equal width with the *Rue Fersen*, which joins it at right angles. Both roads were renamed in 1880, the responsible committee including in their justification for the name change that Fersen had himself paid for nearly all *La Route du Cap* and in the case of JC, that at the time of his death there were 300 men working on his '*embellissements du Cap*.'

Returning to the Journal:

December 14th Desired Herr Bestgen to prepare a complete and detached plan of the Estate, fixing the price at f.250.   Papa

Saturday 17th December Map completed. Gave him orders to draw a plan of the Chateau Antipolis based on the design of the house I had intended to build on Zannone some years ago, had King Ferdinand ceded the island to me, as I asked him to do.   Papa

Wednesday 21st December At 11 o'c Papa called on the Mayor and afterwards on Mr Thuret, the son of the Paris banker with whom Papa had some slight acquaintance when at Le Havre. Mr Thuret offered to assist Papa by giving advice how to plant trees. [*More on Thuret later. His gardens are still world famous.*]
                                                                    James

Thursday 22nd December There are every evening conversations between Papa and Mama about the plan of Villa Antipolis. The Moorish style of architecture is at present thought of, but not decided upon.   William

December 28th I sent Mr Woolfield of Cannes f.200 to be paid to the architect Guishard for the building copy and sections of Vanson's new house at Cannes and for which I offered f.10,000 per annum for three years, and the refusal of which led us to conclude that Cannes was already too dear a place for a family like mine.   Papa

Wednesday 18th January After our lesson Papa went to the Cape with Mama to see the site of our house. Papa performed a miracle. He walked from the Cape to the port, about five kilometres, which he had not done this many a day.   Grace

Tuesday 24th January After dinner Papa took it into his head to visit Vallauris, a village celebrated for its manufactory of building pottery, such as tiles, piping, ovens, balustrades, friezes, stairs and many ornaments of internal architecture of great interest both as to economy, durability and artistic perfection. Papa thinks he can make use of many of these articles.   Papa

[*The following March Miss Esner, Grace and John returned to Vallauris by train and came back loaded with Vallauris pottery. Some 40 years later, when Anne*

Eaden went to Vallauris, Clément Massier, who had been there when JC visited, was still there and had become famous for his lustre ceramics. He showed Anne Eaden a photograph of the Close children dressed in their sailor suits and gave her a vase and an ashtray, the latter being a replica of one of a set he had made for King Edward VII.]

Wednesday 25th January Henry went with the architect to the Cape to work out the situation of the shed and building offices for the workmen. It is to be provided with a soup kitchen. Thus the men will not have to return every day to Antibes and will have better and cheaper food. 					Papa

Thursday 26th January Papa has begun to build a sleeping shed for his men to live in whilst they are working for him. 					Charles

Monday 30th January Papa went to the Cape with Mr Bestgen to mark out the road. 					William

Wednesday 1st February Mr Benery called on Papa this morning to talk about asphalted tubes for the conveyance of water. 					Grace

Tuesday 7th February A gardener arrived on Saturday last from Berlin. He is pleased with the work before him. 					Grace

Saturday 18th February 100 men are working at Antipolis and the workmen's shed is up. The gardener from Potsdam, Mr Reich, has completed his plan for the laying out of the estate, of which Papa approves. 					James

Sunday 19th February At noon we went to enjoy the Cape – some by boat, others on foot. The shed is finished, the lime kiln is getting on, and the well on the military road approaches completion. Another quarry has been opened for stone. The two quarries will be converted into cisterns. The great road through the estate has been suspended, as the *contremaître* (foreman) did not satisfy Papa. Tomorrow Mr Agaud commences the two cisterns. The German gardener has traced out the entire estate into various sites. There will be room for about 30 villas, each with a garden. Papa intends the ground to be in common – a sort of Park, studded with villas. 					Papa

Friday 24th February Henry has taken a small house, being obliged to remain here when Papa goes to Naples for two months. Henry is to supervise the works at the Cape during Papa's absence. 					John

The proposed voyage to Naples was to collect and arrange for the shipment of all their possessions. In fact they did not set sail until the beginning of April, returning to Antibes in the middle of June.

Friday 3rd March Papa went on Henry's horse Cadella to St. Juan to visit a land deposit for making mortar. He offered f.25 per annum to take what he might require for the Cape.

Soon after his return Lord de Ros, Colonel Wheatley and Colonel Gordon called on board, and stayed to dinner. They were agreeable and conversationable, as all well bred men are. They enjoyed themselves greatly – so large a family on a yacht was a sight new to them.

Lord de Ros is Governor of the Tower of London, and invited us to give him a call when we were next there. After dinner Papa and our new friends walked through the rich corn and vine fields separated by allées of splendid olive trees, the birds warbling. From time to time the old Lord turned to the view of the bright blue sea, and the snow capped line of coast beyond Nice, and exclaimed "I had no idea of this!" [*After admiring the view of the coastline to both the East and the West, de Ros said*] "No wonder that the place has seduced you! I had no idea that such a spot existed within an hour's beautiful drive from Cannes". We parted at Rapallo's restaurant after wetting our dry whistles with wine at the bottom of our tumblers, filled up with Limonade gazante; a splendid tipple for heated thirsty and dry throats. Lord de Ros is a yachter, he spoke of a sea life like a seaman. He was Lord Raglan's chief staff officer at the Crimea.   Papa

Tuesday 7th March Papa and Henry went to Nice to present an order on the branch Bank of France for f.5,000, a good proportion of which was in gold, with which Henry was loaded, tomorrow being the day appointed for paying over the purchase money of the estate. It seems that Mr Loudon has concluded his purchase of 50,000 square yards of land, which cost him as nearly as possible the amount Papa pays for his 200,000 sq. yards, and Papa's is far superior in quality and situation. [*Loudon, however, went on to build in 1867 one of the grand villas of the Cap, La Villa Eilenroc, a little to the East of JC's – see map. Loudon was a former Governor of the Dutch East Indies.*]

Thursday 9th March The cold has brought down wolves within a mile of Antibes. Count Fersen's greyhound 'Mussett' and Robroy, a Newfoundland dog, hearing a wolf ran after it, the wolf turned round and bit Mussett severely on the hind leg. Robroy is missing. He killed a wolf last winter.   William

Friday 10th March Mr Senelanze, the Director of a large nursery garden at Lyons came over to see the Cape today for Papa wants to know what sort of trees will thrive best there.

Charles

Saturday 11th March A busy day at the Cape. The cutter was manned for Papa and his friends, and we boys manned the Balinière for Mama and her party. Papa's friends were a distinguished horticulturalist, M. Benery [*the brick and piping specialist*] and, wonderful to say, a M. Beciez, a 'Diviner of water springs' by means of an olive switch or twig. With Mama we flocked round the water conjurer to see what antics the switch would play. It was a long one, which he seized by the ends with both hands, bending it in a loop in the centre. We had not walked ten yards before the switch, that is to say the loop, twitched itself clean over – as if it was suffering pain;. it writhed over. "Where I stand", the man said, "there is water". We followed him over the estate and in some places the same twisting and writhing of the twig occurred.

  Papa brought over the horticulturalist. He said the soil was first class, would grow anything. But, he added, you have too much wind and too little water.

  "Just what is wanted", murmured Papa, "to grow healthy, comfortable chimneys".

  "What's that? Is it a tree or a vegetable?"

Papa

JC was telling the horticulturist that he was planning to build houses on his land. Both agreed that the fresh air and breezes would be ideal for convalescents.

  Later in the month water was found in several places, some of which were in the very spots indicated by the water diviner. For the rest of March, other entries concern mainly the activities of the children, while JC himself busied himself with on-site developments.

  From the start of April until the middle of June there is no information about further progress on the site, as the family sailed to Naples to collect their possessions.

✈ *Last look at Naples*

O N S A T U R D A Y 1st April the *Sibilla* set sail, leaving behind only the dog Lion and Henry, who was to supervise work on the château in JC's absence. During the voyage they missed Lion, the 'universal paintbrush', to clean their plates. On the Monday adverse winds forced them to anchor at Leghorn, from where JC took the opportunity to inspect the marble quarries at Carrara. On 4th April they also visited Pisa. After viewing all the main sights, JC wrote: 'Pisa has evidently seen better days. Its population does not correspond with the space it covers, nor with the monuments it contains'.

On Wednesday they were able to leave Leghorn, but progress was still slow. All but becalmed near Elba, they once again visited the iron mines. 'The shore shines like diamonds. We got iron stones of all colours'. While still on the island, after a vain search for meat, they bought 'about 180 eggs and a supply of milk'.

By Saturday they were opposite Civitavecchia:

> At 7 o'c the bell rang, and the men knelt down to their prayers – it is pretty to hear them. It is a custom with Italian ships to join together at sunset in evening prayer. A sort of litany with responses, invocations to their principal Saints and to the Virgin Mary, followed by a prayer for a safe passage, and concluding with a silent prayer in which they call to mind their home, parents and families. Grace

> *Sunday 9th April* In the afternoon a swallow flew on board which we fed on flies which we caught below and let go near it, for it to chase. It invariably caught them and came back for more; it stayed with us for about an hour and then flew North to England.   Charles

> *Monday 10th April* About mid day we hove in sight of Ischia, Gaeta and Vento-tene. The sailors are all delighted to think of seeing their wives and children. After dinner Vesuvius with its smoking top was seen. The wind was strong and favourable and we put out our scudding sails. About eight we were gliding along the coast of Ischia and the moon shone on the island to show us its beauty. All our flying sails were hauled down as we neared port. Panzera on the forecastle with Michele giving the word of command to the active sailors. The anchor was ready in case we could not get in as we apprehended that the entrance to the port would be choked with sand. Down go anchor, sails, boats and ropes and here we are again in the beautiful port of Ischia.   John

On the 12th JC and Anne crossed to the house to check the furniture and arrange for it to be transported on board. On the 13th and 14th they moored at Baia to enjoy the vapour baths and view the temples of Diana and Minerva. The *Sibilla* did not reach Naples until the end of the week, when they immediately linked up with the their Romano cousins and the boys were sent to spend the day with Aunt Paulina.

Saturday 15th April When we went to the house the journal was discontinued and we boys were congratulating ourselves upon being freed from such a trouble. Unfortunately Papa has discovered it and wishes us to write it from the day we arrived in Naples. We were all up early this morning packing up to go to the house. It seemed so very funny to be in a house again where the rooms are big in comparison with our cabins.   James

The following entry for 20th April mentions Uncle Tom: this was one of Anne's brothers, not JC's elder brother Thomas:

At 10 o'c we got in the carriage and went to the Hotel Washington, where we were to meet Uncle Tom and then proceed to Vesuvius. In an hour we reached Torre del Greco, where we stopped and procured some horses and donkeys to carry us to the foot of the cone. The road was very dusty and it nearly choked us.

We lunched at the hermitage, which is half way up. After we had finished, we mounted our animals and in half an hour we reached the foot of the cone. Uncle took a chair for Auntie and the guides made a tremendous row, fighting about who should carry the chair, so Uncle threatened to smash the head of the first man who kicked up a row and this gentle admonition quieted them. The crater was at work emitting volumes of smoke and throwing up stones to a good height. We saw a stream of burning lava fill a ditch.   James

Tuesday 2nd May Jim went with Mama to the dentist and had four double teeth extracted. He was very courageous about it so Mama gave him five francs for each tooth. They were sound teeth, but the dentist said it was necessary to extract them in order to give room for the others.   Grace

Monday 8th May Mama and Papa very busy packing up the silver and crockery-ware to send on board a merchant vessel which Papa has taken to carry all the things from Naples to Antibes. They usually go in the morning after breakfast to the house and come back at 6 o'c for dinner for they are obliged to superintend the packing all day.   Charles

Friday 12th May Papa now sleeps at the house while the furniture is being packed.   James

It was not going to be possible to load all their belongings onto the *Sibilla* and it must have been during this last visit to Naples that JC chartered a merchant ship to take the bulk of them to Antibes. Included in the cargo were eight Corsican ponies, small enough to be referred to as 'the rats' by the children, for whom they were intended. They were unbroken and, as will be seen later, resisted furiously and were never tamed. They were to be responsible for numerous accidents, but the children adored them and whenever there was a fall, it was the injuries of the pony that were the first consideration.

It is clear that the *Sibilla* remained the family's main home, although the children had various invitations to stay short periods with relations or friends. The ship had now been their home without a major break for over two-and-a-half years.

On a one-day visit to Castellammare, the subject of brigands again came up:

> *Thursday 18th May* The houses which are dotted about are uninhabited on account of the brigands who infest the mountains and seize any unfortunate persons who pass. It was well that Uncle Brooks [*Thomas*] did not visit Paestum with the four boys when he landed at Salerno; the next day Baron Bellili and his neighbour, large landed proprietors of Paestum, were taken and £10,000 asked to save their ears and noses and maybe their lives. We now hear that two Englishmen have been carried off while visiting Paestum. Their wives were allowed to return minus their husbands and dreadful were their wailings!　　　Grace

> *Monday 22nd May* One of the Englishmen taken by the brigands has been liberated on condition of returning with money to free his companion. The English consul according to the papers is gone to look into the affair. Another version is that the remaining Englishman made his escape during a fight between the brigands and the troops, in which three of the former were shot. The papers singularly enough don't name the two Englishmen, nor the sum demanded.　Grace

The story continued on 26th May:

> The conversation at dinner was entirely about brigands. Papa says there are only two ways of reducing brigandage: by unflinching severity or by employing the lower orders at good wages at roads and ports throughout the country, forcing by this means the proprietors to advance the miserable wages of their labourers. Papa says it is just the time to leave Italy for there will be a mess when Napoleon withdraws his troops from Rome.　　　　　　Grace

As JC and Anne were so busy packing, the 'no school' philosophy was relaxed to this extent:

> *Friday 21st April* Papa takes advantage of being in Naples to give us lessons from different Masters. We dance before breakfast and from 9 to 2 every day we

attend Dr. Pioggi's school consisting of 16 boys including ourselves. Immediately after dinner we have to hurry off to gymnastics and so we are well occupied the whole day.   William

Nearly all the Journal entries at this time are by the children. These tell not only of the above unremitting lessons, but also of a full round of visits to friends of the Closes and their children. Increasingly, these became farewell visits, culminating with Mrs Tell Meuricoffre (Harriet) having all of them for the day on 2nd June. The *Sibilla* left Naples for the last time on 3rd June, once Sambo (the pony) had been loaded:

> *Saturday 3rd June* After lunch John and James went on shore with John and Tom Romano to see Sambo and the carriage properly shipped on the barge. Once on board, two hammocks were strongly lashed to two handpikes at the extremities; these were passed under Sambo's belly and with a little struggle and a kick, he at last submitted to the operation and then in less than five seconds was lifted from the barge to the *Sibilla*'s deck safe and sound. All this being done, the sails were unfurled and we went down to dinner. When we went on deck again, we found that we were out of Naples, tacking.   James

She was tacking against a gentle contrary wind, and soon became becalmed in the Bay. Two of the boys attempted a description of their last glimpse of the scene:

> Thus twilight crept on and saw us still in the bay. The view was beautiful. Vesuvius appeared in strong relief against the blue of the sky. The setting sun cast a mellow light over the whole bay and rendered it more lovely and interesting. Gradually the moon asserted her rights, casting silvery rays over the scene, illuminating every little dancing wave   James

> The *Sibilla* was motionless. She seemed loath to quit the scene of her past glory. It was thus that the colour and repose of an Italian night quietly stole upon us.
>   Charles

The voyage back to Antibes was soon delayed by a nine-day stop at Ischia, again saying goodbye to their friends and again taking a last nostalgic look at the island. The only mishap was that the ship got entangled in a tunny net, 'which the authorities have permitted to be placed in front of the port of Ischia. This is an instance out of many which we see constantly of party intrigue, the authorities closing their eyes to the abuse for a consideration.'

They left Ischia on 9th June, John's fifteenth birthday. As the wind was still against

them, the ship anchored at Gaeta, the scene of the siege and final capitulation of
Francis II in February 1861:

> At 6 o'c we let go the anchor in the roadstead. Mama and all of us except Papa
> landed to see the ruins of the town. It was dreadful to see the many destroyed
> houses with the inhabitants still buried under them. A mine was sprung in the
> ramparts, and a breach made by a traitor who was the commander of the powder
> magazine. One of our sailors accompanied us. He had served Francis and had
> been five months at work in the battery. From what he saw of the strength of the
> place, it could not have been taken except by starving them out or by treachery.
>
> Charles

> *10th June* Miss Esner, John, Will and Fred went on shore to see the suburbs of
> Gaeta. The streets are filthy and crowded with pigs lying across them. After a
> great deal of delay and confusion we got two sailors. We started at 8½ o'c with
> the wind right in our teeth.   John

> *Monday 12th June* We scarcely made a mile during the night. The rolling was
> tremendous. Breakfast was left to be eaten by a set of hungry boys, we had ham,
> eggs and sardines. For the sick, the things they like best to eat are sardines, eggs
> and jerkins (gherkins). At noon the sick, one by one made their appearance on
> deck, except Miss Esner who is too ill to get up. At dinner we had cherry fritters,
> two full dishes came in which we boys soon finished. When it is stormy or roll-
> ing it gives those who are not ill a great appetite.   William

The rest of the journey was uneventful, and the *Sibilla* was back in her old berth at
Antibes by 14th June.

🐚 *Back on site*

*O*N THE DAY they arrived back in Antibes, Grace records that 'Henry came
on board and talked to Papa about affairs'; and that is all that is known about
Henry's two-and-and-a-half month stewardship of the building operations during his father's absence. JC now resumed supervision of the works, and most days
would leave *Sibilla* for the six-kilometre journey to the site at six a.m. On 20th
June, for example, 'Papa was over the estate between six and eight this morning. At
ten he was visiting the best places for sand supplies along the shore. At four o'clock
he again visited the estate.'

Water continued to be a problem. The asphalt pipes had arrived, the water diviner had found water, but making it accessible was another problem:

> **9th August** Papa went to the Cape on Sambo before breakfast and was not pleased with the workmen. They are making a new well in hopes of getting some good water, as that in the other well is bad.
>
>   William

Later it was decided that a well shaft had to be imported from Naples: 'The ship that has arrived with the *pozzolano* [*volcanic building material*] from Naples has finished discharging.'

The laying of the first above-ground stone was an emotional affair, and gave rise to the only recorded disagreement between Henry and his father:

> **Thursday 24th August** For better or for worse for the family in times to come this day will be long remembered. Papa was all along disinclined to the idea of laying what is termed the first stone of our new home at the Cape. He thought such ceremonies were only tolerable in great public buildings, that in respect to private houses it was an affectation or a pretension. Mama considered it was less the first stone of our home and more the first stone of the Cape, the new 'to be' colony of Antipolis. Papa assented to the ceremony on condition of it being confined strictly to the members of our own family and as a remembrance which in after years the children might speak of, should the Cape ever become of sufficient importance to hold its own between Nice and Cannes. So after dinner a boat was manned for Papa, Mama and the three young ones. Henry declined being present at so shabby an affair. He had advocated a general blow-out to the department with beer, collations and the band of music, tents and awnings and a dance on the foundations, which are now completed. On arrival at the scene we were met by M. Gérieux, the architect and his staff and the sub-directors of the edifice, transport service, Mr. Reich the chief gardener and old Foukes, the *garde champêtre* [*rural policeman*]. An awning was extended over the stone to be laid, supported on poles entwined with evergreens and surmounted by flags. It was a cornerstone, a fine block well cut, suspended to a triangle overhead. Being all assembled and ready, Papa took a trowel (not a silver trowel) and threw under the stone a quantity of mortar. Mama did the same, and Grace, John, James, William, Fred, Annie and Tom followed. Miss Esner then took the trowel and, throwing in the mortar gracefully, said "in the name and on behalf of Margaret, absent". Upon this Will seized the trowel and throwing in another trowel of mortar said "on behalf of my brother Henry, absent". [*Then followed each of the officials mentioned above as well as Mr.*

Dugos the Secretary and Martin, the Superintendant of Transports.] Finally Mr Durbec, director of the works of the Château, in a masterly manner levelled the mortar and gave the final adjustment of it in the centre and four corners. We then all of us laid our hands gently on the stone, which was lowered finally into its place, Papa saying in French "I pray Providence to spare me until this work shall be completed".

   On lowering the stone, an oblong square recess a few inches deep presented itself; whereupon Mama placed in it a sovereign, a Napoleon, a five-franc piece and some smaller coins. The others followed her example with smaller coins, and a square lid of stone was let into the recess, hammered down and immediately covered with mortar. Another large stone was then laid upon the first, and a third over that, mortared and properly adjusted. Papa gave orders that on the outside of 'the first stone' the ciphers 1865 should be cut in deeply. He has given instructions to supply a bottle of good red wine to every workman then on the estate. We all separated and at sunset were on board the *Sibilla.*

By the end of September it was possible to see Nice from one of the towers, a Journal entry states that it would be possible to see the coast on both sides of the Cape when the building was completed. Mr Woolfield, who had just returned to his house in Cannes for the winter, came over on the 29th to inspect progress. 'He has built several houses in Cannes and could therefore give Papa many hints and information with regard to the size of windows, doors, flooring etc. Most of the houses in Cannes have been refloored, the dry rot having got to the wood. Papa is using iron beams.' On 24th October it was recorded that 'The house is getting up very fast. Mr. Reich has made a wonderful improvement in the garden. He has planted new trees and is cutting out roads.'

> **Thursday 7th December** Early this morning the *Sibilla* arrived with 350 plants and trees from Genoa and at 3 pm Papa, Henry and James went to see them. They are very well chosen, and Papa is pleased.   James

Everyone who visited JC and his undertaking was impressed, even dumbstruck, both by the superb views to be seen from the site and by the progress on the building itself. Lord de Ros's comments on the scenery have already been quoted. Mr Woolfield, with far more building experience than JC, admired the construction as far as it had got and Lord Brougham also expressed his approval.

❧   *Away from the site*

B ECAUSE of JC's preoccupation with the building both before and after the last visit to Naples, the children were no longer under his commanding influence every day and were often left to amuse themselves. How they occupied themselves in Antibes, both before and after the Naples interlude, is now told from their Journal entries. Even over Christmas JC had been busy:

> *24th December 1864* In the evening all was peace and quietness: the boys collected in the nursery to arrange the flowers for Christmas day. There was a great bustle setting the tea out. The Captain [*Henry*] toasted the bread, for there was neither cook nor cook's boy.   Grace

> *25th December* Christmas Day was very different to last year. In the morning we rigged the drawing-room with myrtle leaves and nailed the 'Merry Christmas' up in the saloon in front of Papa's door. Panzera busy hoisting the flags, but the wind blew so hard about 9½ that we were obliged to haul them down. Papa read prayers at 11 o'c. [*Friends of JC then came on board at 3.30 pm to dine.*]
>   Charles

> *26th December* Lessons as usual.   James

> *27th December* Raining Cats and Dogs, Papa is all day shut up in his room writing, reading or talking about Villa Antipolis. Children rather noisy.   William

The New Year had begun with a stinging rebuke from JC, written into the Journal:

> It is a source of regret to me, that instead of progress in their observation and intellectual prowess, the concluding months of the last year's Journal indicated indifference and idleness of mind in all my children, except Grace.

There had indeed been some falling off in the standard of the daily entries. This was partly because JC, busy on site, wrote less of them himself. Also, without JC standing over the children, they were more inclined to spend their free time enjoying themselves in and around Antibes. The family were exploring everything their new homeland had to offer; and the rest of this chapter will tell of their many activities on a subject by subject basis, rather than chronologically.

⚓ *Schooling*

> **Saturday 7th January 1865** Papa has taken a house in the town of Antibes – a
> room is to be fitted up as a schoolroom. We are to clear the *Sibilla* of all the
> books and clothing not in absolute use and send them to the house so that we
> shall have storage room for many things on our return from Naples in the spring.
> [*This was the first clear indication that the plan was to move permanently from
> Naples to Antibes. The street where JC bought the house was re-named Rue James
> Close after his death and is still there today.*] Mama

Most of the time the family, except for Henry, continued to live on *Sibilla*,
although some of the boys were from time to time invited to spend a night or two
in Springfield, the home of the Woolfields. The Antibes house was at first used only
as a storage space, but soon it included the new and well equipped schoolroom.
Towards the end of the year Anne rented some rooms opposite, freeing up space
in their own house for entertaining and the occasional night ashore.

Lessons for the children were extended to include dancing and, for the boys only,
drumming – which must have raised the noise level aboard to an unbearable pitch.
Normal routine was, according to James: 'At five o'clock every morning we get up,
take a header in the sea as a kind of washing and get dressed and set to either washing the decks or wetting the sailors or sometimes throwing the water the wrong way
so Nostromo throws us a whole bucketful of water and then we wet him, and anybody who comes, and by 7 o'c which is lesson time, we are so thoroughly drenched
that we have to dress again.'

A more sober and perhaps more reliable account of the rest of a typical morning
is given in this entry, probably by Mrs. Westropp, now back from India and living
as a guest aboard *Sibilla*.

> The boys went off as usual to their schoolroom, which is large and situated under
> the office, in a nice clean street. The room is furnished with cupboards with
> glass doors to contain the books, and various philosophical and chemical instru-
> ments. In the centre is a large round table, round which stand a just sufficient
> number of ancient highbacked chairs, so that the boys cannot lounge in them.
> They are there from 6 in the morning till one p.m. with the exception of one hour
> for breakfast. Mrs Westropp

> **Monday 31st July** Today the boys have been busy taking their books to the new
> schoolroom and unpacking the philosophical instruments that Papa has just
> given them. Grace

Tuesday 1st August At 11 o'c Papa came into the schoolroom and began rowing us so that we are afraid he will soon have gout.   James

Friday 25th August Lessons go on more regularly now, and the ship is left to Mama, Papa and Mrs Westropp. The boys go off to their schoolroom while the girls are spending their time at the house principally in music. They also give lessons to the two little ones.   John

✺ The rudder and Captain Massa

One construction matter that was not related to the château was the need for a new rudder. On 20th February 'Papa and Henry inspected the rudder, which had been unshipped for the purpose. Orders were given to buy an oak tree to replace the stern and inside piece, which had suffered from nearly 35 years of use.' The wood was chosen and cut by 24th February and fitted by 3rd March.

In June a new captain of the crew, Captain Massa, had been taken on. (Panzera continued in his normal role, but at the time of this next incident was on shore, unwell.) Before starting work, Massa dined with the family in August, and a Journal entry commented that he was a 'great swell'.

Wednesday 6th September When Captain Massa joined the ship one of the first things he did was to deck himself out in his naval uniform, epaulettes, sword and cocked hat. Papa's heart misgave him at the sight of so much grandeur. He felt the *Sibilla* was too small for such a tremendous big fellow. Fine feathers don't always make fine birds. Papa was not wrong in his instinct respecting him, for this morning at sunrise, when Papa went on deck to see where we were, he found the *Sibilla* quickly sailing within pistol shot of the Cape, off our property where the low level of the shore indicated a prolonged shoal into the sea. "Massa you are too near the shore. You will be on the rocks". "I think not, sir, it is all deep water". The last word was not out of his mouth when a grating noise was heard at midships, which increased as it approached the stern to a half sort of roar, the ship moving out of the water until for one instant she stopped. A puff of breeze forced her on with a crashing noise at her stern till, suddenly falling into deep water, the [*new*] rudder flew up with a crash of the quarter deck, quitted her hinges and lay astern, floating whilst the *Sibilla* pursued calmly her course through the blue transparent unrippled waters. The Captain took his cap off his head and seemed petrified. Papa said, mind your sails and proceed ahead to the roadstead in front. We anchored, dragging our rudder after us. The Captain then coolly went to bed. In the meantime Papa superintended the re-shipment of the rudder and the restoration of the broken quarter deck; before noon all was in order again. The broken hinge was sent off to Antibes to be repaired.

At dinner the Captain sent a message to Papa to say that he was off to Antibes. Papa's anger was now fairly roused. He confronted the captain and told him that being in an open sea with a broken rudder neither he nor anyone else should quit the ship until she was again moored in the harbour in Antibes. That point effected, in five minutes he should be out of the ship, never to put foot in it again as commander. At the same time Papa ordered the anchor to be weighed and to return in the best way we could to Antibes.   Papa

Thursday 7th September At sunrise we entered the port. The Captain relinquished his command, was paid off and was superseded by another captain who fortunately was at Antibes and only too happy to obtain employment.   Papa

Later the ship's carpenter dived under it to inspect the rudder: the top of a few sheets of copper were damaged, but not seriously.

🐟 *Comings and goings*

Thursday 15th June We were all up at 5 o'c to see Charlie off by the 7 o'c train – only to be told that the 2 o'c train was the one for the Paris train from Marseilles. Dinner hurried, we again marched off to the station, and Charley jumped into a first class. We bid him adieu with regret, for he has become quite one of us.
                                                                                 Grace

Monday 10th July Papa and Mama went to the station to meet Henry and Mrs. Westropp – who did not arrive. They had been detained at the Customs House and just missed the train. Mrs. Westropp has been ten years in India. Mama did not find her much changed. She is a grand daughter of Dr. Mull of Manchester, who was a friend of Papa's father.   Mama

After her visit to the Closes in Naples in the 1850s, Mrs Westropp had continued to record her experiences in her own Journal during her ten years in India. Now she was to spend nearly five months on board the *Sibilla*.

Thursday 27th July After breakfast Papa rode to the Cape on Sambo. Mama and Mrs Westropp went to the house to put up the pictures, and get the house in order to receive us. The two large paintings of Sts Peter and Bartholomew are too big to go through the entrance and so they remain in the stable in their boxes.   Grace

✤ *Social*

At the end of November 1864 JC had spent half a day with Lord Brougham (three years his senior) in Cannes, and in January Brougham paid his first visit to the site, accompanied by J. Garnett, MP for Lancaster, whose father JC had known. The meeting was 'a merry party and a very happy one' and after the inspection, the party lunched under the ilex trees that lined the road on the way to the site. (It is no coincidence that today the bus-stop opposite the lane that leads down to the Château is called Les Chênes Verts.)

> *Tuesday 10th January* A little bustle in the ship indicated that visitors were expected. At 11 o'c Count Fersen's carriage appeared on the quai and Papa went to meet his friends at the station. He returned with Monsieur le Baron and Madame la Baronne Erlanger from Frankfort. A young couple, she beautiful and lively as a lark. They brought their beautiful but sadly spoilt boy with them. After a biscuit and a glass of Marsala Papa and Mama and the Erlangers started in the carriage for the Cape, visiting Mr Thuret's charming garden as they went. We got two boats out and went by sea to meet them. Papa showed his plans and we joined the party, Tom and Annie bounding over the 'brouipaille' to meet them. At last we all joined, and sat on a rock to eat sandwiches which a sailor had brought from the boats.   Mama and Miss Esner

Another of Lord Brougham's visits was written up by Charlie, in his usual ironic style:

> *Monday 27th February* At dinner we were surprised at hearing that Miss Woolfield and the Reverend Took were on shore. We sent a boat for them – they were merely the outriders, announcing that the King of Cannes [*as JC had facetiously dubbed Lord Brougham*] and Mr. and Mrs. Moss of Liverpool were on the road in their carriage to pay a visit to the illustrious King of Antibes. They were soon on board. Papa had the Gig lowered for the 'quality' and we lowered <u>our</u> boat for the 'quantity', which was composed of the young ladies and ourselves, much the jolliest party.   Charles

Although strangers to Antibes, the Closes soon integrated. JC had no difficulty in keeping on good terms with all classes and local dignitaries soon started to visit him. Count Fersen, whose barouche had collected them from the quay for the sales pitch, invited the whole family to his country house on JC's birthday:

> *Thursday 16th February* Papa's birthday and consequently a holiday. Papa has

completed 66 years ... we could have desired a finer day. Cold and rainy. We had all of us prepared a huge Woollen net comfortable for Papa's birth day. It is handsome and of many colours; every one of us lent a hand in its knitting. At noon we went with Mama to Count Fersen's country residence, and had a game of Fox and Hounds. We dined at four and drank Papa's health with many cheers in Champagne, and no one joined in the toast with a heartier good will than Papa himself. He was merry, and so were we all. He has been to Calixte the Hair cutter, and if at breakfast he looked '<u>Dignity</u>' with his white hair and long beard, at dinner he looked '<u>Impudence</u>' all cropped and docked as he was. In the evening we had to exhibit to him our progress in music. Annie led off, then Fred, then Charles, then Will, James, Grace and John. Papa seemed satisfied with us, tho' at last he was sleeping.   Papa

Fersen had three daughters young enough to play with Annie and Tom, who were invited again to his Château Reynarde. His wife had died a month earlier, but when the two families first got together, his children had not been told that their mother was dead. He himself was already ill with tuberculosis.

They went to local dances:

Tuesday 28th February The last day of Carnival. Here at Antibes Carnival is observed and balls among the small proprietors, farmers and citizens of the town are given by subscription amongst the young men, who invite sisters, relations and neighbours. We receive written invitations to attend them. But as none of the "grandest" or pretentious proprietors attend them, Papa seemed little inclined to show himself. However Harry [*Henry*] was induced by the blacksmith to visit the Ball at Gironde's café on Saturday and was so pleased with the order, propriety and the hearty welcome of the young people and said so much about Papa showing himself amongst good people that he promised to visit the last ball, which was this evening. So at half past nine Papa set out with Henry, John, Will and a posse of sailors with lanterns and off they went to the balls. They were met by M. Bernard and M. Ribaudy at the Café and on entering the room were met by the managers, who led them to chairs in the centre. The demoiselles sat around the room dressed in white with coloured sashes and several of them were fairly good looking. They danced quadrilles, Polkas, Mazurkas, Schottisches – and remarkably well. The quadrilles were walked out, just as the better classes do. They conversed and were led to their places, with as much order and politeness as is witnessed in the higher classes. No smoking, no loud talking, no swilling and all excellent dancers. What wonderful tact the French have too! In England such a thing is impossible.

There is however a meaning in all this. The conservatives of Antibes do not condescend to visit these plebeian occasions. The liberals on the contrary make a point of showing themselves amongst the working classes. It is Papa's desire to stand well with all parties, not to affect superciliousness to the one class, not cliqueship with the other, but absolute independence of all. It was easy to see that his presence at those balls gave the good people great pleasure.   Papa

Tuesday 7th March A musical soiree on board, which Papa treated us to by engaging an Italian from Milan to play on a small portable Harmonicoffre (for it shuts up like a box which the man carries under his arm, and opening it upwards like a telescope places it on the floor and it becomes a three Octave Harmonium). He played delightfully … nothing could surpass the sweetness of the upper tones. He gave us specimens of Meyerbeer's aubar [*aubade*], Rossini and the Last Rose of Summer. On leaving Papa thanked him and slipped a Napoleon in his hand. Mama came into the cabin immediately after and not knowing that Papa had paid him wished him buona notte, and slipped him another Napoleon, but it was too late. The money was bagged and it was awkward to make him disgorge his double fee. Well! It was rather dearly bought pleasure.   Mama

Sunday 2nd July It is the custom here to celebrate Feast days on the next following Sunday when they fall on a weekday. The 29th June was St Peter's day, but it was celebrated today. Last evening after sunset a long procession of mariners issued from the gate of the town to the Quai of the port, each mariner bearing a lighted candle, preceded by a drum and fife. There they set fire to a huge pile of combustibles, and returned in the same order into the town.

This afternoon there were races of men in the principal street. All the town was out, and every window filled. After the races were over the crowds rushed down to the port to witness the duck hunt, and the amusement of a well greased mast. As there were no boat races this year, Papa consented to our boats taking their stations for a race to amuse the people. So we manned the four boats, including the steward and cook's boy. Each boat was commanded and steered by one of the boys. They looked uncommonly well as they took up their stations in the middle of the port, which was lined all around with spectators. The Gig under James's command won the prize of twenty francs. All the others were treated to some bottles of wine.   Grace

JC also kept up with the Woolfields. They brought their daughters with them on their winter sojourns on the coast and in December came their first invitation to the boys for a day's croquet at Springfield with the daughters and their friends.

Before leaving they chose their cleanest shirts, tied 'the mightiest of sailors' knots' in their black chokers and had their ears and nails inspected. They played croquet in the morning and again from dinner – 'where they had to sit still and behave like gentlemen' – until tea. They at once took to the game and to the Woolfield sisters. They took a croquet set back to Naples with them in April.

Tuesday 15th August The Emperor's Fête. At 5 am 21 guns were fired. We went out to hear the Te Deum but found the Church so full we did not go in. Then we went to see the review of the troops by Colonel Schuster. Back at their barracks they had an extra good dinner of roast meat, soup and vegetables.

After dinner the boys went to man their boat, for a race with the champions of Cannes, Antibes and some other boats. A roll of the drum was the signal for starting, and all set off in beautiful order till half way, when our dinghy and the Cannes boat went ahead. Just at the turn another boat tried to get between us and the flag, but we gave one stroke and got clear, Fred taking the rudder beautifully. When entering the port everyone cheered us and we reached the goal, two boats' length ahead of the Cannes boat (the others being more behind). The first prize was given to us, consisting of 20 francs, which we gave to the two boys from Antibes who rowed with us, also of 6 metal plates, in the centre of which was engraved '15 Août, Antibes, 1865'.

In the evening the new road to the railway station was opened, the band played and the mayor made a speech in which he said that Antibes was in a state of progress. In the evening we illuminated Henry's house with Egyptian lanterns.

William

Tuesday 29th August Mama and Grace spent the morning in settling the boys' sailor's shirts, Charley's passing down to James, James to William and so on. John has left off wearing the sailor's costume and has become a midshipman.

Grace

Smuggling

Wednesday 22nd November Rather an eventful day. John had a chase after two smugglers of tobacco! He was out shooting with a friend and saw these two men pass, who looked suspicious and did not seem to like the looks of John's midshipman's cap and buttons. John noticed them quicken their pace and so he and his friend ran after them, whereupon they took to their heels and after being summoned three times and then threatened with a shot, they dropped their bags and soon disappeared. The pursuers were satisfied with the bags which contained about 66 lbs of tobacco and gave up the chase. In the evening we all went to the theatre, which is a moveable one and the little ones were much pleased with the wooden puppets.   Margaret

✿ *Monsieur Thuret's garden*

M. Thuret (the son of the Paris banker) had moved to the commune of Antibes in 1857, built for himself a villa and begun a second career devoted to botany. He was now a rich and eccentric bachelor, and became a friend. He was, according to an entry by Anne in early November, 'a connoisseur in plants, devoting the whole of his time to them. He has plants from all over the world which he acclimatizes. His door is closed against all visits and he never quits the precincts of his grounds except once a year, when he visits Antibes and makes a donation to the poor of the town.'

> *Sunday 29th January* A beautiful day. Papa, Mama and all of us went to the Cape. Papa however stopped half way at Mr Thuret's, who made him lie down on the sofa to rest. Papa always seems pleased after a visit to Mr. Thuret. His conversations and his attainments refresh and exercise his mind. To say nothing of the cheerful but mild expression of countenance, notwithstanding much bodily suffering from a diseased constitution. Papa attributes this pleasing characteristic entirely to the familiarity with God's living works, in which M. Thuret passes his dreamy existence – his plants, flowers and trees looking thankful for his intelligent care of them; and above all to his determination to remain a stranger to the storms and agitations of ordinary life.   Mama and Papa

> *Monday 7th August* At 6 o'c Papa and Grace started off for Mr Thuret's garden to see the trees there and to chose some for the Cape, the time for planting is now coming on.   Grace

> *Wednesday 21st November* Papa called on M. Thuret, who offered to assist Papa by giving advice on how to plant trees.   Mama and Papa

Today the *Jardin Thuret* is open to the public and contains some 3,000 species. According to the *Blue Guide*, Eucalyptus is among the many species introduced by Thuret to the region; but according the Close papers, this particular honour belongs to Woolfield.

✿ *Other sights*

> *20th February* After dinner Colonel Schüster called to take us over the *Fort Carré* opposite the boat, which was planned and constructed by the celebrated

engineer Vauban in the reign of Louis XIV. It is very large and massive, and in running over its courts, bastions and parapets, it seemed strange how such a fortress ever could be taken.   Papa

Napoleon was well acquainted with this fort, as when he was working his way up in the army he had been put in charge of the town's fortifications and the coastal defences on that stretch of the coast. Later, after the fall of Robespierre, he was imprisoned there for ten days in July 1794.

Expeditions were made to most of the villages in the hinterland. On 25th January JC hired an omnibus to take the family to the hill-top village of Biot, where oil vases, known as 'Forty Thieves Jars', were made:

> On the road we stopped at a brick maker's shed and went in. We found a man covered with clay busy at work with a machine for making draining pipes. The machine came from Preston! He set it going to show the children. He also showed us different kinds of hollow bricks, and spoke so well that Papa's curiosity was excited. "Who are you? I supposed you were a brick maker." "And so I am, but only for myself. All the land about belongs to me. I am alone in the world, my wife and child are dead, so it is of little matter. I am a barrister of Grasse!" On our return to Antibes Papa found that this young man's estates yielded £2,000 p.a., which he spends on benevolence and kindness. His pleasure is to work and live like a labourer and whilst his dinner is a plate of beans and lentils, he hands the partridges and truffles to his labourers.   Papa

The man described was M. Benery, who later was a frequent visitor to the *Sibilla*. He was also the supplier of the already mentioned asphalt-lined pipes for the site.

> *Monday 3rd July* After dinner Miss Esner, Henry and three boys went for a ride. They first went to Cagnes, a village between Antibes and Nice. They then struck into the interior and visited the castle of Panis, situated over the village of Villeneuve, returning by a beautiful road near some splendid rocks.

❧ Health

For much of May the children were restrained from going into town because of an outbreak of measles, but their attitude to it was typically robust, particularly by modern standards.

> *Tuesday 9th May* Grace has been in bed since Sunday with a cough and today we think it is measles. Dr Sim came to see her and said we were right, and that

the best thing we could do would be to start for Baja and take vapour baths.

John

Monday 16th May During dinner Aunt and Uncle Romano with our cousins came in a boat near the ship, but were in doubt whether they should come on board, on account of the measles. All the children have them except John and Charlie. Grace has just recovered.

John

Saturday 20th May The children seem better tho' they are all covered with red patches. Tom, Fred and Annie have their worst day today, James has passed his and John is still to come. At 7 o'c Papa, Grace, Miss Esner and Charlie went to the bath. Ladies went first, so as to get on board as quickly as possible to enable Mama and Mayer to take a bath. The rest of the day was spent in reading, writing and nursing the sick ones.

Grace

Later in the year there was a much darker cloud over the region: an outbreak of cholera:

Thursday 21st September Grace accompanied Mama back to the house to put up the blankets in pepper in preparation for departure in case of cholera. The town crier passed through all the town telling the people to wash their streets, and keep them clean.

Grace

Cholera had been very bad in Toulon, with 100 deaths a day. Now the plague was abating and the latest daily count at the date of the above entry was fifty-nine, with twenty-three deaths at Marseilles. As far away as Naples, a Meuricoffre granddaughter had died of it. The disease was capable of getting out of control anywhere. In 1837 the death toll in Palermo alone was 41,000.

The Close family were not affected and the majority of them were in robust health most of the time, the only slightly worrying exception being that John started having bouts of pain in one eye, to which leeches were applied and which sometimes confined him to bed. Another remedy prescribed by the doctor was 'the insertion of small pieces of blue stone, which hurt him terribly'.

Charlie had returned to his family in England on 15th June, very much better although not cured altogether of his asthma. The other children, with competitive riding, rowing and gymnastics, remained healthy:

> *Tuesday 10th January* Before dinner Papa showed us off on gymnastics. John and Will ascended to the top gallant yard, Fred to the top Royal and Jim, seizing a rope, went up it hand over head to the height of 50 feet, all descending by the ropes. We all dined together and when the Baron [*Erlanger, from Frankfurt*] asked Papa how he kept us all in order Papa said it was in this wise: No meant no; Yes was yes – as often as you can with reason and No as seldom. Never break a promise, be it yes or no.
> Mama and Miss Esner

Afternoons were often occupied with riding. John, aged fifteen, had bought his own horse and James had also become a good rider. Even the little ones, Annie and Tom, sometimes spent an hour or two on ponies, and John and James gave them lessons on the Corsican ponies.

Such unrestricted outdoor activities caused the children an unending catalogue of accidents. Fred in particular had always been completely reckless. He had just lost a small piece of his finger while playing with some clay that a visitor from Nice had bought over for Annie and Tom, but this did not inhibit him:

> *Tuesday 27th June* While we were bathing Fred was about to jump from the whiskers of the ship [*two bars, one on each side of the bowsprit*] when he slipped and fell on the anchor and hit himself just above the eye near the temple. A surgeon was immediately called and dressed the wound. It is very serious.
> William

Tom was also accident-prone. On 10th November, when the children had first been shown the proposed site, he could not join the party because 'he fell headlong through the small skylight in the passage and hurt himself on his shoulder. He could not move it.'

A major source of such troubles, and one which caused most members of the family at one time or another to come to grief, were six untameable Corsican ponies, which JC had arranged to be shipped from Naples in the summer along with the rest of the furniture that could not be fitted into the *Sibilla*. Even by November the ponies were still running wild. On the way to the Cape 'the two ponies that took Papa ran away and tho' both the coachman and Papa pulled them in as hard as they could and tho' both wheels were locked, these strong little things pulled the carriage up hill and down as if it were a tin pot! They were finally stopped by a woman standing in the middle of the road and moving her arms about'.

Here is William's accident: 'A dog startled the pony who set off at a gallop and just as he was turning the corner slipped and fell. William's ankle was badly hurt and he will not be able to leave his room for two or three days'. And Tom's: 'In passing by the seaside a wave frightened Tom's pony and he broke away from Margaret who had him on a leading string. It kicked Tom off, Margaret jumped down to see if he was hurt, but he was only a little bruised. Meanwhile the four horses began to fight. James and Margaret separated them, while an old lady took Tom up in her arms and put him on a stone. Tom then got on Sambo and afterwards played as if nothing had happened'.

Anne was not so unperturbed. Her pony buckled under her weight as it galloped downhill and it was some days before she recovered from her bruises. She vowed never to ride anything less than a horse from then on.

JC himself was not immune. On an afternoon visit to the Cape, JC, although warned not to do so by John and by the coachman, was riding one of the Corsican ponies, because the side saddle was still on Sambo. Then:

> *Sunday 25th June* The pony was the most spirited in the stable. Papa nearly came off as he was riding under some trees, he galloped up a very steep hill and stopped at the top, when John begged him to get down and change with Sambo. Papa replied: "Do you think I cannot ride?" and went off at a good gallop. Their coachman Martin said: "Your father will be off" and at the same moment the pony shied and Papa fell off. Water, vinegar, wine and camomile were soon procured and after some time Papa and Mama got into a carriage, which was kindly offered, and drove to the beach, where the boat came to fetch them. Papa received scratches on his head, face and legs, his side gives him great pain, we cannot at present say if he is seriously injured.   John

Over two months later JC had still not properly recovered from this fall. On 29th August 'Papa is not able to accompany us in out walks. He walked too much the other day, and his foot is in a bad state, inflamed on the instep, the shoe having rubbed the skin off'.

Towards the end of September JC's gout broke out in his right elbow, making him 'quite disabled'.

> *Monday 27th November* After dinner Mama was obliged to go to Cannes to

get some medicine for Papa as the chemist here sent back Papa's prescription saying he could not understand it and would Papa translate it! Henry drove her.

Margaret

In the midst of these various activities and maladies, JC managed to fit in a brief visit to England, taking Grace there on 3rd October to finish her education at Miss Nairn's school in Carlisle, from where he wrote that he was not very well, suffering pains in his shoulders. He returned on the 29th with Margaret, who was impressed by how much her siblings had grown; and by Henry, who had been staying with his uncle in Scotland. JC himself retired to his bed until 5th November, but then resumed his supervision of the construction.

Saturday 16th December Mr Merrick the gas man has arrived and has been talking a great deal to Papa.

Margaret

With this entry the Journals come to an end. Two days later JC was dead.

CHAPTER VII

Death and Widowhood

🌿 *Death of James Close*

*J*AMES CLOSE'S prayer at the laying of the first stone on 24th August was not answered: he died of a heart attack on 18th December, when his Valhalla was only half built. There are various versions of the exact circumstances, but the details given by Anne in a letter to a friend written only two days later are surely likely to be the most accurate:

> Sunday was a glorious day; our Sunday service impressed me. All the children were present. James read the service impressively and the music was superior, for Margaret had practised frequently with the children. James joined in with his rich voice. At one o'clock we all went to the Cap. James showed Mrs L. round and explained the house and grounds. He was full of life and good spirits; he took her and Mr Loudon to the Belvedere and pointed out the spot on which he wished to be laid, marking it with his stick. I sent for Sambo – he mounted and rode part of the way home. After dinner we discussed many subjects and books. We then joined the children. I felt so happy, I had not a care in the world. James never passed a better night. He was so bright at breakfast, laughing with Mrs. L. I remained nearly all the morning with him. At eleven he said, "Annie, I feel nervous. Give me some Jeremie" [*a sedative*]. Then he went out to the Mairie. After speaking there, he sat down and was turning over some papers looking for a note, when he suddenly fell on Henry sideways. In two minutes it was all over.

The funeral took place on Christmas Eve. Sailors from the *Sibilla* carried the coffin and James Close was buried at the exact place on the top of a cliff where he had often stood to admire the panoramic view in every direction, and where only twenty-four hours before his death he had indicated that he wished his body to rest. The family surrounded the coffin as they walked, followed by first the musicians and then the entire town in a procession that, accompanied by funeral marches, took one and a half hours to reach the chosen spot. Fred wept, but feeling that this was unmanly, he turned to his still younger brother Thomas and said: 'I wouldn't have cried if it had been you, Tom!' The faithful Lion pined away and the story still persists, even in today's Antibes-Juan les Pins tourist literature, that he died on his master's grave. Later on this spot was erected a gravestone, consisting of a slab resting on four ornamental legs.

On 26th December the weekly newspaper, the *Phare du Littoral,* devoted almost its entire issue to JC's death. The front page was bordered in black, and there the editorial referred to the sad co-incidence that that other benefactor of the Cape, Count Fersen, had also died, only a few months previously. It fully backed JC's defence against the charge (until now not mentioned by anyone) that he was a speculator. "I am not a speculator", said he, on the current burning topic in Antibes, "I came here aged sixty-six to rest in this blessed ground under this radiant sun, and I have no other aim than to repay with good works the hospitality this beautiful country has given me, offering the chance of the tranquillity which I have dreamed of and now found." The inside pages describe the funeral and then give in full the funeral orations of the mayor, of M. Béranger, of JC's doctor from Nice and of Paul Bernard. The mayor, after praising the eloquence of the '*ministre du culte protestant*' who took the service, said that it was not in M. Close's nature to rest, and that no sooner had he sketched out his gigantic plans for villas and gardens on his land than he was working on vast schemes for new roads and gas lighting for the whole town. He revealed that only a few days ago JC had given him f.400 for distribution to those in the greatest need; and then he solemnly enjoined on the noble widow and her son Henry the task of continuing the projects that JC had begun. Béranger highlighted the intention to emulate Lord Broughams's development of Cannes and quoted JC as saying only a few days ago: "Antibes will no longer be the poor Cinderella. She must be smart and stylish (*coquette*) and adorned like her happy neighbours."

The most carefully composed tribute was written by Anne. It is clearly written when he was still alive, although at a time when the handicaps of old age were beginning to tell. She wrote it in her commonplace book, alongside passages she admired by authors such as de Quincey and Dr. Arnold, headmaster of Rugby. Although the tribute is mild and loving, in the main it bears out most of the characteristics – good and bad – that may already have been deduced by the reader. Here are some extracts:

> My husband is a man of cultivated mind, more perhaps by observation and habitual investigation than by any course of reading he can boast of in his school days. His appearance is that of a gentleman, his countenance though not remarkable for handsome features is expressive, vivacious and intellectual. He can appreciate merit, wit and tact almost instinctively. Prone to think

well of people, rather than evil, his good feelings are sometimes imposed upon. Easily roused and passionate, he is easily pacified and the first to regret.

His conversation is highly interesting, full of knowledge and delineations from nature and his own experiences; it has a charm for all who listen to it, so that few who have been in his society for a few minutes retire without deriving a new idea, or some benefit. He scorns everything approaching to meanness, hypocrisy and cant. He is contented with his station in life. To be kind to his relations who need it is to him a duty. Sensitive in extreme to everything that is good and kind, his hatred of injustice, dishonesty, falsehood and ingratitude is absolutely implacable. His religion is rather the religion of charity and good works, than faith. He is a determined enemy to priestcraft, superstition and imposture. He is liberal and generous but promiscuous alms giving he considers a sin. Never obstinate or sulky, he thinks it no disgrace to yield to an argument more powerful than his own. His silvery hair gives him an appearance of age, which wears away after a few minutes spent in his society. His frame is upright and retains the appearance of more power to undergo fatigue than he really possesses.

He has an affectionate heart and is never happier than when it is reciprocated, come from what quarter it may.

The minute details of ordinary life are irksome to him. He is fond of reading, [*particularly*] newspapers and modern scientific publications. Hospitable in a high degree, he neither wants nor cares for any return. Unknown to others, or rather wishing that it might be unknown to others, his pride is intense. I allude to the pride that scorns to solicit the acquaintance of those who circulate in, or who fancy they belong to, a superior class in the social scale; to that pride which rebels at the idea, or fashion, that because a man is a merchant, or engaged in trade, he is not fit for the best society in the world.

As a husband, he has ever been to me more than in my romantic days of girlhood I anticipated. In one word, he has never caused me an anxiety, nor have I known what it is to have a void of the heart unfilled or unsatisfied.

As a father, he has been able to exact obedience and respect without forfeiting the affections of his children.

Other qualities that emerge from the manuscripts and journals may also be noted. JC had an exceptional amount of self-esteem and self-belief. He was well aware of this, and more or less admitted that in his youth he was swollen headed and quick to take offence. His confidence in the rightness of his own ideas was unshakeable and is reflected in the length and assertiveness of his sometimes sententious dissertations on topics such as religion, love and moral duties.

JC had no false reticence about making money. To do so was his avowed intent. He was generous when he had it, but anyone who failed to make his way was often dismissed as a wastrel.

Some of his convictions amounted to prejudices. Disapproval of methodism may have been widespread at the time, but few could have matched JC in his vilification of the sect. He was adamant in his dismissal of the Classics on the grounds that they were of no practical use and gave no consideration to the arguments for their study. His contempt for Italians was remarkable, considering his life was based in Naples and he had distinguished Italian in-laws. They were 'not yet ready for a constitution'. In scorning Cavour's budget for the building of railways, he wrote 'The Italians are poets, singers and dancers, but not men of business'. Yet without such self-confidence, he could never have rescued the firm in Sicily at such an early age (not learning Italian until he got there); organised the education of eight children on a storm-tossed sailing boat, and set Antibes on the road to becoming a rich tourist resort.

His gout was to a large extent responsible for his volcanic temper, still a legend with the family. Perhaps there is something in the proverbial connection between red hair and a quick temper. Yet Henry, Fred (known later as 'Ginger') and Thomas had all inherited their father's colouring, but there is nothing to show that they had his fiery disposition.

He was impetuous. As soon as he got the letter from Christiana telling him that their engagement was off, he left his business in Sicily; embarked for Genoa and from there to England, and without stopping the night anywhere or giving any advance warning, he burst in on her parents' house in Manchester. Seeing that the roads on Ischia were inadequate, he took it on himself to organise their repair. The range of his business activities – cotton, coal, marsala, steamers, a printing works, sewers – shows that he would seize opportunities as they arose. No doubt it is also this impetuosity that made him so free with his fists – from his first day at school until his old age. That he recorded these occasions with pride is perhaps more a sign of the ethos of the times than of aggression.

He had an extraordinarily wide range of interests and made enquiries wherever he went about local industry, latest inventions and techniques, education, systems of government and so on. His observations during the family's visit to the iron mines on Elba show the keen interest of a geologist. While waiting, incapacitated by gout, for the family to return from an expedition near Toulon, he is writing a paper on the cloacks (sewers and waterworks) of Naples – a subject on which he had become an expert.

Although JC was cosmopolitan in the sense that he spent all his working life travelling round the Continent and was quadrilingual, and although it never seems to have occurred to him to work again in England, he would have scorned the idea of assimilating with the local population. He always maintained the air of an Englishman abroad, following English customs of dress, food and etiquette. In that particular trait, his sons in America were to go even further.

Perhaps JC's most admirable quality was his dedication to the care of his family. He wrote approvingly in the story of his early life that his parents only cultivated activities in which their children could join in, such as music; and he noted how all their major expenditure was on making a comfortable home for the family. Although JC could not have set much store by comfort, in a different way his chief concern after his marriage was always his family. He wanted to keep them at home so that they could be loved and given the sort of education that would be of practical use to them in later life. This he achieved – and the use to which that education was put will be seen in the final chapter.

Bust of James Close, taken from death mask

Civic recognition of JC's contribution to the development of Antibes came with the renaming in his honour of the little street where the schoolroom had been and where the family had sometimes stayed while waiting for their mansion to be built. *Rue James Close* is in the old part of the town, in a pedestrian precinct. Referring to his initial purchase of land on the Cap, current (2007) tourist literature says of him: 'In negotiating this purchase he forged very cordial relations with the civil and military authorities and showed himself to be a benefactor of the population with sumptuous gifts that won him popularity and relieved many of the poor.'

Following her husband's death, Anne sold the *Sibilla*. She also sold part of the estate on the Cap, and on this the building that is now the *Grand Hôtel du Cap* was built by a consortium headed by Alexis de Plestcheyeff, Fersen's brother-in-law, executor and guardian of his children. The scale of the Grand Hotel suggests that it was intended to rival JC's adjacent Château Antipolis. Work on that was suspended and it was not finally completed until well into the twentieth century. It changed hands several times: originally bought, unfinished, by King Leopold II of the Belgians, it was sold after the 1914–18 war, by his nephew, King Albert I. (This is stated by both Suzanne Knowles and Anne Eaden; and also by modern guide books and by tourist literature. Yet contemporary records kept at the *Services Archives Documentation* in Antibes however show no record of ownership by the Belgian Royal Family, but this is probably because they wanted their names kept out of financial transactions.) More unconfirmed details are provided by *Soixante années d'expansion touristique* (1953), written by the local Syndicat d'Initiatives. According to this, the remainder of JC's land was divided into two in 1900 and the half containing Antipolis bought by M. Antoine Sella. King Leopold however repurchased it, and after his death it was acquired in 1914 by George Davison, founder of Kodak Eastman in Europe. Still unfinished, Davison completed the mansion and used it for the education of six little girls that he had rescued from the slums in England. It became an orphanage, known as the Maison des Enfants. By 1956 it had become a hotel, *La Résidence du Cap*. Today it is in private hands.

JC's original plan had been to use the same Moorish design that he would have used for his retirement home on the island of Zannone, if King Ferdinand had allowed him to buy it. The photograph of *La Résidence du Cap* in plate 16 shows that at least something of that idea was kept.

Anne ignored the mayor's graveside call, and did not carry on with any of the projects started by JC. She built the Villa Closebrooks, a smaller family home, to her own design, facing towards the sea and the Esterel Mountains and near the building site of Château Antipolis. According to a local description, the house was built in *le style anglais,* with an iron gallery from east to west, its severe aspect accentuated by the fact that it rose from a garden that was like a basket of flowers (see plate 17). 'As to the interior, it has all the comfort that only the English know how to provide for themselves, never mind in what country or latitude they choose to settle.' Villa Closebrooks appears to have been built in 1869–70, as a letter from young Tom in December 1869 says '…we are sleeping in the new house – Grace sleeps in her own room'. Another, in March 1870, reports that the workmen had finished putting down asphalt in the billiard room.

Anne's elder children were now reaching the age when JC would no longer have wanted them to continue their education at home. In 1866 John was sixteen, James fifteen and William thirteen, and Anne's main task in her new-found independence was to visit England to assess suitable schools.

❧ *The family scatters*

Henry also did not want anything more to do with Antipolis. Nor did he fulfil JC's assumption that he would go into the Church. He was a keen and pioneering amateur photographer, but the only job he is known to have done was to serve for a brief period as a Swiss Guard in the Vatican at the time of Pius IX. This must have been some time between his father's death and his marriage in 1869, at the age of thirty-three. He had been slow to marry, but was finally pushed into it by Lady Mainwaring, mother of seven daughters, who caught one of them with Henry, in a rainstorm, sheltering under the same umbrella. She immediately congratulated them on their engagement; they married and produced six children.

Although Henry was called to the Bar in 1871 and had studied at the Middle Temple, he did not practise as a barrister. His eldest daughter Etta Close, whose memoirs have been quoted earlier, wrote this about him:

> My father loathed going abroad. He liked his shooting in England, and a plentiful supply of good food sent up by an excellent French chef at regular intervals. I think he had had too much of foreign parts as a boy, for he was born in Naples and until he was married, lived most of his life on his father's yacht

in the Mediterranean [*except when up at Emmanuel College, Cambridge and when he was a Swiss Guard*]. The sailors were all Italians from Naples, and my father talked Neapolitan as few Englishmen can. I remember years ago my mother and I were shopping in Naples, and we induced my father, for fun, to pretend to be an hotel tout taking round English tourists. Not one of the shopkeepers found him out, and all gave him the recognised tip for bringing in new customers.

Henry was last heard of living in Eaton Square with his daughter Etta. He died in 1913.

Margaret, Anne Close's eldest child, was now nineteen. She decided that the Mediterranean climate did not suit her, and spent much of her time with relatives in Great Britain – mostly with Uncle Henry and Aunt Alice Gaskell (Charlie's parents) at Kiddington Hall near Oxford, but also with Uncle Thomas Close at his shooting lodge in Perthshire and Uncle William Brooks at his home in the Forest of Glen Tanar in Aberdeenshire. She married John Eaden and died in 1887, only a year after her mother's death, giving birth to their second child. John Eaden's brother married Margaret's younger sister Annie.

Grace, on her return from Miss Nairn's finishing school in Carlisle, did return to live with her mother in Villa Closebrooks. When the question of the disposal of the villa arose after Anne Close's death, the family agreed that Grace should continue to live there, since, in view of her health (which had never fully recovered from typhoid), it was thought that she would never marry. She did marry, her husband being the artist Bowen Warrick, and in spite of the subsequent uproar she refused to give up the villa and remained there for the rest of her life, spending her winters in Antibes and her summers in Switzerland. She had no children, and died in 1911.

Anne decided that rather than trying to fit the sixteen year old **John** in at a school, he should be prepared for university by a tutor in England. He went up to Trinity College, Cambridge in 1868.

The photographs of John and his three brothers on plate 1 show that the other three looked remarkably alike, full of fiery determination. John on the other hand, despite the identical sailor suit, has different features and his aspect is more relaxed. Possibly he had inherited more of his mother's looks and calm disposition. Certainly his career would support the theory that he was more of a Brooks than a Close. As Anne's oldest son, he was the one most likely to have been offered a career as of right in his grandfather Samuel Brooks's bank (now run by his uncle William Cunliffe Brooks, who had no sons). Fortunately, he also turned out to be the one best able to offer the steady and reliable qualities needed. John joined the bank in Manchester on coming down from Cambridge in 1872 and was made a partner in 1888. He played a key role in the activities of his brothers in America (related in the next chapter), both by providing finance and by urging caution and restraining them from their wilder exploits. Emphasising his affinity with his mother's family and his bank, he changed his family name by royal letters patent to Close-Brooks. When the bank merged with Lloyds in 1900, he was given a seat on the Board and remained in charge of the Manchester office. He retained his position on the main Board until shortly before his death in 1914.

The links with his mother's family had been still more firmly tied back in 1874, when he married Emily, the daughter of Anne's second brother, the Rev. John Brooks. Emily died leaving her husband with two sons and three daughters. In 1907 widower John, aged fifty-seven, married a very much younger second wife – Grace, also the daughter of a clergyman, the Rev. William Cooke. John celebrated his second marriage by taking Grace, for the honeymoon, on the newly built railway from the South of Alaska to the Yukon gold fields in the North – the railway that had been built at the instigation of his brother William (see next chapter). He and his bride were given an entire carriage to themselves.

As well as being on the Board of Lloyds Bank, John became a director of the Lancashire and Yorkshire Railway, a Justice of the Peace and, in 1911, High Sheriff of Cheshire. He retained the interest in horses and shooting that he had acquired in Naples – he was an accomplished team driver and rented a grouse moor in Scotland each year. His funeral in 1914 was a major County occasion. By the side of his grave was a pair of oars, made of white flowers, with blades of pale blue forget-me-nots. The reason for this will soon be apparent.

James and **William**, after a stint at a prep school in Rutland, were both sent to the newly founded Wellington College, where the headmaster was Edward White Benson, later Archbishop of Canterbury. They both followed John to Trinity and after that both were also offered a job in the Cunliffe Brooks Bank. William declined the offer and James, although he did look after the Bank's interests for a while in West Africa, did not stay with them. They both loom large in chapter VIII and in the section on their time at Trinity – so no more will be said about them here.

While **Fred's** older brothers were at school in England, he (aged twelve), had to suffer the indignity of sharing a governess with sister Annie. However he soon persuaded his mother to allow him to join James and William at Wellington. But when the question of following them to Cambridge arose, he declared that he was 'no good at books', and asked if the money available for a university education could be put instead to the purchase of a ranch in the United States. This was agreed, but Fred, after spending half his life on a boat, had no practical experience of agriculture. So that he would not be completely unprepared, relatives in Scotland found him a place on a farm, and there he acquired some knowledge and skills before leaving for the New World in 1874, at the age of twenty. When he embarked at Liverpool the dockside porters demanded such an exorbitant sum for carrying his baggage onto the ship that Fred carried it on board himself, regardless of their jeers, then turned to them and said: "I am going to make my fortune, not yours!"

Fred was an outstanding sportsman and an expert and fearless rider, never hesitating to take a calculated risk. His gymnastic abilities remain a family legend: on one occasion William Brooks, his uncle, offered his nephew a billiard table if he could walk round the rim on his hands. The table was Fred's in a matter of seconds. He was also hardworking, ambitious, popular and at ease in any social group. At twenty, he showed a self confidence rivalled only by that of his father at the same age. He was also adventurous and daring to the point of recklessness. JC wrote this of him: 'As to Frederic, whose abilities and elasticity are in excess, I may almost say, what of him as a civil or military engineer?' (Right about his talents, wrong about his career.) The rest of Fred's story is in the next chapter.

Daughter Anne, hitherto mostly referred to as **Annie**, stayed at home after the funeral and was the only child never to have any education outside the family. As has been seen, she married her brother-in-law Harry Eaden. They had two sons and two daughters: Anne, who helped to compile this book and Ruth, the author of the *Blackwood's Magazine* article. While Harry and Annie's main home was in the New Forest, the pull of her Mediterranean upbringing never left her: she returned there as often as she could and in later years spent her winters in the south of France. One of her main interests was animal welfare, and with her it was always a question of deeds, not words. In one small town in France she arranged for the demonstration of a humane killer; she canvassed all the butchers in the place and its use was subsequently taken up. Annie was the last survivor of the eight children of James and Anne Close. She died in 1940, aged eighty-three.

🐟 *Anne as widow*

*T*HUS, soon after losing her husband Anne was also deprived of most of her many children, with whom she had lived at such close quarters for so long. But Grace and the boon companions Annie and Tom remained (see plate 4). At forty-five she was still as energetic and adventurous as ever. She also retained her good looks: when in 1869 she attended the wedding of her favourite niece to the Marquis of Huntley in Westminster Abbey, Margaret (one of the twelve bridesmaids) recorded that when her mother entered the Abbey 'everyone turned to look at her'. At home, she devoted much of her time to the care of the sick and needy. She had been left comfortably off, but was inexperienced in dealing with money matters, and her generosity led her into financial difficulties. However William wrote to her from Cambridge: 'Never mind the debts, your sons are talented Samuel Brookses; they will pay them off. Have Philiberts [*family name for Anne's charitable extravagancies*] for ever.' One of the family wrote that her house was 'a sort of general hospital and refuge for sick people from the surrounding country'. When the Franco-Prussian war broke out in 1870 Anne and her daughters joined other ladies in the task of providing comforts for the French troops on their way to the doomed conflict. The conscripts in the local barracks, waiting to go to the front, could be heard singing a song with the bitter refrain: *Marchons, marchons, pour la boucherie.*

Next year brought the greatest sorrow of Anne's life. JC's sudden death had been a tremendous shock, but as Anne was twenty years younger, they had both accepted that he would go first. The death of her youngest child, however, was a blow all the more severe because of its complete unexpectedness. Away from home for the first time, Tom was into his first term at an English school in Switzerland. On 9th November 1871 he died in his sleep, asphyxiated by fumes from a charcoal stove in the dormitory. JC's bizarre claim that life on board ship, with all its hazards, was safer for the children than life on shore, would seem vindicated. In her grief his mother wrote *Night after burial*, a twenty-one-verse poem full of religious thoughts and the conviction that now Tom awaited paradise. Here is just one verse:

> Sleep soft until that blessed rain and dew
> Down lighting upon earth such change shall bring
> That all its fields of death shall laugh anew,
> Yea with a living harvest laugh and sing.

But Anne had many friends and visitors, and her new house was large enough to put up many guests, as can be seen in the family photograph shown in plate 18. And in addition to her charitable works, she still sought new adventures. These could no longer be at sea, so she went on prolonged expeditions inland, calling them 'land cruises'. They involved anyone staying at Villa Closebrooks at the time and would last up to a fortnight. She enjoyed roughing it and seemed impervious to the discomforts of country inns. One particularly ambitious foray took place in the summer of 1875. Anne suffered from an unspecified complaint for which the spa waters of Vichy were prescribed and, seizing the opportunity for an expedition, she decided to go as far as Grenoble by road and take the train from there to Vichy. Margaret was married and living near Cambridge; John was established in the Cunliffe Brooks Bank in Manchester; James was in West Africa, and Fred was farming in the United States. William, then a twenty-two-year-old Cambridge undergraduate, was enjoying the June Henley regatta. Being the nearest, he received a summons to go out to Antibes and lead the expedition.

Besides Anne and William, the party consisted of Grace (27), Annie (18), Annie's governess Miss Carey, a Miss Schmidt (German governess?), two maids and two dogs. The transport consisted of two pony chaises, one drawn by two of her own greys, the other by two of the infamous Corsican ponies, Gazelle and Dagon. Time had not subdued them, and Gazelle kicked one of the greys at the first stop, laming him badly. Yet they did well, seeming untired by the mountain roads and the scorching sun. A landau, with three hired horses, was also taken

All the ponies were fitted with sunhats.

in case Anne felt unwell. Two coachmen shared the driving with William and Annie. William took the precaution of investing 'in a good useful knife and a small revolver'.

When the party of nine people and nine animals left Antibes under William's command, the midsummer heat was intense. As the procession wound its way through mountain passes and valleys there were a number of halts to tend the horses. It seems as if they always came first and had to be attended to before any thought was given to the comforts of the rest of the party. It was a question of taking pot luck in hotels and country inns: some were good, some reasonable and some filthy. Miss Carey's flea bites caused her a sleepless night, while William offended one landlord by sleeping in the landau to get away from the bugs. By 17th July the expedition was making its way through the *Hautes Alpes* with snow and glaciers to be seen in the distance and where there were 'fearful ups and downs and a very hard pull for the horses'. Two nights were spent at Corps, from where four of the ladies on mules and William on foot climbed to a place of pilgrimage, *Notre Dame de la Salette*, some 8,000 feet above sea level.

On 21st July, at the last stopping-place before Grenoble, tragedy struck. At the end of the day, when the horses had been stabled and the rest were about to sit down to dinner, it was found that Borac, one of the greys, had a foreleg broken in two places. There was nothing to be done, and the melancholy task of shooting Borac to put him out of his agony, and seeing to it that he was properly buried, fell to Hardy, the second coachman. A horse was hired to take his place and on their return to Antibes the party took with them Borac's beautiful tail, to be hung alongside those of Sambo and Satan.

The above is a summary of William's twenty-one-page Journal of the Grenoble land cruise. Keeping up with his early training, he had made an entry for every day. Although light-hearted in style and sometimes carelessly written, in writing it at all he was emulating his father's daily record in the Journals.

The Land Cruise diary was of course more mature than the Sibilla entries, but not as good as his later Prairie Journal, extensively quoted in the next chapter; so it has been summarised above. It is not quoted here, except for the following paragraphs telling how he became involved in the journey, and how it began. These extracts show Anne's continuing hold over her family and suggest that at the end of her life she had lost some of her unruffled calm, and was inclined to be irritable:

While at Henley I receive letters from home saying 'We are going on an expedition in our pony carriages to Grenoble ... Come down at once for we must start as soon as possible as it is getting too hot for her [*Anne*] and we shall start as soon as you arrive'. Accordingly after Henley I hurry down, miss the "Varsity" Match and sundry engagements I had made and arrive at Antibes on Tuesday 29 June, find no preparations made for the journey and that we could not possibly start until the Tuesday following. I cussed.

He then spent a week organising the purchase of supplies.

Tuesday July 6th 1875 Day of the start, which we had fixed for 7 am. Called at 5 and left my comfortable bed with regret. Breakfast at 6 and the carriages brought round to be packed before the horses are put to. Confusion in the hall, boxes to be sent to Vichy, boxes to be sent to Grenoble. Boxes to be taken with us lying mixed up in every corner, mingled with bags, rugs and packages for the journey. Mother busy flinging out all sort of things from <u>her</u> own basket trunk, potted tins of all sorts, ham, mackeral, beef soups, coffee and milk tins ... The Mother rolling all that did not suit her Pall-Mall [*sic*] about the place did not add to the order, and she getting hot and seemingly waxy. I say seemingly for she afterwards confessed that she only appeared to be angry to make everyone look sharper.

There are several instances later on in the expedition when Anne shows signs of temper; but, as the above extract suggests, maybe her sharpness was put on, as without JC she had to assert herself more often.

Exactly a year later Anne Close was at Vichy again. While there she was taken seriously ill. She wanted to take her carriage home to Antibes, but was persuaded to go to Paris instead to consult a doctor there. She died three days later, on 19th July 1876, shortly before her fifty-fifth birthday.

✌ *Cambridge Blues*

*A*T TWO-YEAR INTERVALS, John, James and William all went up to Trinity College, Cambridge. There is no record of their academic achievements, as they all took an ordinary degree. They were all bright, and the explanation for not taking an Honours degree could simply be that earlier on they had quite deliberately *not* been taught the sort of subjects favoured by Oxbridge at the time – primarily Latin and Greek. Indeed they had probably acquired from JC a lack of respect for these subjects. On the other hand it could be that the brothers were too busy earning a reputation as one of the greatest family-linked trio of university oarsmen that has ever been known.

When James arrived at Trinity, John had already achieved a striking reputation as an oarsman (hence the flowered oars by his funeral bier). He had rowed in the boat that beat Oxford in 1871 and again in 1872. He was in the University Fours twice and the University Pairs twice, besides rowing Head of the River for Trinity. At Henley he won the Diamond Sculls, the Grand Challenge Cup twice and the Steward's Cup twice.

Unbelievably, this record was surpassed by James, who also rowed in the University Boat: in 1872 with John, and without him in 1873 and 1874. He was President of the University Boat Club in 1873. His triumphs and collection of trophies are too many to list here. While up, his fellow students must have seemed to him callow, after his own adventurous upbringing. The only record available suggests that they in turn thought that he looked down on them. In the minute book of the 1st Trinity Boat Club it states: 'JB Close consented to come up and row. As soon as he came up he of course took the sole charge of the crew and behaved in an (even for him) unusually high-handed and overbearing way'. The minute, which refers to the May bumps in 1874, records: 'His brother was at once installed at four, Mann at two, Dickson at three and himself at seven'. By this time James had already rowed three times against Oxford and was in his last year at Cambridge – so he had some justification for laying down the law for the inter-college bumps. In later life James sometimes found the time to return to Trinity and coach.

William may not have surpassed James, but he also rowed for the University in three successive years to 1877 and he also was President, in 1876, of the University Boat Club. These triumphs of the three brothers arose not from strength and determination alone, but also from the fact that from a very early age the boys had been brought up on and in the water. Even young Tom had been encouraged in that direction: in March 1864 the Journal records 'Tom spends the greater part of the day in the dinghy. He and Annie manage the boat; a sailor accompanies them in case one of them should go overboard. Tom feathers and manages his oar capitally'. Annie was then aged six, Tom four. As they grew older, all the boys were continually racing each other and taking part in rowing races in local regattas.

William's third race against Oxford was in 1877, the year of the only dead heat in the history of the event. At first the umpire had declared the race 'a draw in Oxford's favour', but this equivocation was quickly withdrawn after heated discussions. That William was able to participate in this famous race is something of a puzzle. He was admitted in to Trinity in 1872 and graduated in 1876. In the late spring of the same year he had crossed the Atlantic to take part in the Regatta at Philadelphia, held to celebrate the centenary of the Declaration of Independence. He remained in America for the spring, summer and autumn. He was certainly not studying for a post-graduate degree, so it is difficult to see how he qualified in 1877 for a place in the Cambridge eight. It is almost as if the only reason for coming back to England at all was to participate, as after the race was over he returned to America.

CHAPTER VIII

Close Brothers in America

THE REST OF THIS BOOK will tell the story of James, William and Fred and their achievements in America. If the summary of John's distinguished career in the previous chapter is short by comparison, that is because it is part of the history of the Cunliffe Brooks Bank and its merger with Lloyds. John's part in the exploits of his younger brothers in America was important, as he and his bank supported them financially, particularly in the early days, when money was most needed. On one occasion he even went out there, to assess prospects for himself and buy land. Yet his role was more that of the cautious banker, asking when the loans plus interest were going to be repaid and demanding from William better forecasting and more detailed financial plans. The buccaneering, risk taking adventures of his three younger brothers, on the other hand, read as a continuation of their father's merchant venturer approach and are the link between him and Close Brothers plc in the City today.

In his record of the land cruise to Grenoble, William had begun to develop his early training as a Journal-writer on board the *Sibilla*. When invited to America to row in 1876, he at first wrote lengthy letters back home describing his experiences. Next year this changed to the occasional bulletin, which he would send to England with instructions that it should be passed round selected friends and relations. Thus it was a different kind of Journal to the daily entries written on board the *Sibilla*. It is the main source for the following two sections.

William's style is ironic, self-deprecating, jokey and full of puns. They would have fitted well in the pages of *Punch*, as it was in those days. He records, for example, a small boy asking "What's that tub for?" William: "It's a bath". Small boy: "How often do you use it?" William: "Every day. In England, a gentleman takes a bath every day, even if he has to break the ice to get in it." Small boy: "If I was in England I hope I wouldn't be a gentleman."

Although the Journal only covers a short period, it is quoted at some length, since it is most revealing about William himself and his younger brother Fred, at a turning point in their careers. Moreover William, with his training as a writer, has left a valuable account of the mid-West at that time and the process of opening up virgin prairie.

Fred kept no records himself and most of what we know about him is from the pen of his elder brother. There is little in the Journal about brother James, who later joined them, because he did not appear on the scene until after William had stopped writing it. At that point, which is where the 'Colony' gets going, Curtis Harnack's book *The Gentlemen of the Prairie* will for a time be the main source of information.

The upbringing of the brothers and their dominant father cannot but be present in the mind anyone reading this final chapter. The hardihood and athleticism which enabled them to make something out of the bogs and bugs and other hazards of Iowa; the financial training which enabled William to make a long term marketing plan for the development of his homesteads, the unabashed pursuit of money and absence of any feeling that trade was inconsistent with being a gentleman; the interest in the latest ways of dealing with any mechanical or scientific problem; the audacity with which William at least was prepared to invest in and support almost anything where a good opportunity arose; even the writing of the Journal itself – all these things show how much the three brothers had benefited from the unusual education that their father had provided.

Letters home – Reconnaissance

Early summer to end of November 1876

*W*ILLIAM'S original reason for going to America in the early summer of 1886 was to row. He was President of the Cambridge University Boat Club and had been invited to bring a crew to participate in the Philadelphia-based Centennial regatta. William rowed at no. 2 in the coxless four that was to compete. He sailed to New York with the rest of his team. His crew consisted of A. Jameson, a Scotsman who lived in Ireland and rowed bow; Jerry Mann, a Welshman and a great friend of William; and the stroke, J. T. Penrose, who came from Cork. All three had rowed with William in various Cambridge races.

They sailed on White Star's *Britannic,* which took eight days to cross the Atlantic. Very soon William became infatuated with the liveliness of the American girls on board – a taste which he never lost:

We made special friends with two American families by name Fallys and Van

Dusens, who boasted amongst them of four young ladies, not very pretty, but the most going, larky girls I ever came across. Thorough Yankees with an enormous amount of self-assurance and 'aplomb'. We thought they were about 21 to 23 years old, but the eldest was 18 and the youngest but 16. They did many things that would shock more sensitive people than we, and I confess now and then we were rather startled by them.

When William's party of oarsmen, which included a reserve, a boatman and three boats (probably coxless fours), arrived at New York it was met by a large welcoming party and plenty of champagne. He was astonished at the contrast between life at Trinity and the rough and tumble of America. Far from any rancour that might have remained from the war 100 years ago, they were treated as celebrities and subjected to countless introductions. Yet at first, coming straight from sophisticated and class-conscious Trinity College Cambridge, William in his letters showed a rather priggish disapproval of the democratic camaraderie, the unfinished state of the towns, the transport and the roads. He wrote this about getting through Customs:

> They first make you fill up a form stating how many trunks, boxes, portmanteaus or other articles you have, and what is the nature of their contents. This they require you to swear to. They thought 'three racing boats' was a new name for a trunk or box. They don't seem to take much account of one's oath, for they made me open every single package – but found nothing.

Here is his account of the roads in New York:

> A wonderful coach was waiting for us, more like an old Lord Mayor's than anything else I know. In this we all got in, as well as about a dozen of the committee men, and were driven off. Bejabbers, but we got our bones rattled for something. We were at once struck by the badness of the pavements, great holes here and there, large stones lying about: the driver cared for nothing, went straight ahead, now in a big hole, now out of it with a rush until at last he hit a street with a tramway on it and he put his wheels on to the rails. We congratulated ourselves on running so smoothly when suddenly there was a big jerk, and we all tumbled onto each other. It was only a street car coming along and the driver was getting out of the way. Another jerk and we were on the rails again. These jerks took place at short intervals until we reached the hotel. "What a bad street we came along", I remarked. "Why, do you think so? We came along some of the best paved streets. I guess before you leave this country you will think the pavements

you have just come over elegant" He was right, compared to what we saw in Philadelphia and other places. Why, coming from the steamer we saw a dead dog lying about, rotten cabbage stalks and all sorts of refuse; and as for their boasted Fifth Avenue, one could keep three cows comfortably on the grass that is allowed to grow up in the cracks of the pavement.

But the hotel, where a sort of press conference was held, impressed him:

> In hotels Americans whip creation, everything is about as perfect as it could be. You can get your railway ticket, send a telegram, post your letter, get your money changed, buy your papers and a host of other things, all in the Hotel. You can eat from morning to night if so inclined.
>
>   After feeding, we held unwillingly a sort of general levée in our rooms. I believe every man who had ever touched an oar felt bound to come and be presented to us, and it was sickening to have to answer the same questions time after time. Our answers all appeared in next day's papers with descriptions of our persons. Penrose was slim and graceful, I was blonde with sandy whiskers and moustache.

The party was then joined by New York resident George Rives, who had been one of John's best friends at Cambridge:

> Rives gave us a lot of advice as to the care we should take of ourselves in the heat, and precautions against fever when we got to Philadelphia, where he said malaria was rife. This turned out to be but too true.

On Sunday afternoon, after church, the party was invited to visit the New York Boat Clubs on the Haarlem river, where there were fifteen different clubs, each with its own Boat House, side by side:

> When we got there we found 15 or 20 men sitting about in all sorts of costumes, and very light ones too, bathing costumes predominating. We learnt that the usual way to spend a hot Sunday afternoon was to lounge by the Boat Houses in the costumes we saw them in, and when they got hot, to tumble into the Haarlem and cool, getting out to drink Lager beer, smoke or chat and when hot again repeat the performance. [*They were introduced to every member of this club.*] I am afraid that before we got to the end we were not in a very amiable frame of mind. I confess to feeling very savage at being let in for this sort of thing and shown off to these Americans who, because they sit and smoke in front of their boathouses are dignified with the name of amateur oarsmen. We found out afterwards that there are only two clubs besides the Columbia club

that are exclusively for gentlemen, ie the Nassau and the New York B.C. Carpenters, tailors, shop-keepers etc. abound and predominate in the others.

The papers next morning announced that we had had a grand reception at the Boat Houses on the Haarlem River, and that a sumptuous repast had been provided for us at the Neptune B.C. We had each a glass of Lager beer at that Boat House, and there only being one glass we had to wait our turns. So much for the Grand Reception,

After two or three more days of being lionised, they were escorted to Philadelphia. WB was underwhelmed by the accommodation provided.

On the bus arose a discussion as to where we should drive to, and it transpired that they had not yet engaged rooms for us anywhere. This looked bad. After a lot of talking it was decided we should try the Park View Hotel. This hotel had been run up especially for the Centennial and when this was over would return to lodging houses. Thus the exterior did not look up to much. We were shown to a large room with three beds in it, a washing stand and one chair. "I guess this room will suit all of you first style" remarked the Commodore. 'All' consisted of five of us and our boatman, Adams. A general chorus from the reception committee that it was first style. I then had the pleasant duty of explaining that I did not think it suited us first style, and that we were not accustomed to sleeping two in a bed, nor to have our boatman sleeping with us. They looked very much astonished and seemed to consider this as only one more instance of the prejudices and effete customs of bloated England. However, they provided us with two more rooms.

The crew was now scheduled to train on the river and at Cape May (on the southern tip of New Jersey) using the recent innovation of sliding seats. During one of these sessions, William's seat got stuck, causing him such blisters that he was unable to continue training. While stranded on shore at Cape May, he met Daniel Paullin – a man who was to change the course of his life. Paullin was on holiday with his son and daughter, Mary. He told William that he had made a fortune in the sixties buying land in Illinois, and that he had now made his home there, in the town of Quincy. (It was in County Adams, and both town and county had been named after the fourth American President, John Quincy Adams.) He planned to give his sons the same opportunity in the nearby state of Iowa. He invited William to join him on a reconnaissance of the area. William was impressed – both with the offer and with the looks and sophistication of Paullin's daughter Mary.

William was later to accept Paullin's offer. First he planned to visit his younger brother Fred, and before that, now that his blisters had sufficiently recovered, he had to row in the regatta. His boat might have won it, but for another stroke of ill luck. Half way through the race he collapsed in his seat with diarrhoea and was too ill to continue. 'Those beastly Yankees are crowing over us', he wrote. He was seriously ill, and recuperated at the British Commission in Washington. Malaria is not mentioned again, although it was endemic at the time. Much later, he attributed his illness to the poor sanitation in America – apparently the river from which they got their water was polluted. He did not feel well enough to visit Fred until September.

Fred had now been running a small stock farm for two years in the Allegheny Mountains near Jeffersonville, on the borders of Virginia and West Virginia. The first part of the journey there was by train to Wytheville, about 250 miles away. Travelling with fellow oarsman Jerry Mann, William wrote a page of complaints about the thirty-six-hour journey, including:

> At about 9.30 on the next night we passed through a tremendous storm of rain, lightning and thunder, the wretched car leaked all over, and I awake finding myself sitting in a puddle and water pouring in on me. The train was called an Express, but stopped at every station on the road, some of the stations being nothing more than a cross road or a level-crossing. At last at 12.57 pm we reached Wytheville, and on alighting could see no signs of Fred, but three hotelkeepers are at us, each wanting us to go to their particular house. Getting away from them, and leaving Mann in charge of the luggage, I explored the building that served as the station house, and at last discovered Fred, fast asleep in a chair.

They could not start for three days, because Fred had been summoned as a witness in a shooting case some months ago. But:

> On Monday Fred managed to get off being called as a witness, and having hired a 'hack', we set off for Jeffersonville [*some 40 miles away*]. It would astonish you to see what they call roads here. Why, the roads we used to mend in Ischia are just A1, compared to these out here.
>
> This is a very hilly country and the ranges between Wythe and Jeffersonville run parallel to each other. There are four ranges of mountains to be crossed, their height averaging about 4,500 feet. Fred drove, and down hill we simply went over logs of wood, stones, rocks, holes, nothing stopped him. Every minute I thought was the last and that we must smash, but the strong

hickory wheels stood the tremendous jolting far better than did we, the wretched passengers.

Many well-to-do Victorian families had difficulty in finding suitable careers for their younger sons. For the Close brothers, the situation was worsened by the fact that they had had no early education in the Classics, which would have been a requirement for entry to some of the respectable professions. William seems to have settled on a choice of career without a second thought, on the basis of his talk with Paullin. On the journey to Fred's farm, he was already sizing up the local farming with the eye of a prospector. Between the ranges of the Alleghenies he observed that the soil was played out, often with continuous tobacco crops, and at $14 to $16 an acre, was far too expensive. He was critical of the local farming methods:

> Farms here are very different to English ones, except in a rare case. Here there is no method or system. Nothing permanent, and consequently everything in a very untidy condition. It is a sad sight to see acres of what was once splendid land ruined through want of care until it is quite waste land. They don't trouble to manure, but make land bring up crop after crop of corn until all its strength is gone. They say before the war the farmers used to keep their places tidy, because of their having slaves to do so for them, but now they have to work themselves and have no time to devote to ornamenting their farms.

Moreover, there was a lassitude about the whole area that did not appeal to him. The whites were weighed down with having to do so much for themselves, while the ex-slaves had not begun to take profitable advantage of their freedom:

> It will be years before the traces of the late war are wiped out. Everything seems to have been once better than it is now, and there is no doubt in this part of the South the condition of the negro was far better than it is now, and the great majority of the negroes would like to go back to slavery, for in the old days the greatest care was taken of them, and Captain Perry [*in whose farm they had stayed the night en route*] showed me comfortable log-cabins where each married couple dwelt, and where they had their own plot of ground to cultivate. ... Now the negro is a wretched creature. He will only work just enough to provide himself with food and drink, especially the latter; and when he is ill, he has nothing with which to pay the doctor, and nothing with which to get food, and thus dies off. ... What ruined all these farmers was the fact that the greater part of their capital was in slaves, and that when the slaves were liberated not a cent of

remuneration was given to them. Further South in some States the condition of the negro was pitiable before the war, although not much better now. Then, on the cotton plantations especially, the wretched brute was whipped and worked to death.

Jeffersonville is a small village, I beg pardon, city, of about 300 inhabitants. Although the capital of a county bigger than some English counties, it consists of nothing more than one main street. We stayed there a night, and having procured horses, we made our start for Horse-pen-cove [*presumably Fred's farm, forty miles away*]. Fred's saddle pockets contained all the articles of toilette we required – not more than toothbrushes, however.

There is no record of how long they stayed in West Virginia at Horse-pen-Cove or of what it was like. Fred later returned there once or twice, so he must have retained some interest in his farm; but he did not live there again. They now left to take up their invitation to go to Quincy, but first they stopped off in Washington on the way.

In Washington William was *still* not quite well enough to join the other remnants of the Cambridge rowers and the Irish crew in an expedition to Analosta island on the Potomac, where all had been invited by the local Boat Club. Yet he, Ginger (Fred's nickname) and Jerry Mann seem to have enjoyed themselves just as much where they were. They were shown the sights of the town:

but it was the ladies who especially looked after us, and made much of us. It was so nice to have two or three pretty lively girls to look after one. They <u>were</u> fun, didn't care what they said, full of spirit and in fact regular American girls. I am afraid Anne would hold her hands up in horror at them. They wanted to get up some grand receptions for us, but of course we declined as we wished to remain quiet. However they arranged a pic-nic to Mount Vernon, where Washington is buried close to his old home.

They were much interested in hearing the way English young ladies were brought up, and were much amused and astonished at the strictness of the use of chaperones, and that girls who were not out were not allowed to go to parties and so on. It is not a difficult thing get photographs of young ladies and I have already about a dozen. But the most remarkable thing is the fondness of the ladies for giving one a bit of ribbon, or a bow, or a necktie or scarf and even one lady aged but 17 gave me a small locket (she gave one to Mann as well).

Ginger, after his two years at country life, enjoyed this bit of town life very much, and went in for the ladies' society.

William greatly admired the Governor, Mr Shepherd, for the way he was modernising the city; and had the nerve to call on him and offer him his congratulations:

> I remarked that the city owed everything to him for embellishing it so, but he said he got more kicks than halfpence by it, but thought in time the people would come to their senses. He is a great friend of President Grant and he said he was sorry he was not here to introduce us to him, but he was at Long Branch. The crews, bye the bye, had been asked to Long Branch to meet President Grant, but had already accepted the invitation from Washington and had not time.
>
> Washington has a great reputation for hospitality, and they certainly keep it up, everyone talks of their kindness, and utter strangers come in for it. We were really sorry to leave.

They had only been there four days, but there are several more ecstatic pages about what they did there.

Before taking up the invitation of 'the landowner and his pretty daughter' to go to Quincy, the three of them returned to Philadelphia for a week, mainly so that Fred could see the vast Centennial Exhibition:

> Fred soon got tired of it. He went to the Main Building, the Machinery Hall and the Agricultural Hall, by far the three largest buildings in the place and he announced he had done them very thoroughly – for anyone else to do it thoroughly, it would take about a month for each building.

William, on the other hand, enjoyed himself:

> We had several nice drives. I know nothing pleasanter than to go out with a charming girl in a light American buggy with a fast trotter, and to drive through those lovely woods in Autumn. Oh! the foliage is something marvellous, the leaves turn into such beautiful warm colours from the brightest to the deepest red, scarlet, and all the shades of golden yellow. ... I can only compare it to a continual sunset of trees.

On 17th October the party then left for Quincy, by train as far as St Louis, William writing excoriating criticisms of the organisation of American railways. 'Railway travelling is abominable.' At least as far as Pittsburgh they enjoyed the 'very pretty scenery':

> We skirted along the banks of Susquehana, a beautiful river running between lovely hills, and we passed at the right time to get the benefit of the autumn

foliage. On awaking next morning we found we had got into the Ohio prairie land, and from there through Indiana to St. Louis, it was all this monotonous plain.

We arrive at St Louis at 12 at night and the next morning was a horrid drizzle. It was simply a manufacturing town, very dirty and full of smoke and smuts, so at 4 o'c we got on board the *Golden Eagle*, one of the famous Mississippi steamboats. One can hardly call them boats – it is just as if a couple of funnels were placed on a row of cottages, and these were sent steaming off into the river. There is a sameness in the scenery, but it is a mighty river, so many hundred miles from the sea, and in some places is a broad sheet of water, over a mile in width.

Quincy was near the Eastern border of Illinois. They arrived there on 19th October and were welcomed by the widower Daniel Paullin and his sons and daughters. The idea was to organise an inspection of the western half of Iowa with a view to buying land. Iowa was flat, nearly treeless, extremely cold in winter, and suffered from periodic plagues of grasshoppers which, when they descended in black clouds, would eat everything in sight. Moreover it abutted Indian territory – and the battle of Little Big Horn and the massacre of Custer's Last Stand had happened only a few weeks before William's arrival in America. On the other hand the soil was good and land was still relatively cheap. Grazing was still allowed free in some parts of the prairie. In 1870 a railway had been laid from Chicago to Sioux City in the West, and more lines were planned.

The Closes were by no means the first to take advantage of the opportunities. Paullin himself had started to do so in Illinois in the sixties and even in that decade most of the purchasable land in Iowa had already been sold, leaving only 1.7 million acres available. Prospectors had been moving steadily westwards – hence the need to go to the far western side of the state. The expedition took a week to arrange.

To see what sort of land we should buy and to have an idea of its value we organised our party for a week or ten-day cruise on wheels through the Western and less settled parts of the State of Iowa. Our general idea was to go first to Des Moines, the capital of the State, and inquire there of the land agents as to the pros and cons of the different counties.

Our party consisted of Henry Paullin (one of Daniel's sons), who on the very first day received the cognomen of Grin, chiefly on account of the happy disposition of his countenance, and also because we, each rejoicing in a nick-name, felt it incumbent on us to furnish him with one. Well, Grin, Gerry Mann (now known as Ptolomy), Ginger and self [*now known as Brag*] made up our partie-carrée.

They left Quincy by train at 5 p.m. and arrived in Des Moines at 3 a.m. having had little sleep, as the Munroe cornet band, which had engagements in the capital, were practising in other carriages. William did not like the town – '30–40,000 inhabitants, but roads six inches deep in mud' – but they picked up enough information to plan a 250-mile round trip, starting from Stuart, a three-hour train journey further west:

> We dined there, and hiring a team, we started, the horses balking a little at the Hotel steps (we wished afterwards we had accepted the omen). *The team included a buggy, which was a two-wheel, very light carriage built to hold two comfortably with the driver outside.* We came to a steepish hill and lo, the horses stop, but are induced to move, after some time lost, and we all getting out. Again this happened at another hill, all but Ginger [*the driver*] having to get out and shove. We got them started again and once off, Ginger layed onto them and disappeared, sending up a perfect whirl of mud and looking like Jove in a thunder-cloud – his moustachios come nearer to forked lightning than anything else I have seen.

They only made twenty miles in this first day, but had their first look at the prairies:

> I know nothing like it in Europe. This land is rolling prairie, hardly any level land, but none of the hills arising to above 100 feet. What struck us more particularly was the almost total absence of trees. Hedges were rare and there were hardly any fences, as the Stock laws are in force and the owners of cattle are to keep them in and not let them roam about. The landscape in consequence was a dull monotony. Not a particle of green being visible, it being Autumn, all the grass had been turned into a reddish brown and the only contrast to it was either the pale yellow of the dry stalks of the Indian corn or here and there the dark brown, almost black, of newly ploughed land. It having rained the day before the roads were in a dreadful state, the horses and wheels slithering badly in the mud and making the pulling very heavy.

Having established the price of land ($6–7 an acre), they decided to return to Stuart, but progress was frustrated by the obstinacy of the one-eyed horse who stopped at the foot of each hill. They tried everything. They whipped him, lashed him, kicked him. Talked to him, coaxed him, petted him. Ginger mounted him, to make him think he was ridden and that it was quite absurd of him to think that he had a wagon behind him, but he wasn't to be taken in. Grin suggested filling his mouth and nostrils with mud, we did so but he would not move – I believe he rather liked it. "By thunder" says Ginger, "I'll see if he won't move. Let's put a lot of hay under him and set fire to it". This was agreed, but the only result was clouds of smoke, as it had begun to rain. So they unharnessed the horse, who was prepared to walk on his own to the top of the hill, while the second horse pulled the buggy, helped by everyone pushing.

After further such battles, they made five miles in three hours. The one-eyed horse then baulked at a level bridge. In their attempts to move him on the horse got pushed off the bridge and they broke the springs, the cross bars and the pole of the wagon. Leaving Ptolomy to salvage it, the other three walked the remaining six miles back to Stuart in the rain and the dark. In the morning:

> We thought we should have a bill to pay for the broken wagon, but we arranged to be very high-handed with the Livery Stable keeper and threaten him with damages for wasting our time, especially as we found out at the hotel that the horse was a noted baulker. The man not only didn't charge for the broken wagon, but took four instead of the six dollars that we had agreed to pay.

The next foray, although beset by more accidents, saw some real progress. They took the train still further West, to Atlantic, and there hired a team of two small horses. It had turned horribly cold, but the 'ponies soon showed they didn't baulk by pulling us bravely out of a nasty slough'.

> We started too late from Atlantic, and having missed our way, concluded to stop the night at the first farm that would take us in, as once the sun set we felt it would be too cold to move on. We were glad when at the third application, after some hesitation, they agreed. We found we had fallen into first rate hands, good, intelligent people, who made us at home in less than no time. The family consisted of the farmer, his wife, her mother and five strapping sons, and our advent increased their number considerably, but they were used to it, they said, and sometimes were as many as seventeen, to be divided amongst the three rooms. At 9 o'clock the order came from Mrs Owens "Now you boys, it's time to clear out and get to bed", and we found they had given us two beds and insisted on our taking them. Three of the sons shared another mattress in the same room, so that we were pretty well squashed in the small room.

William could no longer afford to be as pernickety about his sleeping quarters as he had been in Philadelphia; and indeed from now on they exaggerated their poverty, in order not to be overcharged at the farms, The scruffier ones bargained at the door of the farmstead, while the more respectable-looking William and Jerry Mann did the talking when it was necessary to appear important.

> In this way we travelled on, getting into wilder country, but splendid soil, and we always stopped at twelve o'clock for meals at the nearest farm house. We, however, even in the wildest parts seldom lost sight entirely of cultivated land. Sometimes for miles around the soil would be unbroken, save one small patch broken by some settler. This beautiful prairie soil, so wonderfully rich, is from 3 to 10 feet in depth and so fertile that no attempt is made to manure it and it will take years before it will be played out. The soil is vegetable mould.
>
> The people about are very frightened of lightning, and rightly so, there being no trees to attract it; so every cottage and barn possesses its lightning conductor.

On this more successful expedition there was less to record in the way of calamities, the worst being caused by all the tracks having been built in mile-wide squares, so that there was sometimes a temptation to cut across them:

> Our day from Ida to Sac was the blackest day of the whole journey. It was a lovely day, and part of the Indian summer one hears so much about. We were not quite sure of our track, and left it to take a short cut to an emigrant's wagon we spied in the distance and enquire our way, but before we knew where we were, we found ourselves completely sloughed, the horses up to their stomachs in mud. I thought at one time they were going to disappear altogether, but luckily they got to the bottom without sinking further. There was nothing for it but to jump out, unhitch them, get them out and then the wagon, and by keeping hopping about on tufts of grass we kept ourselves from sinking far. The horses struggling pluckily got themselves out, but it wasn't so easy with the wagon. The more one shoved the more one sank, but by each taking a wheel we managed little by little to extricate it. Ugh, what a mess we were in.
>
> Misfortunes never come singly, and Jerry, in drying his hands, flipped his ring off. It must have fallen close to where he was, and although we looked for it for over an hour, and cut away all the grass, we could not find it. With the value of that ring he could have bought about five acres of land. He intends to buy that bit of land if he comes back.

On the same day Fred drove over a hole, snapping the bolt that supported the body of the carriage.

> Sac is a nice little town and has five or six good brick residences of the swells of the place, men who a few years before were worth nothing. Every place we went to is reeking, so to speak, with 'Go ahead'. In Iowa one doesn't see the crowds of idlers that abound in Virginia.
>
> There is not a particle of narrow-mindedness in this State, the people in the remotest parts know what is going on in all corners of the world. In Stuart I was in doubt of being able to get *Daniel Deronda* and not only got it but also the latest number of *Punch*.

With these positive feelings about the prairie, William and Fred returned to England via Chicago and the Niagara Falls. In Chicago they joined a crowd of 10,000 to hear the team of Sankey and Moody sing and preach – a partnership of two gospellers that became almost as well-known in England as in the States. They also visited a massive slaughter house, and William's detailed description of the production line to which the pigs were attached and then killed at the rate of five per minute is worthy of some of his father's accounts of new techniques.

🐾 *The Prairie Journal – Farming and prospecting*

May 1877 – September 1878

*I*T WOULD APPEAR from the previous section that the idea of buying land and farming was first suggested to William by Daniel Paullin and that at no time was any county other than Iowa seriously considered. Yet in the brochure he was to write later, *Farming in North-Western Iowa*, William claimed that before deciding on Iowa he had first ruled out Canada and many other American States. Canada, although still British, was too cold and suitable only for stock farming; Pennsylvania had excellent soil but was too expensive, Nebraska too dry and wells sometimes had to be 100 foot deep, in Kansas there was too much fever and ague – and so on. Only Iowa combined the advantages of cheapness and fertile soil which could be worked without coming up against tree roots, rocks and stones. There is nothing in the letters and Journal written at the time about any of this, and the fact is that William had already made up his mind – quite possibly influenced by the favourable impression made on him by Mary Paullin.

William and Fred did not leave for America again until 10th May. All William tells us about what he had been doing in the two months since the famous 1877 boat race is that he had been enjoying himself. On the day of departure he was called at 6 a.m., having only been in bed for three hours, and very nearly decided to stay there, so 'giving up the grand chance we have of coming back millionaires and letting Iowa and the Yankees go to the devil'.

He did get up, and when they got to Liverpool, they were disappointed to hear that the *Celtic* (which for the White Star line was not a fast boat) was to sail instead of the *Germanic*, a flaw having been discovered in the latter's shaft. 'It was a pity, for the *Germanic* on her <u>outward</u> trip [*usually the longest*] did the fastest time on record between Queenstown to Sandy Hook – seven days, ten hours and thirty-one minutes.' At three o'clock luggage, passengers and those saying a last farewell, including a group of friends and relations of the Closes, went onto the tender that took them to the ship.

> Crowds of lovely ladies got on board the tender but alas!, they all came on board only to see some friends off and went back on the tender. It seemed but a few minutes before the tender began ringing her bells for the non-passengers to retire, and after one more goodbye, those of our party left the ship, and soon these were out of sight, handkerchiefs and hats being waved until they could no longer be distinguished. We left Queenstown at about 4 o'clock, and are steaming along with very calm water. We have just passed the *Scythia*, a Cunarder homeward bound. Fred and I crossed little fingers about her, both simultaneously wishing we were aboard of her.

Steamships were still comparatively slow and were still equipped with sails for use in emergencies. Nevertheless there was a huge volume of traffic:

> **Sunday 13th May** Calm day again yesterday. Passed and met five Ocean steamers, at one time we were exactly between two of the Philadelphia boats, one outward and one homeward bound. At about nine at night there was a report that the *City of Brussels*, who had been due for over a fortnight, was in sight, and everyone rushed up to see, but it turned out to be her sister ship, the *City of Chester*.

> **Wednesday 16th May** Just after dinner we sighted a large ship under canvas coming towards us, and after a while she was made out to be a steamer with all sail set. Then her funnels were made out, black and white. Could it be the *City of Brussels*? I made out through my binoculars that she was certainly not steaming,

and shortly after the Captain gave out that it was the long lost City of B., and we rejoiced. Presently she flew a signal 'Machinery broken down, all well'. When we came abreast of her, we gave them some hearty cheering which they returned. Wretched people, they had been out already over three weeks, and could not expect to get in under another week.

Time passed quickly, with much betting and gambling with black beans, and preparing for an end-of-voyage concert, in which Fred was the only bass, while William 'was shifted about in each glee, sang soprano in one, alto in another and tenor in the third, according as the voices wanted strengthening.' He also sang a solo, *Nancy Lee*. Furthermore: 'I am regularly plighted to Miss Toddie. I have given her a steel ring and she has promised me one of her curls, only after great persuasion, however.'

On arrival at New York on it was even hotter than the previous year, but at least they knew how to cope with Customs:

> We had no trouble with our luggage in consequence of a judicious tip, and having collared our puppies we proceeded to walk to the New York Hotel, as they would not take our dogs in the cars. On landing it was 90° in the shade, we had on warm clothing and it struck us as being 190° at least. Poor Jack suffered more than anyone and at last the poor dog went flop down in the middle of the pavement and refused to move any further, so I carried him into a Lager beer saloon and poured iced water on him.
>
> In the evening Fred and I called on Miss Nelly van Dusen, one of those lively girls we met on the *Britannic* last year. We arranged with her on the following morning (Monday) to call on Miss Fallys, another of those girls, who lives at Brooklyn.

On that Monday afternoon William called on a banker friend, Peabody, who told him that later on the same day a number of his rowing friends would be going by steamer up the Haarlem river to row. William decided to join them on the same steamer. They were making for the New York Boat Club, which was alongside the boat houses that had so displeased William last year, but which was clearly of a better class. He was at once persuaded to do some coaching, and even to row with the 'swagger four' of the Club, for which he found himself badly out of training.

The rest of the week they spent looking up friends and making their wills. Their visit had to be cut short, as they heard from Harvard student Ed Paullin (another of Daniel's sons) that his father and sister were 'at Boston, and were going West on

Monday, so we thought it a capital chance to make the 1,550 miles West together'. They went by train to Boston and stayed with Ed in his rooms at Harvard:

> The Harvard men dress more like Englishmen than the generality of men in the States, and the swells have their clothes sent out direct from English tailors. There is a furore about Jack and Gill, and I expect fox terriers will take the place of the bull terriers, without which no swell swaggers.

William was then asked to coach the Harvard eight that was to row a four-mile race against Yale, much on the model of the Boat Race in England. He did this for an hour on the Monday morning, but that very afternoon he and Fred joined the Paullins on their journey to Quincy.

In the train on the way to Chicago they gave an impromptu concert:

> … and gradually everyone in the car came round our seats and joined in the chorus, ladies and all. Miss Paullin sometimes sang soprano and sometimes second. I alternated with her in the soprano, and otherwise warbled in the Tenor. Ginger was especially basso profundissimo.
>
> At Quincy, Mr Paullin was kind enough to ask us to stay in his house. The town is looking very pretty, everything is so fresh and green. The climate does not suit Jack and Gill, but they have saved their reputation by killing several large rats. Ginger has rigged up Lawn Tennis.

Now at last prospecting began in earnest. William wrote at length but intermittently in his Journal, sending each instalment back to England as it was written. The one below was written on 19th July from the Highland Hotel, Denison, a small town near the Western edge of Iowa.

> About the middle of June, with sad hearts Fred and I, accompanied by Mr Paullin, began business in Iowa. We first went to Des Moines, the capital, and got lists of cheap and good lands from the agents there. As last year, we took a train as far as Stuart on the Rock Island and Pacific Railway. We reached it in the afternoon, and started out for a walk before dinner. We had not gone two hundred yards out of the town, when on the road we noticed thousands of little insects jumping about, and looking closer we found that we had made our first introduction to Messieurs les grasshoppers. Close to was a field of clover perfectly black with them. It was a horrid sight, and I confess to having felt like packing up my baggage and at once beating a retreat out of Iowa. They were all very small, but full of life. We thought the further West we went, the thicker they would become; but it was not so. The last time they came in any quantity was nine years ago,

only then they came earlier, before all the crops were gathered, and completely ate up those that were left.

Wheat and small grain is the favourite food of the young hopper. They commence always at the edge of the field and work their way in, but very few fields in our region were entirely overrun by them. Generally fifteen to twenty feet round a wheat field had been made bare by them and the rest practically untouched. Further North 150 miles they have pretty well cleared out the country and during our voyage we met several 'Prairie ships' coming from the North and fleeing from the hoppers, who had taken everything from these unlucky people.

A Prairie ship, bye the bye, is a covered wagon used for travelling over the Prairies, and for weeks it is often the home of the family immigrating. It is curious to think that all the possessions of the family you see before you are on that wagon, save the cow that follows behind. The way beds, chairs, mattresses, chests of drawers and other *Lares* are packed in the wagon is ingenious in the extreme, room still being left for the family. There is a wise law that however much a man may be in debt, his team and wagon, his cow and some farming implements are exempt from seizure, and thus by migrating he is able to start again.

Doing about 40 miles a day, we arrived at the lands we had come principally to see without adventure. It was while we were visiting these lands that the storm occurred which I wrote you a description of.

William's account had not used the word 'tornado', but that is clearly what it was. He was not familiar with the phenomenon, as are today's television viewers; and this one appears to have been coming directly towards him. No wonder it moved him to write seven pages about it. Extracts are given below. It was June, and he starts by depicting the terrain:

From the creeks slope a succession of hillocks, so that the whole country is but hillocks and dales; there is no method in the way the ranges run, but they go in all and every direction. It is for all the world as if the sea, during a great storm, had suddenly petrified and became covered with a bright verdant carpet. For miles round there is hardly any timber, so that standing on the top of one of these ridges the view to the horizon is uninterrupted.

We had driven all morning viewing lands, the sky perfectly clear, and the sun's rays beating unchecked down on us, making it very hot work, unbearable were it not for a slight breeze that the prairies are seldom without. We dined at 12 o'clock with a farmer located in the midest of these wild lands, his farm being a solitary island in the ocean. We were as usual made welcome and hospitably entertained on bacon and potatoes.

About an hour after we had left him, one of us drew attention to a small dark and angry looking cloud in the N.W. horizon, shot up as it were by an explosion. This cloud, 'as a man's hand', grew with marvellous rapidity and soon spread itself over the heavens, black and terrible. The wind had dropped, not a blade of grass stirred and all round was perfect stillness, save the distant rumbling of thunder.

The storm travelled directly towards us, and soon we could see ominous dusky dark lines, reaching the earth perpendicularly from the clouds and as it neared us these rain lines were merged together, until, rapidly advancing on us, there was but one solid sheet of cloud rent almost unceasingly by the lightning. Far away the distant ridges seemed to us covered in a white foam. At the first appearance of the storm our driver, an old settler who knew the landmarks of the area and whom we had hired, announced his intention of driving to a deserted herds-man's cabin he knew of three miles away. Meanwhile ridge after ridge became whitened with foam, cutting off our retreat to the cabin and rushing towards us. We kept as much as possible in the hollows, but had many ridges to cross, always hurrying over them as fast as we could for fear of thunderbolts. The lightning was indeed terrific, there was no flash, but a series of jagged lines pouring them-selves onto the earth, and the crashes of thunder were unceasing.

On climbing a ridge a terrific gust of wind struck us, it seemed we must be blown over and there, scarce a hundred yards away, was the line of foam tearing on as if to overwhelm us. One, two drops of rain, the only ones we had felt hith-erto, and the storm was on us, rain, hail, wind, darkness. We faced it however, till we got a safe distance down the hollow and turning round, we put our backs to it and let it do its worst. For not more than five minutes did this chaos last, but it was terrific while it did, it appeared to us as a war of fire and water. The lightning was really awful and the thunderclaps deafening – the bolts must have fallen at no great distance from us. As suddenly as it began did it cease, and we could see the rear of the storm disappearing Eastward as plainly as we saw its onset. The rain was not in drops, it was one continuous fall, and where a minute before had been perfectly dry ground was now converted into rushing streams. The sun shone again and where a moment before all was dark and disturbed, was once more bright and serene, with overhead a strip of blue sky. But this bright-ness lasted only a short while, for we saw a second storm coming on, even more vicious and black, if possible, than the first.

The second storm proved to be a repetition of the first, except that it lasted longer. When it began, they had got to within 200 yards of the cabin and managed to sit out the end of it inside. Later it threatened to come back from the East, re-darkening the whole sky except for a strip of light on the Western skyline. But it backed off, retreating again to the East, and William wrote three pages on the effects of the returning light, ending with the sunset:

> The sun sank below the level of the clouds into the strip of clear sky, and suddenly flooded the whole landscape with a golden hue. We were on a higher ridge than most and could see for miles around, ridge on ridge, one after the other lit up by the sun. It was a conflagration extending itself, no sooner was one ridge touched than the next one seemed to catch fire from it. The valleys remained in deep shadows, strongly contrasting with the hills. It was not long before the sun sank below the horizon, then gradually everything was turned into a brilliant blood red, the strip of sky was yet a lovely pale clear green, but the clouded remainder of the heavens was as in a sea of blood, at each instant turning into a deeper hue, until it became dark again.

Returning to William's entry of 19th July:

> We heard afterwards that it occasioned a great deal of damage in the country round. Four miles of the railroad was washed away, they say by a waterspout, and in Denison here several buildings were clean blown over, the Roman Catholic and some other church among the number, and the Episcopal was blown off its foundations and moved East just ten feet: they are buildings capable of sitting over 100 people each, and built entirely of wood. Only one saloon was hurt, and all the ungodly saloon keepers escaped.
>
> We got very badly sloughed while viewing lands, and stupidly too. We sent our guide ahead to examine and he called out it was alright. So in we went with our horses and all, and in we did go, in with a vengeance. The horses quietly lay down and the buggy sank in up to over the hubs. There was nothing for it but to take off our shoes and our stockings and tuck our inexpressibles up and set to work. We unhitched the horses and our first care was to get them out. They seemed well used to the business, for each time we wanted them to make an effort they responded with a will, and struggled hard, but while we waited for them to blow and prepare for another effort, they quietly cropped the grass as if

being sloughed was an every day affair for them. In this way, plunge by plunge, we got them on terra firma. But the real tug of war came when we wanted to get the buggy out. We thought we would try first without Mr Paullin getting down. It was very amusing to watch his face, it was an index of our progress; when we moved a little his face brightened up, and he grew cheerful, but when it seemed as if we were fast stuck his countenance fell at the prospect of his wading out through the sea of mud.

A few more sinkings in the mud are recorded in the Journals and it was a major problem for all the settlers, who eventually co-operated in having the prairies drained by underground pipes into the creeks.

After looking at all the lands we were directed to, we returned to Des Moines via Council Bluffs, and saw the Missouri for the first time. Although it's the longer river of the two, it is not as broad or striking as the Grand Mississippi. Yet it is just as well we haven't it running through England, it might wash us away.

We did not settle terms in Des Moines as they wanted us to take a certain amount if they gave us the land at low rates, so Ginger went back to Denison while I, having some business to arrange at Quincy, returned there with Mr. Paullin. [*Clearly they had made some sort of offer but William does not give away any details.*]

On his return to Denison:

It is rather difficult to write this Journal, for Ginger has all the 'personnel' of the hotel and some of their friends (all of the fairer sex) around him, and I don't know whether it is the effects of the moon, for it is a lovely night, but he is treating them to a concert. He is just telling a tale against himself. With some gay young sparks of Virginia he was serenading some of his fair friends, when at one part of the programme he began a solo. He was rendering this as he thought with a pathos and power and depth of his well known voice, when a window opened and his solo was interrupted by a beseeching voice. 'Hey! down there, please give that calf more rope'. He retired.

Most homes had a harmonium or some substitute for that instrument. Some were used for little more than accompanying Moody and Sankey hymns, so Fred, with a wide repertoire and a good voice, was much in demand.

At one farm which also did duty as an inn, Ginger, as is his wont, was performing on the harmonium to a large audience when the landlord informed us his 'gals could tune a bit'. Ginger was most pressing in his requests to them to favour the company, but whether through shyness or not wishing to play after him, they only giggled and would not. Ginger would not be beaten, and persisted in his efforts to persuade them, still they would not. 'What can I do to persuade you ladies? Why I'd stand on my head if that would make you play.' One of them, thinking he was joking, said on those conditions she would, and without more ado Ginger springs onto his hands and walks about head downwards, and then leads the blushing maiden, fairly captured, to the harmonium.

After seeing another cloud of grasshoppers blacken the air to such an extent that temperature dropped, William wrote:

> We are rather interested in them as if they are to be a permanence, adieu to Iowa, and the castle we have been building in i-o-air!

> ***Written at Denison on 5th August 1877*** Since I last wrote we have remained here looking after the main chances, and before this reaches England we shall each be the lord of 1,200 acres and 80 head of cattle.

William continues with a history of Denison, where they are living. It began only twenty years ago, when the routes of two mail coaches crossed at the top of a hill. A log cabin doing duty as a hotel was built, kept by Mr Denison:

> Mr Denison laid out a town around this hotel, that is put a few stakes about representing streets and modestly called his new town Denison. Being near the centre, Denison was made the county seat and a Court House and School House were erected. This brought in some business and a few 'private residences', or small wooden frame cottages.
>
> [*From there the town quickly developed and by now had*] 900 inhabitants, five churches, two banks, two school houses, 5 brick storehouses, several brick residences, three ice-cream saloons, several common saloons, two livery stables, etc. … When Mr Denison got rich from the sale of his town plots he speculated, and is now a poor man. The richest man in town is the banker, who came here as a small farmer, scraped enough money to buy a thrashing machine and on his earnings started the bank.

> ***In train to Des Moines, 6th August*** I was talking of Denison <u>town</u>. There is no such thing as an American village, all are towns or cities. Denison, were it in England, would be a mere village if one looked at it's size alone, but in every other respect it really is a town. Where it most differs from an English village

is the superiority of the American store over our English village shops. Here it would be difficult to find anything they have not got in their stores. Everything moves up to the age, and everyone lives up to it, as far as buying new things goes. The system of advertising is so perfect (far too much so) that if a new thing comes out, everyone knows of it, and if it is a good thing everyone will have it. Farmers especially waste the greater part of their earnings in buying new machinery.

On 8th August, only three days after writing that they were about to buy 1,200 acres each, he wrote this on his return by train from Des Moines:

> I am back again, and have completed all arrangements for the transfer of 2,593 acres of land to ourselves.

On 10th August he wrote on the differences between an American and an English farm:

> It is as different to an English farm as chalk is from cheese. The soil is of such wonderful richness and fertility, that in some of the oldest farms about here Indian corn has been raised year after year for nearly a quarter of a century and the yield of crops is as heavy now as when the soil was first broken. I know of no instances where manuring has been resorted to for the production of cereals. Manure is simply wasted. Farmers here also prefer cultivating a large tract of land in a slovenly way to taking better care of a smaller tract. And undoubtedly while land is so cheap and the soil unexhausted it pays them.
>
> Indian corn is the great production of Iowa, she producing more than any other State.
>
> The next thing to strike you on coming up to a farm is the smallness of the dwelling house and barns. Although the farmer may be farming 320 acres, yet he is content to live in a cabin, often with but two rooms, dirty and untidy, home being entirely subservient to the farm.
>
> Where then does the money most of them must make go? You can soon see by looking round and coming across the ruins of splendid agricultural machines thrown anywhere, they get a bit out of order through the neglect of the farmer himself, and they are condemned as useless. I almost think the farmer is glad when he has spoilt a good machine for he then has the pleasure of buying some wonderful new machine with the latest improvements. Now no-one thinks of walking behind his plough or harrow or anything else, but all their machines have seats and require the driver to ride, and comfortably too. It is the same with all the new farming machinery, including grass-cutting, and reapers.

William was critical of the German farmers and thought the English and the Scots were the best, once they had 'learnt to unlearn a great deal of their home farming'. He reserved high praise for:

> the best colony [*first use of the word*] around is an Irish Scotch one from Belfast. They came about a dozen years ago, and are now doing remarkably well, and having at once planted trees have good timber about to shelter them and have built neat houses, and live together more like civilized people.

William now reveals his plans for the coming months. He had originally been attracted by Paullin's method of buying up public land and reselling it to settlers, and this indeed is what he was to do later on. But now he became committed to the idea that it would be more worthy and satisfactory, and also more profitable, to convert any prairie land purchased into farmland. He and Fred decided to start by themselves fattening cattle and pigs over winter, while organising preliminary work on 600 acres each of their total holding to get it in a fit state to rent to settlers next year. Fred had been stock farming in West Virginia for two years and had taken to the life. But William, who clearly did all the negotiations on the purchase of the land, was more interested in the renting aspect. His calculations on the return of his investments suggest the mind of a banker and in this he is not a bit like his younger brother. Fred's disclaimer some years ago that he was 'no good at books' probably still held good.

> What we intend to do with our land is as follows. Next spring we shall put each about 600 acres of it into cultivation, and build six or eight small houses or rather cabins, and plant trees around these cabins and call them farms, and rent them.
>
> The first year we shall not get more than a dollar a year [*per acre*] for renting, the second $1½, and the third, $2. Meanwhile the tenant will be bound each year to break up 20 or 30 acres, until all are broke, so that to set 1,200 acres fully going will require about $7,000 and three years time. As farms are rented from March to March, it will not be until next March year that we shall see anything come in from land, so to fill up our time we are going in for cattle, buying cattle that have been fed on grass all summer, and then feeding them with corn until January and fattening them up as well as hogs – voilà tout.
>
> The cattle we buy weigh on average 800 – 850 lbs, and after fattening, 1,200 lbs. We have made our calculations on a moderate basis, and unless very unlucky ought to make 30–35%; but huge hogs are very speculative. If we get cholera

amongst them, which last year caused great losses, we may lose them all, and will have to be content with 15 to 20% [*from the cattle*]. Wouldn't you in England be content with that? We haven't got it yet, but when we have, if we do, I'll let you know. [*This letter was designed to tempt. In England at the time the return on farming was only 2–3%, owing to a series of wet winters and cheap imports ever since the repeal of the Corn Laws.*]

 I think I forgot to mention one thing. As well as a harmonium, no farm is without a croquet ground; often it is not much more than ten feet square, but still it answers for them, and it is a curious sight to see farm labourers playing croquet.

While work on the pigs and cattle was all done by the brothers, it is not clear how much of the preliminary digging of the prairie was done by them, if any. The cost of hiring local men to do it worked out at about $2 an acre.

20th August I think I told you in my last that we had signed the contract for 2,600 acres of land. This makes Fred and me landed proprietors in four differ-ent countries, viz. England, France, Italy and America. Somewhat swagger, but I'm willing for cash considerations to sell my power of swaggering in France and Italy and also England. Make your offers.

Fred bought fifty more cattle at a point sixty miles east of Denison, and wrote to William asking him to come and help drive them over:

So arming myself with my brand new cattle whip, and a toothbrush, I started on my mare, Polly, and as I went along I thought I would practise myself in the use of this formidable whip, the handle of which is not a foot long, and the lash a thick thong 12 feet long. Attempting to crack it, I nearly cracked poor Polly's head, and she replied by rearing and buck-jumping and my first crack with my first cattle whip very nearly deposited me in the dust. I next tried the reverse action and made a sort of cracking noise, but it was against Polly's flank, and I again had to apologise. There's luck in the third attempt, and so boldly whirling the thong thrice round my head in the approved style of the swell driver I tried to produce the pistol shot sound by jerking my arm downwards suddenly (as I had seen them do) and I succeeded in bringing the lash smartly across my face. Ah! didn't it sting.

 I felt as if my face had been cut in two. I shall now always have a certain amount of sympathy for cattle when I lash them.

 Toward evening, just after I had passed a village where I rather expected to

Improve Your Stock!

——THE FOLLOWING——

"Polled Angus" Bulls

——WILL STAND AT——

"THE INCHINNOCH HOME FARM"

Township 92, Range 45,

——FROM——

1st AUGUST, 1881.

LEMARS SENTINEL PRINT.

have found Ginger and the cattle, I heard some way ahead a noise as if a lot of rifles were being discharged, and as I neared the brow of a hillock, I heard a lot of shouting as well. When I reached the summit, below was a thick cloud of dust, and presently, as a little wind blew the dust aside, I saw a herd of cattle and battle going on between them and the two drivers, for on one side of the road was a cornfield without fences – and cattle above all things like green Indian corn [*maize*].

At first the two figures trying to control the cattle were so black with dust that William did not recognize them and moved on. But then 'a voice, unmistakably Ginger's, shouts "Where the (ahem) are you going to, can't you help us? Look sharp, get to the centre". It transpired that Fred and his assistant, around noon, had stopped for a rest under a tree, and had fallen asleep. The cattle had move off to graze a field of Indian corn a quarter of a mile away. Leaping onto their horses, they forgot to put the bits in their mouths, and the boy's horse galloped off in the wrong direction, while Fred in his haste failed to notice a slough in which the horse's legs sank and Fred got his legs stuck under the horse. In the end they managed to round the cattle up and reach their quarters for the night.

> We were on our way early next morning so as to travel as much as possible in the cool, but of all the horrid, dirty, tedious and slow occupations cattle driving is the worst. The drivers have to stay well behind, and thus get the full benefit of the dust. It got into every mortal place it could. We seldom could see the head of the column. Then the sun and the heat, and on that day no breeze. I felt like suffocating.
>   Sometimes there was a corn field on both sides of the road, and then it was the hardest work to keep them straight, and also when once they were in to get them out, for the corn stalks grow higher then our heads, even though on horseback, and it is difficult to see the cattle. We did not get them to the herding ground till past seven, and then had six miles to return here, so we were from 12 to 13 hours in the saddle, and pretty well tired. There is remarkably little romance in driving cattle and a great deal of weariness and dirt.

From the beginning William had seen himself as an investor and planner and this droving experience probably hastened the day when he would make that transition. Fred on the other hand never complained about the hard work and probably enjoyed it. By the time they got back to base he had learned to recognise and given a name to nearly every one of the herd of fifty. This difference in aptitudes between the two brothers was to become more marked, but did not lead to dissension, Fred readily accepting his more humble role.

A further instalment, dated 26th August, shows that luck was with them. The corn was late because of the wet spring, but so far the grasshoppers had not reappeared and it was unlikely that there would be frost before it was harvested in a fortnight's time. Although they had not yet planted any crops, they were interested in the market for corn because they bought it to fatten their cattle with during the winter. In Iowa the price was low and in Illinois, where the crop was not doing so well, it was high. They would therefore be able to sell their cattle profitably in Illinois, which is where the main market was, in Chicago. Also in this year the wheat had done exceptionally well, the yield being double that of the previous best year, 1874. This too augured well for their prospects of attracting farmers to the area.

The rest of the 27th August instalment is taken up with a six-page story told him by a veteran of the Civil War who had made an incredible escape from being a prisoner of war in the deep South. There were hundreds of men in the neighbourhood who had taken part in the war. Iowa had sent over 70,000 to fight, and 20,000 never came back.

> *12th October* We have quite finished our new cattle and hog pen, and have moved all our cattle therein – never to come out again until the day that, rolling with fat, they commence their journey to Chicago and death. They have a nice stream of running water through the yard and ought to be very comfortable.
>
> Ugly rumours of hog cholera having appeared in several localities, we have enquired all round among the farmers who did not lose their hogs last year as to the way they kept them. We found as a rule that those who took care of their stock and hogs did not suffer much. They salted them well, gave them plenty of clean water and plenty of room, while those who neglected them suffered for it.

Just as in 1876, a very sharp frost (just too late to harm the corn) was followed by a hot Indian summer. 'Splendid weather and life during that time is enjoyable in the extreme.'

> I had some time ago promised to take two young ladies here for a ride, and was able to fulfil my promise on Monday last, but it began most disastrously. One of these ladies I soon saw was no rider, for even in walking her hand was never far from the pummel. The other, a Miss Wygant, seemed all right. I proposed a canter, and off they went, their ponies began racing and soon the bad rider was utterly demoralized, her hat at the back of her head and crying woa, woa, and

not attempting to guide her pony. I was not surprised to see her roll off, but almost simultaneously Miss Wygant rolls off twenty yards further on. I found the bad rider in a sad state, her habit torn to pieces and unhooked, and she pale and groaning 'oh my arm, my arm' I looked to see how it had fared with Miss Wygant, and saw her emerge from a ditch, trip on her habit, sit down plump backwards and roll into the ditch again. Before I got to her, however, she was out again, and came towards us, holding in her hand a broken stirrup leather. She was covered in mud. In falling into the ditch she had gone head first and exactly half her face was jet black, the line passing as if painted right up the bridge of her nose. She was very much mortified at having come off, and the indignant expression of her countenance and her eyes (she has pair of A 1 eyes) flashing out from underneath this coating of mud was too much for me, and I fairly roared with laughter. She was half amused and half angry, and I asked her to excuse me until she looked at herself in the glass. She said she wasn't hurt, but would have pulled that pony in, even had she broken her neck, if the stirrup had not broken, and she wasn't going to give up her ride, if I'd only catch her pony for her. [*On examining the damage, the first lady was not badly hurt and was sent home in a carriage; while Miss W. had a lump on her forehead and her upper lip had swollen to twice its normal size.*] So after recapturing the runaway ponies, Miss Wygant and I continued our ride and I found she really could ride well.

Two pages later William tells a story about an anonymous Western family:

The father, Mr W., was a lawyer in town, and having been found out using some trust money was 'wanted', and no one knows where he is. All the property was seized except his homestead and eight acres, which by a wise law in Iowa can never be seized for debt unless mortgaged. On this farm Mrs W. retired with her family: Miss W. and the two sons, aged 19 and 13. Before the catastrophe they were affluent, well educated people, Miss W. decidedly being the best of the young ladies around, and withal rather pretty. She plays the organ, leads the church choir and is an active teacher in the Sunday school (in which I am a Superintendent, if you please). She is but 17. Although very fond of music and able to read well and play fairly, she sold her organ and every spare thing, as did the rest of the family, to enable them to begin farming. This is their first year and they have done pretty well and no one thinks the less of them because Mr. W. was a scoundrel. They are greatly respected by all. They each have their share in the work on the farm, and it was quite a picture to see Miss W. driving in the cows.

It later transpires that Miss W. is the Miss Wygant with whom William went out riding. Now when William went to Quincy later that autumn he became engaged to Mary Paullin, although there is no mention of this in the December instalment. He did not want anyone in England to know about it, and quite possibly did not want the news to reach Denison either.

Reading between the lines of the next instalment, it is obvious that one reason for spending so much time away from Denison was to be near his fiancée. Also during the visit, the divergent roles of William and Fred became more marked.

11th December No more driving of refractory steers as our cattle are being fattened in a yard, and also I have been away at Quincy on business for a month or so [*rather longer than the 'few days' predicted on October 12th*] and while there certainly had not time to write. Fred stayed with the cattle, living out at the farm while I was away. I enjoyed my visit to civilized society very much and there was plenty going on in the way of dissipation.

On my way back I stopped at Des Moines a little while. It is prettily situated on the banks of a river and a busy, thriving and growing town. It is quite likely that I may spend a couple of months or so there this winter in an office, to learn about law relating to lands. At the hotel my waiter was a 'coloured gentleman' indicted for murder and robbery, and his trial was to take place shortly. There wasn't sufficient evidence against him, he informed me, and he was sure to get off. It was only malice on the part of another coloured gentleman that put him in a fix at all.

Although the law for the abolition of capital punishment has been voted, yet it is practically a dead letter, as Judge Lynch has generally a word to say, and few are the murderers who manage to reach the State penitentiary, as the officers are generally saved the trouble of conveying them there – in Des Moines alone there have been two cases of lynching in the last two years.

The Maine liquor laws are also supposed to be law here and the only things lawfully sold are native wine and native beer! But just go to one of these bars and ask for whiskey, gin, brandy, etc. and very seldom do they fail to bring out just the thing you want.

Wine is scarcely ever seen here on a table, or indeed drunk: the man who does have wine on his table is considered a lost sheep. Ladies are strongly opposed to having wines and spirits drunk inside their houses. The consequence is that men are driven to the saloons, where they will drink three or four times as much as they would at home. It is, I suppose, one of the traits of the American character that they can do nothing moderately, it is with most of them either total abstinence or hard drinking.

William himself hardly touched alcohol, at least in this period of his life. He warned prospective recruits from England about the anti-drink climate of opinion, but he was not in the least censorious of those who still partook. He describes with detached amusement the waves of temperance fervour that regularly swept through the state and the meetings where people were urged to 'come out of the gutter' and take the pledge. 'Waves that sweep over the country and leave no traces behind but broken pledges.' Reformed drinkers were brought on stage to tell the audience how wretched they had been when they were a slave to drink and how happy they were now they had given it up. William heard this story about such a occasion in another state:

> During one of their meetings, one old chap got thoroughly excited, and kept shouting "Glory I'm going to heaven now, I'm agoing to climb to Heaven now", and suiting the action to the words, he began climbing up the sides of the log cabin in which the meeting was held. "Hold on", shouts one of the congregation, "before you go further Mr Barrett pay me the dollar and a half you owe me".
>   We are happily free in Iowa from these ranting Methodists.
>   Back in Denison, I found our cattle doing splendidly and fast putting beef on. If the markets are fair we shall ship them about the middle or end of January, but if low then we shall hold on to them, which with Indian corn at 14 cents the bushel we can afford to do. Ginger and I make capital partners in this cattle business I think, for he likes the work of attending to them and I don't. As long as I can get someone else to go into the mud when it is knee deep, I had rather not go myself, but prefer superintending, sitting on the rails.

The entry for 14th December presaged the colony:

> Who should walk in the other morning, while Fred and I were breakfasting, but William Hyndbran Wann, Fred's Virginia friend. [*He had been in Ireland, visiting relations.*] He now intends giving this country a trial. We are very glad he has come, the meeting between him and Ginger was a sight to behold. Henry Paullin intends coming early in the spring, so we are already forming quite a colony. [*Wann then told them about some matters that Fred needed to sort out in Virginia, and by the date of this instalment, Fred had already left.*] He will travel 4,500 miles before he returns, as in default of lines he has to go via Washington.
>   The wonderful crops we have had this year are already showing their effects on

the increased demand for land. Last year, owing to the grasshopper scare, there was little or no inquiry for it, but since the hoppers have disappeared, and the crops have been so good, there is no lack of farmers wishing to rent. We can get $2.50 per broken acre per year, at an initial cost to ourselves of approximately $6.50 per acre. This is a large percentage annual return, but we shall not get any income from the lands until September 1879 for we do not break the lands until June '78.

The $6.50 quoted above included not only the cost of breaking, but also a contribution of $1 as a contribution to the building of a four-room timber-framed farmhouse, barn and well for each of the twenty farms that were envisaged for the acreage bought so far. The houses cost $250 each to build, the barn and well $100. When the tenant farmers were found, they would also be provided with seed and machinery, all of which they would pay for by giving the Closes half their produce.

> *10th January 1878* Trade has suffered a great deal from this unparalleled mild winter, for the roads all being unmacadamised were simply impassable from the mud. Hence farmers were unable to get their produce to market. The people will learn by paying for it that they must have macadamised roads leading to towns.

That was a short extract from one of William's regular outbursts on the state of American roads. It was almost an obsession. Shades of road-mending in Ischia? Just one last example of this will be given, in this extract from his description of Des Moines:

> There are some good stores, the store-widows making a grand display. On the principal street there are two theatres and several hotels, the one I am in now contains several hundred rooms. Altogether, this street would not disgrace any town I know of, yet through the whole of Des Moines there is not a single street macadamised: the roadway is left in its natural state and as the soil varies from 6 to 15 feet in depth, you may imagine what it is like when muddy.

> *Quincy, Illinois 20th January 1878* Shortly after Xmas I left Wann in charge of the cattle [*Fred was still in Virginia.*] and went to Des Moines. I wanted to learn more about the loan business and by sundry wire pulling got the run of the Iowa Loan and Trust Company's office, and saw how they did their business. Nothing can be safer than the security of good farms, and security more than four times the value of the loan is required. I want to see if it is worth while my engaging

in this business at all, in the hopes of persuading people in England, who only get 4%–5%, to send me their money to loan for them. I should propose to do it through the company, but personally select and look over each mortgage and see the land if necessary.

The less William got involved in manual labour, the better. As he has not so far mentioned his engagement in the Journal, it is impossible to say whether that had any bearing on his change of course. Yet it seems probable that the Paullins may have steered him that way. Daniel Paullin had made his money buying and selling land and both he and his daughter Mary may have felt that that was a more suitable occupation than actually farming it.

> As I have nothing in particular to do for a couple of months or so, I thought it best [*after his short spell in Des Moines*] to read up something about the laws of the United States and thus, for that purpose, am in the office of the Hon V. H. Browning, late Secretary of the Interior and as fine a specimen of the gentleman of the old school as you would wish to meet anywhere. One would hardly expect to meet such a specimen out West, but 'I guess' he is about the only one. He is courteous to a degree and very refined in his manners and conversation and dresses in the old style. Mr Browning is considered the shrewdest lawyer in this section of the state, notwithstanding his seventy five summers. [*Moreover, he had also been the US Attorney General and a great friend of Abraham Lincoln.*]

The above entry is a little economical with the truth, as again Mary Paullin must have been an attraction as well as Mr Browning. While in Quincy he must have told his nearest relations in England about the engagement, as he received a discouraging letter from Uncle Thomas Close (the one with whom JC had quarrelled in his youth but with whom he was later reconciled) pouring cold water on the idea that Englishmen could be persuaded to invest in America and expressing disapproval of Mary as a bride, partly because Daniel Paullin was apparently unwilling to provide a dowry, in spite of having persuaded William that he was worth about a quarter of a million dollars. He wrote: 'I cannot sanction a marriage which I am sure that had they been living, both your father and your mother would have disapproved of.' On receipt of this, William made plans to sail to Europe with Mary and argue his case.

Before they left, Fred turned up for a short break in his journey back from Virginia:

Quincy, 29th January 1878 Fred has just returned from Virginia and stayed a couple of nights here on his way back to Denison. He told us that on the way there, he got his pocket picked of nearly all his spare cash in Chicago, but his smart trading qualities came to the fore. Strolling about Chicago, he attended an auction and became the possessor of a handsome gold watch, for which he paid eleven dollars. Luckily he had already bought his train ticket to Wytheville, but after paying his hotel bill, he found himself on the train without enough money to pay for his dinner. When hungry, he asked his neighbour "Don't you wish to buy a gold watch? I am obliged to sell it as I have had my pocket picked, and I must get something to eat." He soon got a crowd round him and was asked what he thought it was worth. "Well, if you ask me what I think it is worth, why I should say $100, but I have to get some money and I am willing to let it go at half that". [*After a lot of hard bargaining and brinkmanship, he settled for $25 – and ate dinner on his profit.*] For bargaining this country is as bad as Naples.

William's account of his two-and-a-half-month absence is confusing, as he describes the journey back to New York before the journey to Europe, and much of what he did there is not told. Some of it is written up on the boat back, but most of it later in May in Denison. The whole instalment will be summarised:

They sailed on Saturday 16th February on the *Republic*. On Monday a terrific storm blew up and Miss Ball, a friend of Mary's, retired to her cabin, not emerging until Thursday. 'Miss Paullin however, although she had never been to sea before, never once felt sea-sick.' It was the worst storm William had ever seen and the log book recorded a 'strong hurricane from the N.E.' Although the ship was over-crowded with saloon passengers of both sexes, 'Miss Paullin was the only lady at dinner' on the third evening.

We arrived in Antibes on March 2nd ... Oh! that month! I left on 8th April. Meant to have seen the University Boat race, only saw a University Procession. Better luck next time. Stayed the greater part of the time in town [*presumably Manchester*] and left Liverpool on 16th April and began this journal in mid-ocean. Be it known that it was only at the urgent and oft repeated requests of the Gynarchy at the Cape that I consented to begin my thirteenth Journal.

There is no information as to the route to Antibes, but we know from Harnack that there he stayed in the Close family house (Villa Closebrooks) and that the two ladies did not come with him to England, but undertook a European tour on their own, not getting back to America until after he did. If one purpose of the trip was to win over the family to Mary Paullin, the family did not include Thomas Close, as the use of the word Gynarchy suggests the family house at that time was occupied by females – and in any case, Thomas was now over eighty. On the other hand he must have been persuasive about his business plans during his short spell in England, for, according to Harnack, 'When he sailed back from Liverpool on 16th April he was in a blithe mood, his battles won.'

On the voyage back to New York William was placed at table at the right hand of the Captain, a young man of twenty-eight. William approved of his conscientious approach: during three days of fog, he never left the bridge. His method of avoiding icebergs was foolproof:

> We must have been very near some ice one night. I woke feeling very cold and next morning the Captain told me the thermometer had been as low as 28°. I have never seen an iceberg. The effect can be felt 60 miles away, and a little bucket is let down every hour into the sea and the temperature of the water is taken.

On arrival, he only stayed in New York two days, but, true to his upbringing, did not miss the opportunity of examining a new invention:

> I heard the phonograph, it certainly represented all that was said very clearly but did not always get the right key. That however depended on the rate the man moved the wheel round. It sounded to me as if someone were in the cellar below and talking up the chimney. The machine is very simple and I could have invented it if I had only thought of it, so could any of you. Some day, perhaps, instead of writing this journal, I shall be relating it to my phonograph, and sending the tin foil round, and you will each have your machine and have the exquisite pleasure of hearing my sweet voice.

He got back to Denison at the beginning of May 1878, with the intention of prospecting for more land that could be broken before the season for that was over. ('Breaking' meant turning over the grass of virgin prairie so that the roots rotted in the sun. He was later to write detailed instructions on how, when and why to do this, and what the first crop to plant afterwards should be, for the benefit of new arrivals from Great Britain.)

> I arrived here at 6 am and was making my way to the Hotel Fred usually boards at, when I learnt from an early bird who had his store open already, that Ginger had built himself a residence (sic) down by Casady's and was living there now.

I soon spied out the new building and knocked Ginger up. He welcomed me, and on entering the building I found myself in a spacious billiard room. "Bravo!" said I, "this is good. Now let us proceed onward and view the other apartments." "Well", said he, with proper pride and a night shirt, "this is the other apartment" and flung open a door and disclosed to view the rest of the residence. In this, Fred occupies the South half and I the North half. We eat with a family next door and get good wholesome food. Mrs Wygant was an Englishwoman and cooks things in a plain way. In hotels in America they give you a tiny bit of every-thing, each bit on a tiny dish on its own, and these are arranged in a semi-circle round you, one large plate being given you wherewith to discuss all these small items. Yesterday I saw the first leg of mutton on the table that I have seen in Iowa.

Ginger is well and has worked well. We have 1,200 acres that are to be ploughed before the middle of July. Fred signed the contracts at $2 an acre.

We shall soon have to be putting up our frame cabins, and find our renters. That will be our chief difficulty, for although we have had applications for our farm that would cover three times the number we shall have, yet the great difficulty is to find good and steady men who are willing to work. The country is filled with tramps, who would be very glad to have a home for a year and when rent time came round would quietly decamp. We take a mortgage on all the renters' goods and chattels, and if caught decamping they are sent to the penitentiary.

It is a great blessing to have a den of one's own, where one can drive into the walls all the nails one has a mind to and just do as one likes. Fred made no pro-vision for having a stove in and no chimney was erected, but last night a sharp frost did enormous damage to the fruit trees and vegetables. We even had snow on 11th May, when for a day the country was under two inches of it.

The frost killed all the fruit. Hopes of cherries from the two cherry trees whose branches could be reached from the windows of their residence/cabin were aban-doned. In June they produced one single cherry, eaten by William.

Although there was much work to be done, William was able to write another instalment on 1st June, because continuous rain had kept them indoors.

All is going well and our breaking is half done. We are contracting to have the frame houses put up and I shall reserve a room for myself at one of them on each farm. The hardest thing to get over when out on our trips is the sleeping at night, when there are only a couple of beds in a house and a bed to oneself is not to be had.

Fred and I have a regular convention. He takes charge of the stables and feeds the horses, while I keep our 'residence' supplied with water and trim the lamps. I am sorry to say the well is a very deep one, and it is quite a labour on a hot day to draw the water.

When the billiard table was first put up, it was amusing to watch the ingenuous way the youth of Denison would be passing by and just stop a moment at the window and have a word to say, and turn the subject on the table and hint very plainly they would like a game.

It is an undoubted economy to live out here. Our three meals a day next door cost $3.50 per week (about 14/6d) and our rooms are swept and made up every morning for $3 a month.

People are very nervous since the last tornado and many of them have had cellars built or 'dug outs' as they are called, as a place of refuge in case one strikes the town.

By now William and Fred had both become well integrated with the community. Fred took the lead in organising various musical occasions and dances, including one major ball – nearly missing this, as he had injured his knee while participating in a local kick about with a kind of football. Raising funds for the church, he organised a 'Strawberry Fair', whereby anyone could come and eat as much strawberries and ice cream as they could for a smallish payment, the food having been donated. He also organised an 'Episcopal Fair' at Mrs Wygant's house next door and 'magnanimously threw open to the public our magnificent suit of rooms', and was quite successful in making a few dollars from the billiards table by charging the gents so much a game of ten points up, with ladies as partners.

William had become a leading figure in the Episcopal Church. When the whole building had been blown sideways in the tornado, there were heavy expenses to be met for moving it back, repairs and replacements; and he contributed to these as well as organising much of the fundraising. When the local priest was away he nervously agreed to take a few services, reading the lesson. He could not argue with the fact that he was the only person available who had both been confirmed and was able to read well. The first time he did this he read a sermon by Vaughan to a congregation of seventy. He was then dragooned into teaching at the Sunday school – 'Aren't you a graduate of Cambridge College?' – and became its Superintendent. He was further distressed when he was pressurised into being a godfather for the second time and declared that if he did not make his fortune in Iowa, it would simply be because of the Church.

In September the great sport and useful provider of food was the shooting of the Prairie Chicken. It was related to the grouse, but looked quite different.

> For quantity of meat I never saw the like, the breast of the chicken being like a small beefsteak. He doesn't come up to the grouse in taste, has none of the gamey flavour, but tastes more like the common chicken. Large quantities are exported to England.
>
> This year all agree in saying that the shooting is not as good as usual, because this spring an attempt was made to burn out the grass hoppers when they were young, and before they could fly, by burning the prairies. The only result of these fires was to destroy thousands of unfledged prairie chicken. Now trapping and exporting are prohibited by law. It is a very wise measure, for were it not so, before long the chicken would be a thing of the past. One dealer in this town told me that sometimes he would receive for exporting as many as 500 dozen birds (trapped) in a day.

What William liked best about Denison was the spirit of enterprise and willingness to take anything on. He wrote about a new local newspaper:

> I send as a supplement the *Evening Review*, the first number of a <u>daily</u> paper started in this village. Is it not extraordinary that Denison, with its ten or eleven hundred inhabitants, should have its daily, besides two weekly papers, one Republican and one Democrat? Of course everything is exaggerated. We had a little matter before the Board of Supervisors – it is magnified as a great legal contest. We are reported as having 3,000 acres being broken, whereas we are only having 1,500, and so on. I told him to advertise for half a dozen Breakers, and he puts a hundred wanted.

The editor of this daily was the German postmaster and he had to hire a sub-editor to put the copy into English. The brothers were relieved not to be vilified in it, as Fred had had a brush with him in the post office. He had been greeted with "Vell, Rost Beeve" and so had replied "Hullo Sourkrout". The postmaster had taken umbrage and said, "Vell sir, if you can't talks like a shentlemans to a shentlemans, vy you had better not talk at all."

> ***Denison, 18th June 1878*** Have been very busy this last fortnight, surveying and superintending breaking. I forget whether I have told you I have bought 420 acres more land and got them very cheap.
>
> A friend of Wann's from Belfast is coming out to join him soon, thus our colony is increasing – the more the merrier.

All the boys in the place are getting their fireworks ready for the 4th July [*Independence Day*] celebrations. Most of the houses in the town are made of wood and there is not the least attempt at a fire department. They have been coming round for subscriptions towards the celebration and Fred and I gave them a couple of dollars to celebrate England's having got rid of them.

While William remained optimistic about the future profitability of his land investments, he wrote a cautionary note on how long it would take for the profits to come in, presumably in order to forestall premature demands for repayment of any funds on loan from England. The quick profits made by others last year could not be expected:

In the first place, we rent this first year on half shares, and secondly, last year was an exceptional year for wheat, prices good and a splendid crop. Still, if next year we have very good luck we could go a long way toward paying for land and breaking. By buying in large quantities and paying cash, we have not given more than $3.25 for any of our lands. Renting on half shares is as follows: I shall provide the land ready broken and also the seed, the farmer doing all the rest. After the first year we intend simply to take a cash rent, as one is liable to be cheated very much in the share system.

I think we came into this country in the nick of time. It certainly seems an anomaly that not 100 miles East of us the same railroad 'raw' lands are sold from 20 to 40 dollars an acre, while here they can be bought from 3 to 10 dollars. It will be but a few years before this will right itself. [*Reference to railroad lands is to the several-miles-wide tracts of land on either side of the line that the State gave to railway companies as an incentive to lay down the lines.*]

There follows a six-page account of the Independence Day celebrations, which William endured with self control. 'At a snorously early hour' the first item in the programme took place, which was the firing of a the Denison gun, accompanied by the letting off of squibs and crackers by boys all over the town, in particular a group of them just under the Closes' window. If this was a show of lingering defiance of the English, there was no further such feeling, and Fred seems to have run away with half the prizes, including the capture of the greased pig.

Events and competitions went on all day, with dancing and jollities well into the night. 'I saw several yokels looking rather beery, but no bad case came under my observation. Thus is the 4th July of 1878 over – Hooray!'

1st August 1878 Since the last number appeared I have been covering a good deal of ground in buggy and on horseback in search of the promised land, which Fred and I want to find and buy to begin breaking on next year. Hearing lands were cheap in N.E. Nebraska [*adjacent to and West of Iowa*], Mr Paullin, who came on purpose to give us the benefit of his advice, travelled in a buggy over five or six counties. [*Paullin was also looking for land for his sons, Ed and Henry.*] We found splendid lands there and at cheap rates, $1.50 to $2 per acre, but the country is not settled enough for our purpose and the renters would be difficult to find. The lands are taxed very heavily, which is the reason they can be got at such low rates. The swindling that goes on is palpable. Each county votes its own rate of taxation but the owners of the land are mostly speculators from the East, and not being residents, are at the mercy of the settlers.

Very high taxes would be decreed so that the locals could allot to each other contracts for building schools, bridges, halls and so on, which were often unneeded. An agent of a railroad land company gave William one example:

In the books he noted the item $2,000 dollars for a school house in such and such a township, and such and such a section. He went in search of it but found no signs of a school house, and only one farm house in the whole township of 36 square miles. He inquired there for the school house and was told he was in it, and was taken upstairs where in the loft were two or three nice benches, and a good assortment of school books, maps, globes and so on. This was the school house that cost $2,000. The man had divided his money with the ring. So much a year is allowed each school house for fuel and he was using it for his own benefit. His three children were the only ones to use the school and his own wife was appointed teacher at the handsome salary of $30 a month.

The enormous taxes that had to be paid made the speculators willing to sell off their holdings at cheap rates to local farmers, who then set about improving them. William concluded that the end result of this widespread scam was satisfactory, as at least the land was finally put to good use by the people who lived on the spot, rather than remaining unbroken in the hands of speculators. But as a non-resident he would have nothing to do with it, and turned his attention back to Iowa:

> We hit upon what may turn out to be the lands we are in quest of near Sioux City, pronounced sue. [*It is in the north-west corner of Iowa, on the border with Nebraska.*] It is a lively little town of some 6,000 inhabitants situated near the junction of the Big Sioux River and the Missouri – and a better course for a regatta I never saw, a wide calm straight stretch of river, 20 ft. deep. It made me long to scull over it. The lands I am speaking of made my mouth water as we drove over them, nothing could be finer. Undulating just enough to carry the surplus water away and prevent any swamps, perfectly watered lands, too abundant springs in all directions – and splendid dark rich soil. It is four to five feet deep even at the top of the swells and I have seen it twice that depth. Even the subsoil will raise a good or very fair crop. As if Nature had not done enough in giving so rich a soil, it is provided with a splendid fertiliser in phosphates of lime; where it has been turned up you can see the phosphates hardened by the sun and lying so thick that you can pick up a handful in the space of a square foot.
>
> It is only a strip of land fifty miles wide on each side of the Missouri river that has this wonderful formation – all the lands we already have are on it, but these near Sioux City are extra fine. There are some fourteen thousand acres which a New Yorker holds and wants to sell cheap if he can get rid of them all at once, but I am afraid it is a bigger bait than we can swallow, and we shall have to be content with less just now. The price he wants is about $3 an acre.
>
> As soon as the lands we want are bought I shall depart for Europe.

The above eulogy on the Sioux soil may have been touched up a bit with a view to raising money in England; but it *was* good, it did become his main land investment and subsequently formed the basis of the family's wealth. He undoubtedly bought

it cheaply: land in Illinois was sold at double or three times the price. Some speculators now had a pressing need to dispose of their investments: they had bought in
the late sixties, when the US government had first opened up virgin prairie for sale.
Then East Coast speculators had snapped it up – and hung on to it, in the hope that
the price would rise. Since then a farming depression had set in, prices stagnated
and speculators began to feel the pinch. They had to pay taxes every year and now,
even although prospects were brighter, they had to cut their losses. However, the
only reason the New Yorker gave William for not having sold it sooner was fear
of grasshoppers; but William took a calculated risk that they would not reappear
in any great numbers, as he thought they only came on the edge of the cultivated
prairie, and that edge was already extending away from his own operations. The
Financial Times, in its 1925 obituary, wrote that 'the lands which he developed and
colonised in Iowa are today the richest cereal producers in the United States'.

At this point a third brother appears on the scene. Not John, who was still doing
well at his uncle's bank and had a wife and family, but James – John's younger
brother. Their uncle, Sir William Cunliffe Brooks, MP, who had taken over the Cunliffe Brooks bank after his father Samuel died, had written expressing an interest in
what William and Fred were doing and hinting that James, who had been looking
after the bank's interests in West Africa but had now been posted to Blackburn,
might come out and join them.

> Jim [*James*] and Lehmann arrived ten days ago and only stayed a day, being
> invited to join an expedition to view the eclipse in the Rocky Mountains. They
> were both looking well and were only a fortnight out from Liverpool on the day
> they arrived here.

William's own attempt to view the same eclipse was frustrated:

> I had one rough night of it at a farm house. It came on to rain heavily and I
> woke to find myself almost swimming in water, the roof above my bunk leaking
> badly – and weren't the mosquitoes voracious too that night. I was glad when
> dawn appeared and calculated that I should reach Denison in time to get a
> piece of smoked glass. So I would have done, but within two miles of the town
> I found the heavy rains had carried away the bridge on a little creek. There
> was nothing else but to start up towards its head, but it soon degenerated into
> a slough some thirty or forty feet wide. [*After floundering a long time in the
> mud looking for a crossing*] ... there was a space clear of the warning weeds,
> I tried it myself first, it was soft, but not very deep and knowing my horse

Kurnil behaved well in a slough I led him in boldly. We were soon hard at it, and by keeping him going fast but steadily, I reached the other side, and for the first time noted a peculiar pink tint – the sun's rays were duller. I had only just begun to notice this when trtrtrtrtr, a noise like the jingling of a number of ladies' bangles, make me throw Kurnil back on his haunches, and sure enough, almost from under his nose, there glided off a huge rattle snake. I marked him make for a cluster of oak shrubs.

He chased after it with a stirrup for a weapon, but it had gone down its hole. Once he got going again: 'I thought I would resume my observation of the eclipse, but the sun was as bright as ever and the great eclipse of 1878 was over'.

A theme that recurs almost as often as Bad Roads is poor hygiene. Diphtheria among children and infant cholera was common, and William attributed this to pigs. Some of his neighbours had as many as a hundred, and everyone kept them in pens in amongst the houses. Every house in town had its open cesspool and the stench was everywhere.

> *10th August* A pig sty was set up with ten pigs in it not fifteen feet from my bedroom window. I complained to the Marshall, who went to the man, and told him he must clean it up. The man turned over the dirt and the stench was ten times worse than before; so knowing it would take six weeks to get those pigs removed by law, I proposed to the man to buy him out. Not a cent less than $20 would he take, and as I thought it best to buy him out rather than run the risk of typhoid fever I paid the money and sold the pigs for $13.
>
> Without hesitation I say that the Americans are the most improvident in sanitary measures of any nation I know of, and I rank many of their municipal bodies in this respect below even that of Naples. The water they give you is seldom clear, especially at Philadelphia, where the drainage from the exhibition grounds and West Philadelphia actually went into the Schuylkill River not a quarter of a mile above the water works that supply the whole town with water and that everyone drank. Yet they wondered at typhoid fever being so prevalent and the newspapers suppressed the facts for fear of stopping people from visiting Philadelphia.

In yet another link with the Wygant family he nonchalantly reports: 'Wann has succumbed already to the attractions of a belle of Denison and is to be married in October to Miss Wygant [*she of the A1 eyes*], of whom I think I have already spoken. She is a very nice girl and will make him an excellent wife'. There is no hint of disappointment in this, but Harnack writes that for some time it had been accepted in

Denison that William and Carrie Wygant were 'keeping company'; and that after the arrival of Wann it was joked that 'Wann is getting closer'.

In an entry dated 20th September, William tells of his attempts to detach six steer from the herd, where he had bought them, and drive them to his own herd, five miles away. Too long for inclusion here, it can be found in Appendix (II). At first assisted by a Mr Brown from New York, William wrote:

> It was quite refreshing to have a man straight from the East and from New York among us. Mr Brown came out here with the intention of selling two or three hundred acres of . . .

And with these three dots the Prairie Journal comes to an end. Possibly he fell ill after rounding up the steers, and was too busy with the events related in the next section to write any more. In any case, he would soon be returning to England, where it was no longer necessary to relate his experiences by post.

❧ *The Colony*

September 1878 to early 1880s

W ITH the end of the Prairie Journal, the main source for the following section on the Close Colony is Curtis Harnack's *Gentlemen of the Prairie*. Harnack was born in Le Mars, Iowa, which in the 1880's had been the centre of the 'Close Colony', and he spent many years researching the phenomenon of English settlers in Iowa and neighbouring States. His book covers not just the Closes, but the whole saga of English prairie settlers.

The main event of 1878 had been the discovery that 14,600 acres of perfect land near Sioux City was on the market, but the abrupt end of the Journal left that in the air. Negotiations had in fact been going on to raise funds to buy as much of it as possible. William and Fred put in what they could, and James, on his return from the Rocky Mountains, examined the soil and not only agreed to come in on the venture financially, but also decided to stay and help run it. Daniel Paullin also acquired a share, but that had to be financed by a loan from his future son-in-law, William. The deal was signed on 1st October 1878. Although at first William had thought that all the 15,000 odd acres on offer were 'a bigger bait than we can swallow', with this further financial help, and by dint of bringing the asking price of $3 an acre down to $2.40, he and his partners did acquire the whole lot. Although there was a down payment on signing in October, the rest did not have to be paid until a year later.

William returned to England before the end of October, with a view to raising funds. His plan was to move his base from Denison to Le Mars, a rather smaller town not far from Sioux City. In London he established Close Brothers Limited as a land agency, with offices in Le Mars (to be run by James), 23 Cornhill in London, and Manchester. As it was the first company with Close Brothers in the name, it may fairly be regarded as the origin of the famous City firm (see Epilogue). In fact the name changed in a number of minor ways in the next few years, whether to take in a new partner, or to differentiate between the American and the British firms or to take on board a new activity. Essentially it was the same firm and the reader will not be bothered with these tactical changes. William acted as the senior partner, and became respectfully known on both sides of the Atlantic as WB. His objectives now were to finance the October acquisition, to raise money in England for still further purchases at a later date, and to recruit new pioneering investors to go out to Le Mars.

For this last task, William was looking for young men prepared to rough it and learn about farming and who were rich and interested enough to at least consider investing in land. He began by working from his 'Manchester office', which was in fact brother John's house. From the start, he was insistent he would only recruit men from his own class, endowed with capital. They would have to work hard, but 'labourers need not apply'. Manchester was the obvious place to start, because so many family contacts were there. Among the well-to-do families it was the normal practice for the eldest son to inherit the major part of the wealth, which meant that subsequent sons needed to find gainful employment. Rather than the Church, the army or the law, William was offering them an adventurous and healthy outdoor life with the prospect of outstanding financial rewards.

By spring 1879 William had produced a thirty-page booklet, *Farming in North-Western Iowa,* describing the living conditions and setting out exactly what the Close Brothers would do for new arrivals. They would be given advice on suitable farmland to buy and how much to pay for it, and help with travel and legal arrangements. The newcomers would be trained on how to break prairie land and/or on stock raising. They would be given food and lodging and attached to a farmer for whom they would work for nothing during their first year. After that they could either take the plunge and buy acreage for themselves or they could be paid a small wage for a second year and be granted some privileges, again attached to a farm. In exchange for all this they would have to work hard, often at tasks that would at home be done by farm labourers, and have a minimum of $5,000 for land investment, on which Close Bros would charge a commission of 5 per cent. He described how this sum could yield a return up to ten times the normal 2–3 per cent return on farming in England. The publication was a fair account of what could be expected – with the excusable exceptions that it made no mention of the bogs and reported that the roads were 'universally good'. The booklet attracted much interest and already in 1880 a third batch of 1,000 copies had been printed.

Shortly before this publication had been written, William had recruited and sent out to Iowa Robert Maxtone Graham, who had been working in Cunliffe Brooks Bank. Son of a Scottish Laird, he had defied his father's ruling that none of his nine children should leave home until they were married. It did not take much to persuade him to leave the bank for the West. Robert arrived there in February 1879, and once he had experienced a few months' hard work on one of the farms, he wrote to William with a glowing testimonial on the life he was leading and how promising it was financially, which William soon put to good use. Other testimonials soon arrived in support, and even while the brochure was being distributed, Robert Maxtone Graham's lead had persuaded about forty adventurers, some of them with family, to go out to Le Mars. William was writing more letters to *The Times* and to Manchester papers about the opportunities in America which attracted a good deal of interest. 'What do we do with our boys?' was a frequent topic of conversation. Now William was making it possible to emigrate to Le Mars without losing social standing. His rowing achievements had already given him a social cachet in England, and his expansionist exploits in Iowa produced good publicity in the newspapers. One emigrant farmer wrote: 'scratch the ground with a toothpick, and reap two harvests a year'.

For the summer of 1879 William returned to Iowa to check on the two farms at Denison that he owned jointly with Fred and to supervise another 2,000-acre farm he had acquired for himself near Le Mars, on the west fork of a tributary of the Sioux river. James was running the Le Mars office smoothly and Fred was developing roles as farm manager and agricultural adviser. New recruits were arriving and all was in place for further expansion. In September it was time to return to England to raise more capital and galvanise the recruitment campaign.

This time Mary came with him, along with two of her siblings, young Bert and Ada. Two disasters followed. In London, often left on her own, Mary went on a spending spree that led to such disagreements with William that she broke off the engagement and returned to Quincy. Then, just as the due date for the payment of the rest of the money for the 15,000 acres was coming up, William heard that Paullin had suffered a bad accident and would be unable to come up with his share of the purchase.

William redoubled his already strenuous work. In November he spent a fortnight at Trinity, where he mailed every member of the University and interviewed thirty to forty undergraduates. One convert would often bring in another for company, as the prospect of going out alone must have been daunting. Because clergymen seemed particularly anxious to find an occupation for their sons, he mailed every clergyman in the country – on Trinity-headed paper, which earned a mild rebuke. He even found time to do some coaching and rowing.

At first William was alarmed by Paullin's defection, and wanted to sell part of the wonderful acreage near Le Mars to make good the deficiency; but as his title to it had not yet been secured, this was not possible. However, he was able to get the final payment date deferred from 1st October 1879 to 1st January. Thousands more copies of the brochure were printed and the contributions of new recruits helped to plug the gap. One, rowing blue Constantine Benson, offered to bring £15,000 capital with him, and William took the bold step of offering him partnership in the firm, which he later accepted. Furthermore, that autumn the amount that each of JC's children were to inherit was finally settled (Anne had died in 1876) and William received more than he was expecting. That he was not now over-concerned is shown by the fact that at the same time as he was struggling to make up for the non-appearance of Paullin's contribution, he instructed James to buy more land by Spirit Lake, seventy miles to the north of Le Mars and just short of the border with Minnesota, where he was contemplating building for himself a lakeside house. This could be seen as somewhat underhand, as brother John had already asked James to buy a slice of the available land around the lake for himself, as an investment. But William (working from John's house) clearly thought that he had priority, since his interest was not just speculative, he wanted to live there, and wanted not just a slice, but all of the land on offer. John could just as well invest in land elsewhere. This in fact John did, visiting Iowa the following year for the first and last time, and buying 30,000 acres in the North-West corner of the State. The Spirit Lake diversion finally fell through, but it shows that when the final payment date came round on 1st January 1880, one way and another the problem had been solved. At that point, Paullin paid up after all.

William was in no hurry to return to America, partly because he was making such a success of raising capital and attracting recruits in England, but also because the thought of being anywhere near his lost fiancée was too painful. He wrote to James in Le Mars asking him to make sure the final details of the settlement with Paullin were generous and asking him if he would keep a paternal eye on Bert, Paullin's youngest son, who had been staying with him in London but had now returned to Iowa.

Meanwhile, in Le Mars the British community was flourishing and developing into the famous Colony that was to become written about in the English press and talked about in society. The *Le Mars Sentinel* later claimed that for a short time Le Mars was the best known American town in England. The Colony was by no means the first, as other mid-west States had hosted groups from a number of European countries, some of them held together by various religious beliefs. But the Close Colony was quite different from the rest: it was an attempt to implant an exclusive upper class English community in the middle of hitherto uncultivated prairie. Within an invisible stockade, it provided the sort of social amenities that the participants would have enjoyed in England – sports, dances, and even a gentlemen's club. All had to work hard during the day, but in the evening could look forward to congenial company. Mothers would bring out their daughters and provide suitable female company – some would marry and settle. Much of the labour force consisted of the first year recruits, who became known as 'pups' (short for pupils). A *Punch* cartoon of November 1881 (see overleaf) mocked the attempt to combine an upper-class social life with drudgery in the fields.

Pups had to pay an additional $100 p.a. if they were lucky enough to be attached to one of the Close's personal farms. James and Fred's 960-acre farm was mainly for sheep, while William's had 1,000 short horn cattle as well as 2,000 sheep – and seven 'pups'.

Many colony members, particularly the sons of parsons, were uneasy about the Episcopalian nature of worship in the town, and raised enough money to build an Anglican church. When in 1881 it was finished and equipped with a vicar, it had cost only $3,200, less than half the estimated amount. It was later described in *Northwest Iowa Pioneers* by Janice Stofferan and Dorothy Warren:

> Two buildings in Plymouth County are well worth visiting if one wishes to view what still exists from that period of English settlement. One is the lovely St. George's Episcopal Church, where services are still held. The church was built

by the English citizens, and followed the general pattern of English churches in architecture. The wooden trays for prayer books, the kneeling boards, and the names of early English folk carved in the pews all serve to take one back in time.

The town of Le Mars had started to grow only in the last five years. Like Denison, it was the capital of its County, and it was built on the junction of two railway lines. Occasionally there was friction between town and colony. While the boost to the economy given by the new arrivals was enthusiastically welcomed by the local press – 'Hail Britannia!' was one headline – neither the Englishness nor the class consciousness of the new arrivals went down well with the American residents. It is not surprising that at the end of a hard day the younger, unattached members of the colony needed a drink. Sometimes this led to over-boisterous or even loutish behaviour in the town, fuelled by drunkenness which deeply shocked

COLONISING IN IOWA, U.S.

(A Hint to the younger Sons of our Aristocracy, and eke to the Daughters thereof.)

Lady Maria. "How *late* you are, Boys! Your baths are ready, and I've mended your dress trousers, Jack. So look sharp and clean yourselves, and then you can lay the cloth, and keep an eye on the mutton while Emily and I are dressing for dinner."

Lord John. "All right. How many are we to lay for?"

Lady Emily. "Eight. The Talbots are coming, and Major Cecil is going to bring the Duke of Stilton, who's stopping with him."

the temperance-minded town. The editor of the *Liberal*, a local newspaper, ran a campaign against the worst of the yobs, some of whom decided to extort an apology. When this was not forthcoming, a group of them, armed with a horsewhip, attempted to use it on the editor: luckily shopkeepers nearby came to his aid and a general scuffle ensued, with no-one being seriously hurt. Smaller bust-ups took place from time to time. The horsewhipping party had been headed by Wakefield, who had always been getting into trouble in England and had probably been deliberately exported, as his family's black sheep. Yet in general, although there was little fraternising between the Colony and the town, relationships between the two were easy. When the Colony formed a cricket club in 1881, a rival club was set up be the citizens of Le Mars, intrigued by this strange game. In February 1882 the *Le Mars Sentinel* wrote: 'Le Mars should delight to do honour to an agency that has done so much to make the young city what it is – one of the most flourishing and popular in the State'.

Soon after their arrival in Le Mars, the brothers acquired The Commercial Hotel in the middle of town, to be used for new arrivals and a meeting place for members of the Colony. They called it *The Albion*. When it was pulled down by a developer in 1910, the *Le Mars Sentinel* ran a long nostalgic article about it, from which:

> *The Albion* was headquarters and when an Englishman landed at the depot surrounded by a pile of baggage ten or fifteen foot high, he was conducted to this hostelry where he was welcomed and fed and got acquainted with the gang, while making up his mind where he was going to locate if intending to buy, or to which ranch if he were going as a novice.

Perhaps to avoid the possibility of any further disturbances, but also because it was closer to his ranch, William decided to found a new town, which he named Quorn, after the Leicestershire Hunt. (It was not so unusual to found a town: it will be remembered that Mr Denison had founded Denison only a few years ago.) Within two years the all-English Quorn had seven shops, a post office, one saloon, a blacksmith, several wooden homes and nine streets. The location had been chosen because the Chicago and North-Western railroad company was expected to lay another new line alongside it. This did not happen: in 1883 it was laid a mile to the East, and the railway company developed their own town, Kingsley. Quorn declined. The other worth-visiting relic described in *Northwest Iowa Pioneers* was William's office. The Kingsley Historical Society restored and refurbished it; and moved it from Quorn to Kingsley. It was opened to the public in the summer of

1976. In the furnished two-storey building are bedrooms which were provided for the comfort of prospective buyers, a dining room, a kitchen, a parlour and an office for viewing land transaction records and old photographs. (See plate 21.)

Also still standing, at least in 1997 when the *Sentinel* featured it, was William's red barn, overlooking the west fork of the Little Sioux River. It was thought to be the largest barn in Plymouth County, big enough to store 18–20,000 bales of hay.

During 1880 Fred, who had been having exploratory talks with another land-owner outside the colony, was persuaded to join the Close Bros partnership. Fearful that he and James might quarrel, William had written to him:

> When you and Jim discuss matters, remember not to try and thrust each other's opinions down each other's throats, and don't think each other fools because you don't agree. Also, don't crow over each other when one of you is right, and for goodness sake don't say "I told you so".

Fred took the lead in organising sports, and before long teams were chosen not only for cricket, but also for rugger, track events, ice hockey, football and lawn tennis (from 1882). There was also hunting and racing. He excelled in this last and had a reputation as an incredible rider. In one race his horse fell at the first barrier, Fred remounted, caught up and came in second – despite having broken his collar bone in the fall. In May 1980 he organised the first Le Mars Derby, attended by people from all over the County; and for the 1881 Derby (it became an annual event) he had a Grandstand built for the grander spectators. William imported a stallion said to be worth $25,000. The winner of the 1882 Derby was none other than Jack Wakefield, he who had tried to horsewhip the editor of the *Liberal*. Another year the 'Le Mars Cup' was won by William Gaskell, related to father James Close's first wife. There was a ball and a white tie dinner, hosted by the Closes, at the end of each Derby day.

There was also a team for polo, which surprisingly was *not* introduced by this upper crust colony, as it had been played in North America since 1875. But Fred, who had played the game in England, claimed to be the first polo player to live in America, as he had been living in Virginia in 1874. By 1885 a 'North Western Polo League' had been formed, with teams in five towns, including Sioux Falls and Le Mars.

By the spring of 1880 £100,000 had been paid in by Close Brothers clients, all handled by James in Le Mars. William issued a constant stream of instructions to him from England, which were sometimes written in such haste that confusion and mistakes were made – compounded by the fact that James was buying and selling for himself as well as for Close Brothers Limited. James had the double job of running the office and supervising the pups. He was working up to twelve or one o'clock every night and sometimes on Sundays as well. Relief came in May 1880, in the form of Captain Reynolds Morton, son of an Irish Earl, who came to live in Le Mars, spending $20,000 on building a mansion just over a mile to the North, on a hill overlooking the town. His property included a sales pavilion, a stock farm, sheep barn and horse barn. He provided a 'Prairie Club' for the Colony and accommodation for the better connected and titled trainees. He founded a YMCA and preached to gatherings of the Episcopal community, rather in the style of Moody. He relieved James of responsibility for, and moral leadership of, the pups. Later, the Club moved to the centre of Le Mars and was run on the same lines as a gentleman's club in England. Within the decade, it had attracted 300 members.

Meanwhile William, having received a tender letter of reconciliation from Mary, had recrossed the Atlantic to spend the summer of 1880 in Iowa and Quincy. That September he and Mary married in Geneva, New York and crossed again to spend the winter in London. Almost from the start Mary took a dislike to the city, and became a semi-invalid, spending most of her time in their London house. This made it difficult for William to introduce her to his friends and to carry out the sort of social life that a newly married couple could normally look forward to. He stayed at home with Mary as much as he could, but had a great deal of work to do. During this time he arranged the creation of the Iowa Land Company Limited, capitalised at $2.5 million, which would act as brokers in the buying and selling of prairie land – not only for the Close Colony, but for any investors in the region. It is not clear how much if any of the capital subscribed came from the Close brothers, although they had a hand in its management. The Colony however still took up much of William's time, and he continued to recruit pups. Last year's had been quick to purchase their own property and new pups were needed to replenish the depleted labour force. This work kept William and Mary in London until May 1881, when they returned to America – she to Quincy and he mainly in Iowa, looking after his own farm and prospecting ever more widely.

One of William's rare setbacks was in the early summer of this year. The Duke of Sutherland (in the eyes of Queen Victoria a disreputable friend of the Prince of Wales), whose yacht it was that had been lent to Garibaldi in Ischia, was now an *aficionado* of the world's expanding railways and decided to cross North America by train. As owner of 1,360,000 acres in Britain, he might have been expected to be interested also in the availability of good prairie land in America, and William, together with *The Times* correspondent W. H. Russell (whose despatches from the Crimea had made him famous) managed to get on the same train and route it through Le Mars. Sadly the Duke, who had perhaps endured too much sales talk from William, would not get off the train at that station. He did however allow himself to be shown round available acreage elsewhere, which was soon to lead to valuable financial support: according to *The Le Mars Sentinel* in May 1881, nearly half the share capital of the Iowa Land Company was subscribed by 'the Ducal party'.

A success was the appointment in April of the Iowa Land Company as the sole agent for the land of the Sioux City and St. Paul railway company, which had been given by the State generous margins of land on either side of their tracks. Since Close Brothers made the travel arrangements for new recruits, and negotiated reduced fares for their emigrants, William had hitherto been hesitant to get involved with any of the railway companies, for fear of conflicts of interest. He now dropped his scruples on that score, and the new Land Company was made sole agent for the railway company's 96,000 acres.

While the Colony continued to be based in Le Mars, William went further afield in his search for new land, as a result of which James moved his office from there to Sibley, seventy-two miles to the North. Fred remained in Le Mars to supervise the training of pups who now, for a fee, could attend an agricultural college which the brothers had set up. The role of office manager there was taken by an ex army officer, Major Charles Ball, who only two years earlier had been on trial for shooting someone in the neck. He got off, on the grounds that the victim had called him 'son of a bitch'.

Back in January 1880 one of the new recruits had been William Humble, 'a young inoffensive smug of 18', wrote William. His mother had been recently widowed, and had responsibility for the remaining seven of her children. She received such enthusiastic reports of life in Iowa from her son William that she decided to come and live there, or at least pay a prolonged visit, with her three unmarried daughters. The daughters were attractive, and a social success. According to Fred's groom, who in his eighties was interviewed by Harnack, Fred when out riding spotted two of them bathing in a stream. 'He was so struck by their beauty – particularly Margaret's – that he fell in love on the spot'. They married later that year and celebrated with a Grand Ball attended by 150 guests including John Walter, proprietor of and frequent leader-writer for *The Times*. He was impressed with the Colony and gave it useful publicity in his leaders. (The other beautiful bather, Susan, married James in 1885 and the third sister, Annie, married Samuel Graves, soon to be a Close Brothers partner.)

The rate of growth accelerated. In 1881 they advertised for 180 tenants. James, based in Sibley, built the farmhouses and organised the breaking of the land for 300 farms, which were for sale or for let. By the end of 1882 Close Brothers, the Iowa Land Company and individuals within the Colony owned between them 135,000 acres. In 1883 they advertised 500,000 acres of land for sale. In 1884 they bought 100,000 acres to the West of another English colony in Kansas (a prototype to the extent that it had been for Englishmen only) that had collapsed in 1873. The Iowa Land Company became the biggest foreign company in America, capitalised at $5.5 million. William had founded this company and the Closes were the exclusive agents, presumably getting a commission on all its transactions.

As this expansion continued, so the three brothers were operating further and further from the Colony, and it was inevitable that they should see less of it. Fred was popular there and stayed on another year. James, having already moved his office north to Sibley, soon needed to move still further North and opened an office in Pipestone, seventy miles into Minnesota, on its western edge. By 1884 he was fully occupied with expansion in that area and had built a hotel for immigrants in the town. Later in the year Fred too moved to Pipestone; and even although he kept in touch with Le Mars and returned there for the 1885 Derby, he started to lay out another new town in Minnesota. By then Close Brothers owned 200,000 acres in that State as opposed to only 70,000 in Iowa. William in particular seems to have dissociated himself from the Iowa scene and everything he had done round Le Mars. He spent much of his time in England, concentrating on the financial side. For his US accommodation, he had a house built for himself and his wife in Pipestone – but most of the time they were living apart, she often staying in Antibes 'on grounds of health'.

The Colony continued in being without the Closes, but gradually faded. The system of pups declined with the diminishing availability of new land. Not all had made their fortunes, and those that failed to do so returned home disgruntled, tarnishing the Colony's shining reputation. Those that stayed eventually integrated with the local community, became American and played their part in the further development of the prairies.

Just as father James had built a successful career based in Naples, keeping his distance from Italians and spending much of his time with his family on board the *Sibilla*, so his sons, in a brilliant but short five years, had managed to make a fortune and open up new lands while working in a close-knit and exclusive community set in the heart of the prairie seas. They were surrounded with compatriots, and did not socialise much with Americans. It is true that William married one, but sadly that marriage did not work, and they were drifting apart.

✥ *The snowiest railway*

*I*N THE MID-1880s, however, the colonisation of the mid-West by the British – and the colony of the Closes was not the only one – began to run out of steam. Americans became uneasy. In *The British in Iowa* van der Zee wrote:

> … bills were introduced into Congress in 1884 to restrict or prevent the acquisition of public lands by these "leviathan squatters". Two members … expressed their alarm … that these foreigners had bought up nearly 21,000,000 acres within the past few years … Subjects of the British Empire … owned an area one fourth the size of the British Isles.

No action was taken on account of these rumblings, but they may have been one reason why the Closes gradually moved away from buying unused land and converting it into farms, to let or for sale. Moreover the best of the virgin prairie had long since been bought, and land was no longer cheap. Instead of buying it for themselves, they acted as buying and selling agents, spending more of their time at their desks. In 1884 they opened an office in Chicago, where they set up a farm loan business. This became the core of their operations: they relinquished their involvement in the Iowa Land Company, handing it over to Constantine Benson. They sold their holdings in the region of Le Mars. They borrowed 'money in England at from 4–5% and realized from 6½–7% on their loans in this country' (van der Zee). Security was in the farms, and no loan exceeded a quarter the value of the farm of the borrower. In 1885 they established a link with the First National Bank of Chicago, and whatever kind of arrangement it was, it must have been mutually beneficial, as it lasted fifty years. The business began to expand beyond farming – for example they financed an irrigation project in Colorado. In 1888 money from England was coming in so fast that a separate company, the Mortgage and Debenture Co Ltd, was set up to handle it. William and Mary (when she was there) and James with his family lived in a house in Highland Park, by the lake to the North of Chicago; and as William was often in London, James again ran the office.

At the end of the decade drought and an incipient depression were getting many farmers into difficulties, and business for the Closes grew slacker. *The Encyclopedia of Iowa* states that 'The drought, grasshopper sieges and higher expenses of the later 1880s and early 1890s caused many of the colonists to lose their enthusiasm'. The purchase earlier of 100,000 acres in Kansas had not worked out well. William looked back on this in a letter written in London in 1921:

> There had been rain for three years before we bought these lands ... but unfortunately a period of drought set in. We also bought another 100,000 acres near Colorado, and another 100,000 of beautiful land in the Panhandle of Texas. But the drought held, coinciding with the financial depression in the United States, and for a number of years there was no demand for these lands, and heavy taxes were paid each year. ... Had these lands been held for a year longer, when the secrets of dry farming were being discovered, there would have been a large fortune waiting, instead of which we did not get the whole of our money back.

1890 saw the end of the three-brother collaboration in the States. First, James and his wife Susan returned to England. Why he did so is not recorded. It may have been because of these less profitable conditions; or possibly his wife Susan, who bore him three children and only survived for ten years after the marriage, wanted to return to her home country. James became manager of Lloyds Bank in Malvern and later manager of the same bank in Margate. So having left the family bank to go West, he now returned to banking in England. His uncle Sir William Cunliffe Brooks died in 1900, and soon after that the Cunliffe Brooks Bank merged with Lloyds. Throughout the last few years James had been the man on the spot running the expanding Close Brothers empire, and his sudden departure must have been disrupting. He remained a partner of Close Brothers, but that was no longer his main occupation.

In the winter of 1889–90 Fred and his wife Margaret (Susan's sister) took a break in England, staying part of the winter at the home of Sir William. During this visit he and his uncle's Cunliffe Brooks Bank raised $3 million to back yet another company that Fred was forming in Sioux City, the Free Land Mortgage Company, scheduled to open in June 1890. Shortly before returning to America Fred, while hunting at his uncle's and reckless as ever, fell and broke his arm. He was by now inured to this sort of accident, and the photograph of him on plate 21 shows him smiling with his arm in a sling. The accident did not put a stop to his plans for the new company, nor did it stop him from participating in the Sioux vs. Le Mars polo match, also in June, although the arm had not healed. In the middle of the match he was seen by the crowd to gallop across the field straight into an oncoming rider: the horses collided, both of them falling on top of Fred. He was mortally wounded and within a few hours was dead. He was thirty-five and his wife thirty. There would still have been time, with his energy and *joie de vivre,* to accomplish again as much as he had done already.

Margaret, very rich and beautiful, returned to England. Welcomed socially at the highest level, in 1902 she was presented to Queen Victoria. Then she became involved with both a lover and a husband, which led to such scandalous and public divorce proceedings that the next Queen, Alexandra, let it be known through the London Gazette that she would no longer be received at Court. This branded her as an outcast and she spent the rest of her life in France with her daughter and second husband, Lord Granville Gordon. Recounting the scandal with some glee, the *Le Mars Sentinel* wrote that 'the lady in the case, who is decidedly "it", was a former Le Mars girl who had hosts of admirers wherever she went'.

Also in 1890 Mary, William's wife, gave birth to a son, Herbert. But the rift between them was not healed. They continued to live apart and within three years they were divorced. William was unsuccessful in his attempts to get custody of the child. His siblings and uncle all rallied to his side and wrote letters of sympathy and support. Anne Eaden's assessment of the situation was that while William had always been in love with Mary, she, who had shown coldness towards him and had at one time broken off their engagement, only wrote the letter of reconciliation at the insistence of her father Daniel, because he had at last seen the money-making potentiality of the Closes. In support of this it has to be said that at the very time Daniel's daughter wrote the bewitching letter, he found that after all he was able to pay for his share of the 15,000 acres of land near Sioux. The divorce was officially on the grounds of William's adultery – but since this was the only possible way to get a divorce, the scenario may have been fixed. Certainly after the divorce it is known that William, although he never married again, was seldom without female company.

With the death of Fred and the departure of James, this chapter on the achievements of the Close brothers in America will now centre on William alone, still at the helm of the firm. Its most striking success was to be in the last two years of the century.

While 1890 was a fateful year for the Close brothers, more generally it was also a year in which the depression in America took a turn for the worse. It was to peak with the panic of 1893, and to last most of the decade. Farmers were the worst hit and William intensified the search for non-farming investments. He was not left entirely on his own to deal with this, as he had already invited others to join the partnership, including Samuel Graves, who had earlier taken charge of some of the outposts and who with the departure of James took over control of the Chicago office. (He showed his affinity with the Closes by marrying the third Humble sister, the other two having married Fred and James.) The letter already quoted from William about Kansas indicates that business in the early part of the decade was a matter of hanging on and not losing too much money. He himself probably spent most of his time in London and it is not known how often he came to Chicago. He was certainly in London when in November 1896 he had a momentous visit by a Mr Wilkinson, from the Klondike.

It was earlier in the year that the Klondike gold rush had started. The nearest port, Skagway, was at the Northern tip of the Alexander Archipelago, a maze of islands and inlets running along the coast from north-west to south-east, with the Pacific Ocean on one side, British Columbia on the other and the Yukon Territory, where the gold was, to the North. Both the latter territories were part of Canada, while the Archipelago constituted the Southern tail of Alaska. Thousands of prospectors, many of them without work on account of the depression, had to get there by sea and then cross on foot a perilous mountain range that straddled the three territories, before continuing their journey for a further 300 miles over relatively flat terrain to get to the gold-studded area in the Yukon. This flatter part of the journey was often undertaken by raft, down rivers and across lakes; but the track over the mountains, mostly only four feet wide, presented problems. At its highest point was the infamous White Pass, half a mile high, and the approach to it was over steeply shelving rock. Horses were blindfolded to stop them panicking, but even so it was estimated that around 1,000 fell – into what became known as Dead Horse Gulch. Approximately 25,000 gold-seekers went over the narrow pass at the top in 1898, and most of the time there was a queue waiting to get through it. Wilkinson's proposal to William was that he should finance the building of a railway from Skagway to the Yukon.

Wilkinson, working on behalf of the British Columbia Development Association, a syndicate based in London, had spent the last seven months negotiating a charter to build a railway over the three territories involved. But on his return to London, the syndicate, unimpressed with the railway's prospects, had been reluctant at first to put up the asking price of £30,000.

To judge from the lack of any notable achievements recorded in the previous few years, William had been languishing, without much attempt to regain the momentum of the firm. The suggestion that he might get involved in the railway reignited his enthusiasm and sense of adventure. He lent £10,000 towards the £30,000. Graves, who was now chief executive in America, was asked to investigate on the spot, together with an American engineer and an engineer representing Close Brothers, Sir Thomas Tancred. Tancred was a friend of William and had been the chief contractor in the building of the Firth of Forth bridge. These three were on the verge of reporting that the project was impossible, when Michael Heney, a young Irish Canadian who had just completed a solo survey of the terrain, returned and with vision and enthusiasm told them that a railway could indeed be built. As a teenager he had run away from home to build railways and was by now qualified to give an expert opinion. They were persuaded and thus the White Pass and Yukon Route Company was created, with Graves as President.

William had responsibility for finding the finance. He loaned the remaining £20,000 to the syndicate, on the understanding that if they defaulted, the building rights would revert to Close Brothers. He then set about raising money for the construction costs, and having extracted as much as he could from contacts in England, he went out to Canada to find funding there. He had hardly started on this when he announced from Skagway on 28th February 1898, much to the surprise of his colleagues in Close Brothers and the members of the syndicate, that the company was ready to begin construction and that he would himself take command. It was clear to all that unless construction began soon it would be too late, as the search for gold was subject to diminishing returns. They acquiesced. The syndicate defaulted on repayments, and the construction rights belonged to Close Brothers.

Of course William, as head of Close Brothers, was in one sense in command already, but in practice his role was to raise the finance and make his firm and their investors believe that one day they would not only get their money back, but make a profit. It was Graves who was the leader of the project on the ground, who recruited the team, negotiated with the State and Skagway authorities, expensively bought off a rival who was trying to achieve the same result by building a road and energetically saw the construction through. At the head of his formidable team were the thirty-four-year-old Heney, Tancred and engineer Hawkings, who had impressed Graves with his skills when masterminding the Colorado irrigation project.

The first men, horses and materials arrived in Skagway by the end of May and already by July 1898 the lines for the first four miles had been laid and used by the first train to run anywhere as far North as that on the continent. From then on the difficulties were immense. It was a thousand miles from supply bases, yet there was such a dire shortage of shipping in the area that discarded wrecks were bought and done up by the undertakers. There were no telegraph lines connecting with Canada or the United States. Labour was difficult to keep, as the men constantly defected to go and join the gold rush. The next sixteen miles were built on the steeply shelving rock (plate 22), great quantities of which had to be blasted away with dynamite and black powder: one 120 foot high cliff had to be removed in this way. Workers with pickaxes had to be tied with ropes hanging from the top of the mountain, and sometimes also tied to each other, in case they slipped or got carried away by gusts of wind. At one point, a bridge had to be built across a canyon, 250 feet below. When work continued into the winter of 1889–90, the strong winds and severe cold made the men torpid and numb, so that they had to be relieved after only an hour's work. 900 had to be taken on just to shovel away the snow. Yet of the 35,000 men that at one time or another had worked on the railway by the time it was finished in October 1900, only thirty-five lost their lives: tragic enough, but a very low percentage in comparison with still more dangerous jobs, such as mining. Fifteen years later the construction of that other ambitious engineering project, the Panama Canal, is said to have caused the deaths of 25,000 workers.

The initial payment of £30,000 was nothing compared with the construction costs. The forty-one miles from Skagway to the summit, which included sixty-seven bridges (more bridges per mile than any other known railway at the time), cost $100,000 per mile, and while the rest of the track cost less, it was still far more expensive than those still being built across the prairies. William's first efforts raised $500,000, but the final total needed was $7 million. It took all William's persuasive powers to find this sum. He was able to call on his brother John, now on the main board of directors of Lloyds Bank, to help raise the money. Finally the required sum was found; but it was not paid off until 1913. Thereafter Close Brothers was in profit. Today's owners are doing well. In 2006 the White Pass and Yukon Route Railway carried 431,000 passengers, nearly all of them tourists.

William, still aged only forty-seven in 1900, had enjoyed the challenge. During the many celebrations to mark the completion of different stages, his gusto and energy, particularly on the dance floor, was noted. He is likely to have been present on 20th February 1899, when the first train reached the pass at the summit, which was on the border of Alaska and Canada. It made the journey in a temperature of 14° below, passing between snow banks thirty feet high and carrying nearly 100 invited passengers. (The photograph on plate 23, taken that March, shows that this must indeed have been the snowiest railway ever.) The party was in a festive mood, thanks partly to the free whisky, but mainly to the awareness that the unspeakable 'Dead Horse Trail' had been made redundant.

In 1902 promising amounts of copper were found, again in Alaska, but still further to the North. William, after surveying the area, prepared a prospectus for building a railway from there to the sea. Unbeknown to him another surveyor, a Mr Guggenheim from New York, had had the same idea and had prepared a detailed plan for the building of the railway along another route. Both proposals were reviewed by the civic authorities, and William's route was chosen – but his competitor won the contract to build it. William was not too disappointed: Guggenheim paid him $450,000 for the use of his plans.

William retained his interests in Alaska for some years after this. In 1912 he was staying by Lake Atlin, to the West of Skagway. In a letter addressed to Close Brothers in London, after some pages describing the great beauty of his mountainous surroundings, he mentioned plans to build a hotel, complete with tennis courts and golf course, and added that the town of Atlin was the centre of new gold-mining activities, which were still 'in their infancy. Only a fraction of gold-bearing ground has been worked.'

Within a year of that letter, he was asked to open the Skagway flower show. On being introduced as a farmer he summarised his Iowan and Alaskan achievements as follows:

> Oh yes, I once owned a number of farms in Iowa, but I am afraid my farming was of the Push Button order. I pushed the button and someone did the rest. In the same way I can claim to be a successful railroad man. … And now I am going to make a bold claim in connection with button pushing on the same principle that Jack built his house. I once pushed a button in London fifteen years ago that set the machinery in motion that caused the railway to be constructed, that caused Skagway to remain a town, and caused it to be inhabited, that caused the present race of gardeners to arise, that caused those gardeners to produce the wonderful flowers and vegetables that you see before you today.

Apart from these two snippets, little more is recorded about William. He returned to England and Close Brothers in Chicago became incorporated as a subsidiary of the London firm, which was in St. Helen's Place in the City. He bought a house in Brook Street. His affection for members of the Paullin family had not left him, and Mary's sister Ada continued to be part of his household, acting as his housekeeper. Tongues wagged, but Anne Eaden wrote: 'There was *no cause* for scandal but naturally the world thought otherwise.' William in fact had a succession of mistresses, and it seems unlikely that Ada was one of them.

William also built for himself Huntercombe Court, a large house near Henley, which still stands today. Here he could keep in touch with the rowing; his advice on that subject was still appreciated. It included eight small bedrooms in a row, where Cambridge eights could stay whenever they were training or racing. According to Harnack, he was practically a fixture at annual rowing events. In one family photograph, he is shown 'among May-week Cambridge revellers, a grey-haired man in conventional business clothes, in the midst of young university men and their girlfriends – a picture apparently taken at dawn, after a night of celebrating.'

Mary had married again, to the military attaché to the British Embassy in Vienna. She lived there, still in poor health, and committed suicide in 1905, ten years after this marriage. Latterly William often stayed with his mistress on the Isle of Wight, and he died there in 1923.

In spite of his rowing preoccupation and other dalliances, William's range of business interests did not diminish. Both he and his father made a point of keeping up with the latest technical developments and William was an innovator. His obituary in *The Times* picked on two of them: 'Against every obstacle it was his perseverance that made a success of expanded metal [by heating it] as a reinforcement for concrete works and roads.' It was this technique which later in the 20th century facilitated the ubiquitous high-rise blocks of flats. The other achievement mentioned in the obituary was his work towards smokeless fuel. He firmly believed that this was a possibility and looked forward to the day when London would be without smog. Just as his father in the last year of his life launched into new realms (with the building of Antipolis), so did William. In the year before his death, he and his partners raised £800,000 for the purchase of the Shipley collieries in Derbyshire, so that they could research low temperature carbonisation of coal, necessary for the elimination of smoke.

William's life had many parallels with that of his father. Both were open-mindedly cosmopolitan, multi-lingual and prepared to work anywhere, while at the same time remaining British in their way of life and never entirely accepting foreigners as equals. JC was never fully reconciled to his sister marrying an Italian, while William made his colony an upper class English enclave. Both were true merchant venturers in their attitude to work, having the imagination to seize boldly opportunities as they arose, in any field.

William Close was responsible for three major legacies: the Close Colony, a glittering phenomenon which sank without a trace but which opened up vast stretches of prairie in what is still one of the most fertile areas of North America; the White Pass and Yukon Railway; and Close Brothers Limited, which as Close Brothers Group plc still flourishes today.

While William may have been disappointed in his failure to replicate the family centred life he had grown up with, James and John, though perhaps lacking William's mercurial business acumen, amply made up for his deficiencies on the family front. Both produced sons whose direct descendants carry the family name to the present day and whose chosen paths in such professions as engineering, medicine and finance embody many of the principles JC held dear.

Close Brothers Group plc

*W*ITH William's death the firm lost momentum and underwent various changes of ownership. Throughout this relatively slack period, however, the name Close was always retained, as it continued to be associated with the striking successes of earlier years.

A return to the pioneering spirit of the original Close brothers began in 1978 with a management buy-out by Rod Kent, the twenty-seven-year-old managing director at the time, together with two young managers, Stone and Winkworth – later known as 'the brothers'. When they first approached their parent company, Consolidated Gold Fields, they were met with incredulity and sacked. They ignored this set-back and pressed on with their offer, finding the capital with second mortgages on their homes and more substantial funds from other City firms.

They prevailed, and set out on a programme of acquisitions and organic growth, fuelled by imaginative ideas for expanding their range of services. By the last year of the millennium the firm achieved profits of £144 million, representing an annual increase of 25 per cent in earnings per share over the previous twenty-five years.

Today (2007) Close Brothers remains, along with Lazards and Rothschilds, one of the three major UK merchant banks that has not sold out in whole or in part to foreign competitors. Unlike the other two, it is a quoted company, with over 2,000 employees and a market capitalisation of £1,278 million. The Close family are no longer involved with the company, but its phenomenal rate of growth now echoes the achievements of its merchant venturer founders.

Six Steers, Five Miles

So that William's mock-modest description of himself as a 'push button farmer' near the end of the last chapter does not leave the reader with the wrong idea, here is one last passage from the Prairie Journal, showing that in his twenties he worked as hard as any cowboy:

We had a tough day's work yesterday, to drive but six steers five miles. It was a much harder job to keep going these six than it was the eighty we drove some time ago. I went the day before with a Mr Brown of New York to try and take them along, but utterly failed to get even one away from the herd. So Ginger and I by sunrise were at the corral, and without much trouble got them out as they thought they were as usual being led out for grazing. All went pretty well until we got past their usual pasturage grounds, then they began to show signs of uneasiness, had evident inclinations to go off in all directions but the right one, kept looking back to see what had happened to the rest of the herd, which they thought had been following behind. We were taking them to join our own herd, and the way lay principally along a ridge in the prairies. At last they seemed to have made up their minds that something was wrong, and turning sharply round, stampeded down the steep hill into the gully below. We were after them in the twinkling of an eye, and after half a mile's chase managed to head four, the other two going off in opposite directions. These four we managed to get in a small side gully, and I mounted guard over them, blocking the entrance, while Ginger went off to help the herder (who had come to assist us a little of the way) to get the others back. One of them had returned very nearly to the corral two miles back, and the other about a mile, before they were stopped; and then they both refused to come back, so there was nothing more to do than to 'run' them, that is not to let them rest a second, keep on worrying them with the whip, until they get tired out. This process, of course, is a disagreeable one for both cattle and owners, for running them takes their fat down very fast, and it takes days to put it on again. But it is consoling how quiet they became for the rest of the journey.

For the next mile it was nothing but a series of rushes on the part of the other four to get off, but by always being on the alert we managed to keep them together, until during a grand rush one got away and down the side of the hill.

He went at a great pace – it is wonderful how fast they go down hill. Before the herder was half down the hill, the steer was careering over the plain below. We could watch the chase from the ridge and far down the valley we could see a small herd grazing, and for this the steer made, knowing that the tug of war would be to get him away from them. We again put the others into a convenient gully, with Ginger stopping to look after them. I went off to help the herder, quite two miles away. When I got up to the scene of action I found three dogs and two herders at work on the obstinate brute. After about a quarter of an hour's fight he began to show signs of having had enough. We at last got him away and for the rest of the journey <u>he</u> was quiet. The herder left us after this and luckily the other three did not require much running to keep in order, still it was all the way a series of attempts at breaking away.

Provisions for the Sibilla, 1851

List of provisions for the yacht *Sibilla* in James Close's pocket book, 1851

Fortnum & Masons £40 2s. 6d.

4	boxes	Figs	3	"	Veal Custard Jardiniere
2	"	Raisins	3	"	Mutton & Tomato
1	"	Stilton & Nuts	3	"	Irish Stew
50	tins	Milk	3	"	Beef Steaks
1	"	Pickled Herrings	3	"	Boeuf a la Mode
2	Bots	Apricots	3	"	Spring Lamb & Peas
4	"	Cherries	3	"	Haricot Mutton
4	"	Green Gages	3	"	Rabbit & Onions
12	"	Raspberries & Currants	3	"	Stewed Veal
2	Bots	Pickles	6	"	Roast Fowls
6	Box	Biscuits	6	"	Boiled Fowls
10	lbs	Currants	6	"	Roast Duck
6	Box	Mustard	3	"	Salmon
6	Box	Prep Ginger	3	"	Turbot
6	Jars	Currant Jam	3	"	Codfish
4	"	Ginger	10	"	Green Prod.
1	Jar	Imp Plums	3	"	Lobster Meat
3	Tins	Grouse	1	"	Oyster Meat
3	"	Partridges	1	"	Sage & Onions
6	Pots	Currant jelly	6	"	Beef Tea
1	Bot	Harveys Sauce	6	"	Mutton Broth
10	Tins	Roast Beef	6	"	Chicken Broth
10	"	Boiled Hams	4	"	Brandied Cherries
10	"	Beef & Vegetables			

Contemporary Report on Fred Close's Death

From the *Sioux City Journal*, 14th June 1890.

A FATAL POLO GAME
Fred Close Killed while engaged in his Favourite Pastime.

The polo game between LeMars and Sioux City came to a disastrous end yesterday in an accident that resulted in the death of Fred B. Close. Fred entered the game with his left arm in a sling, not having recovered fully from the effects of a fall while fox hunting in England last fall, and to that fact was probably due the fatal result of yesterday's game. Notwithstanding his reckless daring, Fred was a splendid horseman, and had he had full use of his arm he might have avoided the collision that caused him to be thrown and crushed beneath the two falling horses.

The Sioux City team had scored three goals, and Fred was congratulating his boys on their excellent playing. Jack Wilson, of the LeMars team, was making a splendid run down the field when, for some unaccountable reason, Fred attempted to cross in front of him, and to the spectators it was evident that the two would cannon. An instant before the horses collided Fred was seen to sway in his saddle, and when the crash came he was already unseated. Watson's horse struck Fred's and the latter was thrown, and falling upon its rider, rolled clear over him. Then, as the horse struggled to regain his feet, Watson's horse fell over him and he also rolled across the body of poor Close. Watson was thrown over his horse's head and escaped injury.

Fred never moved a muscle, but lay as one dead. A number of his friends rushed to his assistance, but he manifested no sign of life. A young Norwegian physician who happened to be on the ground came to their assistance, and succeeded finally in restoring circulation, but was unable to bring the unfortunate man back to consciousness. News of the accident was telephoned to the city and Drs. Bergen and Savage hastened to the grounds, but their efforts were unavailing.

Bibliography

❧ As listed by Suzanne Knowles

Sir Harold Acton, *The Last Bourbons of Naples* (London, 1961)

Josephine Butler, *In Memoriam Harriet Meuricoffre* (London, 1901)

Etta Close, *Excursions and Some Adventures* (London, 1926)

Louise Colet, *Naples sous Garibaldi. Souvenirs de la Guerre d'Indépendence* (Paris, 1861)

Ruth Eaden, 'En Famille', *Blackwood's Magazine*, 1975

Sir Henry George Elliot, *Some Revolutions and other Diplomatic Experiences*, edited by his daughter [Gertrude Elliott] (London, 1922)

Eminent Persons: Biographies Reprinted from The Times, 1880–1889 (London, 1892)

Curtis Harnack, *Gentlemen on the Prairie* (Ames, Iowa, 1985)

Rear Admiral Sir George Rodney Mundy, *H.M.S. Hannibal at Palermo and Naples during the Italian Revolution, 1856–1861* (London, 1863)

George Macaulay Trevelyan, *Garibaldi and the Making of Italy* (London, 1947)

❧ Additional publications consulted subsequently

Barbara Dawes, *British Merchants in Naples, 1820–1880* (Naples, 1991)

Michelle Froissard, *Antibes – Cent années d'expansion urbaines* (Antibes, 2000)

L. H. Grindon, *The Troubles of 1826* and *Manchester Banks and Bankers* (Manchester, 1877)

Julie Johnson, *A Wild Discouraging Mess* (Anchorage, Alaska: US Department of Interior, 2003)

E. Massi, 'Italy in Revolution', in *Cambridge Modern History* (Cambridge, 1909)

Janice Stofferan and Dorothy Warren (compilers), *Northwest Iowa Pioneers* (Iowa, n.d.)

J. E. Westropp, *Summer Experiences in Rome, Perugia and Siena in 1854* (London, 1856) (appendix on the Bay of Naples)

Jacob Van Der Zee, *The British in Iowa* (Iowa City, 1922) [extracts quoted in the *Le Mars Gazette*]

❧ Other sources

'An English Colony on the Prairie', *Country Life Annual*, 1957

A brief history of the building of the White Pass and Yukon railroad and its operations to date (paper from archives of Close Brothers plc), n.d.

From the same source came the unpublished Prairie Journal of William Close, and this has been extensively used.

The unpublished diaries of Miss Wilson, the friend of Anne Close's sister Mrs Burd.

The *Services Archives Documentation* in Antibes supplied information on the location of James Close's purchase of land.

Origin and Authorship of this Book

*T*HREE FAMILY GENERATIONS have contributed to this book about their ancestors.

Anne Eaden was the daughter of JC's youngest daughter Annie, and sister of Ruth, whose *Blackwood's Magazine* article has twice been quoted in the text. It was Anne Eaden who first had the idea of making a book of the Journals. She wrote a curtailed version, with editorial introductions to each voyage, setting the scene, and summarising the entries that had been omitted. She may have intended to write more, but died in 1958, before her work was done. It was entitled 'Log of the *Sibilla*'.

Roger Close-Brooks, great-grandson of JC and grandson of his eldest son John, researched further into the family history and located more of his relations, including descendants of the Romanos, whom he met in Naples. He inherited the Journals and a mass of accompanying papers from Anne Eaden and continued to work towards their publication. He was pleased to find that another relation, **Suzanne Knowles**, author and poetess, was willing to take on the work.

Suzanne Knowles, great-granddaughter of JC, set about writing a second, much longer version of the book. She saw that JC's personality pervaded the Journals and realised that some explanation of his decision to spend his life as a roving merchant based in Naples, and of his extraordinary method of bringing up his family, was needed. Interviewing surviving family members, she acquired letters and other documents. She also quoted in full at the beginning of her manuscript the two documents that JC wrote when nearing retirement – the one on his family background and the other his account of his own life up to the age of twenty-three. Knowles saw however that this left a longish gap in the narrative, between 1822 when JC's autobiography breaks off, and 1859, when JC wrote the twenty-four-page account of a cruise in the Adriatic and also wrote to his brother about his plans for the future. With little to go on as far as his personal life was concerned, Knowles filled the gap with an account of the stormy political developments related to the *Risorgimento*. She covered the tensions arising from JC's business interests at Court and his links with the Republican Romanos. She also reproduced the first hand accounts by family friend Harriet Meuricoffre of the arrival of Garibaldi, of the state of the hospitals in Naples and of King Ferdinand's prisons. She went on to reproduce the Journals in full, and added short summaries of the later lives of each of the children.

Jonathan Close-Brooks continued his father Roger's efforts to get the work published, and following his untimely death in 2000, his wife **Rosemary Close-Brooks** has seen the project through to completion. She asked Julian Potter to edit this third version of the book and the family thank him for turning a variety of manuscripts into something suitable for publication and for his own research and contributions. In particular he was keen to extend the saga to the second generation of Closes, and researched and wrote the final chapter on the exploits of three of the brothers in America.

Rosemary has with her sister-in-law Joanna Close-Brooks further researched the family archives and those on the building of Antipolis on the Cap d'Antibes. A separate section has been made of this, since this episode is poorly covered in the Journals and yet had a major impact on the development of that part of France. Through the kindness of Dott. Carlo Knight, Joanna also obtained a book on nineteenth century British Merchants in Naples, from which the editor extracted facts about JC's business activities during the gap between the premature ending of his autobiography and the start of the Journals some thirty-five years later.

In this final version, the Journals no longer constitute 80 per cent of the text, but have been reduced to but one episode in the saga of James Close himself and the later achievements of his sons in America. The Journals are entertaining throughout and contain many outstanding passages. Yet as the entries were made every day, some are less exciting than others, or too similar to earlier episodes; and these have been cut or summarised. All the highlights have been retained, but the emphasis in the book as a whole has shifted.

The passages written by Suzanne Knowles are so interwoven with contributions by the editor, and in a few cases by Anne Eaden and myself, that it would be tedious and impractical to indicate at each point who wrote what.

Rosemary Close-Brooks

The publication of this family history has been paid for by family members Rosemary Close-Brooks, Joanna Close-Brooks, James (Jimmy) Close (great-grandson of JC) and Precelly Murray (great-great-granddaughter of JC); and also by a generous contribution from Close Brothers Group plc.

Index

Nor end. Got in the cutter & dingay
save them from being carried a
way

Sun 9th   Weather improving &c Sight
Sardinia. Put the Helm up & eas
the ship off to leeward. A great re
lief. Towards evening rounded
the Low for Port Palma. But a
sea having left us & a fine wind
we steered for Cagliari. Sickness
prevailed, but some of us sat down
to dinner

Mon 10 Fine weather, but no wind.
Entered Cagliari Bay in the
afternoon. We returned to our
lessons, & every became cheerful
& lively. After such a storm, our